Wimbledon F.C.

WFC

To Dearest Chaf

on your

30th
Birthday.

Dad & your ever
loving Ma

x x x

2

The Spirit of Wimbledon

The living memories of the Dons from 1922-2003

Niall Couper

CHERRY RED BOOKS

This edition published in Great Britain in 2003 by

Cherry Red Books Ltd,
Unit 17, 1st Floor, Elysium Gate West,
126/128 New King's Road,
London SW6 4LZ

ISBN: 1-901447-19-7

Designed by Simon Joslin
Printed and bound in Great Britain by Biddles Ltd., Guildford and King's Lynn.

✦

Contents

The Spirit of Wimbledon

PREFACE

I had just got an email from John Scales and another from Terry Phelan – both FA Cup winners for Wimbledon – when my fiancée Jenny walks in. She doesn't understand why I'm so hyper, and then my mobile phone goes and it's the club's former captain Robbie Earle. As a Wimbledon fan, it was five minutes that you could only ever really have dreamed of.

To try and explain how I felt I'd ask you to name your 10 favourite heroes of all time. And then imagine that three of them have just contacted you. How mad would that be? Welcome to my world.

Those mad five minutes all came about because of a conversation I had had with my brother Matthew back in November 2002. Around that time the BBC was airing a series on the top 10 greatest Britons. I was also the editor of Yellow and Blue, AFC Wimbledon's matchday programme, and the club had just given us permission to expand from 32 pages to 48. I had to come up with new feature ideas. Matt suggested a series on the top 10 moments in Wimbledon's history. I loved the idea, but I wanted a twist – I wanted to tell the tale through the eyes of the players, the managers and the fans who were there. However, as any journalist will know, writing a ghosted article is no easy task.

I also remember thinking how difficult it would be to choose a top 10. The FA Cup final in 1988 would have to be there, but what would the other nine be, and could I be certain of getting someone to tell me the tale on each of those?

I wasn't convinced, so I made a shortlist of around 30 and began my search. I asked old Wimbledon fans. I searched the web. I chased up contacts at newspapers. I phoned up football clubs. I was asking anyone and everyone I could think of. And then I waited.

Instead of getting the meagre response I had expected, nearly everyone was replying. I reached 10 interviews, then 15, then 20. I was getting players talking about not just one game but two or even three. I had a two-hour phone conversation with Terry Phelan, who was playing for a club in the States. Then there was the call at 7am from Sam Hammam; and the banter with Alan Cork, who was trying to ignore Micky Adams in the background. And so on. By mid-February I had not 10, but 50 different memories. Yellow and Blue simply did not have the space. It was then that I decided to write this book.

If the first 50 had been relatively easy, the remainder would be difficult. The effort that went into tracking down Paul McGee was huge. After several calls, I managed to find a club he had played for in Dublin, and after several posts on their websites, I got a direct telephone number. It was equally difficult to get hold of some of the older memories and sometimes it was simply a case of calling in favour after favour.

But throughout, one theme kept on resurfacing: the special spirit at Wimbledon. It was not just the players linked to the Crazy Gang of the 90s, the likes of Ben Thatcher and John Fashanu, who mentioned it but the players who had played for the club in the 40s, 50s, 60s, 70s and 80s. And it also existed among the supporters.

As a fan of Wimbledon, I had witnessed the never-say-die attitude among the fans. It had been evident at Plough Lane and even to some extent at Selhurst Park, but it came to the fore with the creation of AFC Wimbledon. And the memories behind the formation of the new club and the season that followed are also contained in these pages.

To describe the amount of effort that has gone into producing this book as simply "blood, sweat and tears" would be underplaying it massively. Compiling The Spirit of Wimbledon has been the most difficult task I have ever undertaken in my life, but it has also been the most enjoyable.

Niall Couper

✦

The Spirit of Wimbledon

FOREWORD

Wimbledon will always
bring back happy
memories, whether it's
my playing days back in the 60s
and 70s, or watching AFC
Wimbledon now. The spirit at the
club has always been fantastic.

I was lucky enough to be
involved in some of the greatest
days in the club's history. I was
in goal in 1975 when Wimbledon,
a non-league side then, beat First
Division Burnley 1-0 away in the
FA Cup. In the next round I even
saved a penalty as we held the
League champions Leeds United
0-0 at Elland Road. In those days,
we didn't expect ever to lose,
even when we played at Leeds.
We were fully confident in our
own abilities and that's also part
of the spirit of Wimbledon.

I loved the atmosphere at the
club back then too, and Plough
Lane in particular. We used to
mix with the fans and that
reminds me of AFC Wimbledon
now. We played for fun and for
the love of the game.

Optimistic: Dickie Guy
(Yellow and Blue)

They were great days, and the one continuation throughout it
all has been the supporters. They never stopped loving the club.
For me, it stopped being fun when we turned professional in 1978.
But the atmosphere on the terraces was always there. The fans had
the same never-say-die attitude that we had as players. The move to Selhurst Park hurt
them. They believed Wimbledon should be in Wimbledon. In my opinion it became
even more painful for them when the two Norwegians took over. They weren't
interested in helping the club. They had the money to move the club back to Plough
Lane; they could have built an all-seater stadium there, and I know the council would
have given them permission. If Charlton could have made a success of it then so could
Wimbledon, but the owners were not far-sighted enough.

When I heard that the Dons were moving to Milton Keynes I was devastated. I
remember the news came out at the same time that David Beckham broke his foot. It
was buried; no one in the media seemed to really care about Wimbledon. But I was
really upset. Wimbledon was Wimbledon, not Milton Keynes.

But now AFC Wimbledon is off the ground and I no longer care whether Wimbledon FC are in Milton Keynes or not; I feel far more affinity with AFC Wimbledon. The atmosphere on the pitch, in the stands and at the bar at AFC is simply fantastic. It is like the Wimbledon I knew. I have lost all feeling for Wimbledon FC; I don't feel associated with that club.

The fans are what made the club and it is the fans that have kept Wimbledon alive at AFC. But I am still amazed by how much success they have had. You have to really stop and recall what they have achieved. On 28 May 2002 they had nothing: no players, no manager, no ground, no money and no supporters. They were just an idea. A year later they had an average attendance of 3,000, they finished third in their league and, most amazingly of all, they had bought their own ground in south-west London. The story of AFC Wimbledon is incredible; it's been a fairytale. AFC Wimbledon has got off to a tremendous start. The club has captured the imagination of everyone across the country. Long may it continue.

Dickie Guy

✦

With thanks to

Mark Trowbridge of Getty Images for his research
Lee Martin of Getty Images
John Woodruff and Robert Smith for their help with proofing
All the photographers
All the players, past and present, who answered my calls
The Wimbledon Independent Supporters Association
The AFC Wimbledon board for keeping the dream alive
My brother Matthew for putting up with me
...and mostly my wife Jenny, who suffered more than anyone

The Spirit of Wimbledon

PROLOGUE

T he first 30 years of Wimbledon's history took in just about everything a club could possibly face. There was the dispute with the locals, a period of nomadic existence, international recognition, a meteoric rise, a rebirth and a ridiculous obsession with changing kit. It is a tale that has a lot of parallels with the memories of today's Wimbledon fans. So sit back and let me begin.

It all started in 1889 with Wimbledon Old Centrals. The Wimbledon of the 19th century were no more than a local park team. Formed by the ex-pupils of the Old Central School (hence the suffix), they played on Wimbledon Common, wore navy blue shirts and white shorts and changed in their local pub, the Fox and Grapes – hardly the stuff of legend.

The Old Centrals, however, got off to a winning start, beating Westminster 1-0 in a friendly on the Common on 2 November 1889. But not everyone was happy about the football being played, least of all the Common Conservators. They were fuming. Apparently the ball kept disturbing passing carriages. An official complaint was lodged and Wimbledon Old Centrals were forced to move, admittedly only about half a mile to another pitch on the Common.

That also meant a change of pub. The Swan was to become the new changing rooms. And, as if to celebrate, the club also chose to change their kit to a positively disgusting combination of chocolate and light blue. The games then were all still friendlies and it was not until 3 December 1893 that the club got their first taste of competitive action. They lost 4-0 to Battersea Albion in the

The originals: Wimbledon Old Centrals 1895. Back Row: E Milledge, N Jenkins, A Bates, A Price, H Anstee, F Hossack, J Griffiths. Front row: A Smith, M Ely, E J Anstee, A Edgcumbe, F Jenkins. (Shirley Wootton)

Herald Cup.

The Old Centrals would get revenge a year later, and that 2-1 win in the London Junior Cup also marked their first competitive victory. Wimbledon then flirted with the South London League, before joining the Clapham League and

The first Wimbledon: Wimbledon 1905 (the first side to be called Wimbledon). Back row: E J Anstee, H Beck, A Reynolds, H Jackson, M Podmore, A Vine. Front row: S Kensit, P Drummond, A Podmore, A Astley, D B A Walker. (Shirley Wootton)

the Herald League for the 1895/96 season. They won them both. The Clapham League title, secured just weeks before the Herald, was the club's first piece of silverware.

On the back of this success the club changed shirts once again to green and black. Clearly it had an effect – the Dons would remain trophyless for the next three seasons. But the drought ended in style in the 1900/01 season. They won the Herald Cup, the South Western Cup and the Clapham League to become the first junior club to land a treble.

But success came at a cost. The club could no longer play on Wimbledon Common if their dream of senior football was to be realised, so on 23 August 1901 they moved to a private ground on Worple Road West in Raynes Park.

The nest season they scored 100 goals in 33 games, and although they could only finish runners-up to Clapham the decision had been made: the Old Centrals would kick off the 1902/03 season with senior football in the Southern Suburban League.

After two uneventful seasons, the 1904/05 season would see the club transform itself completely. On the pitch the club won their first senior trophy – the South London Charity Cup – beating Nunhead 2-1 on 15 April 1905. And off it, just two weeks after their success, the club took the momentous decision to drop their "Old Centrals" suffix – from 1 May 1905 the club would be known simply as Wimbledon. Naturally this called for another change of kit, to white shirts and blue shorts. A move to the Mid-Surrey League followed, which they won at a canter at the first attempt. And on 22 September 1906 the club made their debut in the FA Cup, losing 2-1 in the first qualifying round to West Norwood.

Everything seemed on the up for the Dons, but the fall would be almost as dramatic as the rise. They returned to the Southern Suburban League in 1907. But issues over where to play were to prove costly.

They moved to Pepys Road in January 1908, but that was to prove unsatisfactory. And after yet another change of kit – back to green and black – the Dons moved to Grand Drive in Raynes Park eight months later. The restlessness continued, and it was onto The Chase, Merton Hall Road, and then Burlington Road, all before the end of 1909. The Burlington Road pitch, however, was awful and tended to flood, so half the games of the 1909/10 season were held at Malden Sports Ground in New Malden. The nomadic existence couldn't continue and in desperation they turned to the Council to help them find a permanent home. But there was nowhere suitable and on 3 September 1910 football was suspended.

The Athenian Dons: Wimbledon 1920. J C Macey, Martin, G Cannon, T F Goodchild, Gillham, A S Bennett, W Keeble, L F Marlow, E Goodens, H H Allwright, J McEwan. (Shirley Wootton)

Doom and gloom, surely? Nope, for the people of Wimbledon are a resourceful lot. With one team messing up there was really only one solution: it was time to start a new club.

A stone's throw from where the Wimbledon Greyhound Stadium is now, Wimbledon Borough were formed and took Wimbledon's old place in the Southern Suburban League. The side was backed by the old Wimbledon chairman, Mr F Headicar, and a couple of the old players also joined up. The majority of the team, however, were Council workers and the Council's crest was adopted as the new badge.

A year later the "Borough" suffix was dropped, but more importantly there was a new ground. The council identified an area of disused swampland that had once been a refuse site that could be used by the club. It was at the corner of Haydons Road and Plough Lane and would be the Dons' home for 79 years. Wimbledon were up and running again.

The start of the First World War slowed progress. By October 1914, 27 Wimbledon players had joined the forces. And a year later football was again suspended. The club was restarted just before the end of hostilities, and the Dons were back in action on 14 December 1918 beating Hampstead Town 4-2 in a friendly at Plough Lane. Naturally it required a change in kit. This time Wimbledon were really going to push the boat out – they stuck a huge "W" on the front of the shirts. Unfortunately the Football Association were none to pleased and the team had to revert back to the old blue shirts and white shorts.

In a curtailed season, the Dons took part in the United Senior League. A year later they were elected to the Athenian League. The side then included three names that were to go on to far greater things. Firstly, there was W Keeble, who would become the club's first amateur international representing England against Ireland in 1921. Secondly, there was George Armitage, who would also become an amateur international but would make his mark playing for Charlton and England four years later. And finally there was Billy Cotton, who would become rather more famous with a baton in his hand as the legendary bandleader.

Meanwhile, the Athenian League was still deemed too small for the ambitious Dons, and when in 1921 the Isthmian League, the country's top amateur league, announced it was to expand to 14 teams, Wimbledon jumped ship. On the following pages are the living memories of what followed…

Niall Couper

✦

WIMBLEDON
FOOTBALL CLU

The Spirit of Wimbledon

CHAPTER ONE: THE EARLY YEARS

THE BIRTH OF A DON

Football is a global passion, but it takes something unique to turn the individual into a fan of a club. There is a different reason for everyone, and that applies as much to the 1920s as it does now. Back then Wimbledon were on the rise and football was very much part of the community and for one fan it was to become intoxicating.

1922

Plough Lane

By Louise Ellen 'Sis' Martin (supporter)

I was the only girl at home. I had three brothers and most Saturdays they used to go to football. I really wanted to go as well, and one day I nagged them enough to let them take me along. I was only eight. We walked up Plough Lane to the back of the Wandle Valley End where the greyhound stadium was. We were going to bunk in.

There was a hole in the back of the stand there, a gap in the corrugated iron. It wasn't all that big, and Alf Goldsmith, one of my brothers, pulled it open and we all crawled in.

We were spotted straight away. I remember hearing this bloke on the other side. "One, two, three... Cor blimey! There's only a girl coming through too!"

I remember the sound of the rattles and being pushed to the front. I think I ended up sitting on the pitch. I loved it all. I can't remember the game or the opposition, but the excitement of the day made me want to come back.

In those early days we were regulars sitting on the pitch. There weren't really any railings round the edge of the pitch so it was the best place to be. At some away games it wasn't so easy, so we used to take an orange box with us and stand on that to get a decent view.

Casual approach: Wimbledon in the white sleeves take on Casuals away on 15 September 1923. The Dons lost 8-3. (Getty Images)

There was no problem being a girl then. Wimbledon always had its fair share of female fans. The records show that Bill Spiller set up the supporters' club, but it was as much to do with Cath Hardiman. And she wasn't the only one involved.

I loved the football of those days. It was so different to how it is now. There was very little talking on the pitch, almost silent. And it was so much more honest. There was no pinching of yards at throw-ins and free kicks. Then there was the old system of two full-backs, three half-backs, two inside forwards, two wingers and one centre forward. I loved that too.

But most of all we had such great players in the 20s. There was Fred Gregory, our own little terrier. I remember the captain of Kingstonian, May, came off after one match all black and blue. But that was the way Gregory played.

Then there was Sammy Soutter. He used to dribble the ball all over the pitch. He played like Stanley Matthews. We had Whisker in goal. Cath Hardiman's mum used to knit his goalkeeper's jumper. But the hero of the side was Doc Dowden. He was our centre forward and he had everything. He was a leader on the pitch, he could head, he had a powerful shot and he was a total gentleman.

Wimbledon was not just about the football though, it was also about the social side and as I grew older I got more involved with events off the pitch.

In the early 1930s, I used to go to the dances that were held in the dining room above the old North Stand and mix with the players. The football club was the centre of our social life. Our group all used to go: me, my sister Rose, Nell Warner and Peg Potter. The room would be full.

Sometimes the girls and the players used to go out on the stand and do a bit of courting. There were no lights on in the stand. My friend used to say to me: "You will never get a bloke because you won't go out there with them."

That's not to say I didn't fancy some of the players. I used to like Boogie Barnes. He was quite posh. He shouldn't have been at Wimbledon. He should have been at Corinthian Casuals – they were all university types.

Then there was Boy Turner, Jack Turner's brother. Boy Turner's first name was Ellis but he used to not let us call him that.

It was such a great little community club, but that was the case with amateur football all over south London. Each club would be connected to a local business and more often than not the players would all end up working for them. At Tooting & Mitcham it was the gas board, at Dulwich Hamlet it was a company of window cleaners and at Wimbledon it was the Sunlight Laundry on Haydons Road.

Football was part and parcel of life. It was all so integrated back then. If you were part of the Wimbledon community, you were part of Wimbledon Football Club.

✦

A RECORD GATE, 15-2 AND A NATIONAL FINAL

The 1930s was a period of unprecedented success for Wimbledon Football Club. The Isthmian League trophy would become an almost permanent resident at the club. It was a time when the appeal of the Dons was beginning to spread.

THE EARLY THIRTIES
By Ken Randall (supporter)

My dad and my two brothers all followed Wimbledon, but I didn't start going until I was 16 or 17 and that had little to do with my family. I was working at Connolly's leather factory in South Road and there were two lads there who would come in every Monday wearing all blue and white, the club colours in those days, and talk non-stop about Wimbledon. Frank Tinder was one of them and I just got interested and decided to go along. But the Dons were not the first team I supported. I used to follow a side called Colliers Wood, but from the moment I stepped into Plough Lane that all changed.

It could pour with rain at Plough Lane and you would never feel it. I just liked the atmosphere and the way we played. I just took to it and that was that.

I first saw the Dons in 1929. It was the year of Whisker, Balkwill, Dowden, Goodchild, Goodens, Gregory and the like. Whisker was my favourite goalkeeper. He was a thick-set chap; I can still picture him now. He was a good goalkeeper, up there with Dave Beasant who would lift the FA Cup for the Dons nearly 60 years later. It was also the year we beat Polytechnic 15-2 in the FA Cup.

I don't remember a thing about the 15-2. We won a few games every season by a big margin and I never liked those sorts of games. I like a bit of competition. And that's what was generally good about the Isthmian League – it was very competitive with so many local derbies. But winning by six, seven, eight or more was not enjoyable.

The supreme champions: The Wimbledon side of the 1930/31 season with the five trophies they won that season: the Isthmian League, the London Senior Cup, the South London Charity Cup, the South Western Charity Cup and the Surrey Combination Cup. Back row: C Ferrari, H J Sutters, R Hendra, E S Makepeace, E Pratt, F J C Mercer, J E C Stroud, C Preece, V F Rowe, L Lefevre, G H Tingley, W G Hillier, T B Stoakley, A Ford. Third row: S G Rickard, C P Christie, E H Balkwill, A T Bridge, H Minor, E Nailer, H E Williams, B C Corke, S J Meadows, J W Brown, H R Watts, G Philmore, H Butt, J Ciales, J Clement, F N Headicar, J Leach. Second row: H J Blake, J O'Brien, O Parry, W W Dowden, D B Evans, E Whisker, F J Gregory, F Wade, H E Barnes, C Knight, S Worthington, C P Harvey, E W Barnes. First row: W E Gay, H H Bridge, H H Gittens, R Coates, H R Hopkins, F J Roche, F Davenport, E Curnow, P Crate. (Shirley Wootton)

It was also the start of a roll for the club. We won the title in 1931 and 1932, but that was nothing compared to the exploits of 1935. That was the year we got 18,080 at Plough Lane. It was to be the highest attendance there, against HMS Victory in the third round of the FA Amateur Cup.

Plough Lane will always be special for me. There were no real big songs or chants as you get these days, it was more about the humour and there was lots of it. And it's nice to know that's still there now. I think that's always been a unique part of Wimbledon.

But despite the lack of songs, we still had our characters on the terraces. There was a bloke called Leather Lungs, who lived on Grove Lane. He used to just scream "Wim" all the time. Then there was Alfie Mangem, who used to be full of jokes. Those of us who went regularly back then got to know those two really well.

A pair of legends: Frank Wade (left) and Jack Goodchild at Plough Lane on the opening of the new-look ground on 29 August 1931. (Getty Images)

People used to converge on the ground from left, right and centre. It was a 30-minute walk for me from my home at Colliers Wood. There had never been much problem getting in, but the 18,080 against HMS Victory was a different matter entirely.

HMS Victory in the previous round had played Leytonstone at Plough Lane and I went along and watched that, we already knew we were going to play the winners so I went along to judge them. They looked impressive, most of the service sides were in those days what with National Service.

There was a big crowd against Leytonstone, but when it came to playing us it was huge. I used to like walking round the pitch at Plough Lane so I could stand behind the goal we were attacking. But against HMS Victory it was packed, I was stuck next to the North Stand. I couldn't move at all. There were certainly more Wimbledon fans than HMS Victory supporters, but they had bought a fair few as well. It was a great atmosphere.

In defence: A London Caledonians player heads clears under pressure against Wimbledon at Plough Lane on 29 August 1931. (Getty Images)

I remember Doc Dowden got the first from a free-kick. He had a terrific kick on him and was a real favourite with the fans. He hit it as hard as anything from 18 yards, and it hit one of their players in the wall and went in. The poor guy was knocked clean out. Dowden headed the second and we ran out 3-0 winners.

The nearly men: Wimbledon FA Amateur Cup finalists 1935. Back Row: M Batchelor, E Curnow, H E Barnes, I Phillips, C Weller, W D Irish, H H Bridge, A G Reeves, J Chorley, W Miller. Front row: W W Dowden, E C Turner, J K Wright, L Smith, E Zenthon. (Shirley Wootton)

It was part of a great cup run. And we had a great side. Dowden was the goalscorer. Then there was Ken Wright. He was the captain and a school teacher. And Jack Goodchild, who always had his sleeves rolled down and looked a mess. But he couldn't half move.

We went on to meet Bishop Auckland in the final at Middlesbrough. We drew 0-0 up there and the replay was at Stamford Bridge in front of 32,000. After the draw up north, we were the favourites and we all thought we had the game won when Doc Dowden gave us the lead after just three minutes. It was a terrific atmosphere and a massive gate for an amateur game. But I felt so down when we ended up losing 2-1. We went on to win the League, but that was just a consolation.

A year later we won the League again, but I remember that season more for the arrival of Harry Stannard. He was one of the legends of the side. He used to always go in on the goalkeeper and the pair of them would often end up in the net with the ball.

I remember Stannard against Walthamstow. He went in on the goalkeeper and bundled the ball in as he always did. Their goalkeeper was fuming and he charged after Stannard ready to thump him. Some of the other players stopped him first. But that was the sort of forward Stannard was, and the fans loved him. He was physical, but no one really had a bad reputation at the club until the days of Fashanu and Jones.

✦

POST-WAR TRANSFORMATION

With the outbreak of war, football throughout Britain was suspended. It was to return in 1945, but the pre-War ethos of the amateur game had gone. Money was starting to illegally call the shots. Wimbledon resisted the trend and for a while they even defied the odds, reaching the FA Amateur Cup final in 1947. The Dons lost 2-1 to Leytonstone at Highbury despite taking the lead. And after that, although the principled stance remained, the team was changing.

SEPTEMBER 1947
Wimbledon training
By Jack Wallis (player)

I have a lot to thank my late brother Harry for. It was he who persuaded me to come down to Wimbledon. I'd come out of the army in June and I was living at home. Harry was in the Dons schoolboys team at that time and I remember clearly one night he said to me: "I'm going training tonight, do you fancy coming along?" So I did and before I knew it I was in the first team. It was all very simple. You didn't have to register. There was no real commitment in amateur football, you could change your club willy-nilly, but I liked what I saw at Wimbledon and stayed.

Highbury heartache: Wimbledon's Pat Edelston gets in a header against Leytonstone in the FA Amateur Cup final at Highbury on 19 April 1947. Wimbledon lost 2-1. (Andrew Watson)

Before... Wimbledon FC 1946/47. Back row: W W Dowden (team manager), G Jones, D F Walker, A R Head, J Haydock, T Laker, W Magill, J Price (trainer). Front row: C Clark, J A Nash, L J Wallis, F E Lemmer, J F Cousins, H J Stannard, P Edelston. (Louise Ellen Martin)

...and after: Wimbledon FC 1947/48. Back row (players only): Jack Wallis, A R Head, K Lister, J Haydock, A Maggs, C W Mason. Front row: F Gauntlett, H J Stannard, F E Lemmer, W Cousins, J Smith. (Louise Ellen Martin)

That was just five months after the club had reached the final of the FA Amateur Cup, yet most of that side had gone.

"Shamateurism" was rife then. In the Isthmian League only three or four sides were really amateur: Dulwich, Wimbledon and Woking, and, of course, the also-rans like Tufnell Park who finished bottom every year. The rest paid their players and a few from the final side were tempted away.

Wimbledon would not pay their players. Back then we were a very principled side. The likes of Leytonstone and Walthamstow, who were the kings of amateur football then, were willing to pay and consequently they had the best players.

But that wasn't the sole reason for the break-up of the side. Players like me were coming out of the army and were keen to get back into amateur football. There was a new influx of talent into the game.

It meant that the following season only five of the team that had lost at Highbury were still part of the side, and three of those had played for the club before the war: Ron Head, Frank Lemmer and Harry Stannard.

It was a time of transition, but the club brought together a terrific set of individuals, most of whom were to become life-long friends of mine.

There was Arthur Maggs, the right back. He was the epitome of the English gent. He had been in the paratroopers and some of the stories he would tell were legion. He joined at the same time as me.

Doug Munday and Freddie Gauntlett also joined then. Doug was a great character. The right-half. He was a hard man, tough but very very fair. He would mix it when things got a bit difficult. Freddie was a left-winger out of the mould. A dainty player, not very dynamic. He would do no work, but was extremely talented.

It was easy for the new players to gel. We were all coming into something new, but the old players were welcoming too and in Ron Head and Harry Stannard the club had two legends.

Ron was an inside-forward, an intelligent man. He worked in the City then. He was a real dandy. He used to have one of those velvet collars, but he was amateur through and through. He would never have tolerated Wimbledon players getting paid, and the same went for Harry Stannard. He could have gone to any club. He could have got £5 or £10 a game, which was a lot in those days, but he turned all the offers down to stay at Wimbledon.

Harry loved Wimbledon, and after he retired he would still go and watch. His last match was a month or two before he died in 2002.

But we all loved Wimbledon, we loved the spirit and the community aspect of the club, and most of all we loved the amateur nature of the side. It made us feel like the underdogs playing against all these sides that were being paid and that bonded us even closer together. But it also meant we would never be able to compete on a level playing field.

✦

THE WIMBLEDON LADIES
The common misconception of football in the 40s and 50s is that the crowd was made up almost entirely of flat-cap-wearing men. At Wimbledon, at least, the truth could have not been more different.

11 FEBRUARY 1950
FA Amateur Cup third round
Willington 4 Wimbledon 2
By Shirley Wootton (supporter)

There used to be around 20 or so girls who used to travel to all the away matches, and in those days most of the time we would only have the one coach. Among the 20 were my two aunties, Sis Martin and Rose Ball, and Gwen Hall and Peggy. I was the youngest. On the coaches most of the men had their wives with them too and although it was never 50:50, it would get close sometimes.

Even in those days there was no problem with being a woman on your own at football. It wasn't all flat caps and men, and I never felt like I shouldn't be there.

We girls even had our own song: "We are the Wimbledon girls, we are the Wimbledon girls. We know all our manners, we spend all our tanners, we are respected wherever we go. See us marching down the old Plough Lane, doors and windows open wide. We are the girls that make all the noise, damn sight worse than all the boys, we are the Wimbledon girls."

Leaving the Lane: Wimbledon fans prepare for the trip to Eastbourne in the first round of the FA Amateur Cup on 18 January 1947. The Dons won 4-2. (Louise Ellen Martin)

For the away games, me and my aunties would always rush to get the back seat on the coach. Most of the games were fairly local so they weren't that difficult to get to, but there would be the odd one that was miles away and Willington in the FA Amateur Cup was one of those. The town is situated in the North-East of England and none of us had the money to be able to afford to stay overnight, so we had to travel up on the coach overnight.

The ladies: Wimbledon's female supporters pose for photograph on route to the club's third round FA Amateur Cup tie against Willington on 11 February 1950. The Dons lost 4-2. (Shirley Wootton)

The coach left Plough Lane at midnight. I was only 15 at the time, but there was never any problem with me going. My dad had died at the end of the war and my mum didn't mind as she knew my aunties would look after me, and anyway, I slept nearly all the way.

It took ages to get up to Willington. Those were the days before motorways and it must have taken nearly 12 hours all told to get to the ground – and after all that we lost 4-2. But Wimbledon in 1950 wasn't the strongest of sides and we had become good losers. I had my friends with me and that was really all that mattered.

It was such a lovely family club back then. Everyone would do something to help. I would go the club with my friend Sylvia and we used to go to the laundry and pick up the kit and sew on any of the buttons that had come off the shirts.

The club wasn't selling merchandising so it was up to the girls to make most of the stuff. We used to knit all the hats and scarves. Back then of course we were playing in blue and white and not blue and yellow. I remember my aunties making the "Up the Dons" banner on their sewing machine. I was really proud of the banner as rationing was still in place and it was difficult to get the materials. And then there were the balloons. Wimbledon were the first club ever to have them at a game and that was all down to my Grandma.

She worked at Triang Toys, a lot of the Wimbledon supporters worked there too, and I remember the company went and bought a balloon factory. My grandma got them to print "Up the Dons" on a bunch and the Willington tie was the first time we took them to a game.

At Plough Lane I used to stand behind the small Privet hedge either side of the halfway line where the players ran out. There were loads of characters watching the games in those days. They weren't any chants. It was more the noise of the rattles and the general banter that got the players going. We would occasionally sing: "2-4-6-8, who do we appreciate?" But most of the time it was just the odd comment here and there from the fans.

I remember two supporters in particular, the Webb brothers. We played a game at the Oval against Corinthian Casuals. They used to put a rope around the pitch and we would stand on the cricket outfield to watch. But that day the Webb brothers weren't particularly interested in the match and spent the whole game shadow boxing by the halfway line. They had the whole crowd laughing. They repeated the trick many times after and it became just another part of Wimbledon. I also remember being collared by the club secretary Bert Corke at a Tooting & Mitcham game. He said to me and Sylvia: "Are you girls here to watch the football or to find a husband?" I laughed it off at the time, but a few years later I married one of the players.

It was a real family club; we were always having parties round at our house. I loved the players and I'll admit to chasing Ron Wootton, my future husband, as soon as he signed for the club. I used to go to Haydons Road on Mondays and Thursdays when they were training. I'd watch the Wallis brothers and Doug Munday, all Wimbledon legends, but I was secretly spying on Ron. I used to take my 78 records down to the club and play them at the socials after the game. We'd have a meal first and then the music would start. There was one Anne Shelton classic, "Lay down your arms", that was very popular and we used to all sing along to that. But most of the players didn't really pay much attention to the women. They would be playing snooker in another room and then, come 10pm when the football started on the TV, they would all shuffle over move the chairs into place and watch it. That would be as close as we'd get to most of the players.

Ron was the exception. We used to talk in the club room a lot, and one day he asked to carry my records home for me. But nothing happened for quite a while. I remember my mum kept saying: "When is that man going to ask you out?"

Then we started to share drinks together after training, Ron would always have his hot blackcurrant and gradually I won him over. We were married in 1959.

It was a special club back then, and the spirit I knew existed all the way through the 50s and 60s. It diminished a bit in the 70s, and by the time the club turned fully professional it had faded. I was never really interested in the club after that and I stopped going. But those early years will live with me for ever. AFC Wimbledon reminds me so much of those times – all the volunteers, the family spirit – it could so easily be the Dons of the 1940s and 50s.

❖

END OF AN ERA

By the 1950s Wimbledon FC was a club rich in tradition, and central to it all was the boot-room mentality. The management of the club was dominated by ex-players, and training routines had not changed in decades. But in the wider game everything was changing and Wimbledon were being left behind.

AUGUST 1951
Wimbledon trials
By George Coote (player)

Wimbledon were the club to join as an amateur in those days. I left school in June 1951 at the age of 15 and went for trials with Wimbledon in August. I started playing for the juniors in September.

It was strictly an amateur set-up. The ethos was to give talented players somewhere to play and the fans something good to watch. It was very friendly. There were four teams – the juniors, the A team, the reserves and the first team. So there were loads of players around and we used to mix very well.

In 1951, I played at Wimbledon Park with the juniors. The A team also played there and a year later I was in that side. By the 1953/54 season I was a regular in the reserves and I made my debut for the first team at the end of that season.

There was very much a boot-room mentality at Wimbledon in those days. Doc Dowden, the first-team manager, headed it all. He was a lovely old man and had made his debut for the Dons 30 years earlier. But it was the same all the way through the club. The reserve team manager Fred Gregory had been at Wimbledon since 1922, and that was before Doc Dowden. And even Alex Fuce, who was in charge of the juniors, had played for the club before the War.

It was all very simple in those days: we played our game, had a meal and then a couple of drinks and went home. It was a very quiet sort of routine; we all liked to go back to our own little villages and towns to do our own thing.

On match days, we used to turn up at Plough Lane at 2pm, have a cup of tea, have a brief chat about the opposition – discuss who we should look out for and that sort of thing – and then go out and play our own game. There were no real tactics. All that used to be left to the players. I remember frequently talking to Jack Wallis about what we should do and how we could alter the way we were playing. It was up to us to change things if they needed to be changed.

It was the same at training. We had no floodlights in those days and we used to have to use the lights from the back of the stand to help us train. It wasn't very sophisticated. We used to run around the pitch, do a bit of sprinting, a few weights and some press-ups. It was all fitness. There was very little emphasis on anything tactical under Doc Dowden. All he would do was encourage us to shout at one another in matches, so we knew where we were on the pitch and where we wanted the ball to go, but that was it.

I had been encouraged to go for Wimbledon because of the tradition they had. They were a huge club before the war and had reached the FA Amateur Cup final in 1947 under Doc Dowden,

Cup passion: The Dons goalkeeper A Hooper gathers under pressure as Wimbledon are held to a goalless draw by Walthamstow Avenue in front of 14,000 at Plough Lane in the fourth round of the FA Amateur Cup on 23 February 1952. The Dons players (in the white shirts) are Fred Gauntlett, Harry Wallis and Doug Munday. The game was screened by television. The replay was drawn 1-1 and the match was eventually settled at Highbury with the East London side winning 3-0. (Getty Images)

but by the early 50s all the other clubs that had been hit hard by the war were recovering. New ideas were being introduced, they were all moving forward and we were being left in their wake. In my first season the club finished second from bottom. A year later we finished slightly higher but lost three more games, and financially the situation off the pitch wasn't much better.

It was a time of huge transition. The club was broke, results had gone from bad to worse and Doc Dowden spent the last few months of the 1954/55 season sick. Things had to change. The committee recruited Sydney Black to become chairman. He was a property developer, a local Conservative councillor, and he would become the saviour of the club.

Mr Black ran the property company Knight & Co. He was friends with the owners of Chelsea, Myers & Co. So when Mr Black said to Myers he was looking for a manager, Myers spoke to the Chelsea manager Ted Drake and he recommended Les Henley. Ted Drake had been buddies with Les during his time at Arsenal.

Les Henley and Sydney Black were to change everything. The first to go was Doc Dowden. An era which had begun in 1924 when Dowden first played for the club was over. It may have been needed, but you couldn't help but feel the sadness of it all.

✦

THE WALLIS BROTHERS

For the 25 years that followed the Second World War, there would be one surname that would be almost ever-present on the Wimbledon team-sheet: Wallis. And in 1954, the three brothers that would be the centre of the team for the next three years were to play together for the first time.

15 SEPTEMBER 1954
Wimbledon 4 Clacton 2
Isthmian League
By Joe Wallis (player)

I don't suppose anyone can ever dream of having the debut I had. It wasn't a matter of scoring a winning goal or setting up a few goals, it was all about who else was on the pitch. At left-half was my brother Jack and at centre-half my other brother Harry. The pair of them had been integral members of the side for years, but that didn't stop the three of us beaming from ear to ear when I stepped on to the field to complete the trio. It was terrific to play alongside them. I was only 17 at the time.

I don't remember much about the game – at home to Clacton – but I remember my parents beforehand. They were very, very proud. It had never been done, three brothers playing for the same side, certainly not at Wimbledon. It was a huge honour for all of us. Even Jack, who was captain of the side, felt a little humble.

I would never have joined the club if it hadn't been for Jack and Harry. But the team wasn't just about the Wallis brothers, it was also about players like Doug Munday. He was the backbone of the side.

My other abiding memory was the crowd. The fans were great in those days. There were around 7,000 there that day. I had watched the occasional game, but it did little to prepare me for when I was playing in front of them. It was great. I loved Plough Lane. The atmosphere was terrific.

I was outside-right. It wasn't my best position, but in those days under Doc Dowden we didn't really experiment. Doc was vaguely in charge, but we didn't really have anyone running the side as such. We were pretty much left to our own devices.

Joking Joe: Joe Wallis in his latter years with the club heads a balloon at a Wimbledon function as Eddie Reynolds, Les Henley, Peter Kenchington, Ted Murphy and John Martin look on. (John Martin)

Les Henley changed it all around when he came in a year later. Les turned Wimbledon into a professional club. It completely changed, and I went to centre forward or wing. He totally transformed my game, and I learnt a lot under Les. It was my brother Jack who taught me the game, but it was Les that helped me graduate.

I was at Wimbledon until 1969. I left in 1957 for Bromley, but it was like chalk and cheese. I was at Bromley for two seasons, but everything was different there: the atmosphere, the coaching, the lot. I wanted to go back. I missed the players and the spirit too much.

❖

LIFE UNDER HENLEY

With Les Henley now in charge the club was playing catch-up, and everywhere things were changing both on and off the pitch. For some the changes gave them the opportunity to join the Wimbledon story.

AUGUST 1955
Les Henley trial
Possibles v Probables
By Ron Wootton (player)

I went for a trial in 1955. A friend of mine, Brian Fisher, said I should go down to the club. So we both wrote off asking for a trial. We ended up playing in a Possibles v Probables match in front of the manager, Les Henley. Les had only been at the club a matter of weeks. The selection process back then was totally different to how it is now. It wasn't just the view of Les Henley that mattered. After the match, we all had to face a 15-man committee in the boardroom above the

North Stand at Plough Lane. They would decide if you were good enough to join the club. We went in one by one. You had to be pretty neat and tidy.

There was one long table, with seven people on either side and Sydney Black, the chairman of the club, sitting at one end. The club's secretary, Ted Fenton, introduced me to the committee, and I stood there for 10 minutes while they grilled me. It was the real third degree. Les Henley asked me a couple of football questions. "Why did I sometimes cross the ball with my left foot when I was a right-footed player?" was one of them. Then it was the turn of the rest of the committee. They wanted to know what I did for a living, what education I had had, where I had played before, what I thought of this and of that. It was the way most amateur clubs did things back then.

The interview finished with Les Henley stating what I could do on the pitch and how he saw me fitting in. Only three or four got through, Brian and me amongst them. I was very, very happy.

The committee structure was central to everything in amateur football back then. They even used to pick the team, but once Les came in that was the end of that notion at Wimbledon.

Les Henley was the first professional coach to come into the Isthmian League. And he and Sydney Black began the club's great journey.

They were trying to give the club a more professional outlook and they were giving the players the best benefits they could manage.

In those days there were no floodlights. So if we had an evening game at the start or end of the season it would have to start at 6pm, and that made it really difficult for most of the players to make it there in time. So Mr Black used to send a car for us.

The club was run very efficiently and they were even very strict on expenses. Some people might try and get the odd sixpence more, but I couldn't. I came from West Norwood, the same route that the treasurer took.

My Wimbledon career began a week after the trials when I played outside-left for the reserves at Clapton Town. The following week, I went back to the same ground to play for the first team at inside-right.

Les Henley saw me as a utility player. I must have played in about six different positions, but rarely in my favourite position as wing-half.

My debut for the first team was very different to what I had been used to in junior football. I remember Doug Munday, the captain, bellowing instructions all the time. I had never got shouted at as much as that before as a player. I had just come from St Lukes in the Thornton Heath District League. I just hadn't expected that, but then everything felt new.

There were the simple things, like playing with a new ball each week, to the more complicated, like training. Training was so much more organised. Les Henley had all these programmes that I had never known in my time in junior football. Then there was the pace in the games, you just couldn't slack. In junior football you could give the ball away and get away without chasing back. At Les Henley's Wimbledon there was no place to hide.

Then there was also the style of play. Les changed that dramatically in his first year too. He switched Jack Wallis, one of the club's best players, from an out-and-out centre forward to being a midfielder. Wallis would pick the ball up in the middle and play it up the two wing men, who were acting like strikers, and they would create chances in the goalmouth. The system is now known as the "Don Revie formation" after Revie's work at Manchester City and this was the first time I had ever seen it used anywhere else. Looking back, the club were real revolutionaries.

Eventually, I got used to it and got into the routine at Wimbledon. The starting line-up was pinned up on the board on the Thursday before the game. So you knew whether you were playing or not before the match itself. I'd arrive at the ground about an hour before kick-off. The little groundsman would have all the shirts hanging up on the pegs waiting for you.

At half-time Les wouldn't rant or rage, he would just come up and talk to you individually. He would explain what he wanted you to do, who to pick up, what ball to hit – it was all very tactical. He was a mild chap. He didn't have to do loads of shouting from the touchlines. That was all left to Doug Munday.

The worst thing would be if you were sitting on the bench next to Les. When we did something wrong, he wouldn't shout, he would just thump his fist down, but not on his own knee, but on the bloke's knee sitting next to him. I picked up quite a few injuries because of that.

But it was also Les who encouraged the team ethic. It showed in his tactics and in his training. He wanted us all to work together and bond together. We were all working-class lads and we liked a drink, and Les, who could drink a few himself, encouraged it. And that helped build the club's spirit.

I remember Johnny Haynes came to the club for a while and in one game he started clapping Harry Stannard to try and get him to pass the ball. Johnny was way too good for us, but after treating Harry like that we all just thought he was a fancy dan. He ended up at Fulham, but with an attitude like that he would never have fitted in at Wimbledon.

✦

SWITZERLAND AND THE BENEFITS OF MR BLACK

In the 1950s, the club's benefactor, Sydney Black, believed firmly in giving his players the best and it was under his stewardship that Wimbledon began to go on tours abroad. The first of these under Mr Black's stewardship came in 1956.

WHITSUN 1956
Tour to Switzerland
By Ron Wootton (player)

The club was undergoing huge changes. Les Henley was bringing in the professionalism on the pitch, but off it, thanks to the finances of Sydney Black, whole new avenues were opening up that none of us could ever have dreamed of before. The trip to Switzerland in 1956 was one of those.

You have to put it all into perspective. The season before I had been playing for a local junior side and now I was going to be flying to the Alps. It was unbelievable. None of the team or management even owned a motor car in those days, with the obvious exception of Mr Black, who had his Rolls-Royce. And most of us had not been abroad, myself included, let alone been on a plane. So when we were told in the Easter of 1956 that we were all going to be flying off to Switzerland to play FC Lengnau of the Swiss fifth division, we were all really excited.

We went over for four days. It was the first trip the club ever went on under Sydney Black, and he paid for everything.

Most of us were South London lads. We had had our away trips in the Amateur Cup to far-flung places but nothing could prepare us for Switzerland. It was a whole new world.

We flew out on a propeller plane from Heathrow, which was then called London Airport. We were all far too excited to be scared.

I remember when we arrived at Berne Airport it was pouring down with rain. The plane stopped in the middle of the runway and as we got off there was this fleet of stewardesses, every one of them with an umbrella, there to meet us. It was so novel for us. We felt like film stars.

I was amazed by Berne. I remember they had a bear pit in the middle of city – none of us had ever seen anything like that before. That was just one of the many things there that were so new to us.

I shared a room with Jack Wallis and Tom Wright, three single beds. We saw the Swiss Cup final in the impressive Berne Stadium, but in the main we travelled on the coach looking at the countryside.

Alpine experience: Dons on tour in Switzerland in 1956. Back row: Micky Unwin, Edgar Goodens, Reg Oakes, Derek Jeffreys, Les Henley, Fred Gregory, Jack Wallis, Jack Mildren, Gordon Tillyer, Bill Roberts, Tom Wright, Les Bragg, Doug Sayers, Bert Corke, Sydney Black, Walter Bachman. Front row: Joe Wallis, Ron Wootton, Alan Brown, Eddie Jennings, George Coote, Derek Holyoake, Doug Munday, Harry Wallis. (Ron Wootton)

We went to Interlaken, Berne and Basle. We must have looked like kids in a sweet shop. There were the Alps, the beautiful lakes and the wonderful waterfalls. Going up on a ski lift for the first time and having coffee and tea in a restaurant up there was just amazing. All the images from the trip are still so fresh even now.

There then were the socials with all the yodellers. I remember we all had a go on the huge yodelling horn. We all tried but none of us could get a note out of it. And then up stepped Joe Wallis. Joe was the smallest player in the team by a mile. He was only 5ft 4in tall. He was a bit of a joker, the rest of us were a pretty serious mob. He seemed ridiculous next to it, but then he took one deep breath and this note came blasting out. He had a really Norman Wisdom type smile and he was beaming away like anything after that.

That year was the beginning of professionalism at Wimbledon. It was Les Henley's first side and he was doing very much what Terry Eames had to do with the first year of AFC Wimbledon, developing the club in his own image and slowly bringing in new players.

As for the match itself, I don't remember too much about it. I remember the weather was horrible and I think we lost. But given everything else we had experienced it barely mattered.

Later that evening, we were all presented with a watch. Mine was inscribed: "FC Lengnau, Ronald Wooton Whitsun 1956." There are two t's in Wootton, but I didn't mind. I still wear the watch now and it still works.

✦

SHAMATEURISM

By 1956 nearly every club in the Isthmian League was paying their players. It was known as "shamateurism". Wimbledon were among the exceptions, but the club's principled stance had its consequences. In the post-War years, Wimbledon had failed miserably in their attempts to emulate the successful side of the 1930s. They had reached the FA Amateur Cup final in 1947, but that was nine years ago. It was time for change, and for some it was a change too far.

SEPTEMBER 1956
Plough Lane Boardroom
By Jack Wallis (player)

Things were changing at Wimbledon and they were changing quickly. I had Wimbledon in my blood and I had nothing but respect for the early ambitions of the new chairman Sydney Black. He had brought in Les Henley, who was a fantastic coach. Les came in with new ideas and new training programmes which far surpassed anything we had been used to before, and you could visibly see the difference he was making to us on the football field. I was optimistic for the future. That all changed after one meeting with the management at the start of the 1956/57 season.

Ever since their arrival at the club Sydney Black and Les Henley had held regular meetings at Plough Lane with the senior players, which included me. I had been at the club for 10 years and they were keen to hear my views and to sound out their ideas.

And I remember at this particular meeting, Les Henley and Mr Black were in total agreement. They wanted to introduce shamateurism to the club. I couldn't believe it.

I was proud of Wimbledon's insistence to honour the amateur code, against the wider trend. I was playing football for the fun of it, not for any financial reward. And the same was true for a number of us. We had all been offered the chance to go elsewhere and get paid, but we had turned it down to stay with Wimbledon.

But Mr Black was a very ambitious man. He was the sort of chap who would never settle for second best. He had to win at everything and he, along with Les Henley, decided that the way we had gone on previously couldn't continue.

I remember clearly him saying: "We have to start paying players. It's no use carrying on as we are if we want to be successful. We cannot continue to try and make silk purses out of sow's ears. We have to look to other players and we have to offer them money."

They tried to persuade me to accept the new regime, but I told Mr Black and Les Henley that I wasn't prepared to join the arrangement. And we had a parting of ways.

Shamateurism came in very quickly after I left. It was all unofficial. Nothing was really spoken about it. The players used to get an envelope after every match.

My brothers Joe and Harry stayed to the end of that season, but after that they left, along with the club captain Doug Munday.

The next season was when everything really started to change at Wimbledon. Les brought in dozens of new players and there were maybe only two or three first-team players left from my era at the club.

Sydney Black and Les Henley were to change the club dramatically, and no doubt the success that was to follow was down to their decision to adopt shamateurism. I just didn't want to go along with it.

But what pleased me was that the spirit of the club remained. My brother Joe returned to the club two years later after a spell at Bromley and stayed until the late 60s. He always said how much he enjoyed his football and the atmosphere at the club. After I left I played against the club a couple of times and they were always happy.

✦

THE NEW WIMBLEDON

By the late 50s Wimbledon were at last beginning to relive the successes they had enjoyed 20 years before. It had a lot to do with the new management, to such an extent that the club was becoming unrecognisable to the one that had existed just five years earlier.

SEPTEMBER 1959
By George Coote (player)

Everything had changed. I had left the club in 1957 to do my two years' National Service. By the time I came back the club was almost unrecognisable. Les Henley and Sydney Black had begun the process of change when I had left, but that was mainly with tactics. By 1959 we had floodlights, a gym and all new equipment. Sydney Black must have put so much money into the club. It was just so different I couldn't believe it.

The training had also gone to a new level, it was so organised. Mike Kelly and the other goalkeepers used to train on their own with Les Bragg. The rest of the team used to practise defensive and offensive formations. We would sit round and discuss tactics at length. Then we would split the pitch into two halves and put into practice what we had just heard.

The club could hardly have been more different to the side I had played for under Doc Dowden. But it was clearly having an effect. When I had left for National Service the club had progressed a little but we were still no better than a good mid-table side – never in danger of getting relegated, but certainly nowhere near challenging for the title. By my return the club were the reigning Isthmian League champions. The club had last won the title back in 1936 and we were to win it three more times in the next five years.

Football was changing rapidly, and Wimbledon were at the forefront of it all. Our physio invented the modern shin pad; we were playing the Don Revie "M" formation when most other clubs were still playing the old "W" formation. We were starting to use plastic-covered footballs. The studs in our boots were screw-ins. Before that we had had to hammer our own studs in. Derek Holyoake and I used to give our boots to his father, who was a cobbler, and he'd do them for us. The boots themselves had changed dramatically. In 1953 they were still going up over the ankles like old war boots; by 1959 they looked pretty similar to the boots players use now.

The fully amateur ethos the club used to have had gone, the game had changed, and that also meant the end of the road for so many Wimbledon legends.

Doug Munday, Jack Wallis, Harry Wallis and Harry Stannard all retired. All of them had been at the club since the 40s.

Doug Munday had been club captain. He was a cool, level-headed player, very much in the Danny Blanchflower mould. Jack Wallis was a steady sort of player. Harry was a tall man, a domineering sort of player and quite skilful. Harry Stannard was an old-fashioned centre forward. He was a goal-grabber like Jimmy Greaves. He didn't seem to do much, but he always seemed to be in the right place at the right time. But they were all in their 30s, and by the mid-1950s the game had

Champions: John Martin, Roy Law and Bruce Rudge celebrate winning the 1958/59 Isthmian League title. (John Martin)

In training: Les Henley takes charge. (Hazel Martin/WISA)

speeded up dramatically. They just couldn't keep up. The game was no longer the one which they knew. So in came the likes of Roy Law, Les Brown, Geoff Hamm, John Martin, Brian Martin and Bobby Ardrey. These were the players that were to take the club into uncharted areas. And all under the guidance of Sydney Black and Les Henley.

Sydney Black had no great ambition to reach the fully professional ranks, but I think even back then he had the Southern League in his sights, and by the time we won the FA Amateur Cup we had nowhere else to go.

Les Henley, meanwhile, encouraged team spirit. He wouldn't take no for an answer. If you got a knock, he would tell you to run it off. It helped that all the new players came in at the same time – we were all roughly the same age and with similar personalities. We all wanted to win and we all wanted to do it for Wimbledon.

◆

MARTIN GOES FROM THE BRIDGE TO ENGLAND

In the late 50s Les Henley stepped up his search for new players. Henley's search had not gone unnoticed by his friend Ted Drake at Chelsea. And when John Martin turned up at Stamford Bridge, Drake decided he was the perfect player for Wimbledon. Two years on John Martin was to play for England.

SPRING 1960

England v Wales (Goldstone Ground, Brighton)

By John Martin (player)

I did my National Service with the army in the north of England. Up there I had played for the regiment side and I had also played for Evenwood Town in the Northern League. When I got back, a friend of mine wrote to Chelsea asking for a trial. I played a couple of times for their Combination side and then Ted Drake, who was their manager, recommended me to Les Henley at Wimbledon. So I joined the Dons in 1958.

England honours: New caps (from left to right) Brian Martin, Roy Law and John Martin in 1960 at Plough Lane. (John Martin)

I didn't mind as Chelsea kept my registration as well, so I could play for them if they called on me. A few of the Wimbledon team had similar deals. They never called. I found out later that Les Henley refused to release any of us. He had put a stop on anyone playing for any side other than Wimbledon. In hindsight, I didn't mind. I loved Wimbledon. It was a good social life and we all stuck together. The spirit was immense.

I was in the 'A' side to start off with, but I progressed quickly up to the first team. It was obviously so different to what I had experienced at Stamford Bridge. Wimbledon were improving, but the facilities at Chelsea were in a different class. What impressed me at Wimbledon was the camaraderie of the players and the spirit of the club. It went from the management right through the first team, the reserves and down to the 'A' team. And the fact that I'm still friendly with a few of them now, nearly 50 years later, speaks volumes.

The club was really moving forward on the back of that spirit, and two years later I was called up to play for England amateurs. It was an honour and I was well pleased.

Representing your country was something I could only really have dreamed of. I remember getting the letter through the post telling me. Roy Law, the club captain, was expected to get the call, but I was very surprised. It was a nice surprise of course. I have never been an excitable person. I'm not one to jump up and down and celebrate, but inwardly I was very happy and my family were very proud. But to be honest I think that first cap had a lot to do with the style of play at Wimbledon. A lot of clubs were still playing with the old 'W' formation, but the system we had at Wimbledon was very similar to the one used by England. Football after all is not about one player. He needs the help of 10 others.

I started in the squad against Germany in early 1960 as a non-playing substitute. Terry Venables was playing that day for England, but I think he had turned professional by the time I made my England debut a few weeks later. My debut was against Wales at Brighton, and Roy Law made his debut in the same game. I remember the match well. Their left-winger went off injured, and as they didn't have any substitutes in those days I had a pretty easy game at right back. It was to be the first of 22 caps I won for England.

The England amateur caps were part of a legacy at Wimbledon. Brian Martin and Bobby Ardrey were capped later that same year. Les Brown and Geoff Hamm had already played for England. Les had even played for Great Britain in an Olympic qualifier. It was all proof of the growing talent at Wimbledon. We were going places. We had set ourselves the target of becoming England's No 1 amateur club and we were edging closer and closer towards that goal.

✦

THE FIRST LEAGUE SCALP

Wimbledon had been climbing up the amateur ladder. League titles were becoming an annual ritual at Plough Lane, but the Dons had yet to prove themselves to a wider audience. Sydney Black had tried to get the club elected to the Southern League in the summer of 1962, but was thwarted. The vacant spot went to Oxford United instead. Black felt the club needed a higher profile and what better way to do that than to succeed in the world's oldest cup competition?

3 NOVEMBER 1962

FA Cup first round proper

Wimbledon 2 Colchester United 1

By Roy Law (captain)

I remember the game clearly – it was the first time I saw our ground absolutely full. It was a wonderful atmosphere and a great result. The FA Cup always generated a great atmosphere and we didn't have to get gee-ed up for it. We took the lead midway through the first half thanks to Les Brown. Then disaster struck. Bobby Ardrey clashed heads with someone and had to go off. Those were the days before substitutes so we had to battle on with 10, while everyone was busy trying to patch him up off the pitch.

He eventually came back on about 10 minutes into the second half. It had been a Herculean effort to keep them out up until then. Then with about 15 minutes to go the ball found its way out to Bobby on the left. He must have still been dazed, though, as he was supposed to be playing inside-right. He had nothing of a left foot and I remember him having to get the ball onto his right to cross it. It didn't seem to affect him, though, his cross was perfect. It found Eddie Reynolds and we were 2-0 up. It was then that I suspect some of the players realised we were on the verge of making history. Colchester scored almost straight away, but we hung on.

We had been after a League scalp for so long, and now, 73 years after the club's first game on Wimbledon Common, we had finally done it.

My one regret was that I got injured and didn't play in the second round against Bristol Rovers. I was really disappointed to miss that one. I didn't even go to the game.

In those days you could sense that the club was on the up – maybe not quite as far as the Premier League but you could feel we were going places. It

Jubiliant Dons: Wimbledon fans crammed into the Wandle Valley End at Plough Lane in 1962 (above) and (below) celebrating on the West Bank at the same game. (Gerry Cranham)

helped that we were also doing so well in the League. That installed a sense of confidence throughout the team and it meant we never went out onto the pitch thinking we were going to get beaten. We were so full of confidence.

The outlook on football was totally different in those days. People played for their local club and they played for the love of it. I was born in Croydon, so I always wanted to play for Crystal Palace, and that was just natural. I got onto their ground staff, but busted my leg.

I then went into National Service and after that I played on Sundays, with Frank Tolfrey, who was a reserve team player at Wimbledon.

He invited me down for a trial. That was in 1958, and the atmosphere at the club, even then, was great, you could feel it was going places, but it still took four years before we claimed that first important League scalp. From then on there was no stopping us.

✦

REYNOLDS HEADS DONS TO GLORY

The Dons had swept all before them in the amateur game. They had won the Isthmian League, the South of the Thames Trophy, the Surrey Senior Cup and more or less every other tournament they had entered.

But one trophy still eluded Les Henley's side: the FA Amateur Cup, the amateur game's élite cup competition. That was all to change in 1963. One spring afternoon in early May, for the first time in the club's history, the Dons walked onto the hallowed turf of Wembley. The club had reached the final twice before, but this was the first at the national stadium. The opponents were Sutton United. Geographically, the two sides may have been near neighbours, but this was a rare meeting. The Dons were to win 4-2 with all four goals coming from the head of Eddie Reynolds.

5 MAY 1963

FA Amateur Cup final (Wembley)

Wimbledon 4 Sutton United 2

By Geoff Hamm (Wimbledon vice-captain)

I remember the final whistle vividly. I was full of emotion and clamped my arms around Roy Law, the captain. His face was full of joy and we were ecstatic. I don't know why we were near each other on the pitch. He was a centre-back and I was inside-left, so we should have been much further apart. Maybe we were both tired and out of position, but somehow it seemed destined to be. Roy was an inspiration to most of the team, me included.

Then it was up the steps to lift the cup. I can't remember where I was in the line, but I remember the roar from the crowd. That was special. We'd won the Isthmian League for the third time in five years, but this was the icing on the cake.

I had joined the club in 1958 and we won the Isthmian League in my first season. We won it again in 1962 and 1963. It was then the best amateur league. Crook Town and Bishop Auckland in the north were also great sides back then. But the Isthmian was the place to be. And we fancied our chances against Sutton – they were from the Athenian League, and we knew we were better.

We had quality all the way through our side. Roy Law was a hell of a player. Brian Martin at inside right and Eddie up front. Bob Ardrey and John Martin were tough lads who could play a bit as well. You never got an easy game when you played Wimbledon.

The first half was pretty tight, but we roared into a 2-0 lead within eight minutes of the re-start. I suppose then we thought we'd done enough, but we were to get a bit of shock as they got two goals against us to pull level. But I think we still knew we would win, especially with Eddie up front.

Goal: Eddie Reynolds, obscured behind the far post, heads in Wimbledon's fourth goal in the FA Amateur Cup final at Wembley on 5 May 1963. (Getty Images)

Eddie was such a big strong player. He was left-footed and was good on the ground, but he never had the confidence there. He was all up top.

I remember setting up our third goal. I was on the left touchline. I'm right-footed so it was an inswinger – my left leg is just for standing on. And Eddie Reynolds got his head to it. I don't remember how he did it, but I remember the ball hitting the back of the net. It was an important goal for us as Sutton had been threatening.

In the dying seconds, we were all tiring and Sutton were pushing forward. The ball fell to Les Brown, who played on the right wing. He just tried to kick the ball out of the stadium, which was no mean achievement at Wembley. I had never seen him kick the ball so hard or so high. He was just trying to waste time, we were all so tired. I don't think he achieved it though, but he was the sort of person who would try that sort of thing, and I suppose we were all happy to get a breather. Eddie's fourth just before the final whistle sealed it.

I was very emotional. I was fortunate to have won the trophy once before with Woking in 1958, but it was no less special the second time around. The whole day was so special for the whole team. We weren't really an emotional bunch, but that day we were all pleased. It was a great, great day.

In hindsight, the win also led to the end of my career. Wimbledon were the dominant force in amateur football then and the club couldn't go any further. We won the League the year after and the decision was taken to go semi-professional. Everyone signed pro forms except me. Les said I was too old.

It's sad a day when you hang up your boots – it's the worst thing you can do. Once you've done it there is no going back. Your fitness goes quickly and then it's all over. I looked after the reserve side for a couple of years and the club looked after me. They sent me up to Lilleshall for a coaching course and I still had good times at Wimbledon, but it was never like playing.

I went back to Wembley for the first time 25 years later for the FA Cup final against Liverpool. My daughter had got me a ticket and I went on my own. It was an emotional day. I looked at the pitch, where 25 years ago I had embraced Roy Law, and here was Alan Cork doing the same to Dave Beasant to celebrate a win for Wimbledon, my Wimbledon.

✦

MARTIN NAMED CAPTAIN OF BRITAIN

The club were getting twitchy about investigations into payments for players. A move to professionalism was imminent. The management knew it, the players knew it and the fans knew it. For some of the players it would mean the end of international recognition, as back then there were only two international sides: the full national side and the amateur side. John Martin was to earn the ultimate accolade in that final amateur season: he was to be named captain of Great Britain.

SEPTEMBER 1963
Iceland 0 Great Britain 4
Olympic qualifer
By John Martin (Wimbledon player and captain of GB)

had played numerous times for England, but the chance to play for Great Britain in the Olympic qualifiers only came around once every four years. We played four games, two ties home and two away. And I remember them all. The reason is simple: I was captain for all four games. I remember vividly the moment I was told. We were training at Chelsea Barracks before the first game against Iceland, and they pulled me aside. I had no idea what was happening. I thought I was in trouble or something. And then they told me. I was a bit taken aback. It was right out of the

blue. I never thought they were going to make me captain. I thought they would give it to Roy Law – he was captain of Wimbledon at the time and that would have made sense. But it was me they called over to meet the manager and the committee. I couldn't get over the fact that I was going to be captain of Great Britain, yet Roy was captain of my club.

The first game was in Reykjavik in September 1963. We won 6-0 and my Wimbledon team-mate Brian Martin scored twice. Brian and me were often confused as brothers, but to see the two of us you would know straight away.

I was a regular with England then, so I was familiar with the routine. We used to fly in, go straight to the game and fly back. It wasn't that social and it did me no good at all. I used to suffer a lot from travel sickness. So I was relieved when the flight back got delayed. It was an added bonus spending a night there. I could actually relax.

The return was also special, simply because of the location. It was at Plough Lane. I remember that clearly – there were about 3,500 there. I think a lot of Wimbledon supporters turned up that day to give us a cheer. Bobby Ardrey came in at left back so there were three Wimbledon players for the crowd to cheer on.

In the game itself, I remember we picked up a few injuries. Brian Martin broke his leg and another fellow got a bad cut. It was the days before substitutes, so we were left playing with just nine and a half men. But we still won 4-0.

In the next round we faced Greece. The first game was at Stamford Bridge. It wasn't that full

and most of the supporters were Greeks, but my family were there and so were most of my friends. We played amazingly well and won 2-1.

But the return couldn't have been more different. They fielded a totally different side. They were supposed to be an amateur side like ourselves, but we suspected quite a number of their side were professionals. Roy Law came into the side for the return, but it made little difference and we got beaten 4-1. It was gutting. We had played so well at home and to go out like that left a bad taste in the mouth. However, realistically, we

Call of duty: John Martin (far left) captains Great Britain against Greece in an Olympic qualifier in Athens in 1964. Great Britain lost the game 4-1 and went out 5-3 on aggregate. (John Martin)

would never have made the Olympic Games themselves. In those days a lot of countries were still run on a totally amateur basis, and our final qualifier would have been against Czechoslovakia. They were all amateurs behind the Iron Curtain, so we would have been facing their national team.

Back at Wimbledon, the push to turn professional was on. It was Mr Black's desire. I think everyone at the club was for the move up to the Southern League: it was the logical next step forward. But I was a bit hesitant about signing professional forms. I was at the very top of the amateur game. I was captain of Great Britain and England. And it would be a big wrench not to play international football again.

I think the deciding factor for me was the players I was with. We were all happy; we had been together for a long time and we wanted to stay together. We were a happy club and it wasn't just the first team. We used to wait for the reserves to get back, or they would wait for us, and then we would all go off and do the social thing together. There was a unity at Wimbledon. We also had our comedians; the likes of Micky Moore, Joe Wallis and Brian Keats. They were all jokers. You always had to laugh. It didn't matter who you were with or where you were going, they were always capable of making you smile. The whole spirit was what convinced me to stay. We had eight internationals in our first team. All of us knew what we were giving up, but we couldn't really leave. And I intended to get married so the extra money would help out as well.

Things changed when we went semi-professional. Overnight it became more serious, whereas before we had played for the love of the game. We still enjoyed it but it wasn't quite as friendly, and the chance of further international honours had gone.

✦

The Spirit of Wimbledon

CHAPTER TWO: INTO THE SOUTHERN LEAGUE

DEBUT OF THE SEMI-PROFESSIONAL DONS

The victory in the FA Amateur Cup final was the beginning of the end for the amateur Dons. A year later, with the Isthmian title retained, the Dons had nowhere left to go and the decision was taken to turn professional and join the Southern League. The club had tried two years earlier, without success. Now, under investigation for making illegal payments and with three successive League titles already secured, their need was even greater. Clacton Town dropping out of the Southern League had opened a door and this time there would be no rejection – the Dons were in. The side that had begun on Wimbledon Common 75 years before had now taken a giant step and gone professional. This was supposed to be the Promised Land, but for many fans it was a step too far and attendances plummeted. For Wimbledon's chairman Sydney Black, however, it was the fulfilment of a lifetime ambition, and with such a great amateur pedigree expectations were high. They proved to be too high, as Bob Ardrey, a member of the side that won the FA Amateur Cup, recalls.

Dons in training: George Coote, Eddie Reynolds, Brian Rudge, Joe Wallis, John Martin and Roy Law. (John Martin)

I t was the dream of Sydney Black, the chairman, to turn semi-professional. He'd felt as an amateur team we'd gone as far as we could go. We'd won everything from 1959 to 1962. We'd won the League three times in that period, we'd won the Thames Trophy and we were doing well in the Floodlit Trophy against professional clubs. He also wanted the players to dedicate more time to the club. So he decided to go semi-professional. We all kept our old jobs, but now we had a financial responsibility to the club too.

Sydney and the directors had tried to get elected to the Southern League in 1962. But that was more to get a feel of what processes we needed to go through than a real attempt, and the spare spot went to Oxford United instead.

The problem was that to get into the League you had to wait for another team to drop out. Between 1962 and 1964 we kept banging on the door, as we were still winning things, and then when Clacton Town resigned in 1964, the application was put forward and we were in.

And so to the first game as semi-professionals, against Poole Town. To be honest, we were utterly naïve. We were up against it. After all the success of the amateur days we thought professionalism would be a piece of cake.

The whole Southern League set-up was a giant leap away from what we had been used to as amateurs. There was nowhere near the same gulf in wages as there is now, so it was easier for players to drop down from the top divisions. I'd played for Chelsea and Millwall, and we had a few others like that. But all the other teams seemed to be full of quality ex-professional players.

In that first season we played Hereford. Their player-manager was John Charles. They had an inside-forward who had just moved from Leeds and another from Aston Villa. They were in a different class. Even Guildford City down the road were full of class players.

We used to train a great deal for an amateur side: Mondays, Tuesdays and Thursdays at Plough Lane. But that wasn't enough in the semi-professional ranks. Our fitness levels weren't good enough and we'd struggle towards the end of matches.

On the attack: Wimbledon in white shorts go on the attack at Plough Lane. Bobby Ardrey, arm out-stretched, closes in on the goalkeeper, while Eddie Reynolds, centre, looks on. (Gerry Cranham/WISA)

We adapted very quickly, but for those first few games it was very difficult. Against Poole Town we could have played for a week and not scored. Luckily they weren't that great either, and we drew 0-0.

The whole experience was full of irony, for me personally and for the fans. I'd played with Jimmy Greaves at Chelsea in 1955, but I refused to sign a contract as I wanted to stay amateur, so I joined Wimbledon. And here I was nine years later playing professional football. Life I suppose is full of "what ifs".

For the supporters, turning professional was a big, big deal. Most of the people that supported Wimbledon then were fans of the amateur game. And the gates went down dramatically when we turned professional.

They thought if they wanted to watch a professional side they could go to Queen's Park Rangers, Chelsea or Millwall. As an amateur side we'd get gates of 8,000 or 9,000 – far more than the Conference sides get now. We never got close to that once we turned professional.

But not everything from the amateur days disappeared. There was still the family spirit. The wives would go down to all the games, eat in the restaurant at the ground and go to the club functions at Lyon's in Wimbledon. And the club would also hold dances, which most of the players would go to. Then there were the legions of volunteers – the turnstile operators, the tea ladies, and the programme sellers – and that lived on for quite a while. It's very similar to AFC Wimbledon now, and that family spirit helped us survive in those first few years of professionalism.

We may have changed our status, but we were still Wimbledon. And after a goalless draw we knew we had to learn, and we learnt quickly.

By Ken Randall (life-long supporter)

It was a big decision to turn professional. Cyril Black, a Tory MP, was president and his brother Sydney was the chairman. I remember Cyril went on television in the build-up to the decision to join the Southern League, and he was asked: "Did we ever pay our players?" Cyril was a big religious man, but he lied that day and said: "No."

To be honest, players being paid was rife in the amateur leagues in those days, and we were being investigated only because we were successful. Wimbledon were one of the last to pay their players behind the scenes. I remember asking a friend of mine, Brian Fisher, who played for the Dons in 1957, if they were paid, and he said no. He was not the kind of person to lie and I believed him.

The atmosphere was never the same after we joined the Southern League. We used to get big crowds as an amateur side, but we were always going to be squeezed by the likes of Chelsea and Fulham once we turned professional. I was happy as we were – I didn't want to turn professional. I was disappointed as it meant less local derbies. The argument was that we would see much better football, but I wasn't convinced. But it had been on the cards for years and it was always going to happen eventually.

Finance and football never really mixed and, in hindsight, I was far happier before the change to professionalism.

◆

A HAT-TRICK OF HAT-TRICKS SEES DONS UP

It had been a hard transition for the Dons, but once the team began to click, promotion in that first season came into sight. And once more it would be Eddie Reynolds who would prove to be the driving force.

17 APRIL 1965
Southern League First Division
Wimbledon 4 Gravesend 1
By Tom McCready (player)

I always felt that with Eddie Reynolds in the side we could achieve anything. He was a legend. He was excellent in the air, but his footwork was another matter. It was said later that he scored more with his feet than his head, but I can't believe that.

The expectations were massive – everyone thought we would sweep everything before us in the Southern League. So it was essential that we got promoted at the first attempt.

With four games to go that was far from a certainty, and we had to play three of them in four days. We scraped through the first and then the rest was left to Eddie.

He got a hat-trick in each of the remaining three games as we beat Gravesend 4-1, Hillingdon 4-3 and Merthyr Tydfil 4-0. And we were up. Eddie finished the season with 40 League goals – a club record that still stands.

That first season for Wimbledon in the Southern League was momentous for me too. I was the first outside professional to sign for Wimbledon. The bulk of the side was the old amateur team. I was coming up to my 21st birthday when I joined from Watford.

Goal: Eddie Reynolds (No 9) scores against Tooting & Mitcham at Plough Lane. (Gerry Cranham)

Wimbledon legend: Eddie Reynolds. (Gerry Cranham)

The club promised that they would soon be in the Football League, so I didn't mind dropping down. I thought everything would take off from there. I had played for Hibernian before Watford and won Scottish schoolboys honours.

Sydney Black, the chairman and benefactor, was really generous and persuasive, and we had a good side then too, full of amateur internationals. But I was still the new boy and I didn't start initially. We had such a good defence that it was hard for me to break through: they had all played together for years and were a settled unit. Roy Law and Bob Ardrey were the centre halves, then there was Dave Willis at left back and John Martin at right back.

I was a youngster, and it took me nearly the whole season before I got into the team and cemented my place.

Ian Cooke and I arrived at about the same time and we gradually worked up a close friendship. He stayed even longer than I did. I was there for 10 years; he was there for 14 and only left when the club became fully professional.

Coming to Wimbledon also had a huge impact on my personal life. There were four club flats above the pub at the old ground which they used to rent out to the players and staff. Peter Miller lived in one. Eddie Reynolds was also there, and Jimmy Greaves even lived there for a while. And then there was Diane Giles in the fourth.

Diane's mum, Betty, was the barmaid and her dad, Charlie, the groundsman and barman. Diane later became my wife. Betty and Diane used to make meals for all the players, match officials and staff on matchdays – 70 in all, so she tells me. And the romance just blossomed from there.

✦

A NEAR MISS AND COOKE'S NINE IN TWO

After one season of consolidation in the Premier Division, in each of the four that followed Wimbledon would be in the hunt for the title. But as each season neared its finale Wimbledon's form would dip and they would miss out. There were still a number of highlights, including a few huge wins. One of which came in 1966.

10 DECEMBER 1966
Southern League
Wimbledon 9 Folkestone 2
By Ian Cooke (player)

We had always been a team that scored a lot of goals, and the same applied to me personally. But there is a lot, and then there is a *lot*. You can never predict these things. We fancied our chances to score a few against Folkestone, but not nine.

It's nearly 40 years ago, but I remember it very well. It was the first time in my career that I had been asked to play right wing. I'd always had the No 8 on my back and now I was wearing the No 7. Les Henley, the manager, wanted to see what I'd be like on that side.

Well it must have worked as I scored five, and I think I got three of them with my head. I scored quite a few with my head during my time at Wimbledon, despite only being 5ft 7in.

Folkestone I recall had two big guys at the back. They were big but they were also ponderous, and they should really have been able to deal with a little guy like me, but I kept on getting round the back and getting my head on the ball. I felt as if I could score every time the ball came near me.

Bathed in sunshine: Wimbledon go on the attack against Yeovil Town in the Southern League on 27 August 1966. Wimbledon won 2-0. It was the year that Ian Cooke cemented his place in Wimbledon's front line. (Geoff Seel)

It was a great day. To score five in a game was amazing and I still have the newspaper clipping from that game. The Wimbledon Guardian had pictures of three of my goals on the back page.

I nearly repeated the feat the week after, when we beat Corby 6-1. I'd got four and then blazed a penalty over the bar. But nine in two games is no bad return.

Those two wins took us back to the top of the Southern League, but every year with Henley it seemed to be the same. We'd start brilliantly and then fade just before Easter. Certainly in the first few years in the Southern League we always seemed to be at the top at some point, and I suspect it was his biggest regret that he never won the title.

In 1967 we were top until Easter, and then came Romford. We played them twice in three days and lost both 4-1. Even then, if we had won our last two games we would have been champions. First up was Nuneaton Borough. One of their players scored from a stupid distance. The game ended 1-1, and mathematically the title race was over. We lost the final game at Bath 1-0, and Romford won the title by three points.

My own route to the Wimbledon ranks was a weird one. I was playing for my work, Westminster Bank, on Saturdays and Copyc Colts on Sundays. The Colts were a young side, with Jack Goodgame in charge. We weren't playing at the highest level, but Jack saw a lot of potential in the team and told a few of us try for trials at the bigger local teams. And that's how I came to Wimbledon.

I went training with the A squad under Eddie Jennings, and within a couple of weeks I got a telegram at work saying I had been called up to the reserves on Saturday. And that basically meant the end of my time playing for the bank.

I scored a lot of goals for the reserves – I liked to feed off a big forward. I'd played the last six games in the Isthmian League with the first team and that's when the problems started, once the decision was made to turn professional.

My contract at the bank meant I wasn't supposed to take on any other outside employment. I asked them if I could sign for Wimbledon and they refused. So I told Les Henley that I wanted to stay amateur, and after a couple of weeks to consider it he said no, and I was dropped back to the A team.

Sydney Black, the chairman of the club, tried to help out. He sat me in a room and asked me how much I was getting paid. I told him and he offered me £1 more if I went and worked for him. It was tempting, but banking was my career. I really didn't know what to do.

I went back to the bank, and they introduced me to an ex-professional who tried to talk me out of it. The bank finally said that I could sign, but that they didn't want me to. That was enough. I stayed at Wimbledon until 1976.

SYDNEY BLACK

There was no doubt that the arrival of Sydney Black marked a dramatic rise in Wimbledon's fortunes. He rebuilt Plough Lane and helped attract new players to the club. Without him, Wimbledon would never have scaled the dizzy heights that were to follow. He died on 4 April 1968.

4 APRIL 1968
By Ted Fenton (Wimbledon's club secretary)

Sydney was a great influence. I doubt whether Wimbledon would have survived without him. We were struggling before he arrived.

It was Bob Watts, the then chairman, who first approached him back in 1955. Fred Gregory and the then club secretary, Bert Corke, went along too and Sydney agreed to help.

Sydney put a huge amount of money into the club. He brought the floodlights. He covered the West Bank. He had the club house renovated. And by 1968 the whole club bore the stamp of Sydney Black.

We both had our full-time jobs. He had his business to run, Knight & Co. and I had my job to do, but six nights a week we would come together and run Wimbledon Football Club.

It was a great time, but by the end we knew Sydney was dying. Through his smoking he had clogged the arteries going to his brain. He couldn't think straight. He kept going to sleep. He used to lie in bed for days on end. Les Henley and I would visit him in his house. He was up there all on his own. It was very sorrowful.

He still used to come down to matches as much as he could. But he had to be shepherded into the ground and someone would have to keep an eye on him at all times.

I remember the day he died vividly. I got a phone call from his company secretary, Len Hibbard. I had known it was coming, but the shock was still there. He was 56.

His memorial service was a huge affair, and it seemed as though the whole of Wimbledon had come out to mourn him. Most of the players were there and so were a number of distinguished members of the Football Association.

It was difficult to find someone to replace him. His influence with the local Council and Surrey

County Council was hugely important to us. Fred Gregory, who was the vice-chairman, stood in for a while but it was too much to expect Fred to emulate Sydney.

It was a very difficult period and it visibly took something out of Les Henley. Les had achieved so much, but with Sydney gone you could see his enthusiasm begin to drain away.

✦

ANOTHER NEAR MISS

The end of the 1967/68 season had been overshadowed by Sydney Black's death. The passion of the club was on the wane. And it hit Wimbledon badly on the pitch. Once more they were on the brink of League success and once more they faltered.

4 MAY 1968
Southern League
Wimbledon 1 Chelmsford 2
By Roy Law (captain)

The Chelmsford fixture was always a tough one, one I certainly never relished, and this time there was even more of an edge to it. It was the penultimate game of the season and we were more or less level on points at the top. It was a classic winner-takes-all match.

Most of my memories of the day have faded now. I remember vaguely that Eddie Bailham gave us the lead and thinking we were going to win the League at last. The feeling didn't last long – they scored twice and the title dreams were dashed again.

However, the season will be remembered not for the Chelmsford defeat and another year without silverware, but for the death of Sydney Black. He was a Wimbledon man through and through. One word sums him up. He was a gentleman, a thorough gentleman. He would do anything for the club. He was a successful businessman, but football was his love. And the club deserved to be successful under him. We had wanted to win the Southern League as much for him as for ourselves. Ask any of the players from that era and they'll give you the same answer.

Sydney Black and Les Henley were the perfect partnership, and the club thrived under them. It was a wonderful time to be at the club with those two at the helm.

Les took the club from being insignificant to being the leading amateur club in the country. The dressing room was Les's domain. Sydney Black used to come in and wish us luck but he never interfered on the playing side. Les created a good camaraderie within the club. A lot of the players had been successful elsewhere, but Wimbledon was special. All the players were prepared to do anything for Les – they respected him. When he stood up, you listened.

The two were like chalk and cheese. Les was your typical South Londoner. He'd come up the hard way. He had been on the Arsenal staff and had been some player. But in my opinion he was an even finer manager. Sydney didn't get knighted, but if he had lived a little longer he probably would have been. The club was never the same after he died.

We won the last game of that season 5-0 at Plough Lane, against Barnet. It was always nice to win the London derbies, but after the defeat to Chelmsford and the death of Sydney there was a sombre mood over Wimbledon that day.

We seemed destined to never win the League. The Southern League was a tough one, certainly the toughest I ever played in. It was full of ex-professionals and players who were good enough to be professionals, but had chosen to stay semi-professional for one reason or another – those were the days where there was no fortune to be made in football, so for some there was no reason to step up.

✦

THE FAILURE OF 1969

The following season, Wimbledon were once again riding high. Surely it would be third time lucky? Again there was talk of the championship, but again the Dons were to trip on the final hurdle.

14 APRIL 1969
Southern League
Kettering 3 Wimbledon 1
By Eddie Bailham (player)

This was a game we had to win if we wanted to stay in contention for the championship. We had lost the previous match 2-1 against Burton at home, and we hadn't really done ourselves justice. The local press had laid into me. A local reporter had been giving me grief and I was keen to prove him wrong. I was an easy target. I wasn't the type of player who would run around all day – I would only go after the balls that I thought were worth chasing. And for that I got labelled lazy. But many great players were like that. Peter Osgood certainly played like that, and I was aggrieved at all the criticism I got from the press.

We had led the table for a couple of months before the Burton defeat. The fans were expectant, and now the pressure was on us to respond and get back on top.

I scored early on and that was a great start. I thought: "This will show the local press, this will prove that Wimbledon are not to be underestimated." But Kettering came back and scored three times. We couldn't believe it – our title hopes had gone once again.

It seemed like it was always nearly, but not quite. And the Kettering game was just the latest example. As a team it took us a long time to recover from that.

Cambridge United won the League that year. They were a rich club, and they won it again the year after and got elected to the Football League. Without them maybe Wimbledon could have made the breakthrough earlier.

End of the wait: The 1970 Southern League Cup winners. Paul Hodges, Dave Willis, Ian Cooke, Ray Colfar, Dave Harney, Tom McCready, Peter Shreeve, Jimmy Collins, John O'Mara, Dickie Guy, John Martin and Stuart Davies. (John Martin)

A PROFESSIONAL TROPHY AND END OF HENLEY

With Sydney Black's legacy fading, the club was on the wane. Les Henley still had the respect of his players and he managed to lift them one last time. In 1970 the club won their first professional trophy, but it was not enough to convince the Dons board that he was the man to take the club to the next level – the Football League.

2 APRIL 1970

Southern League Cup final

Wimbledon 3 Romford 0

By Tom McCready (player)

I n a way we felt cursed: come Easter, we always seemed to have a bad spell. We always seemed to blow it at the end of the season. You could sense the frustration from the supporters. We were desperate to win a piece of silverware for them.

Each season we would work our way into the top three and then it would just slip away. We just didn't win the vital games. Chelmsford, Oxford United or Romford always seemed to deny us. They were all full of ex-professionals and they all paid more than we did.

In the 1969/70 season, everything at last seemed to be going right. We had our biggest ever League win – 9-0 over Crawley. John O'Mara got a hat-trick that day. He was a big fella, lanky. He was quite skilful, but he couldn't really head the ball. Ian Cooke also got a hat-trick.

In goal we had Graham Roope. He was a great player too. The only problem was that he was a professional cricketer for Surrey and he was always worried about breaking his hands. Gerry O'Rourke – the mad Scotsman – also played that day and he also scored. The goals just seemed to rain in from everywhere. We had talent, and Crawley just couldn't cope with us.

The 9-0 win put us on course for the top of the table. Then there was the Southern League Cup. And that was probably the reason we slipped up in the League that year.

We saw off Dunstable, Dover and Hastings fairly easily in the early rounds. We scraped past Oxford and Bedford 1-0 in the quarter-final and semi-final respectively. And so to Romford in the final.

We won the first leg 3-0 at Plough Lane and at last a trophy was as good as ours. We drew the second leg 1-1, and for the first time since 1964 Wimbledon had some silverware. We always had around 3,000 fans, who really believed in us, and for years we felt we had let them down. Now at last we had won something. We all thought it would lead to bigger things – but it all went sour.

In the last few years I was with Wimbledon everything went into decline. Sydney Black had died in the mid-60s, and in his will he left a seven-year fund for us, but that ran out in the early 70s and the club was broke. We kept changing managers too, and that didn't help.

Les Henley should never have been sacked. We had finally won a trophy and we were riding high in the Southern League at the start of the 1970/71 season. The stigma of always just missing out had gone, but the board obviously saw it differently. In February 1971 they replaced Les with Mike Everitt, but that didn't work out so a couple of years later they gave the job to Dick Graham.

Each new manager would bring in a bunch of his own young players, and the old side that had done so well over the previous 10 years was further eroded. They got rid of Roy Law and Brian Martin, and each season we got worse and worse. In my last season we slipped into the bottom half of the table – it was as bad as I had ever known it.

I had loads of offers from other clubs, but the key was the club's attitude. At the end of the 1973/74 season they forgot to send all our registration forms to the Southern League, and the entire squad became available on free transfers. Many of the players stayed, but I was fed up.

Graham had left and in had come Allen Batsford. I couldn't know what he would go on to achieve, I just saw the same pattern as before: a new manager and a new bunch of players. Batsford phoned me and asked me to come back. We had a long chat, but I thought that the team was poor and there's no money. I couldn't see any future for Wimbledon. I got a really good offer from Dulwich – twice the money – so I went. In hindsight I wish I had never gone – they were even worse than Wimbledon!

✦

The Spirit of Wimbledon F.C.
Wimbledon

CHAPTER THREE: THE BATSFORD YEARS

THE ARRIVAL OF ALLEN

Money was short, Dick Graham had gone and the club had no one lined up to take over. The club were desperate and in Allen Batsford they could hardly have got a better replacement.

SUMMER 1974
By Allen Batsford

I had been at Walton & Hersham for nine years. We had won the FA Amateur Cup and I felt I had gone as far as I could at the club. The club had reached its peak. And then one day I remember looking at the newspaper and seeing an advert for the manager's job at Wimbledon. I rang the club straight away and got through to the chairman, Jack Bevan. Wimbledon were a big non-league club and they were advertising for a manager. It was too good an opportunity to miss.

I went for an interview in June that year. It was all very straightforward and there didn't seem to be any problems. I went back for a second interview and they offered me the job. I was so keen to come to Wimbledon that I even took a slight wage cut.

I was desperate to get the job. I was so naïve. I said yes to it before I had even met the board and before they had told me about the club's financial situation. Financially, the club were in dire straits. They had almost no money to spend and there were only seven players on the books.

It was an almost impossible task. They wanted to restrict the amount I paid the players. They eventually agreed to leave it all up to me, but there was no money available for transfer fees. I ended up signing seven of my ex-players and we began the season with no reserves.

To their credit, my old Walton players wanted to come too. They were a bit surprised by the wages, but they still came. The key, though, was bringing the two groups of players together: the seven old Wimbledon players and the seven from Walton. The two gelled well. Dave Bassett was on one side and Cooke was on the other – they were both leaders and they encouraged everyone to mix in. It helped massively to have players who got on so well.

I didn't know anything about the old Wimbledon players and I was pleasantly surprised. Mick Mahon was an excellent player. He could easily have played in the Football League, but he wanted to be a schoolteacher. We were lucky to have him. Ian Cooke played for 13 years and averaged almost a goal every other game. And then there was Dickie Guy. He was another great character and had a good sense of humour. If there were two people who were going to get laughs among the players, it was Bassett and Guy.

We worked very hard and often. Sometimes we would be training every night of the week. Other clubs commented that they had never seen a club work as hard as we did. Our organisation was superb and we had a great spirit.

Everybody enjoyed winning... and the more we won, the stronger we became.

The new era: Allen Batsford and Ian Cooke in the dug out. (Paul Willatts)

A GAMBLE AND A POOR START

For the players who followed Batsford to Wimbledon it was a huge gamble. They had to sign professional contracts for the first time, and they also had to mix with a rump of Dons players who for the last five years had known only failure at the club.

17 AUGUST 1974
Southern League
Nuneaton 2 Wimbledon 0
By Dave Donaldson (player)

It was a big risk to move to Wimbledon. The club wasn't doing too well, added to which I was 32, but I had worked with Allen Batsford for five years at Walton & Hersham and I knew it wouldn't be the same there once he left.

I knew Allen wanted to take the core of the side to Wimbledon – Dave Bassett, Roger Connell, Kieron Somers and Billy Edwards – so when he asked me it should have been an easy decision.

But for me that meant signing professional terms for the first time. It was very difficult for me; I had a good job at British Airways. It took quite a while for Allen to convince me. He worked out a way to enable me to get to training, and my work colleagues were very helpful. They would cover for me and we'd swap shifts. If we had a game on Saturday then I would swap with someone to work on Sunday instead.

At Walton & Hersham we had won the FA Amateur Cup and many of us had played for England at amateur level. We had been around a bit, but the club hadn't really established itself.

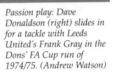

Passion play: Dave Donaldson (right) slides in for a tackle with Leeds United's Frank Gray in the Dons' FA Cup run of 1974/75. (Andrew Watson)

Looking back I don't regret a thing. I ended up playing 60 or 70 times in the League. I would never have had all those great memories if I had stayed at Walton, I'd never have played in the Football League or against Leeds, Burnley and Middlesbrough in the Cup, and I would never have met the likes of Dickie Guy. I owed all that to Allen Batsford.

However, after we lost the first game 2-0 to Nuneaton I wasn't so sure that I'd made the right decision. Selwyn Rice was sent off and the team was totally disjointed. We simply didn't know each other. We gave away a couple of silly goals; Dickie conceded a penalty for one of them. Looking at that game you would never have predicted what was to follow.

But we came back. In training we were determined to learn from that first defeat. The complacency was gone and we realised we had to work hard. I think the memory of that defeat never left us.

David Pleat was the Kettering manager and he said Wimbledon were difficult to play against, even way back then. If only he'd known how much the defeat to his team was to inspire us.

The whole period still seems a bit weird now. It was the first professional contract I'd signed, and three years later I made my debut in the Football League at the age of 35. I was captain for the first-ever game against Halifax (Dave Bassett – surprise, surprise – was suspended). It's been mentioned that I am the oldest player ever to make his Football League debut. I'm not sure whether that's true as no one has ever really been able to verify it, but it's a nice record to claim. I played on for another two years.

✦

THE GREAT CUP UPSET

The FA Cup tie against First Division Burnley was to provide a huge challenge for the club both on and off the pitch. This was the biggest match in Wimbledon's history. Never before had the club faced a side from the country's top division in a competitive senior match. Burnley were eighth in the old First Division, the predecessor of today's Premier League, and Wimbledon hadn't won a trophy for five years. Interest was huge, and the club even organised a train for the journey north, but even in their wildest dreams no one had expected the Dons to get a result. That was until Mick Mahon stepped forward in the 49th minute at Turf Moor...

4 JANUARY 1975
FA Cup third round
Burnley 0 Wimbledon 1
By Mick Mahon (player)

Burnley's goalkeeper parried Ian Cooke's shot and the ball came to me on the edge of the box. I just hit it, and it went through a huge crowd of players. I didn't see where the ball had gone. I wasn't even sure it had gone in. I never saw it hit the net.

It took a few seconds to realise what had happened and before I knew it I was flattened. Everybody was on top of me celebrating wildly. It wasn't the staged celebrations you get nowadays – it was pure joy.

It wasn't the greatest time to score. We had been under so much pressure in the first half and had been happy to go in at half-time scoreless. Scoring straight after the break only encouraged them to come forward even more.

But we had a plan and we stuck to it, despite the relentless attacks. Burnley had Leighton James, the Welsh international, playing on the left. Allen Batsford identified him as their key player so Bob Stockley and Dave Bassett were detailed to mark him.

Normally I'd play on the right wing, but with Dave Bassett playing there I was pushed into the centre of midfield. I didn't like playing there. On the flanks you only really had to concentrate on what was ahead of you. In the middle, you had to look everywhere. I hated playing there, but if you're asked to do a job by your manager, you do it. And it worked. I doubt I would have been in the same place when the ball came back to me after Ian's shot, if I had been playing out wide.

Then there was the final whistle. All the whooping and wailing, people banging into each other. We were delirious. We had a few drinks in the changing room; none of us could believe it. But then something strange happened. It all went quiet. I think that was when we realised what we had just achieved.

We were a non-league side and we had just beaten a team riding high in the First Division away from home. It was unprecedented, and we were speechless. All we could hear was their manager Jimmy Anderson screaming at his players in the adjoining changing room.

That night Ian Cooke, Allen Batsford and I were invited to Manchester for Match of the Day. It was only a quick interview, and unfortunately I never got hold of the tape. I was told that the match highlights were never shown on TV, but I'm sure I saw a snippet of my goal. I'm convinced the tape exists somewhere, but no one has ever been able to track it down. I'd love to see it again.

And then there was the draw for the next round. Away to Leeds. It was too much. The year before I had been playing for Colchester who were top of the old Fourth Division, and we had beaten Leeds 3-2. Everyone was asking me how Colchester had done it. But then misfortune struck – I came down with glandular fever and missed the game at Elland Road. Wimbledon weren't to get the luck I had enjoyed at Colchester and we lost the tie.

Looking back at the two upsets – Colchester and Leeds, and Wimbledon and Burnley – Wimbledon's win was certainly the bigger result. At Colchester we were all full-time professionals, while Wimbledon were just a part-time team. In terms of the global game, Wimbledon's win at Burnley has to go down as one of the greatest results of all time. And I scored the winner!

By Clive Morton (travel secretary)
I took over as the club's travel secretary in 1971 and for the first few years it was a doddle. We had no long Cup runs and the club was stuck in a rut. However, that all changed when Allen Batsford took over, and suddenly my work intensified.

As soon as we drew Burnley of the old First Division away in the third round of the FA Cup, I knew we had to do something special. I thought of hiring a train to take the fans to Burnley. It was a bit far-fetched, but I believed we could do it. I spoke to Paul Howard from the Supporters' club and one of my mates, Graham Kettley, who both worked for British Rail – Paul at Wimbledon and Graham at Euston.

They passed me on to a guy at Euston and I organised a meeting with him. I sat down and explained to him what I wanted to do and how I wanted to do it. I asked him if it was possible. He

On the train to Burnley for the tie at Turf Moor on 4 January 1975: The players (above, left to right) Glenn Aitken, Dave Lucas, Dickie Guy and Bob Stockley. (Andrew Watson) ...and the fans (Yellow and Blue)

said: "Yes, it is." He had even worked out what time the train would have to leave and what time it would arrive.

The biggest problem was the £1,500 cost – which we had to shell out up front. It was a big risk for the supporters' club, but we decided to proceed. I still have the receipt.

Later I had a meeting with the guy who had been in charge of our train and I asked him how it went. I remember his response clearly: "It was like a Sunday afternoon picnic." On the train they had a special carriage in the middle to lock up people if they caused trouble. Only one person ended up in there.

It was such a buzz to see it all come to fruition. It had been a great day and a great achievement. I was so relieved when it was all over and that it had all gone smoothly. That was before I heard the Cup draw: "Leeds United, the champions of England, will play... Wimbledon."

Everyone was excited and for 10 seconds so was I, before it struck me that I would have to do it all over again, only this time it would be twice as big.

We started off with one train and soon realised that we would have to run two. It helped that the Burnley experience had gone so smoothly. We were even allowed hot food on the Leeds train and that was unheard of on football specials in those days. If memory serves me correctly, I think we got mash, sausages and beans.

The only complaint from those who travelled on the Burnley train was that they had to get on it at Euston, so this time we arranged for the Leeds train to run directly from Wimbledon. The train to Burnley took just under three hours, but for the Leeds journey we had to swap tracks at Clapham Junction and Nine Elms, so the trip took about five hours.

The two supporters' trains weren't the only big projects I'd undertaken at Wimbledon. Four years earlier, I devised the idea of a player of the year award. I agreed it with the chairman Jack Bevan and I remember buying the award from a shop in Haydons Road. Roy Law was the first winner in 1971. That trophy and the two trains are my greatest achievements at Wimbledon and I'm proud of them.

✦

GUY DENIES THE CHAMPIONS

So it was on to Leeds United, the reigning champions of England, where Wimbledon would have to play in the fourth round of the FA Cup. Surely the Dons could not repeat the heroics of Turf Moor? Leeds were a class apart from Burnley and had a side packed with internationals. For 85 minutes the two sides could not be separated, but then disaster struck – a penalty to Leeds…

Cup challenge: Ian Cooke (right) under pressure from Gordon McQueen and Frank Gray, gets a header in at Elland Road against Leeds United in the fourth round of the FA Cup on 25 January 1975. (Ian Cooke)

53

25 JANUARY 1975
FA Cup fourth round
Leeds 0 Wimbledon 0
By Dickie Guy (Wimbledon goalkeeper)

I remember it as though it was yesterday. It's still vivid in my mind. The fourth round of the FA Cup, five minutes to go and then it happened – a penalty. I remember thinking: "You prat, Harry." Here we were – Wimbledon, of the Southern League, at Elland Road holding the mighty Leeds United, European Cup finalists the previous year. And Dave Bassett, who we all knew as Harry, goes and does that.

It was typical of Harry. Either the ball or the player goes past him, but never both. The decision, a penalty to Leeds, was inevitable. Afterwards he said he'd wanted to make me famous, so I suppose I can forgive him for that.

The atmosphere at the ground had been fantastic all day. I walked out onto the pitch before the game trying to read the programme, but I was trembling in my boots. I'd never seen that many people in one place before and all I could hear was 46,000 fans banging on the hoardings shouting: "Leeds, Leeds, Leeds."

We had developed a game plan and we stuck to it. In the end it was just 11 against 11. We had no reason to be scared. We did everything that manager Allen Batsford had told us, and it looked like we were going to pull it off. Then Harry goes and does that.

I don't think we'd ever practised penalty kicks at Wimbledon. There's little point as a goalkeeper. To save them you have to be either agile enough to adjust or just lucky.

I remember Peter Lorimer stepping up to take the spot-kick. He had a reputation for having the fiercest shot in football, and I was expecting it to go flying into the corner, so I took off anticipating exactly that. But he scuffed it.

I was in danger of diving over the ball. I had to pull my right arm back to stop it, and I only just managed to scoop the ball out.

Everything then went mental. All I remember is that Jeff Bryant kicked it out for a corner and I was angry with him for that as I was convinced I would have got to it. And once it was out everyone jumped on me. But we still had a corner to contend with and I couldn't even tell you how we got that clear.

I don't remember much about the final whistle. I just got to the dressing room and anyone who was anyone was there. I was dragged out to face the media. I must have fielded what seemed like a thousand questions. I had to have a swig of brandy to calm myself down. Later on the BBC interviewed me.

That night we all stayed in Leeds – I didn't go too mental as ITV had booked a car for me and my wife to travel down to London the next day to take part in Brian Moore's Big Match at the South Bank studios. It was a packed journey as my wife's cousin and the chairman ponced a lift down. It all seemed to happen so quickly.

It was easily the highlight of my career. It wasn't the best game I played. I played better at Burnley in the previous round and at Middlesbrough two years later, but for the sheer emotion nothing will beat that match at Leeds. Even now strangers come up to me and talk about it. I've got the game on tape and I make my kids watch it every week!

Harry had made me famous all right, but he had his revenge in the replay with the own goal that put us out. Now that I haven't forgiven him for.

Exhaustion: Roger Connell collapsed on the pitch at Elland Road after the 0-0 d[...] with Leeds. (Andrew Wats[...]

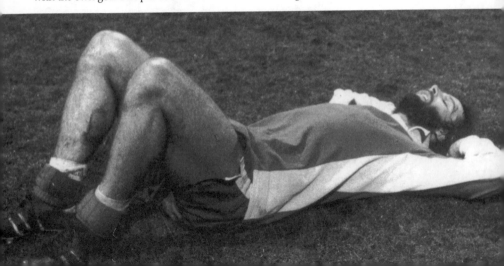

By Ray Armfield (life-long supporter)

It would be tempting to say my favourite Dons' memory is the Cup Final in 1988, but in reality it is still the trip to Elland Road in 1975 to see Wimbledon play Leeds United in the FA Cup fourth round.

I'd seen the Dons in many of the qualifying rounds and also in a tough second round game at home to Kettering. Victory in that one gave us the trip to First Division Burnley, where Wimbledon weren't given a prayer. A single-goal victory was sadly missed by TV coverage and as I couldn't go to Turf Moor, I felt I'd missed out a bit.

My dad probably sensed this. So when he came home from work on the Friday night and said: "Do you fancy going to Leeds tomorrow?" I didn't hesitate for a second. Those were the days before supporter membership schemes, so if you got there early enough you got in.

Trying to be helpful, I woke up the next morning, got dressed and made some sandwiches, before stirring my dad. He said: "It's 3am, son." Oops.

I was aware there were around 2,000 Dons fans going to Yorkshire, many on two special trains. We got to Euston early enough to travel up with one or two other Dons fans and the further north we travelled, the more Leeds fans piled onto the train. We got to Leeds early enough to have lunch and got a special bus to the ground from the city centre.

I recall getting into the ground early enough to virtually pick my spot on the terrace reserved for Wimbledon supporters. Much of the match was a blur, but fortunately I've got the Big Match highlights on video to remind me. The main talking point was, of course, Dickie Guy's penalty save. It was at the Leeds end, but I had a clear view. When I saw Peter Lorimer was going to take it, my heart sank. But when I saw he was going to place the ball rather than blast it, something told me: "Dickie's going to save this." And he did. Cue pandemonium on the terrace.

My dad wasn't an overly demonstrative man, but I can't recall ever seeing a broader smile on his face than when I turned around to hug him. In the final minutes there was wave after wave of Leeds attacks, but we held on for the 0-0 draw. Then came the trip home. Reality sank in when we heard a mass chant as to how we were going to get our heads kicked in, but fortunately we were swept out of the ground and straight onto a bus back to the station with some sensible Leeds fans who congratulated us.

On the platform, we saw one of the Dons' special trains being hit by a few missiles, but our scheduled train a few minutes later wasn't targeted. On the way home, I couldn't stop thanking my dad for taking me to Leeds, but his smile said it all – he'd quite enjoyed himself as well.

✦

DONS SUNK BY BASSETT'S BAD LUCK

After the draw at Leeds, Wimbledon had wanted to host the replay at Plough Lane, but demand for tickets was huge and the tie was switched to Selhurst Park. Again the Dons seemed on course to deny Leeds, but just after the interval Johnny Giles hit a wayward shot and Wimbledon's luck ran out.

10 FEBRUARY 1975

FA Cup fourth round replay

Wimbledon 0 Leeds 1 (at Selhurst Park)

By Dave Bassett (player)

It wasn't the hardest of shots. I was in line with it and all I heard was Dickie Guy shouting: "Keeper". So I turned sideways to move out of the way, but I just couldn't get my left knee out of the way in time and the ball hit it and went in the other corner. It all happened so quickly. It was a horrible feeling. We had come so far, and especially as I'd given away the penalty at Elland Road I really didn't want to make another mistake.

We had played so well up to then. The game was heading for extra-time and then possibly another replay, and the club could really have done with the money. And then that happened.

To be honest, if Dickie hadn't shouted, I would have stood my ground and whacked the ball over the halfway line. But I can't have a go at him for that because he had got me out of jail at Elland Road by saving the penalty.

It was a great cup run, and what most people forget is that it had begun months earlier. It started in the first qualifying round at Bracknell way back in mid-September. Then there were the second, third and fourth qualifying rounds. Then the first and second rounds proper. Then that amazing game at Burnley before we bumped into Leeds. By the time it came to the replay we had played enough Cup games to get to Wembley twice.

It was a bit of a shame that the game was never played at Plough Lane. I'd love to have seen the then League champions playing there. But the weather was really bad and the police didn't feel Plough Lane was really up to staging a Cup tie of such importance. So it was switched to Selhurst Park. There were 45,000-plus there and, yes, there were lots of Leeds fans, but we had a good following too. I think the whole of London was there cheering us on.

Bemused: Ian Cooke leads the Wimbledon team out past two Wombles at Selhurst Park for the fourth round replay against Leeds United on 10 February 1975. (Andrew Watson)

It was an amazing atmosphere. We were confident; we were tough buggers. And we wanted to prove to everyone that we had survived the penalty and now we could beat them on our own patch. We wanted to finish the job. And we were so close to doing it. For a non-league club to hold the League champions and then nearly repeat the feat in a replay is unheard of. It was an amazing achievement, but that night all we felt was disappointment.

Our consolation was that we went on to win the League for the first time, but at the time all we wanted was a victory over Leeds.

*The run ends: Leeds'
Billy Bremner turns
to shake Dickie Guy's
hand after Leeds
United's 1-0 win over
Wimbledon at
Selhurst Park.
(Andrew Watson)*

*Champions:
Wimbledon players
celebrate winning the
1974/75 Southern
League championship.
(Andrew Watson)*

DONS RETAIN THE TITLE

After the successes of the previous season, the pressure was on to reproduce the goods. Allen Batsford would not fail. The team lost only once in their last 21 league games of the 1975/76 season. For good measure they also won the Southern League Cup for only the second time. In the final few games of the season, Wimbledon unearthed a new hero – John Leslie.

27 MARCH 1976

Southern League

Stourbridge 0 Wimbledon 6

By John Leslie (player)

'd arrived with a great recommendation from Vince Parker, my coach at Dulwich Hamlet. Vince said to me that Mick Mahon was coming to the end of his career and that I should go down to Wimbledon and give it a go. He knew Allen Batsford really well and set it up. So I went down and got in. I wanted to vindicate Vince's faith, but my Wimbledon career began really badly. I came on as a substitute against Nuneaton and lasted about 20 minutes before I was stretchered off. After recovering from the injury, I came back in but couldn't really get into it. I played about 10 games in the League and only scored once.

It just wasn't happening. I desperately wanted to prove to Allen Batsford that I was worth it. And then came the match with Stourbridge. It was the turning point for me. We won 6-0 and I scored four times. I scored three in the first half in a 10-minute spell. I remember the second one crystal-clear – I suppose it's about time I owned up to it. It was a mis-hit cross that went in

Night riser: John Leslie scores with a header against Colchester United. (Paul Willatts)

at the far post. I was young. I was new at the club, so of course I told everyone that I meant it. It was a big lie.

My fourth goal was different – I meant that. Allen dropped me back to midfield in the second half. I just wanted to shoot from everywhere and I caught it really cleanly and it flew in from outside the area.

I had vindicated Vince's opinion of me and it obviously impressed Dave Bassett, who was then the Wimbledon captain. He made Vince his chief scout when he became manager a few years later.

After scoring four, I thought that was it: "I'm in, my career is made." But Batsford had a funny way of running things. He'd play me in a load of games, but if I ever did something special he'd drop me for the next game to stop my head getting too big. And that happened after Stourbridge. They drew 0-0 against Atherstone without me, and Allen got lots of the stick in the paper for that decision, but then the same thing happened in the big cup games.

I was looking forward to playing Middlesbrough in 1977 and he left me out. The year after we had Spurs in the League Cup and he did it again. Each time I had played all the games before and I was to play all the games afterwards.

After being spurned for the Spurs game, that was it as far as I was concerned. I was going to walk out there and then. But Dave Bassett talked me out of it. He said I was young and had a long future ahead of me, and that for most of the older players it was their last chance to play in such a match. He said my time would come. He was right and I owe him a lot for that.

But Allen never explained why he dropped me. I suppose he just thought I was young and there was no reason to give me an explanation. Had he dropped Ian Cooke or Dave Bassett then he would have had to say why, but I was just a kid. It hurt at the time, but it also made me stronger.

However, the 6-0 win set us up for the run-in and we just coasted home. I scored twice against Nuneaton in the penultimate game at home and that secured the title.

✦

A BLOSSOMING ROMANCE

In the summer of 1976, Allen Batsford signed a raw 18-year-old, Terry Eames. One of the first people he met at the club was Anne. The pair would eventually marry, and 26 years later form the backbone of a new chapter in Wimbledon's history when Terry became the first manager of AFC Wimbledon.

AUGUST 1976
By Anne Eames

I never thought that romance would blossom between Terry Eames and me. Allen Batsford brought in Terry in 1976. He was just about the youngest player in the club and I was six years older than he was. A year later Ron Noades, the chairman, made me his secretary and that's when I started seeing Terry regularly.

In those days there was only Ron and me in the office. Adrian Cook was the club's secretary, but he worked in central London. He would come in in the morning, give me loads of work to type, head up to town and pick it up in the evening. Eric Willcocks produced the club programme, but he did most of that from home. Allen Batsford was only part-time, so he only came in occasionally, but it was through Allen that I really started to get to know Terry.

I remember Allen saying to me that he was a bit worried about Terry. He said Terry was too shy and he asked me to get him involved with things. There were so many characters around the club in those days and the club was very social. We used to go out together and have fun, very much like AFC Wimbledon, and I think Allen wanted Terry to feel a part of it. I agreed and dragged Terry into the group.

But I don't think Terry was particularly impressed with me in those days. My cousin and I used to walk down to the chip shop before matchdays and pass Terry along the way, and I felt he thought I was snooty.

When we were trying to set up the ladies' team, Terry used to come and watch and help with the coaching. I thought I'd try out for the team just for the hell of it. I was hopeless, and all Terry did was stand on the sidelines and laugh. By that time I remember thinking he was quite cute, but nothing more than that because the age gap was so big.

That all changed when Alan Cork joined the club. Dario Gradi had just taken over and signed Alan and Steve Ketteridge from Derby. I was 26 then and I used to live with my family. I had a flat of my own at the top of the house. Dario wanted to find some digs for Alan and Steve, and asked me if I would let them stay in my flat for a few weeks. I could cope with Alan – he was easy-going and laid back – but Steve was a different story. He was far too lively. So after the agreed couple of weeks were up, I told Dario that I'd keep Alan, but that Steve would have to find somewhere else to stay.

The young couple:
Anne and Terry Eames
in 1978. (Anne Eames)

Future manager: A
young Terry Eames.
(Getty Images)

Family: The Eames girls in 2003, including
Anne on the right. (Alex Folkes)

Over the next few weeks, Alan became good friends with Terry, and that was when I really started to get to know him. Batsford had been right in saying he was shy and I knew he would never make the first move, so I had to. We had a few drinks and I decided to see if he liked me. Fortunately he did.

However, our romance only ended up causing problems for both of us at the club. Dario didn't like the fact that I was in the office and I was also so close to the players. He thought someone was feeding information back to them about certain things and was suspicious of me. I certainly wasn't, but there was no convincing him.

I had no choice, I had to leave. I didn't want to go. I loved my job. I loved working for Wimbledon, but I could always go to another secretarial job. It was different for Terry. He had his professional career. This was his big chance and I knew that. I didn't want to jeopardise it so I left and he stayed. And then, blow me down, but a few months later Terry picked up an injury and a specialist said he could no longer play at that level.

I may have quit the club, but I had Wimbledon in my heart. I'd started to watch the Dons when I was eight years old. I was too young to go to Wembley for the Amateur Cup final, but I remember when they brought the Cup back to Wimbledon Town Hall and paraded it before all the fans. And I remember watching the same parade and the same celebrations at the same place 25 years later, only this time it was the FA Cup and Terry was at my side.

Looking at AFC Wimbledon, you can almost tell that one of the players here is going to end up marrying an AFC Wimbledon fan.

I look back on it all now and it's as if someone up there looked at what was happening to Wimbledon and wanted two people with Wimbledon in their hearts to lead the way, and luckily they chose Terry and me.

Our girls are now both big AFC Wimbledon supporters, and it's up to them and their children and their grandchildren to take the club on in the future. When I was eight I was standing there with my brother getting autographs, and in years to come it will be my grandchildren doing the same.

✦

BORO PUT DONS BACK ON THE MAP

Two years after the glories of Turf Moor and Elland Road, Wimbledon had still not achieved their ultimate aim of a place in the Football League. They needed to put themselves back in the public eye, and an FA Cup third-round draw against Middlesbrough was perfect. Middlesbrough may have lacked the glamour of Leeds United, but they were a First Division club nonetheless.

8 JANUARY 1977

FA Cup third round

Wimbledon 0 Middlesbrough 0

By Dave Donaldson (player)

It was a cold miserable day and they were complaining about everything – the floodlights, the pitch, the changing rooms. League teams never looked forward to playing us, they were accustomed to their luxury. We had nothing to lose. It wasn't life or death for us, but if they got knocked out it would be a total embarrassment. They received good salaries, so the pressure was on them.

They were also used to a reasonable surface and good lighting in the First Division, and we just didn't have that then at Plough Lane. I suppose if you put yourself in their

In pursuit: Terry Eames (left) and Dave Donaldson (right) give chase at Plough Lane. (Yellow and Blue)

situation, they had a view of what was acceptable. They were used to a quality environment, but that is the great thing about the FA Cup. It is a great leveller and the more they harked on about it the more determined we became.

We expected to do things in the FA Cup. The year before the Middlesbrough tie Brentford beat us in the second round, and we were all disappointed. We had got used to reaching the later rounds.

We always felt we would go much further than any other non-league side and that was our aim every year. We felt on our own patch that we were a match for anyone, and that included Middlesbrough.

They had Graeme Souness in their side then, and Jack Charlton was their manager. If we had lost 4-0 people would say it was only Wimbledon and they were playing Middlesbrough. But for a top team to lose to us – now that would be a different matter.

We were a strong side. We had players who could tackle, players who could play. We were familiar with each other, we had been together for many years and we understood what people had to do. We also had a good level of intelligence. I was working part-time with British Airways, Mick Mahon was a schoolteacher, Ian Cooke was a bank manager and Dave Bassett and Roger Connell were also clever guys. We could talk things through on the pitch, and as a lot of us were in our 30s we had experience as well.

We used to drive the ball up to Roger and Ian. It was hard for teams who weren't used to that style to cope with us. That was the case against Middlesbrough.

They just couldn't cope. We felt we had a perfectly good goal disallowed. Roger Connell put it in and the referee harshly chalked it off. It would have been perfect justice for their arrogance.

✦

DONS PAY THE PENALTY

The replay was to provide little joy for the Dons. On a snow-covered pitch at Ayresome Park, a second-half penalty was all that would split the sides. At least Wimbledon had once again shown that they could live with the élite of British football.

11 JANUARY 1977
FA Cup third round replay
Middlesbrough 1 Wimbledon 0
By Ian Cooke (player)

I t all came down to a penalty, just like at Leeds, but this time there was no miracle save from Dickie Guy. What was so upsetting was that there was no reason to give it away. Allen Batsford had a game plan. The midfielders would make sure they always doubled up when a winger attacked the full-back. It meant that if the full-back was beaten there was always someone behind him to kick the ball out or make a second tackle. It had worked brilliantly at Burnley two years earlier, when Bob Stockley and I shut out Leighton James.

Dons on tour: Wimbledon players climb off a coach in 1977. Back row: Ian Cooke and Dave Donaldson. Front row: Jeff Bryant, Dickie Guy, Billy Holmes and Glenn Aitken. (Andrew Watson)

Two years on, and Kevin Tilley was playing right-back and I was in midfield. He was only a young lad and had done well all day.

But with about 30 minutes to go David Armstrong cut in from the right about 10 yards from the goal line and got the ball past him. I was there behind Kevin and I kicked the ball out for a throw or a corner (I can't remember which). I had done my job. But it was too late – Kevin had stuck his leg out and Armstrong had won a penalty.

I just remember thinking it was so unnecessary. Yes, it was a penalty, but I thought there was no need for it, we should never have given it away.

Kevin just went for the tackle, but he was just fractionally too late. Allen didn't berate Kevin after the game. No one did. It was just an unfortunate incident. If Kevin had just held off for a moment, it would have been OK. The worst that would have happened from there was that Armstrong might have got a cross in, but he was never going to score. Armstrong scored from the spot.

To lose was deeply disappointing. I wasn't that impressed with

The finale: Ian Cooke (left) with ex-Wimbledon player Barry Silkman after his testimonial against Crystal Palace in 1977. It was his last season with the club. (Paul Willatts)

Middlesbrough. They had three or four internationals, including Graeme Souness, but we weren't under the sort of pressure that we had been against Leeds and Burnley.

We had the ball for about 50 per cent of the time against Middlesbrough – against Leeds and Burnley it had been no more than 35 per cent.

I was playing as an attacking midfielder, and I felt there was much more room to place my passes. But we just didn't deliver the final ball. The crosses and the through-balls were just falling short or were over-hit. Our defenders were in control, but up front we just weren't clicking.

But we had impressed again, and in hindsight it was decisive in our election to the Football League. For me it spelt the end of my 14-year association with the club.

The board was talking about the Football League; it was gathering support from various places. The club had prepared a glossy brochure to promote the campaign. Everyone knew it was on the cards. We had already won the League twice and if we kept knocking on the door they would have to let us in sooner or later.

Allen had said that if we went into the League, we would stay part-time and that suited my career with the Westminster Bank. But when it came to it the decision was taken to go full-time. I was 32 and that was when I left to join Slough.

It was one of my biggest regrets of my life that I never played in the Football League. I could never imagine being anywhere other than Wimbledon. I felt I had two or three more years in me. I was as fit as I'd ever been. In my mind I had already been thinking how I would get the time off to play in those midweek games in the far-flung northern places, but it was never to be.

LESLIE'S DOUBLE PUTS LEAGUE IN SIGHT

The target remained a place in the Football League, but even to stand a chance Wimbledon had to retain their Southern League crown. The key match was seven games before the end of the season at home to title-chasing Kettering.

25 APRIL 1977

Southern League

Wimbledon 2 Kettering 0

By John Leslie (player)

I wasn't even supposed to play against Kettering. I had gone along just to watch. I was due for a cartilage operation the following day. I'd injured the knee against Maidstone in October and I played on it a few times after, but I knew it wasn't right. So I consulted a Harley Street specialist. He told me I wouldn't be able to play without having an operation.

I was gutted by the diagnosis. Yes, I knew there was a problem, but I just wanted to keep on playing. I had worked hard to get into the team, we had such great players, and I just wanted to keep my place and score the goals that would take us to the title.

It was such an important match against Kettering and I didn't want to miss it even if I was there just as a spectator. Both teams had been chasing the Southern League title all season. We were just ahead, and there was an air of anticipation about the game. It had stuck out on the fixture list for weeks. Then one of our guys pulled out with flu and Allen Batsford asked me: "Can you play?" There is no way a manager today would ask a player to play in that situation. People are far more cautious about injuries now than they were back then.

And equally, there's no way I would have agreed if it had happened in the modern era. But this was 1977 and I was only at the start of my career and full of the naïvety of youth. So I pulled on my boots and probably played my best game of the season.

I suppose what helped me was the fact that I had gone to the game so relaxed and not expecting to play. Everyone else

High flyer: John Leslie rises to head home at the Wandle Valley End at Plough Lane against Huddersfield Town. The Dons won 2-0. (Paul Willatts)

was a little edgy; you could sense it on both sides. But the Wimbledon lads had a special spirit and we thrived on these types of matches. I scored the first and we went on to win 2-0. I have this great picture of me being held up by Roger Connell after I scored. I'd stuck two fingers up to the away fans and the caption read: "John Leslie correctly predicts the final score." The next day Allen cancelled my knee operation.

So much for Harley Street. To this day I still haven't had the operation. After the win over Kettering, there were still a few games left, but that was the decider and both teams knew that. In those days a lot of the games were more or less walkovers. We used to feel upset if we drew away from home. Not many teams worried us, but Kettering were different, they were a class outfit. It was a classic six-pointer and we had won it.

The celebrations that night were great. I don't drink and never have, but a few of the other lads were not shy about putting the drink away that night. We knew then that the title was ours and the focus off the pitch turned to getting elected to the Football League. We cantered through the remaining fixtures and left Ron Noades and his committee to concentrate on getting us into the League. We'd done our bit by winning all those trophies in our last three years in the Southern League. Now it was up to Ron.

✦

DONS 4 DIV 4

After the failure of the last few years, getting into the Football League had become the club's obsession. Back in the 70s clubs could win promotion from the Southern League only if they could gather enough votes from the existing Football League members to be elected. Wimbledon had appointed a new chairman, Ron Noades, who was given the task of garnering the votes. Noades' first move was to form a committee to help him.

SPRING 1977

By Lord Faulkner (Dons 4 Div 4 committee member)

The slogan "Dons 4 Div 4" was all my idea. It just came to me. I think I may have even thought of it while I was sitting in the bath. It was just one of those ideas that come into your head. It combined an improbable football score with a simple message and it works so well as a simple pun.

Before that year, getting into the Football League was all the talk on the terraces. In 1976 there was a big push to get in and we failed miserably – we got only three votes. Yeovil, who had finished six places lower than us in the Southern League, polled 18 and missed out by just three votes. The club had to change their approach.

It was left to the club's chairman Bernie Coleman to sort it out. Bernie had kept the club going when Sydney Black died, but he had never intended to stay on as long as he did. And after the club had failed so miserably to win election to the League he knew the club needed a new injection of energy. He turned to Ron Noades.

Ron had been in charge at Southall, but he didn't think the club had ambition. So he accepted the challenge and took over at Wimbledon. Ron's first action was to call on all the supporters to aid a massive "public relations" effort to help get us into the League. He formed a committee of 13 from the supporters. I was one of the 13. And the push was on.

The "Dons 4 Div 4" slogan came quite early. Noades and fellow director Jimmy Rose backed it and put in £3,000 to launch the campaign. The slogan was on a brochure we produced and sent out to Football League clubs. It was on car stickers. It was everywhere. Then there was the PR coup of persuading the England cricket captain Tony Greig to join the board.

I was given the task of PR organiser. I used to take the media calls and I also did some radio and TV broadcasts. It was all media-led and targeted. We tried to speak to all the clubs that had votes. I met many of them and tried to persuade them. It was a lot of hard work, but it was also a lot of fun.

It aided our cause that at the same time the idea of automatic promotion to the Football League was gaining acceptance, and we were so obviously the No 1 non-league club in the country. We won nearly all the cups we entered, but what put us on the national stage were those FA Cup runs.

There was endless talk of Wimbledon becoming a League side, and as fans we convened meetings about it all the time. We would discuss it on the coaches to away games, in the local pubs and on the terraces. Everyone was encouraged to try everything and anything to help us win votes. There was a huge team of volunteers, stuffing envelopes, making phone calls and writing letters.

In my lifetime as a fan, this was the first real supporters' movement I had seen. We were working every day of every week for our cause. For the first time, the Wimbledon fan base was politicised.

In terms of our Football League campaign, the turning point came as the date for the election grew nearer when we heard that Altrincham of the Northern Premier League had also decided to put themselves forward. We all knew they would take northern votes from Workington. If we had been the only nominees it might all have been all so different…

Pushing for the League: The Dons 4 Div 4 campaign team. Jimmy Rose, Tony Greig, Allen Batsford, Ron Noades, John Reed and Bernie Coleman. (Paul Willatts)

✦

THE GREAT VOTE

So after a year of hard work and 88 years of history it all came down to a meeting in London. Would Wimbledon finally break through and get into the Football League?

17 JUNE 1977
Football League AGM (at Café Royal Hotel)
By Allen Batsford (manager)

It was late afternoon when Ron Noades and I went in. The vote was going to be taken at the Football League AGM at the Café Royal Hotel in central London. We were dressed smartly, collar and tie. In those days there was no automatic promotion to the Football League: you had to stand for election against the bottom four of the Fourth Division.

Noadsie had done loads of work on the "Dons 4 Div 4" campaign – it was his dream. He talked about it endlessly. He had launched a massive campaign. He had had teams of people visiting clubs up and down the country trying to collect votes. It was my job to make sure the team kept winning.

When I arrived at Wimbledon in 1974, the club was destitute. Playing in the Football League was never my ambition. When I arrived we had no money and only seven players. The aim was just to win the next game. And, if at the end of the season you had organised yourself enough and your players had worked hard, you came away with something. We had a special spirit too, and that helped us in the first season.

The second time, we had our pride at stake. Nobody thought we would repeat the feats of 1975 and win the League again. We proved them wrong.

The year after, the pressure was on me even more. But we prepared well, we always did, and we got the results. In that third season we set a new points record for the Southern League, but for me it was never about getting into the Football League. It was still simply about winning the next game.

But we would never have been at that meeting in June if it hadn't been for the three straight championships. I had my job and I had done it. I had my hands full with the team – I didn't have time to help Noadsie.

We had stood for election to the Football League in 1975 and 1976 and had finished last both times, with four and three votes respectively. I suppose Noadsie had learnt from the previous years and that helped him. Once we got to the meeting in 1977 it was out of our hands. There was nothing more we could do.

We were up against Halifax, Hartlepool, Southport and Workington from the Football League, and Altrincham of the Northern Premier League. I remember the Burnley chairman, Bob Lord, getting up and saying: "Workington have had their chance, they have finished bottom enough times. It's time to give this lot a go."

As we weren't members of the Football League at the time, we weren't allowed into the meeting when the votes were counted. So we had to wait outside to hear the

Champions: Wimbledon celebrate winning the 1976/77 Southern League championship. Without the title the Dons would have failed in their attempt to get into the Football League. (Paul Willatts)

verdict. The voting procedure was complex with 48 delegates, comprising one each from the First and Second Division clubs and four others to represent the Third and Fourth Division sides. Each delegate had four votes.

Unlike the previous years, we thought we had a great chance. The wait seemed to last for ages. I was very apprehensive. We were broke at the time; we weren't prepared for the Football League. And then we heard the result of the voting: Altrincham 12, Halifax 44, Hartlepool 43, Southport 37, Wimbledon 27, Workington 21. We were in.

I was full of mixed emotions. I remember thinking: "We aren't ready for this." Instead of being in the Southern League, Wimbledon were now in the Football League.

The media overwhelmed us as soon as the vote was announced. We didn't have to tell any of the players. The reporters were on the phone straight away and it was all over the papers, the radio and the TV.

Ron felt he had done it. And in a way he had. I remained apprehensive: we weren't in the right shape to make the transition, but we had to take our chance.

But my abiding memory of that afternoon was the Workington people. They were devastated. Their whole world had been taken away from them and it was our fault.

✦

The Spirit of Wimbledon

CHAPTER FOUR: INTO THE FOOTBALL LEAGUE

THE FIRST LEAGUE GAME

So, 88 years after Wimbledon were formed as Wimbledon Old Centrals, they had finally joined the Football League. It had been the club's dream for years and now the reality was dawning. The opening match was to turn out to be a damp squib. Halifax were supposed to roll over and let the Dons enjoy the party; they had clearly not read the script.

20 AUGUST 1977
Fourth Division
Wimbledon 3 Halifax Town 3
By Jeff Bryant (player)

I suppose it should be quite an honour, scoring the first-ever League goal for Wimbledon. But I remember the match for entirely different reasons. About four days beforehand we played Hereford United in a friendly and I had four front teeth knocked out in an accidental collision with our goalkeeper Richard Teale, who had replaced Dickie Guy at half-time.

We were about 4-1 up at the time and walking it, when the ball was kicked long into the penalty area. He didn't call for it, so I went for it and that was that. I remember lying on the stretcher and seeing Billy Edwards, my centre-back partner at the time, towering over me. He said: "I told you he was a nutter." To be fair, Teale just hadn't seen me.

But Allen still had me lining up against Halifax. I started the game with a boxer's gumshield in my mouth. It was really difficult to communicate. And I spent most of the game wary of elbows, headers and collisions. Hardly what you want from your centre back!

The game attracted a reasonable crowd, and Plough Lane had a good feel about it. As for the goal? Well, I'd like to say it was a 30-yard belter into the top corner, but it was no more than a six-inch tap-in. At the time, the significance of the goal didn't really sink in. When you are in the thick of it, you don't really think about the historical significance.

To be honest, by the final whistle we all felt disappointed. We had only led once, four minutes from the end, and that only lasted a minute. Halifax were one of the weaker teams in the division and that left us mindful of what was to come. In retrospect, I'm deeply proud of that six-inch tap-in. But we had had so many big occasions in recent seasons, what with all the cup runs and titles, and this was just another big occasion.

We were all part-timers except for Phil Summerill, who came from Millwall, and Geoff Davies, who joined us from the United States. That created a bit of an atmosphere. Those of us who had worked hard to get the team into the Football League felt like we were furnishing their wages.

The Dons' first League goalscorer: Jeff Bryant. (Andrew Watson)

It was just unfortunate that we conceded so many goals in that first game. We had been so used to having a strong defence that it dented our confidence. And, personally, having no teeth for the start of the season didn't help.

I'd like to say that we buckled down and fought hard to lift ourselves, but the reality was that the lack of confidence drifted through the side. It was eight games into the season before we won our first match. Being part-time didn't help and fitness was a big issue. We would continually be outfought.

Off the pitch the relationship between Ron Noades and Allen Batsford began to sour. Over Christmas they had a huge row and Allen left the club; most of us felt that Ron had orchestrated it. The final straw came with the trip to Swansea. We stopped off at Bristol for lunch, before getting on the coach again. When we arrived we realised we had left Dave Galvin back in Bristol. So Dave Bassett came in at right back and I filled in at centre back. Harry was doing all right but then he turned around and curled a shot over Dickie Guy from 30 yards. It just summed up our season. We lost 3-0 and Allen resigned.

Within a couple of weeks of Allen's departure, we all went full-time with the exception of Dave Donaldson. As is often the way with the arrival of a new manager, funds were made available and that just compounded the unfairness of it all. However, it was a good experience to play in front of League crowds. It had been my dream to play League football and I was really chuffed to make it.

Nonetheless, my really fond memories are from our non-league days. I suppose that back then we were the big fish in a small pond.

As a full-time outfit we had to take it all far more seriously. When football is your livelihood, your performance on the pitch becomes a matter of life and death. As a non-league outfit it had all been so much fun. Football is full of ups and downs and that year was a down. Allen deserved a lot better. He hadn't really wanted Dario Gradi as an assistant, and when Allen left the writing was on the wall for most of us.

I was young and was scoring goals, so I stayed on for one more year. Then I was given a free transfer and went to Bournemouth. After that I kept looking for another Wimbledon – but I never found one.

✦

BATSFORD QUITS

The arrival of Dario Gradi had caused strains off the pitch. Allen Batsford was far from happy and he had failed to get any support from chairman Ron Noades. By January 1978 it had all become too much, and Batsford walked out.

2 JANUARY 1978
Fourth Division
Swansea 3 Wimbledon 0
By Allen Batsford (manager)

It was a difficult time. We were not ready for the Football League and Ron Noades had no idea how to run a club. He made my job absolutely impossible. He stopped players coming in for training because he didn't want to pay their expenses. He interfered with scouting. I couldn't put up with that.

He didn't understand what made us tick. When we moved up it was a step too far for some of my players. They had full-time jobs so I had to try and bring in some new players, and Noades wasn't helpful at all. I had some players who could train during the day and some who could train at night, but Noades wouldn't allow them to train during the day. It was all very difficult.

Then there was Dario Gradi. Ron asked me at the start of the year if I would mind if he brought Dario in to help out. The plan was that he would run the youth team and be my assistant. I said we would give it a try and if by Christmas it wasn't working then we would stop it. I kept asking Dario to help me with the coaching, but he kept saying no. He worked exclusively with the youth team.

The ill-feeling reached its peak on Boxing Day 1977. We were away at Rochdale and Ron refused to pay for a coach to go up north. I had to tell the players that they all had to travel by car. We were more professional in the Southern League without Ron Noades than we ever were in the Football League with him.

A week later, after the debacle at Swansea, I just walked out. I'd been placed in an impossible position. Noades just didn't understand how to run a club. From running everything sweetly for three years it all degenerated into chaos, and it wasn't hard to work out who the culprit was. I still loved Wimbledon, but I felt Ron needed to leave before the club could progress again. He wasn't going to go, so I had to.

THE START OF THE GRADI ERA

Dario Gradi could hardly have taken over at a worse time. The players had been loyal to Allen Batsford and most of them felt he had been betrayed. And then there was the small matter of Ron Noades.

7 JANUARY 1978
Fourth Division
Wimbledon 1 Brentford 1
By Dario Gradi (manager)

Ron Noades was worried, really worried. He had worked hard to get the club into the League but he had made loads of enemies in the process. Now we were hovering above the bottom four and Ron was convinced we wouldn't survive a re-election campaign. When Ron put me in charge he said: "Dario, whatever you do, just make sure we don't finish in the bottom four."

I hadn't been Ron's first choice after Allen Batsford. Dave Bassett was offered the job first, but he didn't want it then, so I was offered the job on a caretaker basis. I didn't find out that Dave had first been offered the job until much later. I had come in so quickly that I know some of the fans thought I had been brought in to replace Allen. But that was never my intention.

My first game in charge ended in a 1-1 home draw with Brentford. Given what had gone before I was very pleased with the result. The next week we came back from 1-0 down to win 2-1 at Halifax. Paul Denny got the winner with 10 minutes to go. After that Ron made my position permanent.

I first met Ron when I was in charge at Sutton United. I had just left Chelsea, where I had been in charge of their youth team. And Ron was impressed with what I had achieved there. But I moved on to Derby where I became assistant manager, and once again I was in charge of youth development. However, finances were tight there and I was sacked. That's when Ron got in touch.

He wanted me to become the assistant manager at Wimbledon and start the youth set-up. Crystal Palace wanted me to do something similar, but I felt they were more after the young players I had at Derby, so I joined Wimbledon.

I spoke to Allen at the time and I asked him if he was happy with me coming to the club. He said he was, so I joined. I certainly wouldn't have joined if I had thought otherwise. But it soon became clear he wasn't happy. I was working with the kids and the reserves. I didn't attend first-team games; I was always out scouting. I didn't see the point of being there. Allen disagreed.

I didn't think it could last. Something had to give, and Allen jumped ship just after Christmas. At the time he accused me of stabbing him in the back, but I hadn't done anything of the sort.

Once I was in charge I realised straight away that the team needed some youth. It was an ageing side. I signed Steve Perkins, Glyn Hodges and Paul Fishenden, who had all been part of my youth team at Chelsea, on free transfers. Paul Haverson came from QPR, also on a free.

I got back in touch with Derby. Tommy Docherty was the manager at the time and was a man of instant decisions. I phoned him and asked if I could sign Fran Cowley, who had been with me at Chelsea, and he said: "You can have him tomorrow." I then asked for another player and he said: "You can have him tomorrow." By this time I was getting a bit more confident, so I asked him if I could have Alan Cork and he said: "You can have him tomorrow." He then said: "When you coming up?" And I said: "Tomorrow."

Fran had no hesitation in joining. Corky was a bit nervous, he was a Derby man through and through, but eventually I persuaded him. The other guy refused, so I phoned Tommy again and asked if I could take Steve Ketteridge.

Ron Noades gave me £20,000 to spend – four players at £5,000. So I brought in Ray Goddard for Dickie Guy for £4,000. Dickie was a great guy, but he was coming to the end of his career and his timing was a bit patchy. He would turn up late for training and that just wouldn't do.

I read that Les Briley was being released by Chelsea and that he was bound for Colchester, who were top of the Third Division. Les was another of the kids I'd had at Chelsea. I thought if I could get him he would be my captain. So I asked Ron if I could spend all the money on him. Ron agreed. So I contacted Les and he agreed. When I told Ron, he said: "Bloody hell, I haven't got the money. Give me a couple of days."

I had to stall the deal as long as I could. I think Ron had assumed that Les would opt for a bigger club. I don't think he thought for one moment that Les would join us. In the end Ron sold the mini-bus he had just purchased for the club back to the garage and leased it back to make up the shortfall.

Every player I signed was full-time and I worked hard to get all the others to sign full-time too. Only Dave Donaldson stayed part-time. But he was great. He was working with air traffic control. We could be playing Stockport away and he would say he would be there for 7pm. He never let me down. He used to get a plane up there from London.

Braving the cold: Alan Cork and Dario Gradi. (Getty Images)

He was 36, but he was still quick and he was a great influence on the side. I wanted to keep some of the old players to help balance the side. I knew how important the old Wimbledon spirit was and I wanted the younger players to experience it. In hindsight, I think it worked.

✦

TOTAL HUMILIATION

In the 70s Wimbledon had become used to success. Their exploits in the FA Cup had also gained them a label as giant-killers. In early part of the 1978/79 season the club drew Everton away in the League Cup. The talk was of another giant-killing. Instead Wimbledon were thrashed 8-0. The team had never lost by such a margin.

29 AUGUST 1978

League Cup second round

Everton 8 Wimbledon 0

By Dave Donaldson (player)

For a number of years we had been accustomed to unprecedented success, so there was always going to be a day when we would come unstuck. This was it. It was just one of those days when nothing went right.

I played for Wimbledon for many years and we had some great wins and some great results, yet I scarcely remember them. But I remember the 8-0 loss vividly. Throughout my entire career, with Walton & Hersham and then with Wimbledon, we were never hammered like that.

They were 2-0 up before we could even blink. Bob Latchford got five and Martin Dobson a hat-trick. It was a horror show. At 5-0, with about 10 minutes to go, we all just wanted to walk off the pitch, but they maintained the torture and added another three. Dario Gradi just couldn't believe it and I don't think any of us could.

Afterwards we were dumbstruck. There were a deathly silence. I put my hand up and said I was to blame for one of the goals, but that still left another seven.

Our success over the years outweighs it I suppose, but the night after the game I couldn't sleep and I had to work the next day. My colleagues didn't give me a hard time though. They said Everton were in the First Division and we were in the Fourth, and it was to be expected. But I took it very personally. No one played well that night, and after Burnley, Leeds and Middlesbrough we'd expected so much more. I wrote the whole match off. That year only had 364 days in it as far as I was concerned.

It was to be my last season for Wimbledon. I just wish my one abiding memory of that year wasn't the 8-0 defeat. It was probably my worst performance for Wimbledon and I suspect I wasn't the only one who felt the same way. There was no overall reason for it, no tactical blunder. Basically we all played rubbish. It hurt our pride immensely; no one likes to lose like that.

Thrashed: Steve Galliers (left) and Roger Connell (No 9) in action against Everton at Goodison Park in the League Cup on 2 September 1978. The Dons lost 8-0. (Yellow and Blue)

There was one of two ways we could go. We could either fold, and deteriorate or we could start over again and rebuild our momentum. We regrouped, we won the next game to go top of the table and we went on to win promotion.

Fifteen years later I got a small slice of revenge for the 8-0 defeat. In the match I'd given away a penalty, having tripped their winger Micky Walsh. In 1993, I was playing in the over-50s Umbro Cup for Camberley Strollers and I was up against Walsh again. I scored twice as we won 4-2 and I remember thinking: "That was for the Everton game in 1978."

✦

PROMOTION AND WALLY DOWNES

Despite the humiliation against Everton, Wimbledon were thriving in the League and promotion to the Third Division was sealed with a home victory at York City. The match would also be remembered for the debut of midfielder Wally Downes. Behind the scenes Wally was becoming instrumental in changing the culture of the club.

FOURTH DIVISION

11 May 1979

Wimbledon 2 York City 1

By Wally Downes (player)

It was a great game to make your debut. We came from 1-0 down to beat York 2-1 and that took us up. I scored in the next game; it was a great way to end the season. But it was in the reserves where all the fun was. Dario was in charge of the first team and he liked things to be all serious and disciplined, but with Harry Bassett we were out of sight and we could get away with more or less anything.

I broke into the reserves in 1978. I joined the club in 1977 as the club's first apprentice, but I broke my kneecap in only my second South East Counties game. It took me nine months to get back to full fitness. By the time I was fit again they had agreed to give me a professional contract.

The reserve side was made up largely of the older guys that had been so successful in the non-league days. I was the young one. I was the lad from the Bush. They hadn't really met a character like me before. But those guys also had a spirit about them and I just fed off it. They all had their routines and all I wanted to do was lark about.

I remember one reserve game at Maidenhead. I was 17 at the time and Dickie Guy was playing. He was always done up. If it wasn't collar and tie, it would be a nice pair of slacks and a good shirt, and his hair was never out of place.

Leaping Wally: An acrobatic Wally Downes (centre) attempts to get a shot in against Orient on 4 September 1979. (Paul Willatts)

I wasn't having any of that. I filled up a cardboard box with Harpic and dumped it on his head. None of the other lads had seen anything like that before, and Dickie was none too impressed. He pinned me down on the floor of the mini-bus and beat me up all the way home.

In another reserve game I remember running the whole length of the pitch and scoring with a diving header at the back post. It was a great goal, but Roger Connell was none too pleased. He knew it was a great goal, but he wasn't going to let me have my moment. He picked me up by my collars and said: "Listen laddie, the back post is my domain, not the place for some little upstart." He beat me up on the way back in the mini-bus for having the audacity to be there. It taught me one thing – not to stand at the back post. But it was never serious stuff. It was all just part of the banter of Harry's side.

It didn't even matter if you weren't a player in those days. The geezer who used to drive us to the reserve games also came in for a bit of abuse too. He had a bald head and, well, it was too tempting to avoid. We bought some fish 'n' chips, took the batter off the fish and dumped it on his head. It singed him and he went berserk. He pulled over and it took us ages to persuade him to start driving again.

A week or so later we were off driving again and I was still thinking about his reaction. So I put an empty cardboard box over his head. The trouble was we were doing 80mph. He quit there and then.

Harry loved all those antics. He'd encourage us to mess about. He was a great believer in team spirit, and the more we messed about together the closer we became.

Most of the old players had left. We were a young side and we just loved to lark about. When Dario wasn't looking, Harry used to encourage it. But as soon as Dario was watching Harry would say: "Oh, this is terrible. I can't believe what these guys are doing."

He would take the warm-ups before senior game, and more often than not it would all in end up in a big brawl and we'd come in covered in mud. Dario would ask what had happened and Harry would say: "I don't know, the guys got out of control, but I've disciplined them now and they won't do it again." But he was as guilty as the rest of us.

✦

LURCH'S AWFUL DEBUT

Life in the old Third Division was tough for Dario's Dons. They were out of their depth. The last remnants of Batsford's old guard had gone, and in their place Gradi was introducing a swathe of youngsters. Among them was Dave Beasant. Over time he would become known simply as Lurch and eight years later he would lift the FA Cup as captain of the club. But his first game for the Dons he thought would be his last.

12 JANUARY 1980
Third Division
Wimbledon 1 Blackpool 2
By Dave Beasant (player)

When I was at Edgware Town, we had a few scouts down to watch us. We had Brian Stein in the team back then and he was attracting a lot of interest. In the end two or three of our players signed for Luton and I thought I would be the next one.

One of the boys knew Dave Bassett from Sunday morning football. And after one game he said Dave was outside and wanted to talk to me. I was so keen – I went straight out there still in my kit. I must have stank as Dave told me to go back in and have a shower!

He was assistant manager to Dario Gradi and was scouting for the club. I think he actually came down to watch a winger we had at the time but I had impressed him in the process.

So I went for a trial period. Dario wasn't that convinced about me, so he got Mike Kelly in for a second opinion. Mike had played in goal for Wimbledon in the Amateur Cup final and he had faith in me. The key game came against Brighton in the reserves. They had Martin Chivers in their side and we should have got stuffed, but we won 3-2. Dave Bassett was watching and after the match he pulled me to one side and said the club wanted to sign me.

He asked what money I was on. Now I could have mugged Dave, but he was a tight person and you wouldn't get anything out of him for nothing. I was a printer at the time and I said I was on £25 a week, which was the truth. And Harry agreed to match it. In the end I actually did myself out of some money, as I was earning an extra £12 a week from the non-league stuff. But I was so keen to get into League football it didn't matter.

I spent a long time working hard in the reserves, and then one day Ray Goddard suffered a back spasm the day before a game and Dario gave me a call.

I'd actually been out that night with a girl to the pictures and then we'd had a few beers after, so I wasn't in the greatest of states for the game. I let one in through my legs, I thought: "That's it, I'm finished."

Afterwards, I went dejectedly to the bar. Steve Parsons, Steve Perkins and Wally Downes were there and they would have none of it. I remember Ron Noades came up to me and said: "This will be the making of you, my son. From here you can only go from strength to strength." And none of the lads let me leave the bar until I was utterly paralytic.

You had to be a certain breed of person to survive at Wimbledon. The initiations, the training, the team spirit. It was a unique place.

When we were in the Third Division, Stoke City, who were then in the old First Division, came in for me. I remember meeting their manager, Richie Barker. They offered £30,000, but Harry wanted £70,000. In those days if the clubs couldn't agree a fee it went to a tribunal.

I wanted to go to tribunal. But Harry said if I was not going to stay, I wouldn't start the season and he'd bring in another goalkeeper. So Stuart Naylor came down for a trial. He's a good goalkeeper and ended up having a long career.

But I remember to this day how the lads treated him. All they could understand was that here was this new guy, who was out to replace their mate and they were having none of it. I would have hated to be in Stuart's boots that day. At every opportunity they made his life hell. It got so bad that Harry took them all to one side and said: "Look, if I want to sign a new player it's my decision."

But it made me feel great. It was as touching a moment as you could get from that bunch of lads. And in the end I didn't go to tribunal. I agreed to stay.

Getting the rub: Physiotherapist Owen Harris treats Dave Beasant at Plough Lane in 1980. (Paul Willatts)

INSTANT RELEGATION

Meanwhile, the 1979/80 season was dragging along and would end in abject failure. A draw with Millwall confirmed relegation. They would finish bottom of the Third Division, but behind the scenes a new era and a new style of play was beginning to develop.

22 APRIL 1980
Third Division
Wimbledon 2 Millwall 2
By Mick Smith (player)

The club was bottom of the table when I had arrived five months earlier, so there wasn't really much hope of escaping the drop. The 2-2 draw against Millwall just confirmed the inevitable. In hindsight I think the club had just gone up too soon. It was a big leap from the Fourth Division to the Third and the club just wasn't ready for it.

Relegation had been on the cards for weeks. We had won the week before but that was our first win since the middle of February.

It was a bit of a blow when we finally went down, but we had been expecting it and I tried to put it behind me as soon as I could.

It was very much Dario's team then. Dario was constantly looking to build for the future. I'm not sure if he would have been that disappointed in relegation. He was always looking ahead.

He signed me from Lincoln City in December 1979 for £12,500 when I was just a 20-year old. I was going nowhere at Lincoln City. I didn't get on with the manager there and I was looking for a move. I was only a young professional and I still had a lot to learn and Dario was a natural with young players. His record at Crewe has proved that, but then his talents weren't so widely known. Dario wanted all his players to try and play football; he wanted to improve our technique.

Meanwhile, Dave Bassett, who was Dario's assistant, had cottoned on to the idea that we had to get the ball into their area quickly.

Russian memories: Acting captain Mick Smith (left) shakes hand with the captain of Dynamo Moscow before a friendly at Plough Lane in 1982. (Paul Willatts)

NOADES THREATENS MERGER

Ron Noades had always been ambitious, and dealing with a club languishing in the Fourth Division was not part of his plan. Midway through the 1980/81 season, Noades decided to buy Crystal Palace. He still owned Wimbledon, and rumours were rife that a merger was on the cards. Four years after the successful "Dons 4 Div 4" campaign the Wimbledon fans would step into the fray again, but this time it was to oppose their own board.

2 FEBRUARY 1981
Nelson's Nightclub, Plough Lane
By Mark Curtis (supporter)

Rumours had been circulating for ages. It must have been the worst-kept secret in football that Ron Noades wanted to merge us with Crystal Palace, or at the very least organise a groundshare. He already had a consortium in place to take over Palace and he wanted Dario Gradi to be manager of the new club.

Selhurst Park would be the home of the new team, with Plough Lane used just for the reserves and training. At that time we were in a lower division and had smaller crowds than Palace, so we obviously felt that it would be our identity that would be lost.

I was fuming. You have to remember that at the time there were no internet conections, fax machines or computers to spread information. Protests had to be organised and then publicised by word of mouth and flyers. It would all seem so very basic today. But we had one secret weapon – the Batsford Arms.

Located under the South Stand, the Batsford was the hotbed of the protests. It was no more than a hole in the wall – at the most 40 feet long and about 15 feet wide – but it was our hole. We'd gather there 45 minutes before kick-off, at half-time and for an hour or so after the game. There were young and old alike, and the conversation was solely about how we could stop Noades. Obviously, our thoughts towards Noades were as sentimental as the ones now towards Koppel, the chairman who would 20 years later propose a move to Milton Keynes. The first step was an open meeting, along with Crystal Palace supporters, in Nelson's.

By Robin Rance (supporter)

By the time of the meeting, Noades had taken over at Palace. Back then there were no rules stopping anyone having shares in two clubs, and the concern about a possible merger had reached fever pitch.

It was a Monday night and the place was packed. It was basically an "open mike" meeting so anyone who had anything to say had the opportunity.

The first protest: Wimbledon fans complain against a rumoured merger with Crystal Palace in early 1981. (Paul Willatts)

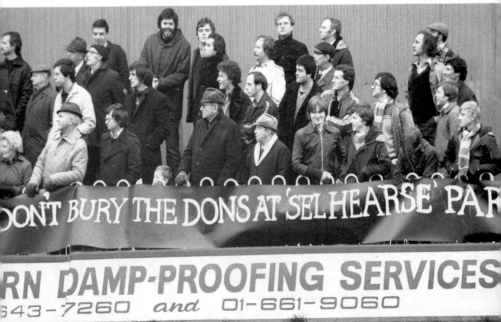

But the one speech that will always stick in my mind came from Chris Wright of the Palace Action Campaign. He barked his fears into the mike with enough decibels to scare anyone within two miles of Nelson's. He was adamant that a merger would never happen. His tone struck a chord. The meeting was always going to be united against the merger, but now everyone was willing to do something.

Anyone who was anything to do with the Dons at the time was there. Buckets were passed round and one individual even put in £300, quite a tidy sum in those days.

Another key speaker was Eric Willcocks, the club's travel secretary and predecessor of Reg Davis, who pleaded with the existing Wimbledon fans to bring their friends to the matches to help swell the crowds – he even came up with a slogan: "Each one reach one". The next match was at home to Crewe and it attracted the highest crowd of the year: 2,782. The game ended with a sit-in and placards were everywhere. We wanted to make it known to Noades that we were not going to go quietly. The fight was well and truly on.

FEBRUARY 1981
Meeting of Football League chairmen, Solihull
By Mark Curtis (supporter)

We had the meeting and we held the sit-ins, but we still seemed to be getting nowhere. It was then that the supporters' club arranged for a coach trip to Solihull where the Football League chairmen were meeting. Eighty per cent of those on the coach were Batsford Arms regulars, with the remainder being officials of the Wimbledon Supporters Club. In fact, many people who made the trip are the same people who fought the Milton Keynes move.

As we were setting out that morning, I really didn't know what we hoped to achieve. I felt that I had to do something rather than just let a new breed of chairman, like Noades, start to dictate what direction football would go. As with the recent attempt to move to Milton Keynes, the proposed merger with Palace was purely for financial gain and not in the best interests of the game.

As for the trip, it was a wet, horrible day when we set out from the Batsford. Spirits were pretty good, and although an agenda wasn't really set we knew that the meeting was taking place at 2pm and we hoped to make our presence known to the arriving chairmen and show them what we thought about the merger. We arrived in Solihull about 10.45am. In typical Batsford style we were all a little thirsty, we had nothing to do for three hours on a rainy day in Solihull. Luckily there was a pub close by. The landlord must have wondered what had hit him when he saw a queue outside his pub at 10.45am. As we were drinking away we came up with plans to go running around the Pebble Mill at One studios with scarves and flags, but nothing really transpired. About 1.30 we left the dryness of the pub and its comforting beer for the rain-drenched picket. Anybody who appeared in a suit and looking chairman-like was greeted with anti-Palace and anti-Noades banter, but the only chairman we wanted to see obviously had a back-door pass.

I don't know what influence our protest had, but it was at that meeting that Noades' plans finally hit the buffers. The Football League ruled that no person could own more than one club. Noades sold his shares in Wimbledon to Joe McElligott, who was to become the chairman of the club.

Noades had hoped that McElligott would favour a groundshare, but within weeks the rest of the Wimbledon board vetoed the plan and we stayed put. It was then that Sam Hammam discreetly became the club's major shareholder.

The Batsford was jubilant. We could get behind Bassett and, for the time being at least, celebrate our independence. There were further battles to fight in the years ahead.

After everything we had fought for and the success we had on the pitch, the eventual move to Selhurst Park 10 years later seemed to be the ultimate betrayal. It was the end of an era, and although the Thomas Farley pub around the corner from Selhurst became the new Batsford, most of the old faces and their memories vanished.

My family had followed the club passionately since the 1920s until the club moved to Selhurst. My father stopped going after one year at Palace. I moved to Florida.

✦

DARIO DEPARTS

With Ron Noades now in control of Crystal Palace, Dario Gradi was given a simple ultimatum: join Palace or face a future with no job. He opted for Palace, and Wimbledon were left managerless.

24 JANUARY 1981
FA Cup fourth round
Wrexham 2 Wimbledon 1
By Dario Gradi (manager)

It was a difficult time for Wimbledon and a difficult time for me. Ron Noades was an ambitious man and he was determined to merge Wimbledon and Crystal Palace. At the very least, he wanted to own both clubs. I didn't want to go and manage Palace, but he called me in and said: "It's either you or Dave Bassett, you won't both be here whatever happens."

I didn't really know what to do, so I spoke to Sam Hammam, who was just a director back then. He said he wouldn't take over the club, but he also advised me not to go.

I thought about it for a long time. I could see Wimbledon blossoming. The young kids I had brought in were beginning to develop and there was more talent to come, and in a way I left to secure their future.

If I took over as manager of the bigger club, it would also mean I could stop the smaller club from being swallowed up, and that thought appealed to me. To be honest, the opportunity to manage at a higher level was tempting too. The key factor was Sam. Had he said he was going to take over I would have stayed. So I went.

In the end, thankfully, the League stepped in and refused to allow the two sides to merge, and Ron had to end his relationship with Wimbledon.

It was obvious that Dave was going to be the next manager. It had been made clear to me ever since I found out that he had been offered the job before me way back in 1978. I had a good relationship with Dave and I could see him learning from what I was doing. I knew that by the time I left that he had it in him to be a good manager.

Farewell: Dario Gradi.
(Paul Willatts)

But our relationship wasn't always like that. When Ron first appointed me he had wanted Dave to be my assistant, but I wanted to run the club on my own. At the time I think it needed it. The club needed to be shaken out of its amateurism.

But at the end of that first season, I spoke to Ron and asked if Dave could be made my assistant. I knew he was hardly going to be able to play the next year and he was too good an asset for the club to lose. Ron agreed, but he also knew I was obviously appointing my successor. By the time it came for me to go, I was happy with what I had achieved. The youth system was working, and I had brought in new players who would hold the club in good stead. The foundations were in place for a great club, and I was sincerely glad that they had their chance to prove it as Wimbledon.

Ron was very supportive throughout my time at Wimbledon; I think we were both moving in the same direction. We wanted the club to be more professional and we wanted it to progress. And that meant having to change many of the old amateur ways.

Despite my friendship with Ron, I have never believed that one individual should own a football club. A football club belongs to its supporters, and back in 1981 I was relieved that the Wimbledon board, for the time being at least, had respected the wishes of their fans.

✦

The Spirit of Wimbledon

CHAPTER FIVE: BASSETT'S BOYS

BASSETT TAKES CHARGE

Dave Bassett had been at the club for seven years. He was captain under Allen Batsford. He was then assistant to Dario Gradi, but he was still an unknown entity at managerial level. But who else would want to take over a club in such crisis? And who else could understand Wimbledon as much as Harry?

31 JANUARY 1981
Fourth Division
Port Vale 2 Wimbledon 3
By Dave Bassett (manager)

There are always some nerves before a game. But to walk in as manager for the first time, it's even more so. I remember the game well, Port Vale away. I can't remember exactly what I said pre-match in the dressing room, but having played with most of them for years I knew what they were capable of and they knew what I expected of them. It was a real battle, nothing pretty. But we won 3-2, Mick Smith scoring the winner with a volley. It may have been just three points, but it helped validate my decision to take on the job.

I always wanted to be a manager. I used to help Allen Batsford. He was a great manager and I learnt a great deal from him. Even from the early Walton days, watching Allen in action, I remember thinking: "I'd like to have a go at it." I didn't know if I'd ever be any good, but it was just something I wanted to do.

When Dario Gradi took over they asked me to be his assistant. I think they wanted me to act as a bridge between the old and the new and I was more than happy to do that. Three years under him was my managerial apprenticeship. Dario was a great coach, and I absorbed his techniques before Ron Noades bought into Crystal Palace and took him as well. The stage was left to me. After everything I'd learnt, I felt I was ready to go into management. The board agreed and that was that.

The players can talk about managers having this or that style, but I just wanted to be me. I wasn't trying to be another Gradi or another Batsford – I wanted to be the first Bassett. As a manager, I tried to get people to help me in the areas where I was weak, while working to my strengths.

Manager marvel: Dave Bassett (right) receives the Fourth Division manager of the month award for April 1981 on the pitch at Plough Lane. (Paul Willatts)

There was no intention to create the Crazy Gang. The spirit had been there before. I just wanted to harness it. Wherever I have been I have tried to create a good atmosphere. But there was always a spirit at Wimbledon. As the manager I got the credit for it, but the players were just as responsible. We had Wally Downes and Alan Cork. But just below them were the likes of Glyn Hodges, Mark Morris and Paul Fishenden.

I could see the potential in the team. I could see where we could go. We were well over halfway through the season and in 12th place at the time of the Port Vale game. From there we went on a great run and finished fourth and were promoted.

By Mick Smith (player)

It was particularly satisfying to get the first winner for Dave. He meant the world to me. There was never any doubt that Dave would take over – and that's when the spirit of the club started to build. There was always an element of that about the club anyway. Wally Downes was central to most things, but even some of the older boys had a certain spirit about them. It's just that Dave brought it out in all of us with his style of play and his training programmes. He liked competition everywhere. He wasn't interested in pretty football; he wanted to see commitment and passion. He wanted players giving their all, even in training. He almost encouraged punch-ups and the like. And it helped to foster the team spirit and atmosphere.

Dario was a great coach, but he was never a great motivator like Dave Bassett. By the time Dave had made Wimbledon his team, we all knew our own jobs and we were all fighting for the same cause.

✦

GAGE'S RECORD, GODDARD AND PROMOTION

The 1980/81 season had been a traumatic one. Managers had come and gone, merger had been threatened, but on the pitch the club was thriving. Wimbledon's 4-1 victory over Rochdale the week before had secured promotion, so the final game of the season turned into a carnival. Goalkeeper Ray Goddard returned for his final game, and a 17-year-old Kevin Gage was to make club history.

2 MAY 1981
Fourth Division
Wimbledon 2 Bury 4
By Kevin Gage (player)

The significance of it all never really dawned on me, but I remember it clearly: Bury at home, 1981, 4-2 defeat. Stepping onto the pitch at Plough Lane for the first time, I never realised that I was the youngest player ever to play for Wimbledon. I still hold that record. For me, it was just my debut and that was special in its own way. I was just 17 and I couldn't see the bigger picture. It was only afterwards that I realised what I had achieved, and it is something that I remain proud of.

It was the perfect time to make my debut. The club had clinched promotion the previous week and there was something of a carnival atmosphere at Plough Lane that day. It was all so relaxed.

I first discovered I would be playing on the Thursday when we all trained together. Dave had this habit of giving out bibs, and if you got one you were in the first team. There was nothing formal about it, no written list on the wall, no little talk. It was just done by the bibs. That was the way you got to know if you were playing.

I was ecstatic, but the game was so relaxed and so light-hearted. We got stuffed, but we were enjoying ourselves. Towards the end of the match we won a penalty, and as it was Ray Goddard's last match for the club the lads got him to come up and take it. It was those sorts of moments that made Wimbledon and typified Dave Bassett's way of doing things.

I had come close to making my debut a few weeks before at Doncaster. Both clubs were vying for a promotion place, and I was on the bench. It was early April and I was still only 16. It was such a tense game, that as much as I wanted to come on, it would have not been a good time to make my debut. We won the game 1-0 and in the end that proved crucial to our promotion.

The youngest Don: Kevin Gage. (Getty Images)

I loved it at Wimbledon. There couldn't have been a better place to be a teenager playing professional football. The best bit about playing football at Wimbledon was Nelson's. At other clubs I have been at they have a players' bar, but at Wimbledon we had a nightclub under the stands. Sometimes you would just fall into there straight after the game and not leave until two in the morning when the cleaning ladies arrived. It was compulsory to drink at the club in those days; the age issue didn't come into it. If I was old enough to play for Wimbledon, I was certainly old enough to drink.

Gradi had turned the club into a professional outfit, but Harry re-installed the spirit of the club. He created the atmosphere. And people like Glyn Hodges, Mark Morris and me just lapped it up. It was a bit like being at school. All your mates were there and you could have a laugh. It was like playing for a really good pub team. Obviously there were times when we had to be professional, particularly on the training pitch. But it was the social side that created the spirit.

The key to it all was that everyone was so young. Most of us had grown up together. We had been in the youth team, the reserves and the first team. We looked out for each other on and off the pitch. Even the senior players, Wally Downes and Steve Galliers, were just 22 or 23 and we all mixed in together, and that created a bond that was to see us through the next five years.

✦

11-0 PROVES BEYOND THE DONS

The first few months of the 1981/82 season followed the same pattern as the Dons' first stay in the Third Division two years earlier, with defeat after defeat. But by February Bassett's young side had begun a run of form which, although not good enough to avoid the drop, would ultimately take them to the First Division.

18 MAY 1982
Third Division
Wimbledon 3 Portsmouth 2
By Mark Morris (player)

The writing had been on the wall long before the final game of the season. We had a late rally, but it was always a case of too little, too late. We were more or less rock bottom at the end of April. But we had won six of our last eight games, and three of those were against teams chasing promotion. Going into the final game against Portsmouth we needed to win 11-0 to stay up. It would have been great to avoid the drop, but 11-0 wasn't even a consideration. Dave Bassett asked us to go out and give it our best shot and go down with some dignity.

All I really remember from the game was coming face to face with Billy Rafferty. He was massive. He must have been 6ft 8in and 20 stone! I thought: "Jesus Christ, this guy is a lump of a man, how they hell do I cope with him." I was just a raw 19-year-old and a newcomer to the Football League. In the end, maybe it should have been him coping with me. I scored the first and we won 3-2. Dignity restored, but still relegation.

The 1981/82 season was really a transitional period for the club. Gradi had gone and Dave was only just beginning to make his mark. We had a successful youth team for a couple of years, and some of us were pushed into the first team before we were really ready But ultimately that may have played into our hands. The nucleus of the side had been together for three years, from the youth team to the reserves and the first team. And it just seemed to click.

And that's where Dario can take the credit. The results had never really come for him while he was in charge, but he was instrumental in the successful youth team set-up. We were all brought into the club under Dario. It was a last-chance saloon for many of us. We'd all played with kids who went on to join Chelsea, Spurs or Palace. Those clubs had rejected some of us, and Wimbledon was our last shot at professional football. We were all local lads too and that also helped.

Wimbledon were the first club to give me a trial. I had no real ambition to be a professional footballer. I was 15 and I thought my chance had gone – I was already thinking about other careers. But my teacher Keith Blunt told me Wimbledon wanted to give me a trial.

After I signed apprentice forms for the Dons, I was almost immediately shipped off to New Zealand for six months to play in their senior league. It was something the club liked to do. Paul Fishenden came with me, and I think Glyn Hodges had a spell in Sweden. It was all about helping complete the transition from South East Counties youth football to the senior game.

I returned in late September 1981 and went with the club the next month to Reading. Peter Suddaby hadn't turned up, and Dave Bassett asked me to get changed and be ready to play. The adrenalin was pumping, but then Suddaby arrived with 15 minutes to go and I wasn't required.

But I wouldn't have to wait too long for my debut. Dave thought I was worth a chance and put me in, in place of Suddaby, against Exeter at Plough Lane. It ended 1-1. And I never looked back from there. I was almost ever-present for the next four seasons.

CROWNED AS CHAMPIONS

After six years without silverware, in 1983 Wimbledon soared to the Fourth Division title in style with their highest ever points and goals tally – two records that would be broken 20 years later by AFC Wimbledon. In front of the TV cameras, the Dons celebrated in style.

14 MAY 1983
Fourth Division
Bury 1 Wimbledon 3
By Gary Peters (captain)

T he Bury game was special for me and it stands out in my memory. In my career I have been promoted nine or 10 times and in hindsight, for me at least, it would be easy to overlook our achievements back then. After all, it was only the Fourth Division championship.

But that would be to ignore what a distinctive side it was. We had quality forwards in Alan Cork and Stewart Evans, a hard-working midfield and a solid defence. And then there was Lurch. But it was the spirit that was so special.

It was the last match of the season, and Bury needed to win to go up. We had already won the title, but the TV cameras were there and it was our chance to show how good we were. I've still got the tape of the game.

We played awesome, but the highlight had to be the reaction of the Bury manager. Match of the Day had a reporter at the pitch side. We scored after a couple of minutes, and the reporter stuck his microphone under the Bury manager's nose. "We didn't want to do that at this stage of the game," was his reply. We scored again just before half-time and the same thing happened. The reporter again shoved the microphone towards the Bury manager and the response was the same: "We didn't want to do that at this stage of the game." He had to say that three times. It was hilarious.

Claiming the Cup: John Leslie with the Fourth Division trophy on the way back from Bury in 1983. (John Leslie)

Champion captain: Gary Peters. (Getty Images)

The journey home was memorable. Now, we'd normally have a beer or two after an away game, but now we were champions. We had no more games to worry about and we had a long journey home. Harry was supposed to get off at Watford, but we wouldn't let him. He was supposed to meet his wife. But we kept him on the train to Euston and left him stark-bollock naked at the station.

A couple of days earlier we'd played Halifax in midweek, and results elsewhere meant that we were champions. And we played awful in the first half. We'd just taken our foot off the gas and Harry was livid. He came in shouting and hollering. He was wearing slip-on shoes and went to lash out at a chair, but his shoe went flying off and clocked Beasant square between the eyes. We all cracked up laughing and were rolling around the floor. Harry couldn't get a grip on us at all. It was all too much for us. But we went out and smartened up and got a 1-1 draw.

They were special times and Wimbledon were a special club. People talk about Fash, Wisey and Vinnie, but we were the real Crazy Gang: the team of Mark Morris, Steve Galliers, Wally

Downes, Dave Beasant and Alan Cork. We must have been the only club in the Football League to still have 10 players at the bar at midnight after a home game. But that was all part of the Plough Lane set-up, and I have very fond memories of the nights at Nelson's after victories.

It was just the way things were done, and Harry encouraged it at every turn. We would play together, we would drink together and we would battle together. That made it all so much fun at Wimbledon. When I look back I have no doubts that my time at the Lane was the highlight of my career.

It may have only been the Fourth Division championship, but it was Wimbledon's Fourth Division championship and we loved it.

I see the same spirit developing at AFC Wimbledon, and maybe that has a lot to do with Terry Eames. He is from the same vintage. He knows that spirit is essential for the club. Belief and spirit are what took Wimbledon all the way to the top. Back in 1983 we were just starting out on that road.

By John Leslie (player)

I remember talking to Dave Beasant before the game. Bury had produced a special end-of-season programme and in it was a picture of a Bury penalty. And Dave said: "If they get one, I'll dive the same way." And sure enough, they got one and he saved it. We coasted through the game after that and won easily. And they were dejected at the final whistle.

I must have been the only sober person on the coach home – beer was flowing everywhere. We had the trophy on the coach and it was being thrown around like a toy. Everyone joined in, but then everyone always did. Dave Bassett, the chairman, the directors… everyone was acting stupid and we were loving it. It was the only medal I earned from football and I'll treasure it for ever.

But the match was also to be my last for Wimbledon. My three-year contract finished after that season and we began discussions about a new deal. The problem was that I had a clause in my old contract that gave me a £20-a-week rise each year, and I wanted something similar again. But Dave Bassett had a strict budget. I was the highest earner at the club at the time, and he said he couldn't give me the payrise.

I didn't want to leave and he didn't want me to go. He even offered me money out of his own pocket to keep me, and I was tempted. That was before Gillingham came in.

Dave insisted his offer stood, but also told me to speak to the Gills. They offered me far more than Wimbledon could, plus a signing-on fee. That should have been that, but the two sides couldn't agree a fee and Keith Peacock, the Gillingham manager, didn't want to go to a tribunal.

So for a while it looked as if I would stay with Wimbledon. I remember Sam Hammam had the right hump with me for having the audacity to leave, and I didn't want the deal to stretch out. So I told Gillingham to sort it out or I'd stay with Wimbledon. They paid up that week and I was off to Kent.

I was really sad to leave. Wimbledon had meant the world to me. But fans have to remember it's still a job, like any other. I had two kids, a wife and a mortgage and I had to look after them.

✦

THE RETURN OF CORK AND A RECORD WIN
Throughout most of the Championship-winning season Wimbledon had to do without Alan Cork, who had broken his leg in early 1982. He was to return in the 1983/84 season with a bang.

3 SEPTEMBER 1983

Third Division

Wimbledon 6 Newport 0

By Alan Cork (player)

I take great credit in being able to remember most of the goals I've scored in my career, and this match is no exception. I had broken my leg against Walsall two years before. It happened when I collided with their goalkeeper Ron Green. Ron spent most of his time in the lower divisions, but he played five times for us after Lurch left in 1988. I mentioned it to him then that I still owed him one.

In those days we didn't have the quality of treatment players get these days, and I was out for a season and a half. That was the hardest time of my career. I returned for the title run-in in 1983 for the Fourth Division. It was great to be back and I got five goals in seven games. But with the long pre-season in mind, Harry wanted me to get some match practice, so he sent me off to Sweden to play for Orebro.

I was gutted at the time. I missed out on the title celebrations. At least in my final game I got a hat-trick against Chester, and I think I left with us needing just six points from our last four games to secure the title. I also missed the first game of the season the following year against Bolton, so I made my return against Newport.

In those days, Wimbledon used to yo-yo between the Third and the Fourth Divisions and I think everyone was expecting the same to happen again. But we had different ideas, and that's what made this victory so important.

I came back from Sweden with a silly haircut – yes, I did once have hair. It kind of looked like a mohican. It was all the rage in Sweden and I suppose it was my fault for trusting a Swedish barber. The guys gave me loads of stick, so I wanted to prove that I could still cut it.

I should have scored with a header, but the ball fell back to me to tap in for the first.

Stewart Evans then got one himself. It was the usual in-off-the-nose job – that's how he scored all his goals. God knows how his nose is still there after the amount of goals he scored with it. That made it 2-0 at half time. Steve Ketteridge made it 3-0 on the hour.

Hat-trick hero: Alan Cork. *(Getty Images)*

My next was a true collector's item. I smashed it from 18 yards straight into the top corner for 4-0.

Stewart made it 5-0 and then we got a penalty. Now Stewart had scored shed-loads the season before and we were both on a hat-trick. There was going to be no debate – it was mine! We weren't the richest club in those days so I had to give the match ball back to the club at the final whistle.

That win was our biggest in the League, and it's a record that still stands. But at the time it also sent out a signal that this time we weren't going to be leaving the division through the trapdoor.

The next game was at home to Bournemouth, and after Chester and Newport I was on a hat-trick of hat-tricks, I scored after six minutes and I thought it was on. But I don't think I got another touch. At least we won the match 3-2.

The team was just starting to gel. And we stuck together all the way to the First Division. We added a couple more players when we went up to the First, but it was basically the same side that had played that day against Newport.

✦

CUTTING DOWN FOREST

The exploits of Wimbledon in the 1970s meant the club still had a reputation as giant-killers, but in reality they had achieved little against the English élite since the draw with Middlesbrough nearly seven years earlier. That was all to change at the start of the 1983/84 season, when Wimbledon beat First Division Nottingham Forest in the Milk Cup. Wimbledon's two central midfielders that day, Steve Ketteridge and Steve Galliers, remember the tie well.

4 OCTOBER 1983
Milk Cup second-round, first leg
Wimbledon 2 Nottingham Forest 0

Steve Ketteridge: It was one of those special nights at Plough Lane. The little ground always came into its own on evening games. I don't think Nottingham Forest really knew what to expect. They were flying in the First Division, a huge club, up against little Wimbledon.

Steve Galliers: Plough Lane was packed to the rafters, and after about 20 minutes I played a neat give-and-go with Stewart Evans. He fed the ball into the area and Wally Downes charged in from the right-hand side shouting at me to leave it. But I wasn't going to do that. I belted it in, and Plough Lane erupted.

We had chance after chance. I have got a video of the game, which I've watched a few times since, and 1-0 would have been a bit unjust. Plus it would never really had been enough to take to the City Ground for the second leg.

The second goal was crucial but we left it very late. There can't have been much more than a few seconds left. Glyn Hodges claims it was a shot, but I'm not so sure.

We beat them 2-0, but it could easily have been four or five. We had all the pressure, Hodger missed a few chances, but so did everyone.

Steve Ketteridge: Unlike Steve Galliers, I can't remember specific moments. I do recall the feeling of playing and being aware of how well we were doing. I remember coming up against Steve Hodge and being amazed by him. He was the first player I've ever played against who'd run around as much as I did. But I kept at it. And I remember the feeling that everyone was doing their job and doing it well. And we thoroughly deserved to beat them. But it was still only the first leg, and most people expected Forest to make amends in the return.

26 OCTOBER 1983
Milk Cup second-round, second leg
Nottingham Forest 1 Wimbledon 1
(Wimbledon won 3-1 on aggregate)
By Steve Ketteridge (player)

Steve Ketteridge: We had worked so hard to get into the second round against Forest, and we weren't going to give up our 2-0 advantage easily.

In the previous round, against Southend, we had lost the first leg away 1-0. The second leg was an epic. The match ended 3-2 and went into extra-time. I remember they scored first in extra-time and we needed two more to go through in the last 20 minutes. I scored first and brought the scores level on aggregate, and then Stewart Evans and Glyn Hodges scored, but even then they got one back to make for a nervy last four minutes.

Now, if you go through a game like that, you're not going to throw it all away in the next round. We may have won 2-0 at Plough Lane, but we still had to focus hard for the away leg at the City Ground.

The build-up to the away leg was amazing. I can remember arriving in the changing room to find all the shirts hanging up in number order. It was an incredible atmosphere.

Steve Galliers: They battered us from start to finish. But our resolve held. Nigel Winterburn had a great game and so did Dave Beasant. Somewhere along the line those two had simply decided that we weren't going to get beaten that day. But the moment that sealed it belonged to Stewart Evans.

I hit the ball

Midfield maestros: Steve Galliers (above) and Steve Ketteridge (both Getty Images)

through for him. Stewart may have been a tall lad but he was great on the floor, and he just bamboozled their centre-half and scored to make it 3-0 on aggregate. There was less than a quarter of an hour left of the tie and for Forest there was no coming back from there.

All credit to them, they tried. I remember they hit the bar and Lurch had to pull off a couple of good saves. Ian Wallace scored a late consolation, but by then we already had our minds set on the celebrations.

Steve Ketteridge: After the final whistle we were all shouting and hollering. Brian Clough banged on the dressing room door, popped his head around the corner, and told us: "Well done lads, you deserved it" and presented us with a crate of champagne.

It was a touching moment from a great manager. Mind you, that didn't stop Wally Downes taking the piss out of him. But we'd always had jokers at Wimbledon. Before Wally it had been John Leslie, who spent the entire time tying people's laces together and putting Deep Heat ointment into people's pants. It was just Wimbledon.

After the Forest victory we headed back to Nelson's at Plough Lane and drank into the early hours. Stanley Reed was also there doing his turn. It was nights like this that made Wimbledon special. As I've always said: "We were like how a non-league club should be, except we were playing in the League."

Steve Galliers: I didn't get home for a couple of days after that. It was just one big long celebration. We were in the Third Division then, and for most of us it was the first time we'd ever beaten a First Division side. And back then Nottingham Forest were no ordinary First Division side. Brian Clough was in charge and they were at their peak, challenging for honours at home and abroad. It was a huge game for us.

Only Harry really had any memories of the club's great cup runs of the 70s, so for most of us this was the biggest win we'd ever known. For me it was just amazing, I had played in the Dons' first-ever League match and now we had beaten the contenders for the League title.

I had joined the club from Chorley. I had played against Wimbledon for them in three FA Trophy matches. I obviously impressed, and Allen Batsford came in for me in pre-season – I had no doubt about joining. When I had played for Chorley at Plough Lane, I just had a feel for the club, it had a certain atmosphere and I felt comfortable. I didn't know then where the club was going to take me.

✦

THE BATTLE OF BRAMALL LANE

As the 1983/84 season drew to a close, Wimbledon, Sheffield United and Hull City were locked in a race for the final two promotion places to the old Second Division – Oxford United were already up as champions. With three games left, the meeting between Wimbledon and Sheffield United at Bramall Lane was crucial. And for Stewart Evans, a Yorkshireman and a Sheffield United reject, the match had a personal edge to it.

5 MAY 1984
Third Division
Sheffield United 1 Wimbledon 2
By Stewart Evans (player)

It was absolutely brilliant. For me, nothing was bigger than that game against Sheffield United. For both clubs, it was the end of the season, we were both battling for promotion and neither side could afford to lose. But personally, it was huge. I had come from Sheffield United. I started at Rotherham, but when Ian Porterfield took over there he gave me a free transfer to Sheffield United. And then a few weeks later he came to Sheffield United and I was sidelined again.

Meanwhile, down at Wimbledon, Corky had broken his leg and I got the call from Dave Bassett. He said he was looking for a big forward to cover for Corky while he recovered. So I went there on loan – anything was better than staying with Porterfield.

I worked hard, and got a few games in. We still went down, but I'd done enough to earn a move there. And by the time Corky was match-fit I had worked my way into the side, and we ended up playing together. I don't think I have ever played with a better centre-forward than Corky. We gelled well. We sailed through the Fourth Division, and now I had my chance to prove to the people at Bramall Lane that they had made a mistake in letting me go two years earlier.

The build-up to the game was awesome. My brother, my mother and all my family are Sheffield United fans. They had been on the phone for weeks before the game giving me stick. For them it was club before family every time.

Goalscorer: Stewart Evans, who scored the vital goal that saw Wimbledon beat Sheffield United, in action against Norwich City's Steve Bruce the season after. (Getty Images)

The atmosphere on the day was great. They always got big crowds, but this was a special game. We were flying at the time and it was one of those we had to win. We were just ahead of them on points, but it was tight.

Harry got the old wind-up machine going and it was brilliant. Harry was a brilliant man-manager. He would put his arm around some players, have a joke with some, and shout and scream at others. He knew how to get us going.

I remember Harry coming over to me before the game in the dressing room. He knew my history. He said this was the one club that didn't rate me, that had released me, and this was the chance for me to make amends. He needn't have bothered. I was up for the game, I wanted it badly. For Ian Porterfield, for my brother, for my mother and for the Dons, I wanted it.

I remember my goal that afternoon as if it was yesterday. It was a long ball, a Gary Peters special from the halfway line. The ball ended up between their centre-half and their goalkeeper at the near post and I don't think either of them fancied it. They must have thought we'd all end up in a heap, but I ghosted in with a diving header and it just flew in. It was a great goal. I don't think I've ever felt happier in football before or since seeing that ball fly into the net.

After scoring I ended up in front of the home end. I was on the floor and as I clambered up on to one knee, I was covered in spit and everything. It was disgusting. But it was worth it and it only served to gee us up even more. We weren't going to lose then.

In the second half, Corky got a second for us. It was a typical Corky goal. He nipped in front of the defender and scored. It was a good finish, but in those days he used to get one like that every other week.

I remember Colin Morris got a late penalty for them, but we weren't in the mood to go down.

It was a big win for us and I'll remember it for as long as I live. We had a brilliant side and you could tell that as the players all went on to bigger clubs. The spirit was excellent. We would play as one and make it hard for other teams.

I got abuse from the family for a couple of weeks after the Sheffield triumph. I stayed up there for a couple of days after the game and they were fuming. But I was as happy as Larry. From that day on I used to always score against Sheffield United, but nothing will beat that day in 1984.

✦

DEFEAT, PROMOTION AND LESLIE'S RETURN

Despite the victory over Sheffield United, Wimbledon still needed another three points to secure promotion. Plough Lane was packed as the crowd anticipated a promotion party; instead they slumped to a 3-1 home defeat to Gillingham. The mood was downcast before news filtered through that Sheffield United had lost as well. The Dons were up, and for former Wimbledon legend John Leslie, playing for Gillingham that day, the emotions could not have been more mixed.

7 May 1984
Third Division
Wimbledon 1 Gillingham 3
By John Leslie (player)

It was a really difficult game for me. I had spent all those years at Wimbledon and they were on the brink of the seemingly impossible – promotion to the Second Division. I was full of mixed emotions. I wanted Wimbledon to go up, but I was playing for the opposition.

It didn't make any difference to us as we were destined to finish mid-table. It was the penultimate game of the season and Wimbledon needed to win. They must have thought it was in the bag when Kevin Gage scored after about 10 seconds, but we came back strongly.

I was playing against Nigel Winterburn. I gave him a torrid time, and that's a story I've related many times when Nigel was winning all those medals with Arsenal. Bassett said later that Nigel had the flu and didn't want to play. I'm not so sure.

We went on to win 3-1. I was upset that we won, but then the news reached us that Sheffield United had lost at Bolton, so Wimbledon were up. I can't imagine how I would have felt if we had denied them. The emotion in the boardroom and with all my old teammates was amazing. But I felt down too. I felt I could have been a part of it and I regretted ever leaving. Wimbledon will always be a special place for me. I remember Corky giving me a kiss on the lips. That was painful!

I don't drink, so I was on orange juice and lemonade, but the old Wimbledon boys made sure I bought a few for them. It was like being back with them. They didn't give me any stick for leaving and I didn't give them any for winning the match. But there was a part of me that wanted to be truly part of it. I had been there the year before when we had won the Fourth Division championship, and it was very strange not to be a part of it again.

Wimbledon were the best club I ever played for. I never missed a day's training. I had eight great years there. The spirit was special, and that day in 1984 when they went up without me will always hurt because I was no longer part of it.

◆

HODGES: THE DONS' FIRST FULL INTERNATIONAL

Wimbledon's surge up the divisions had not gone unnoticed by the home nations, and in the summer of 1984, Glyn Hodges made a piece of Wimbledon history – he became the first Wimbledon player to win a full international cap.

6 JUNE 1984
International
Norway 1 Wales 0 (Trondheim)
By Glyn Hodges (player)

All the players were booking their holidays. We'd normally either all go off to Magaluf or San Antonio. I can't remember exactly where we were off to that year. I just remember that I was really looking forward to it and then, unfortunately, I got picked for Wales to play Norway and Israel and I had to cancel everything.

My first cap was brilliant, all five minutes of it. I actually remember it really well. It was in Trondheim in Norway. Andy Dibble and I were on the bench and we were desperate to get on and make our debuts. It was fantastic, but the one thing in my mind was to get a second cap. I didn't want to be labelled a one-cap wonder. Thankfully, I got half an hour against Israel in Tel Aviv later that summer.

It was humid and hot in Israel. I was playing in front of Joey Jones and I was running around, desperate to impress. I remember Joey shouting at me to calm down. I reckon that was the only time in my career that anyone said that to me. It turned out to be a great game to play because it was played at such a slow pace.

I don't know what I expected when I came back. I was the first Wimbledon player to win an international cap and I was a local boy, born and bred in Merton. But there was nothing – it was a bit of a let-down.

I didn't get any recognition until Nigel Winterburn played for the England Under-21s in 1986. Then we were both presented with solid silver commemorative plates. They were thinking it was only Wales.

I got my last full cap in 1996 under Bobby Gould. I had a 12-year international career, but I was only capped about 20 times. I must have been on the substitutes' bench for 40 others.

My international career actually began back in 1980, when Dario Gradi was in charge of Wimbledon. I was chosen for a trial squad of 40 for the Welsh youth team.

I remember Dario coming round to my house with the letter and talking my dad out of letting me go. He said I was too young to commit to play for Wales and that there would be other opportunities.

Wales then qualified for the European Championships in Germany. I was only 17 at the time and I think I was the only one playing regular first-team football, so they picked me for their 16-man squad to face Germany, Belgium and Greece. Again my dad and Dario didn't want me to go. But I spoke to my nan, who was from Swansea, and I went against my dad and Dario's wishes and played. It was one of my better decisions.

The first game was against Germany in front of 50,000. I played in central midfield with Mark Hughes. It was live on television and we lost 5-0. I scored in the second game, a 3-0 win over Belgium. And then I netted the winner in the 1-0 win over Greece, in the final game. I loved every moment, and four years later I won my first full cap.

It was one of a few records I set at Wimbledon. I'd been the first youth international for the club in 1980, three years later I won the first Under-21 cap, and in 1984 I was the first Wimbledon player to score an international goal. Lawrie Sanchez had his eye on that one.

And there is one other thing: I'd like to set the record straight. Who was the first Wimbledon player to score in all four divisions? Alan Cork? Wrong – it was me. That's another thing I never got an accolade for. I scored in our first home game in the First Division against Aston Villa, four days before Corky scored against Leicester.

But despite everything, I'm not bitter. I have got my caps and some great memories. No one can take those away from me.

◆

BEERS, BASSETT AND BORO

Wimbledon's spirit was not just about the players, it was also about the fans and how the two sets mixed. In the mid-80s the players and the fans couldn't have been closer. For supporters of a small club like Wimbledon, the long treks to the north of England hardly appealed. More often than not the club would only need the one coach for such trips. But those who went were Dons to the core, and their loyalty after one trip to Middlesbrough was to be rewarded by the manager.

18 SEPTEMBER 1984
Second Division
Middlesbrough 2 Wimbledon 4
By Ray Armfield (supporter)

Wimbledon travelled to a crumbling and virtually deserted Ayresome Park for a Second Division fixture, accompanied by just one coach-load of fans. Middlesbrough were in trouble, beginning a downward spiral that would lead to liquidation, and were fielding a team of veterans and kids in front of sub-5,000 crowds. The hosts took an early lead through David Mills only for Stewart Evans to equalise on half-time. After the interval a defensive mix-up gifted Boro the lead.

Home seemed a long way away, but the Dons' faithful – corralled in an empty, open corner – sang their hearts out for the lads, and the cavernous, empty stands nearby made their echo sound more like 600 voices than 60. Wimbledon responded with two goals in a minute.

Northern trek: Wimbledon fans at Ayresome Park, Middlesbrough, on 18 September 1984. (Ray Armfield)

Alan Cork cleverly set up Steve Ketteridge to fire home from the edge of the box, and from the restart the Dons came straight back up field to win a penalty for handball. Steve Hatter crashed home the spot kick via the underside of the bar and ran to our enclosure to "give it large". Another sweetly struck shot from Ketteridge put the result beyond doubt.

A good win, you will agree, but memorable? Well, that came afterwards. The club's travel supremo, the late and dearly missed "Mr Wimbledon", Eric Willcocks, boarded the coach with a bigger than usual smile to inform everyone that Dave Bassett had been so impressed by the travelling support that he had given Eric enough money for a pint each at the local hostelry – the cue for more songs and an eventual arrival back in SW19 at around 3.30am!

Harry and Eric repeated the trick at the end of the season, arranging a social evening in the Batsford Arms for regular away supporters as a "thank you" for their efforts.

✦

A STUDENT FARE AND A SKINFUL OF BEER

Wimbledon were not the richest club in the world in the mid-80s, and occasionally players and fans would meet on the train home. For the supporters it could turn into an enlightening experience.

26 JANUARY 1985
FA Cup fourth round
Nottingham Forest 0 Wimbledon 0
By Matthew Breach (supporter)

After securing a creditable 0-0 draw away to Nottingham Forest in the FA Cup fourth Round, I left the City Ground with the remainder of the Dons faithful and headed back to the station. Unfortunately, I had travelled from London on a student fare and was refused permission to take the football special back to town with everyone else, so I spent 90 minutes on my own waiting for the next London-bound train.

After eventually leaving Nottingham, hunger pangs struck and I headed for the buffet to sample the delights of British Rail catering. I was amazed to come across the entire Dons team occupying the buffet car in varying states of drunkenness.

There was Corky, dead sober, fleecing several team-mates at cards; Harry was holding court, explaining to all how his tactics saved the day; and Lurch sitting quietly in a corner with four cans of Special Brew in front of him. As I passed through in a typical student attempt to look cool and unimpressed, several of the players waved on seeing my shirt and muttered thanks for coming. I queued at the counter wondering how to act on my way back past through the team, and on reaching the front was just about to order my sandwich when Glyn Hodges jumped in and asked for four cans of lager and a couple of Mars bars.

"Oi!" I spluttered. "Just because I support you doesn't mean you can push in – I'm starving here!" Just as it was dawning on me that the first words I had ever exchanged with one of my Wimbledon heroes was an argument, Glyn turned to me apologetically and said: "Whoops, sorry mate, come and have a drink." He dragged me back to his table. Two hours, six lagers, 20 autographs and a Mars bar later I staggered off the train at St Pancras in the knowledge that this Wimbledon were not just a great football team, but a special group of people too. And to top it all we won the replay 1-0.

✦

GAGE CELEBRATES AFTER PALACE CRUMBLE

After the club's rapid rise from the Fourth Division to the Second, few gave the Dons any chance of survival. But the 1984/85 season was to prove the critics wrong: Wimbledon could certainly hold their own in the Second Division. A 5-0 away win over Crystal Palace hinted that there was still more to come from the Dons. The victory itself was celebrated in style by fans and players alike. And for Kevin Gage that meant an unusual encounter later that night.

24 FEBRUARY 1985

Second Division

Crystal Palace 0 Wimbledon 5

By Kevin Gage (player)

It was one of those unforgettable matches. Every pass we hit went to feet, every tackle was won and every shot seemed to go in. Just about anything that could go right did. We absolutely annihilated them. In any derby game you are always aware of trying to do well for the fans. You always want to beat a neighbour, and Wimbledon against Palace was no different. And that day must have been so sweet for the fans. Everything came off… they just couldn't live with us.

But I remember the game far more for what followed than for the match itself. I went to a party later that night in Croydon with Wally Downes. It was some friend of Wally's, and Jim Cannon was there. He'd just played against us for Palace and we were just gobsmacked. I can't remember any of the goals that day, but the look on his face when we walked in will live with me for ever. And let's be fair – Wally and I milked it. We gloated. He would have done the same to us, so it only seemed fair.

The little I do remember of the match centres on Paul Fishenden. He got a hat-trick that day, and he and I were flat-mates. Fish lived on that for weeks after. We had bought the house together. On our wages we couldn't afford to get a place by ourselves, so it made sense to get it together. He was a good lad. The boys christened us the Wham boys back then and we lived up to it. We were single, we were young and we were professional footballers. We weren't flash, but we liked to enjoy life.

That year we finished mid-table, but we were all growing up. We had had a bit of success getting up to the Second Division and none of us knew anything different. The younger players like myself were coming of age. The team was blossoming, we were all maturing. We were getting wiser to the game and that's what pushed us on. Results like the 5-0 win at Palace showed our capabilities. They were markers of what was to follow. The team that day – Beasant, Gage, Winterburn, Galliers, Morris, Mick Smith, Evans, Fishenden, Cork, Sanchez and Hodges – had seen it all yet none of us were at our peak. You only to have look through that list of names. Every one of them would go on and play in the top division.

✦

THE NAMING OF THE CRAZY GANG

The name "the Crazy Gang" has been synonymous with Wimbledon for years. But the first time it appeared in the national press came as part of a preview of Wimbledon's fifth-round FA Cup replay with West Ham United at Upton Park in 1985.

6 MARCH 1985

FA Cup fifth round replay

West Ham United 5 Wimbledon 1

By Tony Stenson (Daily Mirror journalist)

I used to cover Wimbledon for the local newspaper when they were in the Isthmian League, and over the years I developed a deep affinity for the club. I used to call Alan Cork "the White Pele", and every year I voted for him in the Football Writers' Awards. And that includes a few years after he retired too.

The Crazy Gang: The Wimbledon first team prepare to take on Wimbledon cricket club in July 1986. Back row: Stewart Evans, Mark Morris, Andy Thorn, Dave Beasant, Alan Cork, Kevin Gage, Wally Downes. Front row: Andy Sayer, Glyn Hodges, Steve Galliers, Mick Smith and Paul Fishenden. (Andrew Watson)

Anyway, eventually I started doing Harry Bassett's programme notes. I did it for eight years unpaid and I continued doing it even when I got my job at the Daily Mirror.

Harry used to allow me a bit of license to write what I wanted. And it was there that I first started referring to "the Crazy Gang," but it never went beyond the programme. The turning point came with the club's run in the FA Cup in 1985.

Wimbledon had drawn 1-1 with West Ham at Plough Lane and had gone away for a few days to Bisham Abbey to prepare for the replay. I remember having a conversation with the Daily Mirror sports editor at the time. He wanted to know what Wimbledon were all about, so he asked me to go down to Bisham Abbey and introduce the players to the Mirror readers.

I went down there and got Wally Downes to do pen pix on all the players. It's a familiar format these days, but in 1985 it was totally new. There were no guidelines for Wally to follow so he just went with whatever came into his head. I remember the entry for Dave Beasant vividly: "We all call him Lurch. He gets his wife to put £1 behind the clock each week. He's so tight. He won't let a ball through his gloves." They were all like that.

But the key was the standfirst. They asked me to write one. I wrote: "Meet Dave Bassett's barmy army, meet the rag tag and bobtail, the team that is so skint they nick towels from hotels. Let me introduce soccer's Crazy Gang."

It was the first time the phrase appeared in the national newspapers and it was picked up and used by my colleagues. Within weeks, all the papers were using it.

✦

INTRODUCING FASH THE BASH

The following season, Wimbledon surpassed all expectations and stood on the brink of the unthinkable, winning promotion to the First Division just three years after leaving the Fourth. To help complete the final push Dave Bassett persuaded Sam Hammam to part with £125,000 – a new club record fee – to buy John Fashanu.

29 MARCH 1986
Second Division
Portsmouth 1 Wimbledon 1
By John Fashanu (player)

I was kicking nine bells out of everyone at Millwall. People who saw me then used to say I was the man. No one could live with John Fashanu – all within the rules of course. And then dear old Harry came in for me. He loved the fact that there was this 6ft 3in black lad running around the Second Division, causing all sorts of havoc and knocking in goals left, right and centre. He said: "Listen, Fash, we could do with you. You could take this club from the Second Division to the First Division."

George Graham was in charge of Millwall at the time. And in his wonderful generous way he said: "Off you go, then," and that was it. Actually, there were about four clubs in for me at the time, including Aston Villa, but I liked Harry's spirit. Harry talked the same game that I played, which was no nonsense and straight at 'em.

I remember my debut really well. It was a great game against promotion-chasing Portsmouth at Fratton Park. I absolutely loved it. I came on as a second-half substitute and I scared them. They had Noel Blake at the back, Alan Knight in goal and Micky Tait. They were a nasty little firm and they really thought they were it. They had this reputation, but I wasn't going to respect them. I had knocked the hell out of them for Millwall four days earlier and I was up for doing it again.

It was at Millwall that I was first called "Fash the Bash". I just continued playing the same way and against Portsmouth it was brilliant. It was a game full of incident and it was important for me. I was a new Wimbledon player. I had to cover my own back. I wasn't sure whether the Wimbledon boys would back me up.

After every tackle there was a punch-up. I was having a non-stop battle with Blake and their goalkeeper. It was never-ending. It was psychological warfare all over the pitch. Everything was going on off the ball. The referee just took the attitude to ignore it all. The players couldn't believe it; my style was new to them. But at the end, Sanch, Corky and everyone were right there steaming in.

I had cut eyes and bruises everywhere. I can't remember the score – I am not even sure if I touched the ball, but it was a great game. A great battle. The lads immediately accepted me.

Wimbledon has always been famous for its initiation ceremonies, but I remember giving all the boys the Fash stare. After that there was only one person who ever dared to do anything to me, and that was Wally Downes.

He filled my tea with salt and tried to burn my socks, my favourite silk socks. We had a bit of a confrontation after that, nothing too serious: that was left for Lawrie Sanchez later – the famous clash of the titans. At every club I have been at there has been a confrontation with someone. At Millwall it was Steven Lowndes. He needed six weeks in hospital. At Aston Villa it was Dalian Atkinson.

After those first few weeks at Wimbledon, I used to go in every day wearing a suit. No one was going to pick on me.

At Wimbledon we had our own way of doing things and the players respected that. I remember Vinnie and I dragging Steve Cotterill around the pitch in the snow with no clothes on. It was just the way we did things. He took it well and it made him stronger.

I remember the shock on Terry Gibson's face when we all charged in for a punch-up against West Ham before half-time. It was his fourth game for the club since joining from Manchester United. He went in to break it all up and succeeded. He thought everyone would congratulate him for calming it all down. But he ended up getting a slap from Vinnie and Sam Hammam. We had an agreement at Wimbledon that we would never stop a fight if it started. You can join in, but you can't stop it. Terry just looked shocked. But that was Wimbledon and I loved it.

◆

THE BUST-UP

The animosity between John Fashanu and Lawrie Sanchez is legendary. The two were strong characters and refused to back down. Their stubbornness led to an inevitable clash just a month into Fashanu's career at Wimbledon in April 1986. Sanchez had expected a punch-up, but Fashanu had other ideas. The battle was to make the national press, and the pair have not seen eye to eye since.

The new arrival: John Fashanu, who fell out with Lawrie Sanchez immediately. (Getty Images)

APRIL 1986
By Tony Stenson (Daily Mirror journalist)

The battle between John Fashanu and Lawrie Sanchez was probably the most famous fight ever to happen at the club. John had just arrived from Millwall and he wanted to take control, but Lawrie is one of the strongest players mentally you will ever meet and he was having none of it.

John was fuming and the pair agreed to settle it once and for all. So, in true schoolboy style, they went behind the shed to fight it out. I think Lawrie and everyone expected a fist fight, but Fash went in using his kung-fu skills. He had one aim – to try and break Lawrie's leg.

Lawrie was furious and he phoned me straight away. He wanted me to take a statement from him and send it to the Press Association. I did just that. It said something like: "John Fashanu and I had a disagreement and I thought we were going to settle it like men with a fight, but he tried to break my leg and I cannot forgive him for that."

Lawrie was never really part of the Crazy Gang at Wimbledon. Most of the players respected him. He was the intelligent loner, but after the incident with Fashanu the two never saw eye to eye again.

It was the worst incident I'd ever known at Wimbledon – and I had seen a few. The only one that ever came close was the day they hijacked Paul Fishenden, tied him to the top of a transit van with bandages and drove off down the A3. They went all the way to the M25 and back with Paul tied to the roof. It was just incredibly dangerous, but no one batted an eyelid. They just couldn't see the danger in it. It was just one big laugh for them.

Fights were common at Wimbledon. They always had been. Harry encouraged them.

A few years later Robbie Turner, arrived at the club and he fancied himself a bit. So Fash set on him, they exchanged a few blows and Robbie got knocked down. As he fell, he gouged a huge chunk of flesh out of his thigh and was out for months. Then there was the fight between Keith Curle and John Gayle. John chased Keith around the training ground with a baseball bat. But each time the two aggressors made up. That was the way Wimbledon were supposed to work. Fash and Lawrie just didn't read the script.

✦

SANCH'S STRIKE SENDS THE DONS UP

On the pitch in 1986, Wimbledon were flying. With three games left they needed to win just one to gain promotion and take the club into wonderland. The vital victory came at Huddersfield. It was a scrappy game on a dire wet afternoon in Yorkshire. The scene was set for Lawrie Sanchez's belter

3 MAY 1986
Second Division
Huddersfield Town 0 Wimbledon 1
By Lawrie Sanchez (player)

I wasn't on free-kicks. That was usually Glyn Hodges' or Kevin Gage's job. I can't quite explain what was going through my mind, but I just asked them to knock the ball square to me. And I hit it. Both my feet were off the floor and it flew in. It surprised everyone including me. It secured our promotion. I've got a photograph of me wheeling away celebrating, with Mark Morris, Glyn Hodges, Steve Galliers and Kevin Gage chasing me. It's got pride of place in my study.

We had three games left going into the match, all away. We only had to win one to go up. It wasn't the prettiest of games, and they had a couple of players sent off late, but all that mattered was that we had got the three points and I had scored the winner.

In those days, however, the television coverage was nowhere near as extensive as it is now. I scored over 50 goals in my career, but I'll be lucky if 20 of them were caught on video. I once saw the grainy newsreel of the goal against Huddersfield. It was from an appalling angle, but you can see the emotion and it was definitely a good shot. But it also showed how bad the weather was that day.

It was chucking it down. Those Wimbledon fans on the terraces were the true Wimbledon fans at Huddersfield that day. Not the ones who swamped Wembley in 1988 or the town centre the day after. They were great too, but it's those huddled few on that wet afternoon in Yorkshire that I associate with. It was the supreme moment of the season. We just savoured it, fans and players alike. We were excited, we were overjoyed.

That season was epitomised in that one goal. The two most important goals in Wimbledon's history – and I scored them both, the other, of course, was the winner in the FA Cup final two years later. But in my opinion the one against Huddersfield was the most important.

Nobody outside the club thought we would fare well in the top division, but we had an excellent side then. The next few seasons were to prove it. We never quite got the credit we deserved.

On the way home from Huddersfield, the celebrations were great. But none of us were quite sure what was going to happen. We were looking forward to Liverpool and Old Trafford. What we never realised was that we would go to those places and win.

But in terms of the promotion itself, I took it all in my stride. I had been promoted and relegated before at Reading. And it was the same for most of the team.

I never quite realised how special it all was. When you are in the eye of the storm you never realise how big it is until you step outside. I knew we were doing something, but it's only when I look back now that I think what we had achieved was phenomenal.

✦

The Spirit of Wimbledon

CHAPTER SIX: THE FIRST GREAT SEASON

TOP FLIGHT DEBUT

So Wimbledon were to kick off the 1986/87 season in the First Division. It seemed beyond reality, but could the club survive amongst the élite? The Dons first game in the First Division was away at Manchester City. The experience was to be an eye-opener for the club's players. Andy Thorn made history by becoming the first Wimbledon player to score in the top flight.

23 AUGUST 1986

First Division

Manchester City 3 Wimbledon 1

By Andy Thorn (player)

I had always wanted to play in the First Division. It had been a dream. We travelled up the night before, but I couldn't sleep – I was so nervous. We did well for about an hour. We were awarded a free-kick out wide. It was the usual routine: hit the ball high, aim for the far post and hope someone gets a touch. No one did and it went straight in.

I used up a lot of energy celebrating. I didn't know what to do, so I just went mad. I remember Harry shouting at me to calm down and perhaps I settled down too much. They equalised almost immediately, and I remember thinking we would have to start all over again. But before we could even pause for breath we were 3-1 down and the game was lost.

It was such an eye-opener. Every time we had given them a chance they scored. We hadn't been accustomed to that level of ruthlessness. On the way back from Manchester we realised we had blown it. Harry was furious. But he was more frustrated as we had done enough to win.

Back home we had lots of meetings. We worked out what we needed to do and we focused again. We went back to basics, to the football we knew, and it worked. We were determined.

Personally, I had battled so hard to get into the First Division that I wasn't going to let it all go in one season. I was educated at Raynes Park High School and four of us went to Wimbledon as schoolboys: me, John Gannon, Steve Payne and Kevin Wedderburn. I was the only one not to be offered apprenticeship terms. I was gutted. I remember my dad saying it would be all right and that he'd get me a job on the buses.

I had resigned myself to that fate, but a couple of weeks later Wimbledon rang up and said they could offer me a place as part of the new youth opportunity scheme. That was 1984, and I was offered £25 a week.

Goalscorer: Andy Thorn, who scored Wimbledon's first goal in the First Division. (Getty Images)

The other guys were getting a lot more than that. But I wanted it so much, I wanted the chance.

The others were on two-year deals, but I only had a year to prove myself. I was playing regularly in the reserves, and in late March 1985 Bassett pulled me in. It was a Thursday, and he said: "You've done well. I want to send you to Sweden for six months to see how you get on there." Then on the following Saturday, Wally Downes, who had been playing as a sweeper, broke his ankle. On the Monday Harry told me: "You're no longer going to Sweden." On Tuesday, a couple more players picked up injuries and the next day Bassett said: "Andy, you're playing on Saturday." I stayed there for the rest of the season.

So after all that, I was the only one of the Raynes Park High four to break through.

◆

ON TOP OF THE WORLD

After the defeat to Manchester City, Dons supporters could have been forgiven for fearing the worst. Instead, what followed went beyond their wildest dreams. Wimbledon won their next two games – 3-2 against Aston Villa and 1-0 over Leicester. And in the first few days of September came the unthinkable, after a 1-0 win over Charlton Athletic... Wimbledon were top of the League.

2 SEPTEMBER 1986
First Division
Charlton Athletic 0 Wimbledon 1
By Steve Galliers (player)

What I recall most was seeing the papers the next day. We were on the back page of them all. We had achieved so much throughout my eight years at the club, but this was totally unexpected and unprecedented. It was amazing. I had played in the club's first-ever League game, and now here we were on top of the whole thing. Roy of the Rovers would have struggled to write that script. But I was far more concerned about the immediate future.

We were under no illusions that we were going to win the League, but we were keen to prove the critics wrong and I wanted to make the most of it. I was 29 and I knew that the whole experience had probably come a little bit late for me. But it was a great time and we were having so much fun.

My only regret is that we didn't get into the top flight sooner. I would love to have played a couple of years at that level. But it was great to have got a taste of it, however brief.

Our strength was that we had all been together for so long. We had spent the early years slogging around Rochdale and Hartlepool, so we were going to make damn sure we enjoyed playing the likes of Manchester City and Tottenham. From Spotland to White Hart Lane, it just didn't compare. We were going to lap up every moment.

◆

HODGES STRIKES LATE TO KEEP DONS TOP

The midweek table was viewed as just a blip. Wimbledon were top and Manchester United were bottom – surely by Saturday a degree of normality would return? No chance. A Wimbledon win at Vicarage Road kept the Dons on the top.

6 SEPTEMBER 1986
First Division
Watford 0 Wimbledon 1
By Glyn Hodges (player)

It was the crowning moment for Harry and for all of us. We went top in midweek, but it was Saturday's game that made people sit up and take us seriously. In the final minute of a scoreless game there was a ricochet in the box and it fell to me. I had one shot on my right foot that came straight back to me. I remember seeing John McClelland and Tony Coton, their goalkeeper, blocking the way.

I was at inside-left, and the only shot on was one with my left and the pair of them had it covered. But I knew if I shot that John would go to block it. So I hit it between his legs. It wasn't the most powerful shot, but Coton was unsighted and it sneaked in. The guys later said I didn't mean it, but I did.

To be honest, I was lucky to still be on the pitch. Harry was trying a new formation of 4-3-3, playing Dennis Wise and me a little deeper. But it wasn't working and we weren't causing any problems. I half expected to be substituted. And then the ball came to me – the only chance I had all game.

On top: Glyn Hodges celebrates scoring at Watford on 6 September 1986. (Getty Images)

The celebrations were mad – "Airplanes" flying all around the ground, it was great. Some people look back and point to the Liverpool cup game in 1993 as the first time the Dons wheeled away in an airborne celebration, imitating a squadron, but that's not correct.

We'd given it a go on the Tuesday at Selhurst Park, when Wisey scrambled home the winner against Charlton. Going top was unbelievable, but there were some matches on the following night and most of the papers dismissed our achievement as temporary. But all our rivals slipped up, and we were still top. That's when it began to hit home and we made the decision to celebrate in style if we defeated Watford as it would leave us top of the table with no doubts. I remember seeing Bryan Robson on television afterwards talking about Wimbledon as the leaders. We felt invincible. We had great self-belief, we were untouchable. We'd had to pinch ourselves when we won promotion, and now here we were sitting on top of the First Division. It was almost too much. We were labelled long-ball merchants, but we had some fantastic players who could open up the play. And we didn't get to the top of the table by playing bad football: we were organised, we had a game plan and we could play. And in Nigel Winterburn, John Fashanu and Wisey we had excellent players who would all go on to play for England.

✦

GAZZA SPOILS MICK SMITH'S SWANSONG

Mick Smith had been at the heart of the Wimbledon defence for the best part of a decade. His final game for the club was against Newcastle, his home town club. And in the opposing team's starting XI was a young Paul Gascoigne.

20 SEPTEMBER 1986
First Division
Newcastle 1 Wimbledon 0
By Mick Smith (player)

It was a dream come true to be playing in the First Division. I missed the first game against Manchester City, but I played in each of the next six. They were to prove to be my last for Wimbledon and my last in the top flight. Injury hit after that. I had hernia and then pelvic problems, and I wouldn't play for the club again. I finally left in January 1988. But I will treasure for ever every game I had in the First Division and the last above all others. It was against Newcastle, my home town.

I had never dreamed that I would return there as a First Division footballer, even more incredibly playing for a team at the top of the First Division. We probably deserved to win, but for once the luck was against us. A young kid scored the winner, a delightful lob early in the second half. His name was Paul Gascoigne. I loved my time at Wimbledon. I loved the players around me. We had been together for years and our playing system was almost instinctive. We knew the role of every position. I could have played in any position and known what to do.

But there was also the competitive side to Wimbledon. I knew if I wasn't playing well there was someone willing to step into my place. But we still passed on information to each other. It sounds strange now, but we wanted to see whoever was in the team do well. It was up to you to get your place back. In those days the win bonus was a major part of your pay packet so there was plenty of incentive. But the No 1 priority was always the team.

✦

INTRODUCING VINNIE JONES

After a great start, Wimbledon's first season in the top flight had stalled. Top at the start of September, Wimbledon had lost seven of their next 10. Dave Bassett wanted to add some passion to his side. He turned to non-league side Wealdstone and signed an unheralded midfielder for £15,000. His name was Vinnie Jones.

22 NOVEMBER 1986
First Division
Nottingham Forest 3 Wimbledon 2
By Vinnie Jones (player)

My first game was away at Nottingham Forest. I played in midfield with Wally Downes that day. I will always remember it. I remember Dave Bassett saying to me: "You have to mark this Neil Webb in midfield; he's the business, a great player." I followed him around the whole day. I didn't play my own game at all, and then Franz Carr did a one-two with Nigel Clough and chipped the ball to the back post. I couldn't get there in time and I handled it.

Barely quarter of an hour had gone. Carlton Fairweather had given us an early lead and I had blown it. It was a penalty – up steps Cloughie and it's 1-1. Andy Thorn then got an own goal to give them the lead. Hodges brought it level, but I was still getting the run-around. And then there was Johnny Metgod's free-kick. It was from miles out, but Dave Beasant never had a chance. We lost 3-2.

People said to me after that: "Do you think you will be back in?" But I never gave it a thought. It was all happening too quickly. I never had a chance to do my shoelaces up.

The next game at home to Manchester United Bassett played me, but I really did have an awful game at Forest. A lot of managers would have said: "That's enough, he ain't good enough." But he kept me in and gave me a good talking-to.

He said: "You are not in here to chase people about all day. You are here to do your bit. You are good in the air; get the ball into the channels like how we play." And so I did.

I went loose, and in the first 10 or 15 minutes I hit the post with a volley and that gave me a buzz, and then the next minute Glyn Hodges whipped a corner in. Kevin Moran was marking me, and I gave him a bit of a shrug and powered it in with my head. Remi Moses tried to clear it off the line, but he couldn't stop it and we won the game 1-0. That was the only time I have ever had any good press. I scored in the next two games too, against Chelsea and Sheffield Wednesday.

The Manchester United game was also the first time Wimbledon fans saw the Vinnie Jones commitment. What the fans like is firstly goals, secondly skills – good passing or a good header – and thirdly they want you to play the way they feel, with passion and a desire to win. I have been a supporter on the terraces looking down saying: "How can they just stroll about?", "How can they not fancy it when you are on a stage like that?" A lot of players are like that, but a lot of players have had it too easy. They haven't seen the other side of it. They don't get the fans' view. I've always got that.

✦

STORMING THE BRIDGE

Both geographically and in the footballing world Wimbledon had always lived in the shadow of Chelsea, just a short trip up the District Line. After a 4-0 victory at Stamford Bridge in 1986, the Dons stepped out of the shadows.

6 DECEMBER 1986

First Division

Chelsea 0 Wimbledon 4

By Glyn Hodges (player)

If there is one match in my career that stands out, it has to be the win at Chelsea. I had been on their books as a kid, but I chose to join Wimbledon as an apprentice, and this result was the vindication of my decision. It felt really good. My one regret is that I missed a sitter late on that would have made it 5-0. I kicked the post in total frustration and hurt myself. We wanted it so much and we didn't stop for the full 90 minutes.

The game started well for us. They had Doug Rougvie sent off in the first minute. As manager of Barnsley, my side played against 10 men and lost a few times. You still have a job to do.

Chelsea were the big glamour club and we were little Wimbledon, it was perfect. We just went for it. We wanted to rub their noses in it. At Wimbledon you could sense it when another club didn't fancy playing us. I've never felt that anywhere else. It happened a lot in the lower divisions. We used to dominate teams, intimidate them, bully them, but it hadn't happened against a top team. But that day you could feel it. They didn't want it. I wouldn't say they were scared, but we could feel the game was ours for the taking.

Schoolboy returns: Glyn Hodges, who was on the books at Chelsea, thrived on his return to Stamford Bridge. Here he gets a cross in against Nottingham Forest. (Getty Images)

Ken Bates had installed an electric perimeter fence, but he hadn't been given permission to turn it on. Fash had put us one up and the ball broke down the left-hand side. One of their players kicked it out and it bounced back off this high fence. I took the throw quickly. It went to Corky, he crossed, and Carlton Fairweather put it away to make it 2-0. I remember thinking: "Thanks, Ken – that fence just cost you a goal." They were never going to come back from that.

Winning 4-0 is impressive in any league. But winning 4-0 away, and in the First Division, and at Chelsea, now *that's* impressive.

It was all part of an amazing season. We went on to beat Liverpool at Anfield, we beat Manchester United home and away, but that win at Chelsea topped them all. We had shown the whole of London and England that Wimbledon deserved to be in the top flight. We weren't just a long-ball team.

But that's not to take away from what it meant to be Wimbledon. We were aware of our roots, our humble backgrounds. I was an apprentice, and there were a few of us who had come through the ranks. Nigel Winterburn was a free transfer from Oxford United. And we had Plough Lane. It was tiny and cramped, it wasn't the greatest stadium, but it was Wimbledon.

Plough Lane helped create the spirit. We'd drink in Nelson's after the game with the fans and we'd stick together. I remember the likes of Ivor Heller from those days. It was what made us so hard to beat and we took that wherever we went, whether it was to Anfield or Old Trafford. And that spirit was there with us that memorable day at Stamford Bridge.

The day they dug up Plough Lane was a sad day for every player who ever graced that stadium wearing the blue of Wimbledon.

◆

DONS RISE TO THE CRITICS

After the victory over Chelsea, Wimbledon were back on track and the good times continued to roll. The Dons have always been keen to prove their detractors wrong, but when one of them is playing for the opposition...

10 JANUARY 1987
FA Cup third round
Wimbledon 2 Sunderland 1
By Glyn Hodges (player)

We equalised late and I got the winner. It was a great comeback, typical of those times. It wasn't the warmest of nights and some of us probably weren't up for it. Sunderland had a good team. Eric Gates was up front, Alan Kennedy was in defence and there were a few other experienced players. It was Gates who fired us up. Just before half-time he got in between our defence and scored. He went berserk. As we were coming off at half-time he was giving it large, saying we were this and that and weren't worthy of being in the First Division.

We'd all expected a roasting from Harry to get us all going again, but after the spray from Gates, Harry didn't have to say a thing. He knew we were up for it for the second half.

That was Wimbledon back then. We were all young lads, we didn't respect anyone, and we were playing our way and to hell with the rest of them. Pele could have come down and played against us then and we would have hammered him.

We were all used to the banter in the lower divisions. But this was the first time we were taking on players of that standard and we didn't expect that sort of comment from Gates. It was a real eye-opener for us and we were determined to make sure they wouldn't forget us.

Sanchez got the equaliser with three minutes to go. I'd swung in the corner and he got his head on it. I didn't fancy a cold night at Roker Park for the replay. I don't think any of us did. I'd made up my mind that the next time the ball came my way I'd go for it, and luckily I got the chance. Dave Beasant hit the ball downfield, and I picked it up and went for it, rounding the keeper and scoring.

There was only one place I was going to run to after that: I made a bee-line straight for Gates. And we gave it to him large. That was sweet.

That was the mentality of those days. No one was going to get away with degrading us and we weren't going to give in. We caused problems for all teams and we just kept going. If someone dropped off there would be someone else to pick him up and drive him on.

Dave Bassett would wind us up. But we had a couple of leaders on the pitch. That's the way Harry wanted it. It all began with Gary Peters years before. He wouldn't take any crap and I had a few run-ins with him. If he thought I wasn't playing well he would tell me. He was a great captain.

And then there was Wally. He was another motivator and he took on Gary's role when he left. It was Wally who rubbed Gates' words into us that night. He had the drive and desire to win and that was instilled in all of us.

I've still got a lot of tapes from those days. Vince Craven used to make a special compilation for the players, and I still put them on to remind myself of those times. The quality isn't that good, but the goal are all there and the Sunderland game is one that I always fast forward to.

Looking back, God knows what would have happened if Gates hadn't spouted off, but as soon as he uttered those words there was only going to be one result. The fans might not have known it at the time, especially as we left it so late, but we certainly did.

◆

DONS STEAL THE LIMELIGHT

It was a crucial time for Wimbledon. On the pitch, a mid-season blip in form had passed and the Dons were now cranking out the wins again and pushing for a top-six place and an unprecedented FA Cup quarter-final appearance. Off the pitch, Sam Hammam had spoken about his desire for Wimbledon and Crystal Palace "to marry". His intention to proceed with a merger incensed Dons fans. A live televised game was the perfect opportunity to voice their concerns.

22 FEBRUARY 1987

FA Cup fifth round

Wimbledon 3 Everton 1

By Andy Sayer (player)

It was the first time the club had been shown live on TV. The build-up to the tie was massive, and then there was the talk of merger. As a club we'd got into a habit of doing something special the week before each round. We'd been to Portugal and somewhere on the South Coast in the earlier rounds, and this time we spent four or five days in Spain before the game. A couple of journalists flew out with us. Martin Tyler, from Football Focus, followed us the whole week. It also helped us escape from all the protests back home.

Everton were much stronger then. They went on to win the championship that year. And we were huge underdogs, but we always felt we had a chance.

They took the lead early, and then Kevin Gage won a penalty just before the break. It was saved but Glyn Hodges knocked it in at the second attempt. In the second half John Fashanu put us ahead, but it should have been my goal. I had a great chance, but the keeper saved it and Fash tucked it away.

Our third goal was the best – yeah, OK, I scored it. Dave Beasant put in a booming kick, John Fashanu won the header and I picked it up and went around Kevin Ratcliffe before slotting home. My goal made the game safe at 3-1. There was no way back for them.

The fans created an incredible atmosphere at Plough Lane – it was buzzing. It was one of those special days when you could really sense the Wimbledon spirit. But the fans were still fuming and they protested long and hard, and we could really understand their feelings. We were Wimbledon. We didn't want to merge.

Personally, it was the start of a great week. I scored a hat-trick six days later against Newcastle United and ended the month as the FIAT Young Player of the Month. I think I'm the only Wimbledon player ever to win that award.

The hat-trick was special. It was the first by a Dons' player in the top flight, and that's my bit of history. Newcastle were struggling then, but they had a big away support. So it was a big day for Wimbledon. None of my goals were particularly great; they were all tap-ins, scrappy goals.

The last one was the best and I remember it well. It was a volley from a Glyn Hodges cross, which I should have headed but by the time the ball reached me it was too late for that. I still have the match ball.

My team-mates were as proud as I was about me getting a hat-trick. That was part of the spirit of the club. They were a brilliant set of blokes. The lads used to socialise a lot – we would drink and joke, but at the end of the day we were all professionals. When we needed to be serious, we were. We worked hard and played hard.

The footballer's life at Wimbledon was an eye-opener, yet it actually corrupted me. As an apprentice I'd been away with the team to Magaluf. The team had just carried off the Fourth Division championship, someone dropped out of the trip and Dave Bassett told me to pack my bags and come along. I was just 16.

I loved Wimbledon, but things changed under the new manager. Bobby Gould had definite views of how he wanted the team to play and I didn't fit into those plans. If Bobby hadn't taken over I would have happily stayed at Wimbledon for ever.

◆

Personal triumph: Andy Sayer, who scored against Everton in the fifth round of the FA Cup on 22 February 1987 and was then named FIAT Player of the Month for February. (Getty Images)

THE BATTLE AGAINST MERGER

The Everton protest was the pinnacle of the anti-merger campaign, but there was much more to come after. At the heart of it all was David Lloyd.

By David Lloyd (supporter)

We were savouring playing in the top flight of British football. Life was as good as it could get, but then news filtered through that Sam Hammam, the owner of our club, wanted to merge with Crystal Palace.

The fans were devastated. There was a hastily arranged meeting organised by the club at Nelson's. Peter Miller, who later became a director, spoke to us.

At the time he was an opponent of the merger to create a super-club in South London – Wimbledon Palace or South London United or whatever. He was deputy news editor of the Sunday Mirror at the time and was a big fan. He told us we had to get organised and we took it from there.

We were livid. But out of the fans' rage the "Save Wimbledon Action Group" was born. A central core formed the committee: Laurence Lowne, Dennis Lowndes, Lord Faulkener, Paul Willatts and myself.

It was the classic political committee. We used to meet regularly in a smoke-filled back room of the Irish Club on Wimbledon Broadway, with pints of Guinness on the table. From there we plotted and planned to stop the merger.

We had our own specialist skills. One of us looked into the ownership of Plough Lane and the adjoining land, and the issue of shareholding at the club. This was against a backdrop of a number of property developers buying into London clubs, whose grounds were situated on prime real estate, most notably Fulham and QPR. We discovered that Hammam owned significant tracts of land behind Plough Lane. It looked all set for one big property deal.

Another job was to work in liaison with the Crystal Palace Independent Supporters Association. They weren't as organised as us, but they spoke passionately at a few meetings, including one memorable occasion at Wimbledon Town Hall. Chris Wright from the Palace Action Campaign, who had been there in 1981, spoke eloquently about the need for the two clubs to maintain their independence. "This was no business deal, this was football," he said.

Richard Faulkener, who later became a lord, was the most influential member of SWAG. He was active in politics and was a member of the Football Trust. He raised questions about the merger in the wider world of football. Should anyone be allowed to own two football clubs? Was there a conflict of interest that needed to be resolved? At the time Robert Maxwell had been involved in both Reading and Oxford and he was talking openly of creating a merged entity, Thames Valley Royals. We set out to question the legality of it all.

I am an ex-journalist and work in the PR business. I was charged with the responsibility of getting our message across to the fans and to the media. For every home game that season we produced a series of open letters to challenge Hammam's plans, to put him on the spot and make life as uncomfortable as possible for him, and we handed them out for free. With everything going on, it wasn't particularly difficult to find something new to write about each week.

We kept asking: "Where's your evidence that Palace will rally to support this new club? Where's your approval from the football authorities?"

But Hammam could have easily ignored the fans, so I kept going to the media and they took up the baton. They were able to ask the difficult questions, the ones Hammam had refused to answer when we put them to him.

What he had failed to realise was that the never-say-die attitude of Wimbledon applied as much to the fans as it did to the players, and the fan base was solidly behind us. The spirit of being a Wimbledon fan has always been a David versus Goliath battle.

Looking back, it was the perfect continuation of the battles waged to get us into the Football League and the original protests to stop the first proposed merger back in 1981. Every time we had been faced with threats, cometh the hour, there were always plenty of people who were willing to fight, which is one of the reasons why the Wimbledon Independent Supporters Association and AFC Wimbledon are so successful now. We will never know when to give up.

The SWAG campaign was to last for six months. And then one day Hammam called Laurence's father, Alf, a veteran of all the great Wimbledon supporters' campaigns. He invited Alf and me to his offices in Mayfair. I still remember getting the call from Alf to join him. I didn't really know what to expect. Hammam was behind this desk. He was a different character to his public persona. He looked reflective when we entered his office.

He said he regretted deeply what he had done and admitted he had been naïve. He hadn't realised the passion of the supporters and the importance the community plays in a local football team. And then came the words we had waited for six months. He said our campaign had been effective, so much so that he had thought things over.

He no longer wanted to fight us; he wanted to work with us. Use us. And that was the first time he showed us the plans for Wandle Valley. "If you really want to campaign," he added, "help me get planning permission for this and I will drop the Palace thing."

And he unveiled a plan for a multi-sports facility, with a sliding roof and an artificial pitch. He spoke of hosting rock concerts and boxing matches there. He believed there was a real desire for such a venue in south-west London. But he wanted an outside developer to help, which would make Wimbledon effective tenants in their own stadium.

We could see what he wanted, and I and a few others tried to assist him. It was Hammam's first direct involvement with the fans and he had come to realise that the fans shared his passion for the game and the club.

But two things effectively scuppered the Wandle Valley move. The first was the Football League's decision later that year to ban artificial pitches, although I still thought we could go ahead with a grass pitch. The second was Hammam himself.

I went to a meeting with Hammam and a Mecca Leisure director, someone I knew from my work. Hammam was a disaster – he ranted about the council and about how they had betrayed the club, when all he needed to do was show them the plans he had shown us and given Mecca the chance to consume it all.

He must have learnt a lot in that year. If only he had seen it all before, how different things could have been…

◆

CORK POPS ANFIELD'S BUBBLE

Back on the pitch, by the end of the 1986/87 season Wimbledon were thriving. Everytime a big game came along the club just seemed to rise to the challenge. The biggest then was a trip to Anfield. Liverpool were the team of the decade. Anfield was the greatest arena in England and Wimbledon were the scruffy upstarts. A Wimbledon victory at Anfield seemed preposterous. Someone had forgotten to tell Alan Cork. With 12 minutes to go he headed home the incredible winner.

28 MARCH 1987

First Division

Liverpool 1 Wimbledon 2

By Alan Cork (player)

It was about the only time in my life that I have ever outpaced anyone. From the moment the ball hit the net I was off, and no one was going to catch me. The Scousers are a special bunch and the atmosphere that day was great. While I was warming up, this one guy was giving me loads of abuse. He was shouting "Spamhead" at me non-stop, but he had me in stitches. That's the thing with the club in those days. We were all supposed to concentrate on the matches, but just sometimes something stupid would happen and we'd all end up laughing.

We had no particular form going into our first visit to Anfield, but we always fancied our chances against the bigger clubs. Nigel Winterburn gave us the lead just before the break and at half-time we were buzzing. But then Kenny Dalglish cracked a curler straight after the interval to wipe the smiles off our faces. Mind you, we were still playing well.

Harry threw me on with 15 minutes left. I'd barely had a touch when the ball went out for a corner on the left-hand side. I can't remember who took it, probably Glyn. The ball floated over, Mark Morris got the faintest of flicks past

He's got no hair: Alan Cork, who scored the winner against Liverpool in 1987. (Getty Images)

Gary Gillespie and I was there to head it into the top right-hand corner. I've got a picture of it on my wall in my office.

And that was it – I was off, straight to the guy who'd called me a spamhead. And to his credit he loved it, he clapped me. And at the final whistle I went over to him and we had a laugh about it. That's the Scousers for you.

I scored loads of goals for Harry from the bench, but it never did any favours for my wage packet. And that was the same at Leicester. He is as tight as anything. I remember Bassett and Glyn Hodges arguing over a £5 pay rise. And they decided to settle it over a toss of a coin. Glyn lost, and I'd never seen Harry looking happier.

Anyway, that day in 1987, as we walked off, I remember Stanley Reed clear as anything. He was so excited. It was probably the biggest team we'd ever beaten. Liverpool were massive – no one else in Europe could come close – and we had just beaten them at their place. Stanley wore the biggest grin.

The journey home was mad. Stanley, Tony Stenson, Thorny and I popped out and bought a bottle of Scotch, a bottle of vodka and a couple of other bottles before getting on the coach. And we were wrecked by the time we got back to Wimbledon. After most away games the whole team would generally end up back at Nelson's, but we could barely walk as we stumbled off the coach at the Sportsman.

It was all a bit too much, Wimbledon FC going to Anfield and winning – unbelievable. It was just a great occasion, especially for Stanley. He loved that sort of thing. Stanley was Wimbledon through and through. I miss the old boy. He would do whatever he could for you. If you wanted a quiet chat, he'd make time. If you had a few problems, he would try and sort them out. And if you wanted to have a big drink, he'd be with you. Stanley was top dollar. They don't make people like that any more. And for that reason, I'm delighted that we were able to give him all those great memories. He deserved it.

✦

UNITED TAMED AT OLD TRAFFORD

Reduced to 10 men, up against a team full of internationals, most teams would have no chance. But with Bassett in charge there could only be one winner.

2 MAY 1987

First Division

Manchester United 0 Wimbledon 1

By Mark Morris (player)

Hard worker: Mark Morris, who was part of the team that won Old Trafford. After this victory, Morris was to play just two more games for the club. (Getty Images)

We were on a great run. We had beaten all the teams at the top away from home: Liverpool, Chelsea, Tottenham and now Manchester United. We were playing unbelievably. At the start of the season, the media had said we were going to be the worst side ever to play in the First Division. But that just spurred us on.

We had several other great results, but the win at Old Trafford sticks out for me more than any other win. It was like a dream. We had been used to playing at Rochdale, Mansfield and Hartlepool just two or three years earlier and here we were playing United.

They had a team full of household names, all internationals. And to go there and win wasn't part of the script. They expected to turn us over. But we worked hard, a lot harder than people give us credit for. We had a lot of grafters, but we also had a couple of players who could produce the tricks.

We were seriously underestimated. You only have to look back at the players we had then and take a look at where they finished to realise how good Wimbledon really were. But it was the last fairytale in football and it will never be repeated.

I remember the match crystal clear. I played midfield that day and I was up against Bryan Robson, who was arguably the best midfielder in the country at the time.

Brian Gayle was sent off at 0-0 and we were under the cosh for the last 20 minutes. We got a free kick. It was swung into the box and Wisey got a touch and it went in. It was hard to believe, after all the defending and effort, we were winning.

With 10 men against a team of internationals, a lot of sides would have been overwhelmed, but not us. We had an inner-belief that just swelled through the years. We used to listen to those moaning about our style of play, but we used to gain strength from that.

Dave Bassett was the catalyst for the famous Wimbledon spirit. Wally Downes got people going, but Dave had this way of getting us to do things for him. We would have run through brick walls for him.

In his final season at Wimbledon we finished sixth, the best position the club ever achieved. The next season he wanted a couple of more players to really go for it. But the club wasn't willing to do that and that marked the parting of ways, an end of an era.

Sadly, it was also to be my last season at the club. My contract expired during that summer. I had been at the club for nine and a half years. If I had been offered a contract it would have been a big wrench to leave, but none was forthcoming.

✦

BASSETT AND GAGE BID FAREWELL TO THE LANE

The writing was on the wall and word was getting out after 13 years Dave Bassett was leaving the club and for a number of the players they were also heading off. A victory over Chelsea was the perfect send-off.

5 MAY 1987

First Division

Wimbledon 2 Chelsea 1

By Kevin Gage (player)

I remember Harry getting chaired off and all his clothes getting ripped off. Wimbledon fans loved Harry, they knew he was going and this was their way of saying good-bye. It was a fitting send-off as we had beaten Chelsea 2-1, another big scalp for the little club. I also knew my time at the club was just about over. I had a feeling I would be moving on.

I remember looking around the ground at the final whistle trying to take it all in. Plough Lane was an integral part to everything that was Wimbledon. It was absolutely vital to our success, especially in that debut season in the top flight. Teams just didn't want to play us at the Lane. They were used to the big stadiums with the big crowds, with all the facilities and add-ons. And then they'd come to Plough Lane on a cold Tuesday night in front of a few thousand fans. It must have been akin to playing a non-league side in the third round of the FA Cup. Plough Lane was intimidating and it wasn't just the way we played. The fans were right on top of you. We may have only ever got a small number down there, but the atmosphere was crackling. You didn't need many there for it to feel packed. We always felt we could turn people over at home.

An end of an era: Kevin Gage, who played his last home game for Wimbledon against Chelsea on 5 May 1987. (Getty Images)

We were also criticised for our long-ball game, but our playing style was far more complicated than that. And if people thought we were just playing a simple game then that was all the better.

It was a special club, but the time had come for me to leave. I hadn't signed a new contract. We had finished sixth, I knew Dave Bassett and some others were going. I thought this was the end of an era. I couldn't see the club getting any better. They proved to be famous last words. A year later they went and won the FA Cup.

I joined Aston Villa, so there was no jealousy. I was more than happy to go. I remember watching the Cup Final in Magaluf on an Aston Villa promotional trip. I was in a bar full of neutrals and everyone was cheering on Wimbledon.

It was a strange feeling watching the team. It still felt part of me, but my time had gone. And I didn't regret a single moment.

✦

BASSETT LEAVES

The time had come. Dave Bassett was off after 13 years. Victory over Sheffield Wednesday was to secure Wimbledon sixth place in the League. The club would never finish higher.

9 MAY 1987
First Division
Sheffield Wednesday 0 Wimbledon 2
By Dave Bassett (manager)

It was very difficult. Part of me didn't want to go, but Sam and I had fallen out. My contract was up and I felt Sam wanted me to go. I think Sam felt I was too big for the club and he felt he wasn't getting enough credit.

We had achieved so much in that first season in the top flight. We'd won our last four games and finished sixth. We won the last game away at Sheffield Wednesday 2-0 and Glyn Hodges scored an amazing goal. We'd also reached the quarter finals of the FA Cup for the first time and had our first exposure on live television. The club was going places.

I knew that, but I also knew that the trip to Hillsborough was to be my last senior game in charge. We had a friendly a few days later against Scarborough, but I had already said my goodbyes, to Plough Lane at home against Chelsea when we won 2-1, to the Dons fans at Hillsborough, and to the players and staff in the days in between. It was just a sad time.

I had been a player, an assistant manager and a manager at Wimbledon. I had been with the club for 13 years and it was painful, Wimbledon was in my blood. But in the last 12 months, it had all gone sour behind the scenes.

"Don't go Harry," still rings in my ears from the last two games. At Plough Lane against Chelsea, the fans had invaded the pitch and sung it for ages. The match at Hillsborough and the same song. It was a poignant moment. I had tears in my eyes. And I didn't really know what to tell the players.

There was Nigel Winterburn, who I had signed from Oxford United. He wasn't even the left back I had wanted to sign. Originally, we had gone in for Brian Sparrow from Arsenal for £10,000, but at the last minute they upped the price to £15,000. So we turned our attention to Nigel. I had my eyes on him since his Birmingham days. He was released by them and when I found out he wasn't getting a game for Oxford we moved in. And he turned out to be a far better defender than Brian. And after my last game at Wimbledon, I knew he would go on to become a great player.

Then there was Lawrie Sanchez, whom I had signed from Reading. He was always under-rated. He was a great player and I was glad he got his moment with the Cup final a year later. And then there was Vinnie Jones and John Fashanu. Those two were unique.

But most of all there were the players who I had known for years and had been with me at the start – Dave Beasant, Kevin Gage, Glyn Hodges and Mark Morris. I didn't know what to say to them. They knew it was the end of an era.

I loved my time at Wimbledon. It was a homely club. There was the Nelson's nightclub, where the fans and the players would mix. I remember the characters among the fans as much as the players. The players, the management and the fans, it was unique. There was a feeling at Wimbledon that everyone was in it together.

In that last year it went wrong for me. I think Sam had never really forgiven me for walking out and joining Crystal Palace for three days after we had won promotion from the Third Division. But I came back because I loved Wimbledon too much and I knew I still had a job to do. And then it was over and all I was left with was the sound of "Don't go Harry".

By Glyn Hodges

I've always wondered what would have happened if we had stayed together with Harry in charge. We finished sixth that year and then Nigel, Gagey and I left.

That team really could have gone places. We were young and there was so much we could have achieved. The team went on and won the Cup a year later. We had so much in us and I honestly believe that side could have won a number of trophies if we had stayed together.

By Mick Smith

I never fitted into Bobby Gould's plans. Sam had promised that I would get a testimonial. I had been at the club for eight years, my wife's mother was ill and I did all this for the club and suddenly I didn't matter any more. I never got my testimonial.

I wrote to Sam and he didn't even bother to reply. It was simply a case of out of sight out of mind. After everything I had done for the club that saddened me.

But I still have memories of all the good times and I still see Steve Ketteridge, Alan Cork and Dave Beasant. I even see Wally every now and then. It's like we are still playing when we meet up, the camaraderie from 20 years ago is still there. No one could take that away from me and that's the legacy of Harry's side.

By Mark Morris

The lads were earning peanuts at Wimbledon at the time. We were on about £180-a-week and we were playing against top internationals. It had been a dream come true to play in the First Division, but I woke up and I had to start looking after my family. We were so far behind what all the other clubs were paying, it was ridiculous.

Dave just called me and said: "Do you fancy coming to Watford?" At the time I thought it was a good career move.

✦

The Spirit of Wimbledon

CHAPTER SEVEN: GOULD AND THE ROAD TO WEMBLEY

THE ARRIVAL OF BOBBY GOULD

The departure of Dave Bassett had been unthinkable. Yet now he was gone, the question was who would replace him? Bassett's managerial team had all left en masse to join Watford so there was no option of promoting from within. The board turned to Bobby Gould.

SUMMER 1987
By Bobby Gould (manager)

I was at Bristol Rovers when Dave Bassett moved on. And I let it be known that I would like to be considered for the job. I was with my family on holiday in Corfu when the phone rang. It was little Stanley Reed, the Wimbledon chairman, and he asked me if I would be interested in the managerial vacancy at the club. I said I would be extremely interested. Stanley was a fabulous fellow – a pleasure to work with. A great front man for Sam and the pair of them were a great team.

It was June when I arrived to deal with the fall-out from Dave Bassett's departure. He had taken nearly all the staff with him, and half the squad had left. Ron Suart was my first appointment, a great man and a great scout. I'd known him from my Chelsea days and he covered my backside.

And then I invited Don Howe, the best coach in the world, to the dance. Don said he would come and help me out for a month. He ended up staying for two and a half years.

New manager: Bobby Gould peers out of the dug out at Plough Lane. (Getty Images)

Almost as soon as Don arrived, we went off to Sweden on a pre-season tour. I remember we were booked into a motel, and me and Don looked at each other. We were four-star operators, and this wasn't what we were used to. So we phoned the club and got them to move the whole team to a four-star hotel. We wanted the players to get used to higher standards and to expect more from themselves.

That night we held a team meeting, and the players came down the stairs all full of themselves. Me and Don didn't have to say a word. As soon as they'd sat down, Lawrie Sanchez, Vinnie Jones, Alan Cork and Dave Beasant stood up. They took over the meeting.

They told everyone what they expected from training, what they expected Don to do, what time players should arrive, how they expected us to play – getting the ball into the box 104 times each game, with 44 crosses. It was that precise. They just totally bossed it. And after that Don said he wanted to stay for ever more.

In management, that's exactly what you want. You want your players to take over, to make yourself almost redundant. All it needed was a little bit of tinkering here and there. Terry Phelan, John Scales, Eric Young and Clive Goodyear were my own additions, and very early on they were all told what was expected of them – not by me, but by the likes of Lawrie and Vinnie.

It didn't take long for me and Don to see that the club had a special spirit. And it was very much a case of: "If it ain't broke, don't fix it." We just filled in the holes and kept the club going in the same vein that Harry had.

Don was making more and more jokes and becoming even funnier. The players grew to love him. And both of us really got into the spirit of it. It was fun – it wasn't like working at all.

Eric Young used to come to work with a Brighton club bag, which got the other lads more and more annoyed. He should have realised what was coming.

One day the lads got hold of it and set fire to it in the dressing room as part of a Red Indian ritual. The bag with all its contents was burning in the middle of the floor while all the players were dancing round it.

It set off a fire alarm that was connected directly to the local fire station. And this big fire engine turned up to see all these top-flight players dancing round a burning bag. It was hilarious.

My first game in charge wasn't that great. We lost 1-0 away at Watford, but that year was to end in pretty good fashion...

◆

GIBBO CELEBRATES SPURS' RETURN

At £200,000, Terry Gibson became the club's most expensive signing over the summer. It didn't take long for the little forward to make an impact.

31 OCTOBER 1987

First Division

Tottenham 0 Wimbledon 3

By Terry Gibson (player)

I always liked playing against Spurs. They were the team I supported as a boy. But I also felt I had something to prove whenever I faced them. I'd been on their books as a youngster and I even broke into their first team in the early 80s.

I didn't really want to leave Tottenham, but they kept signing big-name centre forwards: Steve Archibald, Alan Brazil, and Garth Crooks. I felt the young players never really got a chance at Tottenham. I was 19 and frustrated, and when Coventry came in for me I didn't see the point in staying, so I left.

Tottenham were a team that suited Wimbledon. They didn't like the way we played and they would always make a point in the papers the day before the game, saying something like: "You always need a strong referee when you play Wimbledon." And it would always be one of their stars saying it: Gary Mabbutt, Chris Waddle or Gary Lineker.

That sort of attitude wound the team up, me more than most. So to win at White Hart Lane was always going to be special, but to win 3-0 and score as well – that was just perfect.

And then there was Tony Parks, the Tottenham goalkeeper. We had been best mates since my days at the club and he had been best man at my wedding.

I was pleased that Parksy got the game. The year I left he had come in for Ray Clemence and had become a hero in the Uefa Cup final. But he never really got a run in the team. He should have left earlier, but he was stubborn and I think that harmed his career.

Ian Crook, Mark Bowen, Iain Culverhouse, myself and Parksy were all in the same youth team, and only Parksy really failed to get to the level he could have reached.

Record signing: Terry Gibson who scored at home and away against his former side Tottenham in the 1987/88 season. (Getty Images)

Over the years we faced each other a few times, but there was never any rivalry. Between real mates you don't get any. Still, that didn't make scoring against him any less sweet. I have this picture of me sitting on the ground celebrating after the goal.

Dave Beasant had hit the ball long – just the kind of ball Spurs hate – and I had got on the end of it and slid it in. That was just after half-time to make it 2-0. John Fashanu had put us ahead with a header in the first half. And then, with time running out, John Gannon scored from miles out to make it 3-0.

It was just a great all-round performance. To top it off, in the game at Plough Lane the same season we repeated the trick, winning 3-0. I remember Terry Fenwick played in that game. He stamped all over me when the referee wasn't looking. That happened a hell of a lot then. They'd never pick on John Fashanu or Vinnie Jones, but the little guys like me, Dennis Wise or Terry Phelan.

Fenwick was an intelligent player. He knew when he could get away with fouls. But I was livid. I went storming in to him and said: "If you want to start, you will have 11 players after you, all backing me up. How many of your mates are going to back you up?" You could see from his face that no one would.

Terry Fenwick knew then that a tackle could come in from anywhere and at any time. He didn't touch me after that. He knew that at Wimbledon we stuck together.

✦

THE THIRD ROUND: WISE MADNESS

The FA Cup run of 1988 that was to make Wimbledon famous began on a cold January afternoon against West Bromwich Albion. The win was comprehensive, but it gave little indication of what was to follow.

9 JANUARY 1988

FA Cup third round

Wimbledon 4 West Bromwich Albion 1

By Clive Goodyear (player)

The FA Cup is special, but this was just the third round. We had no idea then where it would lead to. The latter games of the run probably live long in the minds of most of the other players and the fans, but for some reason this game sticks in my mind. At home to West Bromwich Albion was a good draw, and all we were looking to do was win the game and get into the next round.

It was one of those dark, cold, early January afternoons. They were well up for it – any lower-division club always is when they play a top-flight side – but in the end we were far too good for them.

I remember John Fashanu's header gave us the lead just before the break. But it's what happened straight after the interval that I remember best.

Dennis Wise took a thumping great knock and had to be stretchered off. He limped back on, and seconds later unleashed a screamer into the top corner of the net from fully 25 yards.

It was typical of the club at the time. There was no way Dennis should have been on the pitch – he was injured. But that wasn't going to stop him. Bobby Gould finally managed to drag him off after Robbie Turner made it 3-0. We ended up winning 4-1.

I was so happy to be at Wimbledon. I'd had a few years in the old First Division with Luton Town, and I was desperate to get back up there. After Luton I spent three years at Plymouth. In 1987 we had just missed out on the play-offs to get into the First Division. And in my opinion Plymouth seemed to lack ambition. When Bobby Gould gave me a call out of the blue, I knew it was a great opportunity.

However, I didn't turn up to see Bobby looking my best. With Plymouth we had been doing some training with the army – lots of sides did pre-season with the forces in those days. Anyway, I got a kick from a rifle and ended up with a huge black eye.

Bobby took one look at my eye and said: "You'll do."

I think it just said to him that I had the battling spirit he wanted at Wimbledon. And that was it – I was a Don.

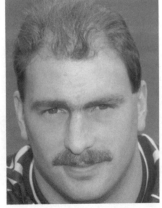

Starting out: Clive Goodyear, who would play a crucial part in Wimbledon's FA Cup run in 1988. (Getty Images)

THE FOURTH ROUND: THE BELIEF ARRIVES

Bobby Gould's side was full of young players picked up from the lower leagues. None of them had experienced a decent Cup run, but the win at Mansfield gave some the belief that perhaps the unbelievable was about to become reality.

30 JANUARY 1988

FA Cup fourth round

Mansfield 1 Wimbledon 2

By Terry Phelan (player)

I t was one of those games, full of passion. It was a tough, tough game. They really wanted it. You could feel it. It was an old-fashioned cup tie. They spent the whole day keeping the pressure on. And then there was the pitch – it was awful. It wasn't just muddy; it was in a terrible state. It made it almost impossible to play football, but ironically that suited us.

We just played the balls into the channels and that was how I got my goal. A long punt from Dave Beasant, a flick-on from Fashanu, goal.

That was what Wimbledon was about in those days. I'm not saying we couldn't play, because we had the likes of Alan Cork, Dennis Wise and Terry Gibson – they could all knock the ball about a bit. But we had our own game plan and we stuck to it.

The goal was the turning point for us in the cup run. Corky had given us the lead, but we were under so much pressure that we knew we needed another to be sure.

And that's how it proved to be. They scored almost straight after I'd made it 2-0. And then Lawrie Sanchez gave away a penalty, but thankfully Beasant saved it. That was crucial for us. I barely remember the save, but it was a blessing (we all know what happened later in the final).

It had been a hard game, but it gave us belief in ourselves. And as we were travelling back on the coach the feeling grew that this side was destined for Wembley. It sounds silly looking back that a 2-1 win at Mansfield would give us that belief, but it really did. I would pinpoint that game as the one that took us to the final. And I knew my goal had done it. It was a sweet goal, slotted in at the near post. I don't score that many, and that one was good.

But it wasn't just the goal that was unusual for me – I was playing on the left wing. Bobby wanted to try something new. He wanted to take the game to them. I had played there as a kid, but not since. It was a big risk, but I'm like any full back, you just want to get forward when you get the chance. It was great.

It was probably one of the best games of my career. And it was a big turning point personally. Wimbledon had a close-knit core when I arrived, and it was hard at the start. I was in digs and didn't know anyone in London. If you didn't give everything they wouldn't accept you. And I went for it against Mansfield.

After the game the other players patted me on the back, and I could feel I was finally being accepted into the family. It gave me a lot of confidence. You had to be able to take a joke at Wimbledon. You had to go along with it. If you didn't, you weren't accepted.

✦

THE FIFTH ROUND: KEYSTONE ANTICS

It was hardly the draw Wimbledon wanted: away at Newcastle. But it was to be arguably the club's best performance on their run to Wembley. In front of a passionate home crowd, the Dons turned it on and silenced the Newcastle faithful.

20 FEBRUARY 1988

FA Cup fifth round

Newcastle 1 Wimbledon 3

By Andy Thorn (player)

W e went up on train on the Friday morning. It was a brilliant atmosphere. We got into the hotel then did a bit of training. And as some of the press boys were staying in the same place, we had a few beers with them. Bobby Gould didn't really mind as long as we relaxed. It wasn't a big session, I didn't get bladdered. It wasn't like the night before the Cup final, when I played with a hangover. We just had a chat and a few beers.

Alcohol has never been a million miles away from football. Later in my career, when I was playing for Newcastle, there would be a bottle of whiskey in the changing room. It was like, nine below up there and some of the players used to have a sip of it before going out to play. I didn't. I liked to do all my drinking after the game.

It was even colder for the cup tie. They were redeveloping the stadium, and we got changed in a Portakabin – it was freezing. This was the fifth round of the FA Cup, and it was like changing for Sunday morning football.

The core of the side had now been together for a long time. In the old days we might have gone up there naïve and go down 2-0 or 3-0, but we handled it perfectly.

We had a load of strong characters. We were never going to get beaten that day. We just steamrollered them. Gibbo gave us the lead after about six minutes and that was it – game won.

They couldn't deal with us. When other people talk about Wimbledon, they talk about Vinnie and Fash, and yes they were our flag-bearers, but inside the group it was a different story.

We knew our strengths and weaknesses, and the talented players and key players were not those two. They were important, their job was basically to scare people, but the rest of us had our jobs too. And together we were far stronger than we were individually. We were a special team, from the players to the coaches.

It was a big year for me personally. I was in the first team playing regularly. Thanks to the help of Don Howe's coaching, I won my first England under-21 cap and that extra experience helped me deal with the likes of Paul Gascoigne and Mirandinha of Newcastle.

I remember that after the match Mirandinha spat at Lurch. That made Lurch mad, and we ended up chasing Mirandinha round St James' Park. It was like the Keystone Kops, like kids in a playground.

We came straight back after the game, on the only train we could get. We weren't going to be in the changing rooms any longer than we needed to be. The police gave us an escort straight to the station, and we must have been on the train within 30 minutes of the game finishing.

The Cup run had really kicked in. What I didn't know, of course, was that the next time I was to play in Newcastle I'd be wearing the black and white of the home team after becoming the first British defender to be sold for £1m.

✦

THE QUARTER-FINAL: SUB CULTURE

On the route to Wembley Wimbledon would have to overcome a number of difficult challenges. The trip to Newcastle was tough, but the next round against Watford was tougher. Losing 1-0, reduced to 10 men and with just 45 minutes to go, the omens were not good. Bobby Gould and Don Howe had to do something. They turned to substitute Eric Young...

12 MARCH 1988

FA Cup quarter-final

Wimbledon 2 Watford 1

By Bobby Gould (manager)

To put it bluntly, things weren't going right on the pitch, and we knew we had to change things round. They were 1-0 up, they were dominating, and Brian Gayle had just thumped Malcolm Allen and we were down to 10 men.

We knew we had to bring on Eric Young, but we couldn't work out who to take off. Don Howe and I were scribbling madly trying to work out what to do. Who to go up front, who to go out wide, who to drop back. We weren't really paying attention to the names and when we finished we had 10 players left on the sheet.

It was then that we realised that we'd left Corky's name off. I couldn't believe we had left out a forward when we needed to chase the game, but it seemed the only way. Four minutes after the break, Eric Young headed in the equaliser from a Dennis Wise free-kick and the gamble was fully justified.

We were always good from dead balls. Something like 84 per cent of our goals came from set pieces and most of them came from Wise. This was no different. And then Fash got the winner with about quarter of an hour left.

It was all about the mental strength of the team and the players had it in bucket-loads. You had to have it at Wimbledon or you wouldn't survive.

Early in his Wimbledon career, Terry Phelan couldn't handle it. One day he came into my office in tears. At Wimbledon if you couldn't do something the players told you so, and Terry was finding it really hard to get his confidence going and to fit in.

Even John Scales had problems. I remember John Fashanu having a right go at him: he said he couldn't cross and he couldn't tackle. If he was going to do anything, at least try and get the ball on Fash's head and if he couldn't do that he should get out of the club. John coped, but Terry didn't.

The comeback begins: Eric Young (arm raised) is swamped by team-mates after his equaliser against Watford on 12 March 1988 in the FA Cup quarter-final. (Getty Images)

Don and I knew that Terry was talented, so one morning we set up an exercise we knew he would really excel at. It was all running and sprinting. He and Dennis beat everyone, and after that his confidence picked up and he was accepted into the team.

As always, it was about the psychology of the team. It infected us all and was the main reason why we managed to come back against Watford when the odds were stacked so firmly against us. We were mentally tough as a unit. I would have gone to the end of the earth for them.

✦

THE SEMI-FINAL: THE KNOCKOUT HOOK

The draw had been kind. Liverpool and Nottingham Forest met in the other semi-final. Wimbledon would never have a better chance of reaching Wembley. The fans knew it and the players knew it. But it was only late in the second half when the dream became reality.

9 APRIL 1988

FA Cup semi-final (White Hart Lane)

Wimbledon 2 Luton Town 1

By Alan Cork (player)

I remember the winning goal vividly. We'd just got a throw-in and it came to me on the right-hand side. We'd been practising hooking the ball in, and here was my chance to do exactly that. I just slung the ball in the middle and Wisey threw himself at it two-footed and it went in. Then he was off, and we were all after him. He jumped on Gibbo, who'd been substituted, we all fell into Gouldy. It was one almighty bundle. God knows how we composed ourselves for the last 10 minutes.

It was a bit of an unusual game for me. Don Howe had told me to go and play on the right wing. There's no arguing with Don – he knew the game far better than any of us, and we all had the utmost respect for him.

I didn't quite get it, but he always knew what he was doing. And early on it seemed to be working. I'd played Gibbo and Fash in quite a few times, and we should have been at least 4-0 up at half time. But they just couldn't finish.

And then Luton went and scored through Mick Harford. We had been running the whole game and now we were 1-0 down. I felt gutted. None of us wanted to come this far and not make it to Wembley.

We needn't have worried, though. Eight minutes later, Gibbo gets dragged down in the box and we get a penalty. Up steps Fash. I don't recall him ever missing before then, so we were all pretty confident. And then he walks up. I don't think anyone has ever kicked the ball slower. Andy Dibble almost had time to get up after diving the wrong way and walk over and stop it.

Jubilation: Vinnie Jones celebrates after the 2-1 win over Luton Town. (Getty Images)

It gave us a massive lift, and we just went for it from there. And with 10 minutes to go there was my cross, Wisey's lunge and the winning goal.

The celebrations at the final whistle were mad. Vinnie went crazy, ripping his shirt, screaming and hollering, and I just couldn't believe we'd done it. My late mum and my dad were there and they were just so pleased. And I was delighted to see them; it made the day that extra bit special for me.

The whole team went back to Plough Lane after the game, and into Nelson's. It was non-stop drinking. No one went home. There must have been 25 of us at the bar all night long. That was the heart of the club. We played together, we battled together and we drank together.

After the semi-final it was hard to concentrate on the League, and a few of us picked the games we wanted to play in. Off the pitch, we just couldn't stop messing around and looking forward to the final.

Thorny loved the whole build-up. Then there was Vinnie and Fash's group, and they were up for the whole thing too. And next up was Liverpool and Wembley.

✦

The Spirit of Wimbledon

CHAPTER EIGHT: THE CUP FINAL

A WEIRD AND WONDERFUL WORLD

A thousand things came together on that fateful day in May to produce the greatest moment in Wimbledon's history. Wimbledon had done the unthinkable. They had beaten the best team in England, Liverpool, 1-0 and won the FA Cup. In the joy that followed John Motson uttered the immortal line: "It's a weird and wonderful world if you come from Wimbledon." And indeed it was. Here, the players and their manager Bobby Gould recall what happened from a few days before the final, to the game itself and the days that followed.

14 MAY 1988

FA Cup Final (Wembley)

Wimbledon 1 Liverpool 0

Clive Goodyear: A few weeks earlier, I had thought my Cup dreams were over. Against Spurs the week before the semi-final I damaged my knee really badly. I knew it was serious, and the thought of missing out on this big occasion in my life was shattering. I had to work so hard to get fit. I managed to play the last three League games of the season, but even then it was not certain that I would get into the team or even the squad. I was told on the Thursday before the final that I would be playing. I was bubbling inside, but I also felt so sorry for John Scales. We were good friends and he was tremendous about it. He was still part of the squad, and that took some of the sting out of it.

Royal introduction: The Wimbledon captain, Dave Beasant, introduces Diana, Princess of Wales, to his team-mates before the start of the FA Cup final on 14 May 1988. (Getty Images)

John Scales: I remember the build-up to the final. I wasn't 100 per cent fit. I'd been playing regularly in the team and then I got injured against Forest. Me and Clive Goodyear had been battling for a place in the team, but with the injury I wasn't even sure I was going to be in the squad. Although I did make the squad, I was utterly gutted not to be playing. Nowadays, top-level football is a squad game, but back then, being in the team was the be all and end all. It was difficult sitting on the bench. I remember the preparations before the game, and the beer in the hotel the night before – and it being perfect for our group of lads. And it obviously worked to our advantage.

Vinnie Jones: Me, Brian Gayle and Dennis Wise were sitting in the hotel the night before the game. We were playing cards and the boredom was starting to set in. We had to do something so we went for a walk just to get a change of environment. So naturally we ended up in the pub for a quick pint. We didn't think anybody would notice.

Bobby Gould: They thought I hadn't spotted them, but I had. Meanwhile, the rest of the lads were getting edgy and nervous. So I just said: "Here's £50 – go down the pub, and once you've had a pint of shandy come back."
Then Gayley, Wisey and Jonah came in through the back door. I spotted them straight away. I said: "Don't think I don't know where you haven't been."
They were looking all smug, like naughty schoolboys. And then I said: "Well, you guys are the mugs, I've just given the other lads £50 to go to the pub, and you had to pay for your own drinks." I've hardly seen them move quicker as they left to catch up with the others.

Lawrie Sanchez: That night was easily one of the highlights of the whole weekend. You see it wasn't just any old pub. It was the Fox and Grapes, the pub which 100 years earlier had provided the club's first changing rooms.
Anyway, the bar staff wheeled in this 90-year-old woman from next door. Her father had played in the Old Centrals team, and she told us how she'd watched them play on the Common. It was humbling. You could see her eyes glisten with the memory.

Clive Goodyear: After the old woman's story, the beers really started to flow. I often think back to that night and try to imagine what we must have looked like. It's the night before the most important game in the club's history, and the entire squad are in the pub wearing club tracksuits and drinking to their heart's content. I stayed until about 11pm supping my Guinness, while most of the other guys tucked into their lagers. There were still a lot of them at the bar when I left.

John Fashanu: I may have been the grumpy one in the corner drinking coke, but I was there. I had to look after Jonah. He was screaming and hollering as usual. All the lads were having a craic. I was milking my soft drink – I used to be able to make one last all night. I don't know whether it was because I liked drinking slowly or whether it was because I was being tight.
I just liked to mind my own business. When it all kicked off, I would join in. But I liked to watch from the sidelines. Something was always going off. Someone would pull someone else's wife or someone would stamp on someone's foot, and it would all kick off. That night we were all up for having a laugh and enjoying ourselves. But it turned nasty when I got back to the hotel.

Bobby Gould: They weren't that late back, but I remember being downstairs when the phone rang and it was Vinnie Jones. He was sharing a room with John Fashanu, and Fash had just put his fist through the door.
He had just been told that the News of the World were going to do a splash on him on the day after the final about some sex scandal he'd got himself mixed up in. That's their way of doing things – ring you up the Friday before it goes in. Fash was livid. If you watch a recording of the final you can see that his right wrist is all strapped up. It took ages to calm him down.

Vinnie Jones: The reporter had been hanging around all day. I wanted to chase him up the road. I was going to bang him. Fash was fuming, but I had the key to the door. Fash was first to the door and he just wanted to hit something, so he hit the door. It was solid oak. It must have been four or five inches thick, but he left a hand print in it. You could see his knuckles pop back when he did it. He played in so much pain the next day.

Bobby Gould: But that wasn't the only problem that night. Down the corridor there was Gibbo. I stuck my nose round the door and all I could see where what looked like huge feet under his bed. Gibbo had gone to sleep wearing his boots. He'd been given a new boot deal for the final and was trying to break them in. He'd even sat in the bath with them on to see if that would help.

In every room there was something I had to deal with – that was the real hard part of being a manager of Wimbledon.

The next day, the papers were saying that if Wimbledon won it would set the game back centuries. They criticised us for taking free kicks on the left with the right foot, and on the right with the left foot. And then there were the long throw-ins. In the years that followed, every club in the top flight followed suit. Now even Italy and Brazil do that.

But those sorts of comments just helped us. We thrived on them. It just added to the build-up of the whole day.

Terry Gibson: As a kid, I always remember waking up at 9am on Cup final day. I used to rush downstairs and watch the build-up to the big match from start to finish: the "It's a Knockout" special, meet the players, the TV cameras with the coach and everything. That's what made the FA Cup final so special. Millions of children around the globe had the same routine.

Me and Clive Goodyear were in our hotel room putting on our suits, watching the build-up to the final – our final. And the TV cameras were outside our hotel filming our coach and I remember the reporter saying that in 10 minutes' time the Wimbledon coach was due to leave. I had a lump in my throat, and I looked at Clive. He had a lump in his throat too. Neither of us said a word.

That's when it hit us that this was the day we had spent our lives looking towards. There were loads of people at the hotel, all in yellow and blue, all wishing us well and wanting to see us off.

Andy Thorn: On our way to Wembley, we were watching Liverpool on their coach on TV. Alan Hansen was being real cocky. He said: "Can you see any Wimbledon fans? This is all Liverpool." That's what kicked off the stuff in the tunnel. He was so arrogant. We couldn't wait to ram it down his throat. Bobby Gould didn't have to say a thing. Just listening to Hansen on the coach lit the touch paper.

Terry Gibson: The week before we had played Manchester United at Old Trafford, and I chatted with Gordon Strachan and a few other United players after the match. Gordon was a good friend of mine from my United days and he said to me: "Whatever you do, make sure you enjoy the day. Soak everything in – it may only ever happen once in your life."

And those words were ringing in my ears when we arrived at Wembley. I walked alone on the pitch for about five minutes, taking in every blade of grass, every seat. I wanted to remember every moment.

Bobby Gould: Everybody had been given a job to do. We didn't change much from our usual play. I remember Don saying he wanted to switch Dennis Wise and Alan Cork to counter the threat of John Barnes. We just wanted to deny him the ball, and Don's plan worked. But to be honest, being manager of that side that week was not really about tactics or about who was going to do this or who was going to do that, it was more about keeping an eye on them and making sure they didn't burn themselves out emotionally.

Terry Gibson: The week before, Liverpool had played Nottingham Forest, who at the time were one of the best clubs in the country. They absolutely destroyed them, 5-0. I remember thinking they would murder us.

But we then spent the whole week watching that video. We found that all their attacks had stemmed from Alan Hansen. Obviously they had the likes of Peter Beardsley and John Barnes, and Don Howe had plans for dealing with them, but the key was to stop them playing the ball out of defence.

Clive Goodyear: Dennis Wise and I were told by Don Howe to stop the ball getting to John Barnes. That year he had torn so many defences apart. We didn't want Barnes to end up one-on-one against me. The idea was to make sure he had to face Dennis first and then I would clear up if he beat him. It was simple, but it made a huge difference.

Terry Gibson: My job was to mark Alan Hansen man to man. It was the most defensive role I'd ever been given, and yet I was still playing centre forward. We planned to just let Gary Ablett get the ball. The rest of their team could pass, but we had worked out that all he ever did was hit the ball long – and that would be meat and drink for our defence.

John Fashanu: In the changing room, Vinnie pulled me to one side and said: "None of this old shaking hands stuff, let's just stick it straight up 'em." He knew me well. I was a gentleman really. If someone was nice to me I couldn't hurt them. If one of the Liverpool players had said: "Are you

The winners: The Wimbledon team with the FA Cup in joyous mood. (Getty Images)

OK, John?" after a bad tackle, or "Don't worry about it, it's part of the game," after I crunched them, I wouldn't have done anything. Vinnie wanted to get me going, get the aggression pumping – and it worked.

Bobby Gould: Liverpool feared us – I don't care what anyone says. They couldn't cope with us. We spent the entire day trying to get under their skins, and it worked.

It started from the moment we went to meet the ref. We put all the clocks and our watches back five minutes and convinced Liverpool that their watches were wrong. That meant they were left waiting in the tunnel for five minutes. Then there was our yell of euphoria: "Yidaho!" They were petrified. Despite what they've said since, it did upset them. I saw it in their eyes.

John Fashanu: "Yidaho!" It was a wild war cry. We were all shouting and hollering, but everyone remembers Vinnie more than most. He spits when he shouts.

Terry Phelan: Even Vinnie was scaring me with his shouting. Wisey and Fash joined in, but we were like that every match. It was like our Haka.

Vinnie Jones: The shout "Yidaho" actually came from my mates down the pub. We all used to shout it when we did something well – won at cards or something like that. I had got all the boys in the pub tickets, but they didn't want to go. They wanted the tickets to go to real Wimbledon fans, but I couldn't stop thinking about them. So when we were in the tunnel it just came out: "Yidaho!" Fash and Wisey joined in and then everyone else. And once we won we couldn't stop shouting it.

John Fashanu: I had said to everyone that nobody should shave or wash for 24 hours before the game. In the end it was only me, Jonesy and Wise that didn't. My thinking was that if we are going out there looking like fancy dans, we will play like fancy dans. I wanted us to play like Raggedy-Arse Rovers.

I felt so mean and aggressive on the pitch. And then there was Vinnie. At 3.01pm Vinnie went in for a tackle with Steve McMahon – and that was the key moment. The tackle started at his throat and ended at his ankle. That was the game won; psychologically we had made our mark. Vinnie had hit them like an express train.

We were in the FA Cup final, how could we go too far? We were either going to win or we were going to get sent off. We were not going to hang around. We didn't want to be there at the end with sad puppy-dog eyes as Liverpool got the trophy. We were not going up those stairs as losers.

Vinnie Jones: The papers were all saying Steve McMahon was going to do this and that to us and I had had enough of it. I said to Fash a couple of days before the final that I was going to get him. And Fash said: "If you whack him early you'll be alright. It's the Cup final, you're playing in front of 100,000 people, he can't send you off that quickly." That said when the referee reached for a card I was bricking it.

That tackle was the first key point of the game. It set the tone for what was to follow.

Terry Phelan: The game was won with Vinnie's tackle on Steve McMahon. That was our mark on the game: it said that no one was going to come through the middle.

Dave Beasant: The key moment for me? Ten minutes in, and my fingertip save. The penalty save in the second half, of course, was crucial, but that was in the second half and we were already 1-0 up. At 0-0, though, had they scored it would have been all over.

It was a nothing sort of a shot from John Aldridge, but it took a slight deflection off Eric Young. I managed to adjust and block it with my thigh, but it looped up in the air. I can remember it as clear as day – the ball was above my head, just hanging there. I can still see John Barnes charging in, ready to volley it in. He must have thought this was it, this was 1-0.

Then the old Go-Gadget-Go arm came out and I managed to get my fingertips to the ball and scrape it away. Vinnie Jones did the clearing-up job and we were safe once again.

Liverpool were the "Team of the Decade", everyone's favourite. A goal then and our dream would have died.

Terry Phelan: Then came Peter Beardsley's disallowed goal. Everyone talks about it, I don't know why. Andy Thorn fouled him. Everyone heard the whistle, Peter heard the whistle. We stopped as a back four, why Peter went on I will never know. If Dave hadn't bothered to try and stop the shot, the argument would never have happened.

Andy Thorn: Had the referee waited just a second or two more, the whole story could have been so different. I'd switched off a bit, and Beardsley got the run on me. He had a good first touch and he took the ball across me. I grabbed his shirt and the referee blew. But my grip was slipping and Beardsley shrugged me off and went on and put the ball in the net. If the referee had just held on we would have been 1-0 down.

Vinnie Jones: I have spoken to the few of the lads about it and I would have given the goal. You're supposed to play the advantage rule at times likes that, but that was just our bit of luck.

Terry Phelan: Our goal came seconds after Beardsley's effort had been chalked off. I was pegging it down the left flank with Ray Houghton. The ball was played over the top and I just played dumb. We were looking for free kicks.
Don Howe had told us to head out wide and look for the overlaps and if we could get free kicks, we would get free kicks. Liverpool were terrified of us in the air. They had all the big six-footers, but once the ball was swung in the air, we were always favourites.
    We were never going to score from neat passing outside the box. We were going to score from a free-kick or a corner. We had worked on that ploy all week and for all the time I was at Wimbledon.

Alan Cork: There was a bit of an argument over what we were going to do with the free kick, and in the end we decided to go for our usual routine. Such was the quality of Dennis Wise's deliveries that we almost expected to score every time. Nine times out of 10 it would have been me who scored the goal. And yes, it was disappointing that I didn't get it. It missed me by maybe an inch. But it was destined to be Sanch's moment.

Terry Phelan: And then it happened. Dennis's free kick, Lawrie's flick-on, and it was in the back of the net. I just stood there watching. It reminds me now of Ray Houghton's goal for Ireland when we beat Italy in the 1994 World Cup. I felt the same way both times. The world stood still – it was as if what I was watching wasn't real.

Vinnie Jones: I was standing on the edge of the area as it came in. We rehearsed free kicks over and over. We knew the routine. I didn't actually see the ball go in. My view was obscured from where I was standing, but I remember seeing Bruce Grobbelaar's face. It told the whole story. And once it was nestling in the net that was it – game over.

Lawrie Sanchez: Everyone talks about the goal – but it was my job and you just get on with it. I'd scored against Chelsea the week before with a header from a Dennis Wise free-kick from the same side. I knew how Dennis took the free kicks, and it was the same in the Cup final. I scored, we went 1-0 up, and I had this feeling then we were going to win.

Andy Thorn: When we won the free kick, I looked to Eric Young and said thank God for that – we can have a rest. I didn't even run up to celebrate the goal. It was too far to run – 45 yards there, 45 yards back. He wants me to run 90 yards to say: "Well done"? No way.
    At half time, Don Howe pulled off a master stroke. Because it was so hot he had got us all fresh shirts and loads of ice in bags to cool us down. It was brilliant – better than having sex! We were all chatting away and Don said: "Don't sit back, don't start wasting time, keep playing the way you are and you'll win this."
    Five minutes into the second half, the ball drops to Vinnie Jones and he just boots it.

Terry Gibson: It wasn't all Liverpool. I remember I had a glorious chance to make it 2-0. It was on my weaker side. Bruce Grobbelaar ran out of the goal and I just touched it round him. In hindsight I should have hit it with the outside of my left foot. Instead I miscued it horribly, but thankfully it wasn't too costly. Sanch was the only one who was happier with 1-0. I think I probably got my job as his deputy because of that miss!

Clive Goodyear: Then there was the penalty. I couldn't believe what had happened. I clearly toed the ball back to Dave Beasant, and the whistle went. Peter Beardsley had played a nice reverse pass but I read it and slid in and won the ball. John Aldridge had just fallen over my leg. As far as I was concerned I had done what I needed to.
    And then it clicked – the referee had given a penalty. As far as I was concerned it was ridiculous, and that's putting it politely. I was not one for ranting or raving. I vaguely remember Eric Young, Andy Thorn and Dave Beasant tearing after the referee, but I was just stunned.

Terry Phelan: You could sense that something like that was going to happen. I remember it as clear as daylight. Clive Goodyear got the tackle in. It was a good sliding tackle and the ball went straight to Lurch. But the referee clearly wanted to make amends for the Beardsley goal and gave the penalty. My veins were pumping and there must have been 80,000 scousers in the stadium all mad for it.

Andy Thorn: The referee just gave it to make up for Beardsley's "goal". John Aldridge was nowhere near the ball when Clive got the tackle in and slid it back to Dave. I have spoken to the referee since, and I said to him: "Bad decision that one." He said: "Which one?"

Dave Beasant: It was never a penalty. Anyone who has seen the game knows that. Clive Goodyear got the ball cleanly.

I don't know what. Andy Thorn and Eric Young were incensed and went charging after the referee. But I am a bit more level headed than those two, so I pushed them aside and said to the ref: "Look, he got the ball." But the referee just said: "Penalty." And that was that, there was no changing his mind.

I headed back to my goal line and suddenly I couldn't breathe properly. I had to put my hands on my knees and try and get some air into my lungs.

Clive Goodyear: I remember lining up on the edge of the box, looking at Dave on his line. We had battled so hard and they were putting us under so much pressure. I thought: "If this goes in we will probably lose it. Miss, please miss!"

Dave Beasant: I've always studied penalties. Throughout my entire career I've tried to learn something about the opponents' penalty-taker. When we were in the Fourth Division it wasn't easy. I used to look for pictures of penalties in the opponents' programmes, and I could normally tell by the angle of the penalty-taker's foot where the ball had gone and how they had hit it.

But against John Aldridge it was easier. Liverpool were on the TV every week and he had scored something like 13 penalties that season. I had seen his technique over and over again. A little shuffle and it would go to my right; no shuffle and it would go to my left. There was no shuffle, and I saved it.

Andy Thorn: Aldo knew it wasn't a penalty. I later played with him when I was up at Tranmere and I know the miss affected him really badly. He was taken off straight after and he was never the same player again. The players at Tranmere used to pester me to ask him about it, but he would never be drawn.

We rode our luck in the game. If you get all your tackles in and all your blocks in, then you deserve your luck. But when a short, fat, bald referee gives a penalty that isn't a penalty, that's sickening. If John Barnes had volleyed the ball in from 30 yards or one of our players had made a mistake that led to a goal, we would have coped with it, we would have accepted it, but this was crap. Lurch's save was justice.

Terry Gibson: I came off with 20 minutes to go. I was so physically drained. I didn't want to come off, but I had rolled my socks down and Bobby Gould just knew then that I was knackered. John Scales came on for me, and although it seemed absurd to put him on up front, he was just taking on my defensive role.

John Scales: It was Wembley. It was the Cup final and we were winning. There were 20 minutes to go and Bobby Gould tells me to get warmed up and then he throws me on up front. Me up front? I was as shocked as anyone.

Now, normally you charge on with instructions from the bench to tell people to do this or that. Instead, I had to explain that I was going up front and that I was as surprised as they were. For that last 20 minutes I ran around trying to make it as difficult as possible for their defenders.

Terry Gibson: Being on the bench for the closing stages was nerve-racking. I didn't fancy our chances if it went to extra-time. They kept on having all these near misses, and each one was like another heart attack.

John Fashanu: Ten minutes from the end I was delirious. I was physically and mentally exhausted. I couldn't move. I had cramp in both legs and I was praying that the game would end. I have never experienced such pain before or since.

Dave Beasant: The last 10 minutes went on for an age. With two minutes to go, Scalesy was caught offside. The referee blew, and half the team thought we'd won. Bobby Gould and Don Howe leapt off the bench and I think Vinnie punched the air – the tension was immense.

Momentous moment: The most famous goal in Wimbledon's history: Lawrie Sanchez's header against Liverpool. (Getty Images)

Bobby Gould: I was jumping up at every whistle thinking that was it and Don Howe would pull me down and tell me to keep an eye on the clock. I was just a kid in management compared to Don – he knew how to deal with everything.

Andy Thorn: I was getting delirious with the heat. We kept asking the referee how long was left and he kept saying: "Not long." But how bloody long is not long? "Not long."

Then the ball dropped to Vinnie Jones in the last minute, and I was thinking: "Just leather it Vinnie, just leather it." In the same moment I remember seeing out of the corner of my eye the referee putting his whistle to his mouth. I had my hands in the air before he blew. As for the ball, it must have landed on Mars.

Terry Gibson: It was a huge feeling of relief. I remember looking up into the clear blue sky above Wembley and thinking: "I've done it, I can pack up now."

Dave Beasant: I didn't leap. I didn't jump. I just turned round to get my gloves bag from the back of the goal. And then there was this hefty weight on my back – it was Thorny. We were off, me carrying him and him hollering and shouting.

John Fashanu: I fell to the floor at the sound of the final whistle. Everyone thought it was a form of celebration, but I was shattered. I remember seeing Vinnie doing all these antics and normally I would have stopped him, but I just couldn't move.

Clive Goodyear: It was a schoolboy's dream and it had just come true for me. But the main emotion was relief, especially after the penalty.

Alan Cork: In 1977, when we got into the League, only a nutter would have said that we'd get into the First Division and win the FA Cup. Yet 11 years later here we were, winners. It took us 11 years to do it and it will never happen again. It's impossible now; the gap financially is too huge. No club will ever emulate Wimbledon.

Bobby Gould: I just couldn't believe what we had achieved. Personally, it meant so much. My father Roy was born on the same date and had died 12 years earlier. The win was for him as much as it was for me.

Terry Phelan: We'd done it. I was a 20-year-old standing on the pitch at Wembley and my dream had just come true. As a kid you try to imagine what it must feel like, and here I was and it was happening for real. It just didn't sink in. I remember Bobby Gould and Don Howe telling us to walk around the stadium as slowly as we liked and to soak in everything and savour it all as it might never happen again. They were right and I'll thank them forever for telling me to do that.

Dave Beasant: I remember trying to make sure I shook the hands of all the Liverpool players. I doubt it meant much to them, but to me it was important. They were the greatest team of the decade and they deserved respect.

The happiness: Vinnie Jones, clutching his winners' medal, lifts his arms in defiance. (Getty Images)

Terry Phelan: Watching Liverpool climb the steps as the losing team was surreal. I was from the north of England. This was the greatest team in a generation. They were supposed to have won the Double. I felt terrible for them. But it was our day to savour.

Dave Beasant: Then it was our turn. I hadn't paid much attention to Liverpool when they went up – I was too busy jumping up and down and going mental. Then the man from the FA came over to us – Adrian something, I can't remember his second name. And he said simply: "Dave, get your boys together and go and get the Cup."

It must have been the dream of millions of people to climb those steps and lift the trophy. The steps were lined by Liverpool fans, but that didn't matter. They were brilliant to us.

And to get the Cup from Princess Di, the one royal everyone could identify with, was extra-special. I remember picking it up and lifting it and all I could hear was Wisey swearing away in front of royalty. He didn't know where he was, but it didn't matter. It was our day.

Opposite above
The save: Dave Beasant dives to his left to save John Aldridge's penalty. (Getty Images)

Alan Cork: I remember walking up the steps. I was behind Thorny in the line and I have the image of Lurch lifting the Cup fixed firmly in my mind. I've got a nice picture of me and Princess Di shaking hands and her giving me my medal. It was a great moment.

Opposite below
The relief: John Fashanu (jumping) leads the congratulations after Beasant's penalty save. (Getty Images)

Terry Phelan: It was like a dream, walking up those steps and getting my medal. And then there were people throwing their scarves and hats at us. It was all so unreal.

Liverpool had all these fabulous players, all at the peak of their careers. Every one was an international. We had nothing to lose. We never thought we would get to the final, let alone step onto the pitch. That one game made Wimbledon known around the world. I live in the States now and even here I get kids talking to me about that game.

Vinnie Jones: All I remember after I got my medal was press everywhere. I was choked up. They had dismissed us as scum. They had said we weren't even fit to be on the same pitch as Liverpool. And we had shown them. I went to them all screaming and hollering showing them my medal. "That bloody shows you," I shouted. That day was the day when Wimbledon came of age.

Terry Gibson: The medal means the world to me. My life would never be the same without it. The actual game itself I didn't enjoy. I had a hernia earlier in the season and I knew I needed an operation, but I decided to put it off as long as we stayed in the FA Cup. By the time of the final, I was in so much pain that I wasn't even training between games. I was one of the first people to use cycling shorts to try and keep a hernia under control.

When we got to the final, I was a little bit short of fitness. I remember Bobby Gould asked me a few days before the game how I was and whether I'd be fit enough to play. I lied through my teeth and said I was fine. It was the hardest game of football I have ever played. I was in hospital the Tuesday after the final.

The joy: Dave Beasant (left) and Alan Cork embrace after the final whistle. (Getty Image)

The Cup final meant a lot to me and Bobby Gould. We had both left Coventry a few years earlier and in 1987 we had to watch as they went and won the Cup. I was in Malta with Manchester United and I honestly thought I had missed the boat. I never knew what was going to happen at Wimbledon. I had gone there just to get first-team football and I came away having fulfilled a life-time ambition.

John Scales: It was just a great occasion. It's a special memory, but it went by all too quickly. I was just 21. I was playing in my first final. There was the hype and all the build-up. I had just come from Bristol Rovers and here I was playing at Wembley.

You hear it all the time, but it's true: the first time you play in a Cup final it all flies by. You can't sit back and enjoy the whole occasion. After 1988 I promised myself that if I ever went back I would take it all in. And I was lucky – I was back with Liverpool in 1996 against Manchester United. We lost, but I really enjoyed the game and I can remember every moment. But the 88 final is just a blur.

Dave Beasant: As we walked around the pitch with the Cup, some of the lads spotted Harry Bassett in the gantry. Waving the Cup to him meant a lot to us.

John Fashanu: I remember it clearly too. Harry was our man. Bobby

Gould was the grizzly bear with his big eyebrows, but it was Harry's side.

Vinnie Jones: I remember seeing Dave Bassett and waving the Cup to him shouting: "This one's for you Harry!" I'd known Harry since I was 12. When he was still playing at Wimbledon, he used to come down and take training. He had faith in me and I had nothing but for respect for him and this was my moment, my chance, to say thanks.

Dave Beasant: Bobby Gould knew he had inherited a great squad. Harry may have gone, but we wanted to make sure he knew he was part of this. And I can remember as clear as day seeing him waving at us.

When we got to the dressing room it was quiet. That was when reality finally set in. We had just beaten the Team of the Decade, the mighty Liverpool, the favourites for the Double. Little-fancied Wimbledon from tiny Plough Lane had just produced one of the biggest upsets in Cup history. We were shell-shocked.

We'd always done things OTT. If we went drinking, everyone went drinking. We would stay out until everyone else had gone. Now we were stunned.

Andy Thorn: We had done our celebrating on the pitch and this was like a huge come-down. We were shaking each other's hands, but it was subdued. And then in walks Alan Cork.

Alan Cork: It was deathly silent. I didn't expect that at all. It was funny really. The spirit, the passion of the club had made us famous. Little Wimbledon had just beaten Liverpool to win the FA Cup, the most famous club tournament in the world. And not one player could muster a word in the dressing room as I walked in.

I suppose, looking back they were all dazed and exhausted. Since the semi-final this moment was all we had lived for and now it was over. But I wanted to make the most of it. There was a massive bar in the corner of the dressing room and I strode up to it, past everyone, and said: "Anyone fancy a beer?"

Andy Thorn: And that it was it. We must have been drunk solid for the next week. We drank the bar dry and were diving in and out of the bath – it's more like a pool at Wembley.

Alan Cork: By the time we had clambered on the coach everyone was singing. We were singing all the way back to Wimbledon, and I reckon some of us didn't stop until halfway through the next week.

John Fashanu: By the time we got on the coach, reality was starting to set in. You bastards have just won the FA Cup. Raggedy-Arse Rovers have won the Cup. It was simply fantastic.

Lawrie Sanchez: It is an amazing feeling to score the winning goal at Wembley. But I spoke to a journalist friend before we got on the coach. And he said: "Shame it was such a drab final, no one will remember your goal."

That comment saddened me at the time and I believed it. It hadn't been the prettiest of finals. But since then I've done two television programmes solely on the goal, a documentary, and numerous radio shows around the world – and I'm still being asked about it now. That goal is as well known as any other from an FA Cup final. It pisses off everyone else from the team.

It may not have been a great game, but it was a famous final. It was the highlight of my career. We were a good first division side, a top 10 side. We weren't the pub team everyone made us out to be.

I was never a fans' favourite like Vinnie Jones, or Glyn Hodges before that. I had 10 years at Wimbledon. I was a limited player, but I used what ability I had. I came back as reserve team manager a few years later. And I have only happy memories of the 15 years I spent there.

What we achieved with 7,000 fans, going through all the divisions and winning the Cup final, will never be achieved again.

Terry Phelan: That day in May, Wimbledon came of age. I was speechless – it was a moment to savour and one I will always remember. Playing in the First Division was immense, and then a cup final – it had all happened so fast.

The celebrations that night were mad. We went back to the Cannizaro Hotel after the game. The Cup was placed on the floor and we danced round it. And then it was onto the marquee at Plough Lane. I barely remember anything from after we got to Plough Lane. I had had quite a lot by then. I vaguely remember all these stars and models who all wanted a piece of the action.

Dave Beasant: Stanley Reed had wanted to take us all to the Hilton no matter what the result, but that wasn't our style. So we went for a marquee on the pitch at Plough Lane. Every player had a table for 10 full of family and friends. It was a quieter night because of that. If it had just been the lads, God knows what would have happened.

Alan Cork: The marquee back at Plough Lane was fantastic. My late mum wasn't the greatest at staying out late, so I'd booked her a cab for midnight. But by the time midnight came round she wasn't going anywhere. She didn't leave until 3.30am. The rest of us kept going.

Andy Thorn: It was about 5am. But there was no public transport and we couldn't get back to the Cannizaro Hotel, where we were staying. Corky and Wisey were there with their other halves. There were still a few policemen around and one of them called back to the station to help us out. We had swiped loads of wine and we gave them a couple of bottles.

Alan Cork: So we ended up getting a lift in the back of a police van. I must have had three bottles of red and two of white, and we were swigging away with the police in the back of the van. And then it was back to the Cannizaro to keep going. By 9am I don't think any of us knew where we were.

Andy Thorn: We only managed about an hour and a half's kip before we had to head off back to Plough Lane for the parade through Wimbledon.

John Scales: It was a late, late night to say the least. Me and Wisey were on Frost on Sunday the day after. I'd love to see a video of that; we must have looked in a pretty awful state. Then there was the bus to Wimbledon. We left Plough Lane and there were no crowds. We were thinking: "We're just little Wimbledon, no one really cares." And then we turned the corner into the town centre.

Terry Phelan: There were all these yellow and blue flags waving. We wanted to know where they had all appeared from – we'd never seen that at a game.

John Fashanu: I didn't get drunk the night before; it would have affected me badly. I was so exhausted, I would have collapsed and I wanted to enjoy the moment. The parade was amazing, seeing so many Wimbledon fans. I couldn't believe it – none of us could. The whole of Wimbledon a sea of yellow and blue. And for that reason alone, I'm glad I stayed sober.

The antics: Inspired by Vinnie Jones, the Wimbledon players partake in a mass moonie at Alan Cork's testimonial. (Getty Images)

Andy Thorn: We got up to the balcony. It turned out the mayor had a bar in his chambers, so we went through that too.

Alan Cork: Anyone who's seen pictures of the victory parade will have noticed that I was just sitting at the back of the bus with sunglasses on. I could barely bloody move. But the drinking just carried on, all the way through the reception at the town hall and on to my testimonial on the Monday.

Then there was the mooning incident. Vinnie started that. The crowd were singing: "Vinnie, Vinnie, show us your bum!" So he did. And the rest of us thought, what the hell, and we mooned as well. And it was us lot who all got charged – Vinnie got away with it!

But those were good times and that night at my testimonial was another amazing one. I can't imagine any club ever celebrating like the Wimbledon of 1988. We were special.

Andy Thorn: The only downside of it all was that Bobby Gould refused to take us on a pre-season trip. He said we were uncontrollable and right then I suppose we were.

Those few days were like a dream come true and the good thing about Wimbledon was that it felt like all your family were there too.

Clive Goodyear: The final and the celebrations afterwards at Plough Lane proved to be the highlight of my career. I damaged my knee in the Charity Shield and was out injured for the next 13 months. The lads were great. Vinnie Jones organised a whip-round and they raised enough money to pay for a holiday to Portugal – that was a nice gesture. I battled hard to get back, but I never again reached the standard I would have liked and that was the reason I left. I managed four more games for the club and then I went to Brentford. I had never wanted to leave, but I just knew I would never be able to do the team justice again and that hurt.

Dave Beasant: I didn't figure that the Cup final would be my last game for Wimbledon. When Dave Bassett had left the year before, I felt it was my time to go as well. I didn't envisage Wimbledon ever reaching the FA Cup final. I spoke to Bobby Gould and he persuaded me to stay, but we made an agreement that if any club ever came in for me he would let me know. I remember we played Newcastle a couple of times in the cups that year, and we beat them both times. And after the League Cup tie they offered £350,000, but Bobby told them to come back with an offer of £750,000, which would have been a record for a goalkeeper back then. And, I thought, that was that. I was happy at Wimbledon anyway, so it didn't bother me.

I didn't even think about leaving after the Cup final. But then Bobby called me and said the club had accepted an £850,000 offer from Newcastle. And I suppose there was no better way to leave Wimbledon than having just won the FA Cup.

Andy Thorn: It was my last game for the club too. I never wanted to leave. I'd read all these rumours linking with me with a move to Newcastle.

Dave Beasant was already there by then, and I'd been made club captain. That's a quiz question for you: "Who was the Wimbledon captain after Dave Beasant?" It wasn't Vinnie Jones, it was me.

About two weeks after Dave left, Bobby Gould told me they had accepted an offer from Newcastle. In the end it was to work out at over £1m.

Lawrie Sanchez: What saddens me is the situation now. My history has been extinguished with the demise of Wimbledon FC. With the move to Milton Keynes, how can they claim a credible line to Wimbledon?

I have a great respect for what AFC Wimbledon have done – and the fans have the same great memories as I do – but AFC Wimbledon have never won the FA Cup. The 1988 Cup final has been consigned to history – it belongs to neither club. It belongs solely to the players who played in it and the fans who watched it.

✦

The Spirit of Wimbledon

CHAPTER NINE: PLOUGH LANE'S SWANSONG

BIG ONE HANS!

After the joys of May, Wimbledon had been brought back down to earth with a bump. The loss of Dave Beasant had left a huge hole in the team. By the start of October, the club were bottom of the table and were about to field their third goalkeeper of the season: the Dutchman Hans Segers.

1 OCTOBER 1988

First Division

Wimbledon 2 Everton 1

By Hans Segers (player)

I was so keen to make an instant impression. The club was fresh from its FA Cup success, and Dave Beasant had been the hero. But he had been sold in the summer to Newcastle United for £850,000 and his absence left a huge hole at the club.

Wimbledon had tried a couple of goalkeepers before I arrived and they simply hadn't come up to scratch. The club had lost four and drawn one of the first five games of the season, and the doom-merchants were circling, wanting Wimbledon to fail.

Beasant, at the time, was the only keeper taking free-kicks from outside the penalty box. During my first week I spent every day in training doing a lot of kicking, trying to emulate him. And then came my opportunity, barely 15 minutes into my Wimbledon career, a free-kick just outside the area. It went straight to John Fashanu and he headed it in. I was an instant hero.

I think that sealed my relationship with the Wimbledon fans. With that one kick I was accepted. And that was the start of my fisted salute to the Dons fans. We played in quarter-finals, and we finished sixth in the League one season.

Direct football: Hans Segers kicks the ball long. (Getty Images)

But that first game, that kick, that goal – that was my highlight. Alan Cork added a second, and although we conceded a goal in the second half we won 2-1 and the club was back up and running again. To be accepted by the crowd so quickly meant so much to me and from then on I went from strength to strength.

Moving to Wimbledon, though, had been far from certain. I'd had two or three offers from Belgium. My wife was homesick when I was at Forest. I played 70-75 games for them, but we never really settled. Then Bobby Gould rang.

My wife and I talked about it. It was another challenge – coming to London, a big city. It was something different. So we decided to give it a go and I never looked back from there.

I'll be honest, Wimbledon's reputation petrified me. I'd heard about them cutting up suits and other shenanigans. I spent the whole first week waiting for something to happen. After a week I thought I'd escaped.

Then there was Aston Villa, my first away trip with the club. We went up on the Friday night, had coffee and dinner in the hotel – the usual stuff, and then I went to my room. They had ransacked it. My television was in the bathroom and my clothes were all over the place, but the main thing was the bed. It wasn't there. The boys had opened the window wide and pushed the bed out of it. Can you imagine the call to reception: "Excuse me, can you help me? Erm, my bed has been pushed out of the window!" It was my welcome to the club. There was a committee among the players that organised the pranks and the jokes flowed from there. In time, I was to become a member of it. It was all part of the team spirit. You had to be able to take it. I did, and so within seven days I had become an integral part of Wimbledon, accepted by the fans and players alike.

◆

NICK HORNBY OWES IT ALL TO McGEE

Nick Hornby's best-seller Fever Pitch was to spark a renaissance in football. The book centres on Michael Thomas' injury-time winner at Anfield in the final game of the 1989 season that was to win the closest title race in living memory. What Nick fails to do is credit a diminutive Irishman wearing the blue of Wimbledon who made it all possible.

17 MAY 1989

First Division

Arsenal 2 Wimbledon 2

By Paul McGee (player)

I remember everything about the goal. After Hans Segers' kick-out, Lawrie Sanchez picked it up on the right wing and fed Roger Joseph, who slipped past Nigel Winterburn and got to the by-line. He pulled the ball back to me on the edge of the box and I came on to it and just hit it. I can see it now, nestling in the bottom corner of John Lukic's net.

I went mad – I think most people remember my celebration far more than the goal. But there was good reason for it. Not only was it my debut and away at Highbury, but it was also my 21st birthday.

I only found out half an hour before the game that I was playing. I'd gone to the toilet, and Bobby Gould had followed me in. He asked: "How are you feeling?" I said: "Fine." He said: "Right, that's good you're playing No 8." I said: "Feck off." And he said: "Yes you fecking are."

I couldn't believe it – and the rest, as they say, is history. It all sticks with me. I signed for Wimbledon in February 1989 and made my debut on 17 May 1989 – a Wednesday night. It was a huge game for Arsenal. If they won it, it meant they would only have to draw at Liverpool in the final game of the season to win the title.

Nigel Winterburn gave them the lead. Alan Cork brought the scores level. Then just after the break Paul Merson put them back ahead, and then came my goal. Nick Hornby, the author of Fever Pitch, probably owes me something for that.

The lads knew it was my birthday. And when I ran off to celebrate, Vinnie Jones rugby-tackled me and all I can remember is about 10 guys on top of me, all going mental.

It was a feeling I will never ever forget.

At the final whistle, David O'Leary wouldn't shake my hand. He said he had waited 15 years to get a championship medal and now some little Dublin runt had gone and ruined it for him! But he was to get his medal with that memorable win at Anfield and Micky Thomas' injury-time goal. And my goal had set it all up for them.

I ran into O'Leary a few weeks later, and he apologised to me and said it was a great goal. I'm not sure if he would have said that if they hadn't got the 2-0 win they needed at Anfield.

By Matt Couper (supporter)

One of the great things about being a Dons fan is that you know that everyone around you at matches has had the same experience – of being looked down on. It's no wonder that we can count DJs, actors, prominent businessmen and a rocket scientist among our number, as we've all got something to prove. I for one took a lot of stick at school for being a Wimbledon supporter, as everyone around me supported Charlton – which was a bit rich as we always finished above them.

However, I wouldn't swap my childhood ridiculing for the world, as no one else I knew was able to live out a real-life version of Roy of the Rovers. When I started supporting Wimbledon the Dons were about to get relegated to the old Fourth Division. We needed to win our last game against Portsmouth by 11 clear goals to stay up. We won 3-2.

The next season we won the Fourth Division championship, and I played my part by leading the team out against Hull (as a mascot – we lost 2-1). Before you could blink, we had won the FA Cup.

Along the way there have been many amazing games, but one that sticks out for me is the away game at Arsenal in 1989, not just because of the circumstances of the match, but also because it was the moment that football threw off its dodgy 80s reputation and became fashionable.

I was at Highbury with my brother and a few hundred other Dons fans, and I assume that somewhere in the crowd was Nick Hornby. We were crowded into one corner of the ground, as was commonplace at the time for Dons fans, and I was so near the pitch I felt as if I was on the subs bench.

I could hear every player's voice and feel the pitch jump under their feet as they rattled across the playing surface. The atmosphere was intoxicating, and the match seemed to be being played at an alarming rate. I can't remember specifics, but I do remember thinking that the Arsenal fans should be a lot louder for a team chasing the championship.

There is of course one moment that will live with me for ever – Paul McGee's goal. At the time it seemed to fly through the air and smash the back of the net. In truth, it bounced along the ground before nestling in the corner. We went nuts, but not nearly as nuts as Paul McGee, who sprinted like a lunatic before being jumped on by the whole team. I watched the highlights later that evening and heard the commentator say: "Anyone would have thought it was Wimbledon challenging for the title." At the time it felt like we were.

The one other moment I remember from the match was in the first half when either Corkie or Gibson headed the ball goalwards, and it hit the post and rolled along the line. Vinnie Jones watched it, not wishing to take the credit for a goal, but by the time he realised the ball wasn't going in, it was too late. Like that Gazza lunge against Germany in Euro '96, Vinnie Jones could have changed history and we would have been looking for another literary football genius to make football fashionable.

◆

THE FIRST FULL ENGLAND CAP

It had taken three seasons in the top flight, but at last Wimbledon were to get the ultimate accolade from the footballing establishment: an England cap. Sixty-eight years after W Keeble had won the club's first international cap as an amateur, Wimbledon had their own full England international.

23 MAY 1989
Rous Cup
England 0 Chile 0 (Wembley)
By John Fashanu (player)

Don Howe and I had a love-hate relationship. He hated me. He'd criticised me, the way I did things, the way I played, but I loved him. And then out of the blue he told me I was in the England squad. I couldn't believe it.

I was playing like three men at the time – I felt I was able to carry two people on my back. I knew I was on the fringe of international recognition. There wasn't a defender in the whole league that was able to win a ball in the air against me.

It was still a big deal to finally get selected, and I knew that I was making a piece of history for Wimbledon. But I never realised how much pressure there would be playing for England. I was to play in the Rous Cup against Chile and Scotland. Playing for a small club made it even harder, and I was lucky that I had a big profile. You need to have a big-club mentality when you play for your country.

But I held my own with the likes of Paul Gascoigne and Bryan Robson – if you couldn't, you might as well forget about it. You had to be able to live with them, you couldn't be intimidated. For me it was like: "All right Gazza?", "How you doing, Bryan?" And they'd come back with: "Yeah, fine Fash. How's things?"

But it was more than just talking. The boys would spend £5,000 or £6,000 a night on gambling or drinking without thinking about it. And you needed to be able to go in and play with them.

It wasn't Bobby Robson who picked the team. It was the captain, the vice-captain, and the coaches, and you needed to fit in.

I would have hated to come from a small club without a big profile into all that.

I felt I was in. My first cap was against Chile at Wembley. A tube strike meant the crowd wasn't that big. But that made no difference to a Wimbledon man. I was proud to put on the England shirt. I spotted a few Dons fans in the crowd and that was nice too.

Against Scotland I got the nod ahead of Steve Bull. But I went off injured, and then the bastard came on and scored a great goal. And that was it – my England career over.

That year I was scoring goals for fun, but it wasn't good enough to earn a recall. But it didn't matter to Sam Hammam. He couldn't believe it: Wimbledon, his Wimbledon, had an England international. I opened doors for him that previously he couldn't even reach. We had made the big time. It was a dream come true for him.

My England career may have been over, but the spirit of Wimbledon just grew stronger and stronger. After my call-up, the critics came back even harder than before and that just made us even more determined. We began to steam in even more. Technically, if we tried to *play*, we might lose. But as a team we were among the best. The bigger the game, the harder we battled and the more of a team we became.

A lot of the boys from that era still keep in touch now. We all met up for Stanley Reed's funeral a few years ago. We turned it into a ball – he would have loved all that. He wouldn't have wanted anything else. Stanley Reed was unique, and my England caps belong as much to him as to me.

❖

THE BEGINNING OF THE END OF THE LONG BALL

The 1988/89 season could never match the achievements of the year before. But more worryingly, sides were beginning to work out how to play against the Dons. By the 1989/90 season, it was clear that the club had to change. Bobby Gould did the unthinkable – he dropped John Fashanu and decided to play the ball on the floor. It worked.

2 DECEMBER 1989

First Division

Chelsea 2 Wimbledon 5

By Terry Gibson (player)

I can picture the whole game as clear as day. I've got it all on video, but the problem is it's in Dutch. I was one of the first Dons players to get satellite television. Lawrie Sanchez still takes the piss out of me for it. He came round once and saw the size of the dish and he just loves telling everyone about it. It was so big, and to get different channels you actually had to physically go outside and move the dish.

I was up late the night after the game watching Dutch TV, as you do, and the highlights of English football came on so I shoved a video in and recorded it. It was well before they had extensive highlights on British TV, so the foreign channels were the only place to watch our games.

Chelsea were top of the League, and we hadn't really been playing that well up until then. So Bobby put me up front instead of Fash and we played the ball on the floor. Chelsea just couldn't cope with it – they had been ready for an aerial battle and instead we stuffed them on the deck.

Chelsea took the lead after about 10 seconds, but before they could even celebrate I equalised with a near-post header, of all things. Not bad for a midget. I remember Graham Roberts threatened to kick me in the air after that. I knew him from my Spurs days. Even in training at Spurs, when we would do reserves against the first team he would still go in full throttle. When I see him at dinners and the like now, I make sure I have my pads in the car!

Wisey then gave us the lead, before I made it 3-1. Roberts pulled one back from the spot and we went in 3-2 up. At half-time Bobby told us to keep playing the ball on the floor, and in the second half we just destroyed them.

I remember that about 10 minutes into the second half, this perfect cross came in. I was going to tap in to complete my hat-trick and Dennis Wise dived in in front of me. He had the cheekiest grin on his face after that – he knew he had denied me a hat-trick and he just thought it was hilarious. That was 4-2, and then Dave Beasant, who was in goal for them, dropped the ball onto Corky's head and we were 5-2 up and laughing.

I think we shocked a lot of people in the footballing world with that display. Not so much that we scored five goals at Stamford Bridge, which in itself was a shock, but more in the way we had done it.

We had played the ball on the floor. It was going away from the image of just lumping it forward, the one-dimensional side that everyone had pigeon-holed us as being. On the back of that display people began to realise that we had good players.

We had grown up a lot as a team. And it was the first time we had gone anywhere and got credit. Chelsea had no excuses. They hadn't played badly, we had just played better. We played good football. We had scored good goals and we had beaten a good team.

✦

BENNETT'S DREAM DEBUT

Even after the victory at Chelsea Wimbledon's form was still erratic. And after defeat to Second Division West Bromwich Albion in the FA Cup, Bobby Gould dropped half the team and gave debuts to Brian McAllister and new signing Micky Bennett.

13 JANUARY 1990
First Division
Wimbledon 1 Arsenal 0
By Micky Bennett (player)

It was an amazing few days for me. Leaving Charlton, where I had grown up, to come to Wimbledon was a bit of a surprise. It all happened in the space of an afternoon. I was called in and told Wimbledon wanted to sign me, I met Sam Hammam and Bobby Gould, and that was it. One minute I was playing in the Second Division at Selhurst Park for Charlton, the next I'm up against Arsenal at Plough Lane in the First. I thought I'd spend a few weeks in the reserves first and then maybe get my chance, but it was straight into the first team.

So there I was against a team full of stars and internationals. Faces I only really recognised from television – and I was playing against them, the likes of Michael Thomas, David Rocastle and Tony Adams. I just couldn't believe it. I wanted to leave a lasting impression on the game, to show everyone what Micky Bennett was capable of.

The game had been delayed by 15 minutes through crowd congestion, and it was almost 5 o'clock, the final minute, when I got the ball on the right side. I've always been told to mix it up a bit when going forward. I was up against Nigel Winterburn and I'd been going out wide every time, so I thought I'd cut inside this time and the pathway to goal just opened up for me. I could see Tony Adams coming at me, and I didn't know whether to shoot or not, but I gave it a go and it crept into the bottom corner.

It was a great goal, but I just didn't know what to do. I was around new players, playing at a new ground, in a new shirt. It didn't sink in. The dressing room at Wimbledon was all about the team, so I didn't feel particularly special in there. We were all celebrating together. Then, as I

Gould's replacement: Ray Harford makes a point during his reign as manager of the Dons. (Getty Images)

left the dressing room, all the cameras were flashing and microphones were under my nose: "How did it feel to score the winner against Arsenal?" It was unreal.

I remember my debut for Charlton and playing for England, but scoring that goal edges all that. I am a winger. I'm used to setting up goals. So to score on my debut, against Arsenal, the champions, in the final minute, and to win 1-0... It's what dreams are made of.

✦

GOULD DEPARTS

SUMMER 1990
By Bobby Gould (manager)

I loved my time at Wimbledon. And of course I was sad to go, but it was all to do with finances. I had twisted Sam Hammam's arm after the Cup final, but a year later he offered me £10,000 less than what I wanted – and that was that. He'll deny that to this day, but that was the situation.

It hurt to leave, but that was my decision and I knew that whatever happened I could take my memories with me from a great two years at Wimbledon. And in Ray Harford the club had a good replacement.

✦

CANARIES CLIPPED

Ray Harford may have lacked the charisma of Dave Bassett and Bobby Gould, but it was under his stewardship that Wimbledon cemented their place in the top 10 of English football. An early highlight was the trip to league leaders Norwich City.

1 DECEMBER 1990
First Division
Norwich City 0 Wimbledon 4
By Warren Barton (player)

My arrival at Wimbledon was a bit of an odd one. Bobby Gould signed me in pre-season on a Tuesday, and by the Friday he'd left the club. But luckily Ray Harford stepped up pretty quickly and he calmed me down before I could really worry about the situation.

Ray was great with young players – like myself, Paul Miller and Paul McGee. I have a lot of time for Ray. It must have been a difficult job for him. Bobby Gould was still being lauded for winning the FA Cup and he had a bunch of maniacs to control. But Ray managed to strike a balance, and we finished that year in seventh place. The spirit in the side continued to thrive, and the trip to Carrow Road was the greatest example of that.

Norwich were flying high at the time, but we weren't worried. It was the Wimbledon way. The bigger they were the harder we went for them. But it was also one of those days where everything went to plan.

John Fashanu barged forward and gave us the lead after 26 seconds. We couldn't really have got off to a better start – maybe 10 seconds earlier would have been better! Then I made it two. It was a long bouncing ball that fell between their goalkeeper Bryan Gunn and one of their defenders outside their box. I nicked it off Micky's toes and slid it into the empty net.

John Scales got a third and Fash added a fourth, and that was it – game over, and we hadn't even played the first 30 minutes.

We always fancied our chances against teams like Norwich, teams that liked to play football. We used

Player of the Year for 1990/91: Warren Barton. (Getty Images)

to mix it against them get stuck in, and that was totally alien to their way of playing. And then there was Fash – they just couldn't handle him. But to win 4-0 at the League leaders wasn't really in the script. A lot of it was to do with our spirit, and that came out with all the antics we used to get up to.

We played Sheffield United away about eight games into my career at Wimbledon. We won 2-1, and I said in the papers that we were a far better side than them. The lads didn't really like show-boating like that. So on the Monday I got stripped and thrown in a huge muddy puddle. For a 21-year-old that's quite embarrassing!

When I was involved with England, Sam Hammam would let my tyres down. Sam was a right character, he used to go in goal after training and we'd play for money over penalties to see if he could save one or score one past us. The game has got a lot more serious now.

I remember there was this fracas at Everton at home. John Scales was involved and I went in to stop it, but Fashanu pulled me away and told me to stop. "We either go in to help our players, or we let the fight go on, we never stop it," he said.

I was delighted to have the likes of John Fashanu, Vinnie Jones and big John Gayle in my team. I could push whoever I wanted and I knew I could hide behind them if it got ugly. It was all part of the Wimbledon way. We went out to intimidate sides.

But we had a decent side back then too. Keith Curle, Roger Joseph and me were all part of the England set-up. Dean Blackwell was in the England under-21s, Fash was on the fringe of the England team and we had loads of others who would win caps. We may have been intimidating, but we were also talented – and that's what accounted for Norwich back in 1990.

✦

THE RELUCTANT SUBSTITUTE

As the season drew on, a 1-1 draw at Villa Park earned Wimbledon a replay at Plough Lane in the FA Cup. On a miserable night the game seemed destined for penalties after 119 minute of scoreless action. The stage was set for Alan Cork.

9 JANUARY 1991
FA Cup third round replay
Wimbledon 1 Aston Villa 0 (aet, score at 90min 0-0)
By Alan Cork (player)

N ow, you might think that as a substitute all you ever want to do is get out there and play. But that's all lies. That night it was pissing down with rain, it was freezing cold, and frankly I didn't fancy it. And the thing about the dugout at Plough Lane was that it was below pitch level, so it would get soaking wet and freezing in there. I was wet through.

I'd been sitting on the bench for nearly the entire tie when Ray Harford turned to me and asked me if I wanted to come on. I replied: "I'm freezing cold, it's windy, it's raining and I'd rather not." But he was insistent. I had a big jacket on, and a hat and gloves, so I tried to make a deal that I'd only play if I could keep them on. He persuaded me to lose the jacket and the hat.

It was cold – very cold, especially when you're just drifting around up front. We had held them 1-1 at Villa Park. That hadn't been the greatest of games, and I suppose some people expected better the second time

Extra-time winner: Alan Cork. (Getty Images)

round. They must have been very disappointed until the final seconds.

It was a dour, dour game. The pitch was slippery and I don't think there had been one clear chance all game. The ball was just getting whacked from one end to the other by two tiring defences.

We must have been seconds away from penalties when Warren Barton launched the ball towards me. I just went for it, a full diving header. Well, I say "diving header", and I know some of the fans might remember it as that because it was at the away end, but to let you into a secret it came off my shoulder.

It was cold, and it wasn't as though my timing was going to be the best at nearly 10pm. But the records will say the same whatever. It makes no difference whether it was a 30-yarder – not that I ever scored goals like that – or in off the shoulder. In the record books, it'll say: "Wimbledon v Aston Villa, goalscorer Corky".

I was delighted, and I did the old Mick Channon celebration, running for miles. Normally I'd be quite happy just to stand up and shake hands, but it was freezing and running was the only way to keep warm.

I also knew it was near the end, so I wanted to get as close to the tunnel as possible and head straight for a warm bath. Neither team really wanted the match to go on any longer. I think the Villa players were just as happy as us when I scored.

It wasn't the greatest of games, but it was a great time to score, and afterwards we were all buzzing. It was one of those special nights at Plough Lane. The weather was miserable, the floodlights barely lit the pitch, but the place was alive.

Plough Lane helped make Wimbledon Wimbledon. I never liked Selhurst Park. Plough Lane and nights like the one against Aston Villa – that's what Wimbledon was about.

✦

WHAT'S IT LIKE TO BE OUTCLASSED?

The Cup victory spurred on the Dons and Ray Harford's side were now firmly on the up. But no one was to predict what was to follow when Tottenham paid a visit to Plough Lane. For Wimbledon fans of a certain generation that game sticks out above all others. The Dons won 5-1.

23 FEBRUARY 1991

First Division

Wimbledon 5 Tottenham 1

By Joe Blair (supporter)

Provider: Paul McGee in action against Tottenham. (Getty Images)

Spurs? They are the very antithesis of everything Wimbledon stands for: their moaning fans, their big-club mentality, their sneaky cheating players (Nayim, Claesen, Ardiles, Klinsmann, et al). My personal dislike of Spurs stems from our first victory against them. That was back in 1986. We won 2-1 in a bitter game. Lawrie Sanchez and Graham Roberts were both sent off. And afterwards, despite our success, we were belittled by their manager, their players and their fans. No matter how many times we beat them they always had some naff excuse: injuries, the referee, the grass being too long, and so on. This, however, was a victory that well and truly shut them up.

The star-studded Spurs side back then came complete with jellyfish Lineker himself and attracted 10,500 people to Plough Lane to witness the most one-sided victory the Dons ever enjoyed in the top flight.

This was the season in which Ray Harford transformed the evil

Dons from a bunch of thugs with a worse press than Saddam Hussein into a team somewhat patronisingly compared to AC Milan. This was the one time Spurs couldn't complain about the pitch, the referee or long-ball tactics. They were out-thought, out-passed and outclassed.

The Dons' scoring spree started in the ninth minute when John Fashanu scrambled a low cross along the six-yard line to Paul McGee, who stabbed home. McGee then nearly injured himself in the subsequent celebrations when he vaulted the 6ft 2in Fashanu. The game remained quiet for some time until we were awarded a free-kick for a foul on Detzi Kruszynski in the second half. Keith Curle lived up to his name and beat the Spurs keeper with a beautiful strike.

Spurs pulled a goal back through Bergsson, and for about five minutes it seemed they might put up a fight. Terry Gibson had other ideas. With 12 minutes to go, he back-heeled the ball into the path of Warren Barton, who carried the ball down the left wing. Barton waited long enough to allow the ex-Spur to take up an unmarked position in the centre of the box. Gibson's glanced header past Erik Thorstvedt was a formality.

At 3-1 serious cracks started to appear in the Spurs defence, and Wimbledon exploited them to the full. On 82 minutes Fashanu was allowed three bites at the cherry before he finally bundled in Barton's cross. Alan Cork concluded the scoring five minutes later. Barton played in John Scales, who beat two men before chipping a ball to Cork at the far post, who finished with a brave header.

The stuffing complete, we had a few minutes to savour the victory. "What's it like to be outclassed?" taunted the West Bank. Spurs had no answer, and in any case most of their supporters had shuffled off home at 3-1.

Terry Venables refused to attend the press conference. Ray Harford sent his assistant Joe Kinnear in to take the plaudits from the press – enough to annoy anyone, let alone those dispirited Spurs fans.

✦

THE ARRIVAL OF A ROUGH DIAMOND

Ray Harford lacked the charisma of previous Wimbledon managers, but he had a great eye for talent. And in March 1991 he plucked Andy Clarke from non-league football. He was to famously describe the young striker as his "rough diamond".

30 MARCH 1991
First Division
Wimbledon 3
Nottingham Forest 1
By Andy Clarke (player)

I knew very little about my move to Wimbledon. I knew a few clubs were interested, but that was about it. I had heard Wimbledon were one of them, but I hadn't given the Dons a second thought. And then it all happened. It was far more to do with Joe Kinnear than Ray Harford. Joe was Ray's assistant at the time and it was his job to do most of the scouting. Apparently he'd been to watch me quite a few times. It didn't take much to convince me to join. I was playing non-league football, and this was my chance to play in the top flight. I didn't even think about the price tag – it was only much later that I realised that £350,000 was a non-league record.

The first day I arrived at Wimbledon I was really shy. It was at the game against Spurs at Plough Lane in late February, and I was just watching. I didn't know what to expect. But after the match the lads made me feel really welcome – it probably helped that they had just won 5-1. It was a good day, and everything fell into place after that.

I had my first reserve game in mid-week and on the Saturday I was on the bench against Norwich.

I was a late substitute for the next four games, and each time I was playing that little bit more. The turning point came against Forest. I was running against Des Walker, and I beat him and hit the ball past Mark Crossley.

The next match was against Manchester United at Old Trafford, and Ray pulled me to one side and said I was starting. I'll be honest, my legs were wobbling. I just couldn't believe what was happening. Playing at Old Trafford – it was just amazing. God knows, I enjoyed it. And then I scored, and I remember thinking this is it. This is really it.

I was on a roll. I scored against Everton away and everything seemed to be going right. I remember that Ray Harford described me as a rough diamond that year. I just wanted to go on and show him and the fans the finished article.

Record arrival: Andy Clarke holds a Wimbledon shirt up to the cameras at Plough Lane on the day he signed for the Dons from Barnet. The fee of £350,000 was a non-league record at the time. (Getty Images)

ARDLEY'S FIRST START

Wimbledon's strength over the years had come from within. And more often than not that meant bringing players through the youth ranks. Towards the end of the 1990/91 season Ray Harford gave two – Neal Ardley and Neil Sullivan – their debuts away at Aston Villa. Both would become mainstays of the team for the next decade: Sullivan in goal and Ardley in midfield. To cap the day the fledgling Dons guided Wimbledon to an impressive 2-1 win.

20 APRIL 1991

First Division

Aston Villa 2 Wimbledon 1

By Neal Ardley (player)

About an hour and half before kick-off, Ray Harford dropped the bombshell: I was in the first team and I was starting. I had travelled with the team a couple of times but I never expected to start. I hadn't even progressed to the bench. I thought I might make a brief appearance as a substitute before the season's end, but not go straight in.

No one, least of all myself, expected me to play. I had no family there to watch me. They would never have been able to make it to Birmingham in time. That perhaps was my one disappointment on the day. I had joined the club at 11, and from that day I had dreamed about making my first-team debut and having my family there to share it with.

When it came to getting changed I wasn't sure what to do. I had changed hundreds of times before for the youth and reserve sides. I remember thinking: "Do I get changed early and risk looking too eager, or do I delay it and risk looking arrogant?" It sounds ridiculous now, but that's the kind of thing that goes through your head when you're making your League debut.

In the warm-up, I tried not to do too much. I was worried that I might wear myself out. But before I could work myself up into a nervous wreck the game had started. God knows what I would have been like if I had been given more than 90 minutes to think about it. It was a master stroke from Ray – the art of management in action, and he was one of the best at it. I was told to take all the corners, and to hit Fash every time. It was that simple.

We had Keith Curle, John Scales and Terry Phelan in the side then. It was a good team, and that helped me relax. It also helped that Neil Sullivan was making his debut.

It all seemed so far away from the day I first played for the Wimbledon under-11s side, but at that level the link to the club is fairly loose. I was also playing for my school, Carshalton High, and I was in the district side. I became captain of Surrey, and all the scouts started taking notice of me.

It was then that I had to make a big decision – which club to sign

Young Don: Neal Ardley makes a jump start to his Wimbledon career. (Getty Images)

schoolboy forms with? I had a choice of four: Spurs, Chelsea, Luton or Wimbledon. I sat down with my dad and we talked about it for ages. In the end, we settled on Wimbledon as we thought it was there that I had the best chance of breaking into the first team. In hindsight, it was the right decision to make.

So to Villa Park, we won the match 2-1. Ray Harford brought me off 16 minutes from the end. Aiden Newhouse came on and he scored the winner. I remember Ray Harford saying: "Well done." I thought I had done OK but I wasn't really sure. But then I spoke to Terry Burton, who had been my youth team manager. He was beaming. He was very proud, and told me that Ray Harford had said I'd done brilliantly. I couldn't believe it.

SO FAREWELL TO THE LANE

While results on the pitch were going well, rumblings off the pitch were beginning off it. The Taylor Report commissioned after the tragic events of Hillsborough in 1989, when nearly 100 fans were crushed to death on an overcrowded terrace, had decreed that the age of standing had to come to an end. For the Plough Lane of 1991 that would have meant a reduction in capacity to 6,000. That prospect was simply unacceptable. Rumours had been rife for weeks that Sam Hammam was planning a move of some sorts, but no one knew where or how soon. The announcement came in his final programme notes of the 1990/91 season: Wimbledon would be leaving Plough Lane and would kick-off the next season at Selhurst Park.

4 MAY 1991

First Division

Wimbledon 0 Crystal Palace 3

By Andy Clarke (player)

The last game at Plough Lane was a sour occasion. The players loved the ground, but with all the protests and the uncertainty, our minds just weren't on the game. It would have been good to have left with a win, but it just wasn't to be. The bitter irony was that our opponents that day were Crystal Palace, our future landlords.

To be fair, it was all about Ian Wright then – he was simply unstoppable. He was scoring from all angles and we just couldn't cope with him. He ended up with a hat-trick.

MEMORIES OF THE LANE

Terry Burton (manager): I first joined Wimbledon back in 1988, when the Crazy Gang and the spirit of Wimbledon was reaching its peak. It was just after the Cup final, and Don Howe was having a few heart problems, so Bobby Gould asked me to join as reserve team manager

I knew Don and Bobby well, and it was agreed that I would join if the club could get a place in the Football Combination, the Premier League of reserve football at the time. They did and I joined. My first game was the Charity Shield.

The reserves finished third that year, just behind Arsenal – the team I had just left.

We played most of our reserve games at Plough Lane. My memories of that little stadium, like all memories, have become rose-tinted over time.

I remember the ground as a quaint little fortress, but the reality wasn't like that at all. It was a ramshackle dump: the showers didn't work, the whole place stank of pee and the dressing rooms were tiny. I had just come from Highbury – it couldn't have been more different.

But it had a good atmosphere. The place had a buzz and it could be intimidating. From a purely footballing point of view it had a lot going for it. Aesthetically it was awful.

Jason Euell (player): I was spotted by Wimbledon scouts at the age of 12 and I used to go training at Plough Lane. I played a lot of games for the youth team and the reserves down there. I got a buzz from playing there.

I remember the old Portakabins, the dressing rooms, the tunnel and everything. I think about the old place a lot. It has a special place in my youth and in my development as a footballer.

The club had a great family spirit at Plough Lane, but then I couldn't have gone down there at a better time. My first visit was in 1988 and I was hooked. I loved Plough Lane.

Andy Clarke (player): Plough Lane was intimidating and that was a huge advantage to us. People were frightened to play us with the crowd right in your face. And it was so homely – everyone seemed to know everyone.

After that last game, I remember feeling really sorry for the fans and seeing them tear the old ground apart just to get a piece of their history. But there was nothing the players could do about it. I had been at the club for only a few months, but I grew to really love Plough Lane.

I loved that first season at Wimbledon: the little ground, the family atmosphere – all those great memories. I wanted it to get better and better. But then we moved to Selhurst Park. I didn't really like Selhurst Park. Plough Lane suited our small-club mentality. I was surprised that they never redeveloped the ground. It stood derelict for ages, and even having a small capacity there would have given us such an advantage. But no one ever had the foresight to go ahead and do it. I've often thought what would have happened if we had stayed.

Paul McGee (player): I had six great years at Wimbledon. It was like another family, so I never felt like I was away from home. We had a phenomenal spirit – we were different from everyone else. I didn't come from a wealthy background and that was the same with all of us. We all played for each other.

Sam always wanted us to get into Europe. Wimbledon would have been a real force, I reckon, in Europe. If the First Division couldn't deal with us, God knows how Europe would have coped.

Then there was Stanley Reed. I have this lovely picture of me, Stanley and Bobby Gould at Plough Lane. He was a great character and is sadly missed.

But the key to it all was Plough Lane. It all began to change when we moved. I didn't like Selhurst Park – I would have rather stayed at a redeveloped Plough Lane. It was home, part of Wimbledon. At Selhurst Park the spirit was still there but something had gone.

Micky Bennett (player): I loved my time at Wimbledon. I felt at home straight away – I felt at ease and at peace, and that had a lot to do with the character of the place.

Plough Lane had a family feel about it, from the fans and the players right through to Bobby Gould and Sam Hammam. The likes of Dennis Wise, Lawrie Sanchez, Scott Fitzgerald, Neal Ardley, Roger Joseph and Warren Barton were all welcoming. I may have spent most of my time in the reserves there, but the place was special. I loved it. That's what saddens me about the Milton Keynes move. Wimbledon belongs in Wimbledon.

I scored on my debut against Arsenal at Plough Lane. The memory is special to me, but it belongs to the people of Wimbledon and those fans who stood at Plough Lane.

Warren Barton (player): The spirit in the side then was awesome. It had a lot to do with our small-club attitude. People used to knock us for our ramshackle style and our ramshackle ground. But I had been playing at Maidstone, so I liked Plough Lane. I thought it was a decent stadium.

I used to love the atmosphere there, the way the fans used to be so close to the pitch. The ground always seemed packed. You could get 8,000 or 10,000 there and it would feel like 50,000. My first two games were against Arsenal and Liverpool. We lost the first one 3-0 and the second 2-1, but the atmosphere at both was brilliant.

I remember getting the Player of the Year award at the end of that first season. We started off drinking in the player's lounge, then drifted through to Nelson's and kept going. That was also the last game at Plough Lane.

I don't suspect other teams liked Plough Lane much though. Salt instead of sugar, cold tea and cold showers. It was a special place. It saddens me to see it gone.

Darren Stokes (supporter): I have so many fond memories of Plough Lane from the first game I remember going to, in 1977, until the last one there in 1991. I can remember vividly the 10-minute walk from my parents' house past the dog track to the football ground. Even though it was only a

Lost love: Evening falls on Plough Lane in 1991. (Getty Images)

short walk, we had to run the gauntlet of away fans had assembled for their pre-match pint, in either The Plough or The White Lion.

Once past the away fans, a short stroll past the petrol station and over the bridge and I arrived at the ground. My first action was always to have a glance up to see if I could spot any fans at the Wandle End. If I could, it meant that whoever we were playing had probably brought quite a few, especially if I could see fans in both away sections.

Another couple of hundred yards and there I was at the home gate. I would pay my entrance fee (in the 1977/78 season as a junior I used to pay 40p to get in and 15p for a programme) and squeeze through the antiquated turnstiles. Then I was on the West Bank.

The first noise I would hear was somebody shouting "Gold-digger Lotteries". I must confess that in all the years I went I never once bought a Gold-digger Lottery ticket (sorry!). Then I would take my place towards the front of the terrace to the right of the goal, and watch the players warming up.

One of the things I used to love about Plough Lane was how close you were to the pitch, the way it really felt like you were part of the club, like you mattered. I defy anyone to tell me they ever felt like that at Selhurst Park.

It always seemed that the number of people on the West Bank increased dramatically just as the teams kicked off. I think that must have had something to do with The Batsford Arms and its inhabitants.

Half-time was an experience in itself. There was the queue at the tea bar, which I religiously joined 10 minutes before the break. I could buy a burger the size of a hub cap or a hot dog as long as your arm. Everything brought from that tea bar seemed bigger than anywhere else.

Once the refreshments were finished it was time to go to the loo. A memory of Plough Lance cannot be complete without recalling a trip to the gents. It was pitch black, it seemed you were standing in a pond, and the smell…

After the final whistle it was back home. The problem was that the West Bank was never known for its subtlety, so the away fans used to get a fair amount of stick. This, coupled with the fact that we always seemed to have the habit of scoring last-minute winners, meant that the away fans were often not best pleased at the final whistle. As the crowd left the ground, most people seemed to head towards Wimbledon town centre, leaving me and a few other hardy souls to head off towards Earlsfield, towards the disgruntled travellers. By this time the away team coaches would be parked up outside the ground, and running the gauntlet of away fans once again was the order of the day.

I always remember one Sunderland fan shouting out how much of a dump Plough Lane was, and I thought: "Yeah, it might be a dump, but it's *our* dump."

✦

THE PROTESTS THAT FOLLOWED

So after 79 years, Wimbledon left Plough Lane. The promise was that the move was only temporary and the club would return to the London Borough of Merton in the fullness of time. It never happened. Fears were also growing that the club would merge with Crystal Palace. They were fears that were to spark the fans into action.

SUMMER 1991
By Laurence Lowne (supporter)

This is a story that is painful for me to recall, and those who know my family will understand why. The 1990/91 season promised something and delivered a little. A respectable seventh-place finish in the old First Division, the usual early-season exit from the League Cup, 3-0 on aggregate at the hands of Plymouth, and one or two rumblings in the background about lines of communication between the supporters club and the football club, which meant Sam Hammam.

It is a little-known fact that Sam used a number of people to bounce ideas off, my late father Alf Lowne being one of them. At short notice a telephone call would come, and dad would disappear for four or five hours and meet with Sam to act as a sounding board.

It is often said that the Big C is triggered by an event. I feel in hindsight that the move of Wimbledon FC to Selhurst was that catalyst for my father, for by the autumn of 1991 he was terminally ill, and passed away in February 1992. It is perhaps for this one reason alone that I have been reluctant to put my feelings down on paper.

If the move had not happened, would my father have lived for many more years? It is a question I cannot answer.

My father never knew in all those discussions that took place as they walked and talked around the Plough Lane pitch that the ground would soon be gone and for that reason I shall never trust a majority shareholder again because he can say all the things you want to hear, but do exactly what he wants instead, with no come-back for you.

So to that fateful last day of the season at home to Palace. A game lost 3-0 to Ian Wright, and the announcement in the programme that the club would be moving. A decision had been taken, and not for the first time, Peter Cork, a director of the club, was out of the loop since no board meeting had been convened to ratify the action. This meant that the supporters' club, chaired by Mike Winning, did not know either. It also meant that my father was as much in the dark as every other supporter of the club.

There was anger and disbelief among the supporters. The club had spent 79 years at Plough Lane, full of memories of good and bad times, of favoured positions on the terrace or in the stand, of drinks in Nelson's or The Sportsman, of incidents on and off the pitch, of happiness and sadness.

Talk after the match centred upon the possible merging of Wimbledon and Crystal Palace. It had been mooted before, in 1981 and 1986/87. Very soon supporters were organising, and by 7pm that evening a group of fans had called a meeting to discuss what to do. The result a few days later was an organisation called Supporters Against Merger (SAM for short – deliberately chosen, I might add).

Sam Hammam also knew of this anger, and had called for supporters to attend a meeting with himself in the executive lounge at Plough Lane.

It was the first time Sam and I crossed swords, and that clash is well documented in the fanzine Grapevine, of which I was editor. I was threatened with court action for libel, and would have been happy to have my day in court, but sadly it did not come to pass.

The meeting did not quell the anger of supporters, but saw us turn upon ourselves. We were split on what action to take: whether to boycott or to go and fight the possibility of a merger. Either way the supporters' club was, in my opinion, hopelessly disorganised and wasn't in the position to campaign. So six of my friends stood at the AGM to force out the "Old Guard". We won and a decision was taken to support the club's move. It was a decision which saw me persuade a supporter by the name of Marc Jones to continue to follow the club. We had become friends through our respective fanzines, and both of us recognised that we had to ensure that Sam would never be able to merge CPFC and WFC.

That summer saw a special issue of Grapevine, which encouraged supporters to attend the open days at Selhurst Park and to continue their support. It worked to a degree and helped create a new layer of supporter voice. The seeds of the Wimbledon Independent Supporters Association (WISA) were sown that summer, though we did not know it then.

The threat of merger eventually subsided, but Wimbledon never returned to Merton. Looking back to all those years ago, were we naïve? Yes, I think we were, because we genuinely believed that the Taylor Report would force our relegation from the top flight if we had not moved from Plough Lane.

Would I change any of the actions we took that fateful summer? No, since the supporters didn't have a proper voice and we couldn't have done much at the time. But perhaps more importantly, that summer a lot of friendships were formed – many of which have stood the test of time, and without that move WISA might not have eventually found its voice.

The question then arises – where would we be now?

✦

THE LEGACY OF THE LOST LANE

In the years that followed, claim and counter-claim over the reason for the club's decision to leave Merton came to the fore. And then there was Sam Hammam's decision to sell the ground to the supermarket chain Safeway. It was to sour his relationship with the fans and the fans' with him.

By Sam Hammam

I gave every penny back to the club. People at Wimbledon need to realise that. In 1978 we first applied to the council to build a 12,000-capacity all-seater stadium at Plough Lane, and that was turned down. Then there was Wandle Valley South. I used over £500,000 of my own money to produce a detailed plan, but that too was rejected.

Then we had to leave Plough Lane because of the Taylor Report. Then there was Beddington Lane. I wanted Wimbledon to be in Wimbledon. And unless people can accept that, then I do not know how I can reconcile myself with the fans.

You can look at the records and see their rejections of our plans. The architects who drew up the plans in 1978 are still in Wimbledon. George Watts, I believe you can ask them.

Maybe Merton Council is good now, and helping AFC Wimbledon to find a home, but the ones of yesteryear, of 1978, 82, 88, 89 and 90, were not in my opinion.

I only sold Plough Lane when I was chucked out of the club by the Norwegians. Why else would I have hung onto it from 1990 to 1998, when it was finished?
I didn't take a penny from it.

By Tony Stenson (Daily Mirror journalist)

There was never any need to leave Plough Lane in 1991. I remember looking into it all at the time. The club had been given five years by the Football League to get the ground up to scratch.

Wimbledon were offered 13 sites by Merton Council back then, and they had planning permission for two of them – Wandle Valley and Tanden Works. After five years the planning permission on both sites lapsed.

Then, of course, redeveloping Plough Lane was always an option too. Sam also owned the gypsy site at the back of the ground and that would have allowed for a significant expansion. There was also no restriction on how high the Wandle End could have gone. At a relatively small cost Plough Lane could easily have become a 25,000-capacity stadium.

Selhurst Park was a disastrous move for Wimbledon. I remember walking down Wimbledon High Street over the years. In the early days all you would see were Liverpool shirts everywhere, but by 1991 mothers had started buying Wimbledon shirts instead. There was a whole generation coming through – you could see it. The club had the chance to grow in Wimbledon and they blew it.

If it was about leaving Plough Lane, why didn't they move to Fulham? Craven Cottage is just four stops up the District Line, and they could have still kept those young fans. But instead they went to Selhurst Park, and the logistics of getting there from Wimbledon are horrible. Sam must have got a better deal from Ron Noades at Palace.

The club lost its virginity by moving to Selhurst. The big stadium just betrayed what Wimbledon was all about. Suddenly it was all about money: the players were talking about it, Sam was talking about it, and no one was talking about Wimbledon.

I'm not going to deny that football is about money, but it's also about heart, and somewhere along the line Wimbledon lost that.

✦

Gone: The Plough Lane site as it was in 2002. (Neil Presland)

CHAPTER TEN: CLIMBING OUT OF THE CHAOS

THE SHORT REIGN OF PETER WITHE

The Dons supporters were still reeling from the loss of Plough Lane at the start of the 1991/92 season. Six weeks in and they were to recieve another blow: manager Ray Harford was off. Harford had fallen out with Sam Hammam and left to become Kenny Dalglish's No 2 at Blackburn Rovers. It left Wimbledon with a vacuum. Joe Kinnear, Harford's assistant, seemed the obvious replacement, but Sam Hammam opted for the untried former Aston Villa player Peter Withe. It was to be a big mistake.

8 OCTOBER 1991

Rumbelows Cup

Peterborough United 2 Wimbledon 2 (Peterborough won 4-3 on agg)

By John Scales (player)

I t was obvious very quickly that Peter Withe wasn't the right man for the job. He didn't understand the way Wimbledon worked or the mentality of the club. It was his first real managerial position. He had been brought up on the ways of Brian Clough at Nottingham Forest and that couldn't have been more different than the way things operated at Wimbledon. It was clear to me that there was a problem from day one. He got off on the wrong foot and never really recovered.

He had his set methods that he wanted to introduce and the players didn't take to it. He banned us from wearing trainers and jeans. He also wanted us all to be clean-shaven. They were all little things, but they don't really endear you to a new club and especially a club like Wimbledon.

When you come in you need to understand the sensibilities and the appreciations of the new club. You need to talk to the players; take time to understand how things work. But that wasn't Peter Withe's style. He was very authoritarian. He wanted to be the boss and he could have been, but he lacked the necessary subtly to win us over. You can't come in to the Wimbledon set-up and go crash, bang, wallop and expect everything to be alright.

His big problem was that we were a very opinionated group of players. You could name every player in the side as an example of that character. You had to have a strong character to survive at Wimbledon and that had been our strength throughout the years. The strongest characters were the likes of John Fashanu, Vinnie Jones, Alan Cork, Robbie Earle, Warren Barton and myself – the more experienced players. We had a system and a hierarchy that worked and Withe was trying to break it.

I liked him, but he didn't seem the right fit for Wimbledon. It was all about man-management. The players needed to be managed in a style that wasn't Peter Withe's. He would have been right for another group of players, but not for Wimbledon. In the space of a few days the harmony we had enjoyed for years was broken. He tried to fix it with a few gimmicks, including a ridiculous tie competition, but he failed.

Football's all about confidence and spirit. If you have disquiet and rumblings of dissatisfaction in the dressing room, it is bound to affect the performances on the pitch and that's what happened. His first game in charge was against Peterborough in the League Cup and we drew 2-2 and went out on aggregate. It was the start of the worst run of results I'd ever known.

We didn't speak to Sam about it; I don't think we had to. Sam knew how the club worked and he would have got a feeling that things were going wrong and that's why he acted so quickly. Withe was sacked in January and Joe Kinnear came in to replace him.

Joe understood the mentality that made the players tick at Wimbledon. He had been Ray Harford's assistant. He knew how to make the team work. He won us over very quickly. He was a very good coach and a great man motivator. And that was a big contrast to Peter Withe.

Ray had been a great manager and was seriously under-rated. He was a good coach and he got his respect that way. He was very similar to Don Howe. And both Don and Ray helped develop Wimbledon. Don gave us a tactical understanding, but it was under Ray that we added the footballing element to our game.

In the big scheme of things Peter's reign was just a blip in our progress. Joe knew what we were really about. He capitalised on all the work Ray and Don had done before and took us to another level.

Opposite above
Lack of respect: Peter Withe (centre) tries to make a point in training at Selhurst Park. Neal Ardley listens in, while Alan Cork (left) struggles to take it seriously. (Paul Willatts)

Opposite below
Laughter: Players gather round to show off their bad ties as part of Peter Withe's competition. (Paul Willatts)

VINNIE RETURNS TO SEE OFF WITHE

Peter Withe's record was atrocious, just one win in 17 matches. Ironically, the final nail in the coffin came with the visit of Chelsea who included Vinnie Jones and Dennis Wise in their starting XI.

WIMBLEDON 1 CHELSEA 2

First Division

18 January 1992

By Vinnie Jones (Chelsea player)

After leaving Wimbledon, I went to Leeds, Sheffield United and Chelsea, but Wimbledon fans followed me wherever I went. It's always been my home, my roots. I remember when I was at Chelsea we played Wimbledon in their first season at Selhurst Park. You could feel that the old spirit wasn't there. Maybe it was Selhurst Park, but maybe it was because Peter Withe was in charge.

It felt wrong and it ended up being quite an easy game for us. We won 2-1, but it could have been three or four. I never celebrated one of our goals. I never cheered. A part of my heart was still with the Dons and I didn't like seeing them that way.

It was Peter Withe's last game in charge of Wimbledon. On the Monday after the game he was sacked. Joe Kinnear was brought in. He restored the old passion and within nine months I was back at Wimbledon.

By that sort of time, my reputation went before me. I had this hard man image and everywhere I went people were giving me grief. Mainly it was 14 or 15 year olds who were a bit lippy and would ride their luck. But I'd just have a giggle and ignore it.

The worst thing was when there was a crowd of lads in the pub and one of them had had a but too much to drink and would start effing and blinding at you. You have to pull them and that would cause problems and consequently you would have to leave the pub.

When I went out back then I would only ever feel relaxed when I had had a couple of beers. If I went to a pub and didn't have a drink I would always find myself looking around all the time to see if someone was going to have a go or something like that. So in the end I tended to stay on my own patch and drink in my local in Hemel Hempsted.

I think a lot of people had a misguided image of me from the way I played my football. If there's a bit of a bad tackle and a lad has got injured I was always the first to get him a beer after the match. I never took the malice off the pitch. That was the Wimbledon way.

Withe's replacement: Joe Kinnear. (Paul Willatts)

KINNEAR MAKES HIS MARK

After Withe, Joe Kinnear could hardly be any worse. His reign began with a draw at Queen's Park Rangers, followed by victories over Aston Villa and Manchester City. But they had been unconvincing and doubts still remained. Victory at Anfield changed all that. Joe Kinnear had arrived.

8 APRIL 1992

First Division

Liverpool 2 Wimbledon 3

By Andy Clarke (player)

It was such an important time for Joe Kinnear. Peter Withe had left the club in an absolute mess, and Joe was charged with turning it all around. I do not have one good memory of Peter Withe. He tried to get on with us, he tried to be one of the lads, but it just didn't work. He tried to change our style. He wanted us all to be clean shaven, with no earrings, and to wear suits, but that just was not us.

We hardly won a game under him. He just didn't understand Wimbledon and we were sliding away. He didn't get the spirit of the club. And then Joe came in. He never actually said: "Go back to the way you were", but we all did. The laughter was back. Now we just had to get the results going too.

Travelling to Anfield was always a big occasion and we used to do well up there, but this time everything was not going to be quite so smooth. In Joe's first game we got a draw at QPR. A couple of wins followed but they were against teams in trouble, and we all knew that the trip to Anfield would be the real test.

Micky Thomas gave them the lead, Lawrie Sanchez equalised, and just before the break Ronnie Rosenthal made it 2-1 to them. Under Withe, I doubt whether we would have come back. But Joe had got the old Wimbledon spirit going again and we refused to lie down.

I remember clearly the cross coming in and just waiting for it to arrive. I'm not the tallest of blokes, but I was so keen to score. I out jumped one of my own team-mates and that made it 2-2. Playing against one of the best teams in the country and then scoring a goal at the Kop End sent me rocking. That was with about 20 minutes to go, and then 10 minutes later Fash won a penalty and we were ahead. The celebrations afterwards were fantastic. It was one of the best nights ever. And Joe was central to it all. He urged us on – not that he really had to. Fash jumped up and down and we were all up for it. Wimbledon were back. Yes, it was a job, but it was a great job and Joe was turning us around.

Celebration:
Andy Clarke.
(Paul Willatts)

HOLDSWORTH'S HIGHBURY HAPPINESS

In the summer football in England was to enter a new era. After a series of financial rumblings, the country's top echelon broke off from the Football League and formed a new division. The Premier League was born and Wimbledon would be founder members. With Joe Kinnear at the helm, Wimbledon were firmly on the up, but there are still some matches that belong to a single player. Wimbledon's victory over Arsenal in 1993 was one such game. Dean Holdsworth had joined the club from Brentford for £750,000 and this was to be the highlight of his time with the Dons.

10 FEBRUARY 1993
Premier League
Arsenal 0 Wimbledon 1
By Dean Holdsworth (player)

It wasn't the prettiest game, but for me it meant the world. I may have scored the winner, and in normal circumstances doing that at Highbury would have been pretty special on its own. But there was all this other stuff as well. My son Bradley was the mascot. They didn't normally have away mascots at Highbury, but Sam Hammam liked to pull a few strings if he could and he agreed to let Arsenal have a mascot at Selhurst Park in exchange. I don't think Bradley really realised how special it was. I have some pictures of it and I know he loved it. But I don't think he had a clue about how difficult it had been to organise.

And then there was my wife Samantha's family. They were all born in Islington and every one of them was an Arsenal fan. There were all pleased when I moved to Wimbledon, but I suspect that was because I could get them tickets at Highbury when we played there!

It was also my first season at the club and the first time I'd played at Highbury. So put all that together and I was more nervous than anyone.

I couldn't have dreamed of a better start to the game. About halfway through the first half the ball dropped to me in the middle of the area and I just scrambled it home. I think I spent the rest of the game with a smile on my face. I remember looking up after I scored to where my wife was, and she was celebrating, but all around her her family were unmoved.

Sure Arsenal came back at us, but we held firm and they just got more and more frustrated.

After the final whistle, I didn't make much of it with the lads. We were a team and we'd won as a team. The same really applied to Samantha's family. I met them in the players' lounge after the game. I didn't want to gloat about it. But then there was the smile on Samantha's face…

That goal was the start of a great first season for me at Wimbledon. I had joined the club from Brentford. It wasn't really a difficult decision. There were a few clubs interested in me, but I wanted to stay in London. And Joe Kinnear and Sam Hammam were very persuasive. I also knew Robbie Earle – I'd spent a while on loan at Port Vale – and I'd grown up with Warren Barton. I wanted to feel the Crazy Gang spirit. I went down there and I loved it.

Then there was Sam Hammam's promise. When I joined he said that if I passed 15 goals in a season he'd make a bronze statue of me. I scored 17 that season. And at the club's Player of the Year awards, he honoured his promise. I remember vividly Stanley Reed handing it over. But what was even madder is that Sam said that if I scored 15 the year after, he'd kiss my arse. All the players knew about it, and when I got my 15th goal at Newcastle in the 1993/94 season, Sam was dragged in. I think John Fashanu held him down and he was made to kiss my arse in front of everyone!

◆

DONS LORD IT OVER THE LANDLORDS

In Joe Kinnear's first full season in charge the Dons would finish 12th in the inaugural Premier League. And there was little doubt as to what the highlight of the season was. The 4-0 victory in the Selhurst derby stuck out a mile. It was also a result that would prove decisive to Palace's hopes of survival.

7 APRIL 1993
Premier League
Wimbledon 4 Crystal Palace 0
By Dean Holdsworth (player)

It was a horrible wet and windy Sunday morning, a local derby live on TV. The atmosphere was fantastic. Sam Hammam had given out all these red cards to the Dons fans – I can't remember what for – and they were waving them around. It was like a carnival. We were the tenants, the paupers, and that made it special. We won by four clear goals and the fans just loved it, probably even more than we did.

Goal time: Dean Holdsworth celebrates after scoring Wimbledon's third goal against Crystal Palace in 1993 (top), before Robbie Earle powers in the fourth to complete a 4-0 win. (both Paul Willatts)

I had a part in the first three goals. The first came early on, I was holding off Richard Shaw (who's a good mate of mine now). I got a nice diagonal ball away to Neal Ardley and he hit it back in for Robbie Earle to head home. The second wasn't the most spectacular, but it was all to do with the way we played. Neal whacked the ball in, and all the pressure was on Nigel Martyn. He dropped the ball at my feet and I scrambled it home.

I remember the third really well. The Palace fans used to slaughter our supporters for not having a ground of our own. So we knew what it meant to them to give them a good hiding, and the third sealed it. Andy Clarke charged forward on a counter-attack just after half-time and skipped past a couple of players before slipping the ball into my path, and I slotted it home. I was beaming and I could see all the fans in front of me, and they loved it. It was awesome. There was no coming back from that, and from then on it was just a matter of how many we were going to score. We may have been tenants but we were lording it that day.

Robbie Earle headed in the fourth from a cross from Gerald Dobbs, and by the end of the game we were both chasing hat-tricks. We both would have loved to make it 5-0, but in the end we had to settle for two each.

The next three years at Wimbledon was one big pleasure ride. I loved it there. We just lived for Wimbledon and for having a laugh.

John Scales, Robbie Earle and Steve Talboys all became great mates of mine, but everyone got on with everyone there, right down to Stevie Allen the physio. There wasn't one person down there who didn't fit in, and if they didn't they weren't there long. It was like 30 guys going on holiday for three years.

But we also trained hard and worked hard on our tactics. Joe Kinnear and Terry Burton would get us well prepared for matches, but sometimes it was the team spirit that got us through.

Against Palace everything just clicked. It was one of those days where we were going to enjoy ourselves whatever the weather. I like to remind Richard Shaw of the match. I give him a nudge every now and then and tell him how we tonked them, the year they went down. The result had a huge effect on their season. The week before, we lost 6-2 to Oldham. And Oldham and Palace finished that season level on points, but Palace's goal difference was two worse and they went down while Oldham suvived. I bet the Wimbledon fans are well aware of that stat.

✦

SQUADRONS CELEBRATE SEGERS THE HERO

The 1993/94 season began slowly, but it was kick-started by a dramatic victory over Liverpool in the Coca-Cola Cup. A late Robbie Earle equaliser at Anfield had earned Wimbledon a replay at Selhurst Park. And for 89 minutes everything seemed to be going well. The Dons were 2-1 up and had one eye on a place in the quarter-finals. Then disaster struck…

14 DECEMBER 1993
Coca-Cola Cup
fourth round replay
Wimbledon 2 Liverpool 2
(Dons win 4-3 on penalties)
By Hans Segers (player)

I wanted the world to open up and swallow me. I couldn't believe it – I had played so well and we were just seconds away from victory. It was a harmless-looking corner, but it moved in the air and I misjudged it. I had wanted to catch it originally, but I changed my mind and went for the punch. It slid off the back of my glove and went in.

Tension: Hans Segers can barely watch as the Coca-Cola Cup tie against Liverpool on 14 December 1993 goes into penalties. (Getty Images)

Relief: Vinnie Jones (left) swoops in to congratulate Neal Ardley (centre) after Ardley's successful spot-kick saw Wimbledon edge past Liverpool on penalties in the Coca-Cola Cup. (Paul Willatts)

Ecstasy: The Wimbledon players celebrate in front of the Dons fans after their dramatic victory. (Getty Images)

We had been the better team. It was just unbelievable – we had deserved to win in normal time. Dean Holdsworth had given us the lead, they equalised, Robbie Earle put us in front and then I did that. I had blown it for everyone. I was distraught.

But I was to get my chance to redeem myself. In extra-time they won a penalty, and John Barnes stepped up to take it. I had to prove something to the team, to the boys. I guessed right and saved it.

They'd had the upper hand after my own goal, but my penalty save swung the tie back our way. We held out for the rest of extra-time, and so to penalties.

I saved two, and Neal Ardley struck the winning spot kick – and we were off, airplanes everywhere. We had rehearsed it in training, and as soon as the ball hit the net Neal reeled away with his arms spread wide like a plane, soaring around Selhurst Park, and we all followed. I have never witnessed anything like that. I had many great matches at Wimbledon and this was one of them. The celebrations went on late into the night.

The bigger the club, the more determined we were to beat them. That was the strength of Wimbledon. In those days the press used to get on our back too. They used to slag off Wimbledon week in week out and to be honest the players loved it. For that reason we really wanted to beat the big boys – Liverpool, Arsenal, Chelsea, and Manchester United. We didn't have world-class players, but we had the best team spirit.

When someone was not doing their job we could tell them, and they would accept it and try harder next time. At every club I have been with since that's not been the case. There are too many players now who find it hard to accept criticism. And too many football people are afraid to tell people off.

Sometimes we would have fights in training, but at the end of the session we would all walk off as good friends. It was as important at Wimbledon that you could take it as well as give it. And then there were the jokes and the committee – the boys loved it.

It was a lot to do with Fash the Bash. And then there was Vinnie and Wisey too, they were the main characters. They were involved in everything. But everyone was part of it, we had that special spirit. And I thought that my display against Liverpool that night was just another example of it. I messed up, but I learnt from it, picked myself up and made amends. That was Wimbledon.

◆

BLACKBURN SUCCUMB TO DONS' REVIVAL

Joe Kinnear's side was beginning to gel. The fearlessness that had epitomised the Dons of old was back. The visit of the League leaders Blackburn Rovers was the casing point. They arrived with a huge reputation and left humbled.

29 MARCH 1994

Premier League

Wimbledon 4 Blackburn Rovers 1

By Robbie Earle (player)

Scramble: Dean Holdsworth (centre) scrambles in Wimbledon's third goal against Blackburn on 29 March 1994. (Paul Willatts)

t was a huge game for Blackburn. They were leading the table and wanted to extend their lead over Manchester United. It was just the sort of match we thrived on. A couple of days before the game Sir Alex Ferguson gave Sam Hammam a call. The pair of them are good friends, and Alex said: "Do us a favour and I'll send a crate of champagne down." Sam told us about the promise, but it didn't really matter. We were not the sort of team to do anyone any favours – we wanted to beat everyone.

It was a cold March evening, and Blackburn got on top early through Jason Wilcox – I think he made a bit of a mug of Warren Barton. And to be honest, we weren't really in it in the first half.

Joe Kinnear got hold of us in the interval, and that second half must rank among the best displays ever produced by a Wimbledon side. Everything clicked into place: our athleticism, our team spirit, our direct style. It was all there, and they just crumbled. It could have been eight.

Fashanu got the first five minutes after the break. Hans Segers kicked it long, I picked it up got into the area and Fash just hit it in. It's not a feeling you get every week, or even very often, but from the moment we drew level we knew we were never going to lose the game. It stayed level for a while but we were on top – we could sense it.

Then Vinnie launched a long throw, the ball got bundled in, and we were off, we were flying. You could see it all over the pitch: everyone was bombing forward. We just felt we could score at will. We felt untouchable. Peter Fear swept up the right fed Dean Holdsworth to make it 3-1. I volleyed in the fourth in the last few minutes. It was comprehensive.

The team then was just full of strong characters, from Sanchez to Cork and from Vinnie to Fash. We had a never-say-die attitude. It was a great job being captain of that side and I took it very seriously. Once we stepped over the touchline I became the manager's eyes and ears. Off it, I was always the link between the players and the manager. It was my job to keep people on track and steer the player away from trouble, and I relished it.

If people needed a gee-up, it would fall to me to do that. Equally, if people needed a kick to get them going then I'd do that too. It was a really difficult role when we were struggling, but when we were on form and flying, as we were against Blackburn, it was easy.

The crate of champagne arrived a few days later.

✦

ACCUSATIONS AS EVERTON SURVIVE

It should have been a celebration of Wimbledon's greatest ever season. Under Joe Kinnear the side would finish sixth, but the season would be tarnished by allegations of match-fixing by Hans Segers and John Fashanu. At the centre of the prosecution's case was the final game of the 1993/94 season.

Everton needed to win to stay up, but after 20 minutes they were 2-0 down. A disputed penalty gave Everton hope, the second was unstoppable, but their third and the winner – a mis-hit shot that somehow deceived Segers – appeared a little too convenient.

7 MAY 1994
Premier League
Everton 2 Wimbledon 3
By Hans Segers (player)

A lot has been said about that match. I've seen it on video hundreds of times and I'll hold my hand up. Yes, I was at fault for their third goal. Graham Stuart's shot was soft, but the ball hit a divot and went over my arm. Nine times out of 10, I would have saved it. It was the last match of the season and they needed to win to stay up. We had stormed into a 2-0 lead after 20 minutes, a Dean

Rescue act: Everton's fans and players celebrate after coming back from 2-0 down to win 3-2 on the final day of the 1993/94 season. The win was just enough to keep them in the Premiership. (Getty Images)

Holdsworth penalty and an own goal. We all thought then that we had it wrapped up. They got a penalty to pull one back before the break, but with so much focused on their third goal, I don't even remember it.

I couldn't have done anything about their second. I remember that well. It came midway through the second half. Barry Horne hit it and it just flew into the top corner.

Then there was Graham Stuart's effort with nine minutes left. The boys at Wimbledon all knew I was a winner. I would never let in a goal on purpose, and that's been proven in a court of law. I have no problem talking about it now. It was just one of those things.

I was gutted. I wanted to win, and it was a howler. It put Everton in front for the first time when they shouldn't have even been in the game.

They held on and Goodison Park erupted. They had stayed up. We had no sympathy for them. We'd wanted to beat them – we would have happily sent them down. It was always Wimbledon first.

It had been such a great year for Wimbledon, we finished the season in sixth place, equalling the club's highest ever finish. It was the greatest achievement in my time at the club. I was so proud of that sixth place, and I would have loved even more to make it fifth.

The accusations didn't really surface until later. The club was unique, and some people were out to tarnish its image. And then there was the trial. The Wimbledon supporters were great to me throughout that. They knew me. I got loads and loads of letters from them and not one was negative. Wimbledon had made my career. It was the first time I'd been the first-choice goalkeeper at a club. I had been in and out of the team at Forest, but at Wimbledon my career really took off. The club meant the world to me, and I was so relieved when my innocence was proved.

◆

ON-LOAN LEO MAKES INSTANT IMPACT

The 1994/95 season begun really badly for the Dons. John Fashanu had been sold to Aston Villa for £1.3m and he had left a huge hole in the side. Wimbledon had won just three of their first 13 games. The poor start persuaded Sam Hammam and Joe Kinnear to take a Norwegian on loan: Oyvind Leonhardsen. Trailing 3-1 to Aston Villa at home was hardly the perfect start for Leonhardsen. What was to follow wrote him into Dons folklore. Aided by the his excellent display in midfield, Wimbledon pulled back to 3-3. But there was still more to come from Leo...

9 NOVEMBER 1994
Premier League
Wimbledon 4 Aston Villa 3
By Oyvind Leonhardsen (player)

It was deep into injury time. The ball was hit in from the right and Efan Ekoku trapped it about six or seven yards out. I just nicked it off his feet and fired it in. I ran to the fans. The atmosphere was great and the fans just grabbed me, it was a great start to my career in England and it is a moment I will always remember. I'm not sure if Efan will ever forgive me!

Warren Barton had given us the lead with a penalty, but Villa came roaring back. I seem to remember Dean Saunders scoring twice as they went 3-1 up. Neal Ardley pulled one back, and then Vinnie Jones levelled with seven minutes to go. It was all set up and I got the winner.

Everyone gave me a great reception. I remember Sam Hammam ran onto the pitch full of smiles. I'd signed on loan for three months, but after that game against Villa I think they decided there and then to keep me.

The loan move to Wimbledon had happened quite quickly and I knew very little about it. It was all conducted through my agent – Joe Kinnear knew more about it than I did! I had played for six years in Norway and three at Rosenborg. I wanted to go abroad and Wimbledon gave me the chance. Rosenborg weren't that keen to release me, but I had made up my mind.

At Rosenborg it was very different: we won the league and the cup almost every year. We played neat passing football. At Wimbledon the tempo was so much faster – and then there were all the long balls.

I was awarded the Player of the Year in the Norway, so I was full of confidence. I didn't have any doubts in my ability. I adapted quite quickly, but those first few games were really fast and the ball just seemed to be flying past me. I just wanted to go out and do my best. At Wimbledon I went on to learn that style. But I also learnt about camaraderie and spirit. I've been at many clubs before and since, and none can match what we had at Wimbledon.

I'd told Sam Hammam that I saw the club as a stepping stone to a bigger club, and I said to him: "If a big club comes in for me, please let me go." But to be honest, my biggest ignorance was that I never realised what I had at Wimbledon. We finished sixth and we reached two cup semi-finals. I can see now how good and how special those times were.

I'd been used to winning things at Rosenborg, so to not be as successful was almost a disappointment. But Wimbledon were a small club in a big league, and to compete and to do as well as we did was an amazing achievement. I wish I had realised that then.

Sam Hammam was a great guy. He loved the club. For him it was important that I and everyone he signed also loved the club. "You have to love the club to play for it", he said. The club was that little bit more special because of Sam.

I have quite a few good memories of my time there, but my debut will always stick out. A winner in the final minute – I couldn't have dreamed of a better start.

By Trevor Pearce (Supporter)

There's a bit in Nick Hornby's Fever Pitch which describes the perfect game: plenty of goals, with your team getting slightly more of them, and of course a big 21-man brawl at some stage.

This game didn't have the brawl as such, but after Warren Barton had scored on five minutes, and they had replied with three goals and a performance which promised a severe drubbing, we did get a bit of a flashpoint. From where I was standing, it was perhaps the only example in history of us getting the better of a contentious decision. Andy Townsend's tackle may have been a foul, but flashing an instant red card at him was the kind of ridiculous decision I'd have made if I'd had managed to get hold of the whistle before the game started. But who cares?

Norwegian joy: Oyvind Leonhardsen celebrates scoring in the final minute of his debut on 9 November 1994 to give the Dons a 4-3 win over Aston Villa. (Getty Images)

We were instantly transformed, getting a quick goal, and then from 35 yards out Vinnie crashed a shot into the post, right in front of me, for what would have been the best goal I'd ever seen a Wimbledon player score. But no matter, he went one better five minutes later by cracking a shot straight at Paul McGrath's ample posterior, and the ball rebounded past the prostrate keeper and trickled gently into the opposite corner of the goal. And when Leo popped in his 91st-minute winner, I think we all had one of those moments you get in football when you forget who you are, where you are, what the health and safety regulations of football stadia are, and just go absolutely stark raving mental.

◆

A DOUBLE NIGHTMARE FOR BARTON

In the second half of the season, Villa were to get ample revenge for the 4-3 defeat. But for Warren Barton, playing in his final season for the club, there was even worse to follow in the close season…

11 FEBRUARY 1995
Premier League
Aston Villa 7 Wimbledon 1
By Warren Barton (player)

We started off flying, we always did. But it turned out to be one of those days. They had seven chances and took every one. We just walked off and tried to forget it. When you lose 7-1, you just try and block it out of the mind as soon as possible. The harder we tried, the worse it seemed to get. Nothing was going right. We had turned them over enough times, so they were due a time to beat us.

We had started so well. Mick Harford won a header and it got knocked over to me. And I volleyed it over my shoulder and into the top corner.

A big stadium, a big crowd, and Wimbledon turn up and take the lead. We'd done that hundreds of times and we just thought we'd get another win, but we ended getting a big spanking. Joe wasn't happy – and for the sake of decency I won't reveal what he said after the match. But he came in on Monday and just told us all to forget it. There's no point reliving games like that.

At Wimbledon we always responded well to crisis. Next up was a trip to Anfield in the FA Cup, and I suspect every pundit in the world would have backed Liverpool. We came away with a 1-1 draw – and that's typical Wimbledon.

That was my best season at Wimbledon. I was named Evening Standard Player of the Month twice, and every week there was speculation linking me with one club or another. But that was nothing new. In my first year with the club, Brian Clough came in for me with a bid of £750,000. Sam turned that down. And to be honest I didn't really want to go then.

It was all different in 1995. I knew before the final game of that season that I was leaving. I actually thought I was off to Celtic. There was nothing concrete, but the rumours all seemed to indicate a move to Scotland. But the transfer speculation had been rife all year.

Earlier that same season, my agent had told me to get myself together and go and meet Graeme Souness at Blackburn. He said a deal had been done for me and Robbie Earle to go there, but Sam called it off. David Dein at Arsenal was also interested in me, but they didn't have a manager at the time. So that wasn't really on the cards.

In the end it was Newcastle that signed me. I found out later that the actual negotiations had begun after our 1-0 win at Sheffield Wednesday in mid-March. Kevin Keegan watched that game and got in contact with the club almost immediately. But Joe kept it between him and Sam. I didn't have a clue what was happening, but Joe and Sam were great. They just kept saying that they would look after me and see me right, and I trusted them. The move didn't go through until the summer.

My biggest regret at Wimbledon was the final game of that season at home to Nottingham Forest. I had won the Player of the Year, but I had picked up a slight injury and couldn't play. I had to walk onto the pitch to get the trophy with no Wimbledon shirt on. I'd wanted to play one more time for the club; I wanted to show the Dons fans what they meant to me. And to have to walk onto the pitch to get the award in a suit was a shame.

I used to have a laugh with the fans at Wimbledon – they were a great bunch and I miss them. I didn't want it to end like that. I was to play one last game as a Wimbledon player, but it's one I'd rather forget. It was my debut for England.

I had been in the squad for five or six months. I'd been itching to get my first run-out, and then I was told I would start against Ireland in Dublin. I was ecstatic. My girlfriend (now my wife) and my whole family came across. I was so excited.

It should have been the highlight of my career, but a small minority of so-called England fans had other ideas. Pumped up by racist hatred, they tore up seats and sparked what I can only describe as a full-scale riot. I was petrified. I was just shell-shocked – I couldn't believe what was happening.

I knew the Irish people – they just wanted to enjoy the game and have a Guinness. They didn't deserve this. I was worried for my girlfriend and my family. I was just stunned.

The England players were whizzed out of the stadium on a coach. I was almost in tears. Peter Beardsley came and sat next to me and was great. He told me to forget what had happened and said they would be other times.

Peter is one of the few great people in football. I remember when we played Liverpool at Plough Lane in 1990. They won 2-1, and he called me aside in the bar afterwards. He wasn't

Hooligan woe: Warren Barton in action on his England debut against the Republic of Ireland in Dublin. The match was abandoned after 30 minutes due to crowd trouble. (Getty Images)

even in their side that day. He said: "Forget the result – you played well, son." It was only my third game for Wimbledon. Now, five years later, his words were just as soothing, and in a month we would be team-mates at Newcastle.

◆

EUELL HEARS THE MUSIC

The 1995/96 season began well but five defeats in six games and an injury to Efan Ekoku gave a chance to a young Jason Euell. In the film Escape to Victory, Pele comes on and scores a superb overhead kick. Euell's debut will be remembered for a similar effort – except his was better.

28 OCTOBER 1995
Premier League
Wimbledon 1 Southampton 2
By Jason Euell (player)

As debuts go, I could hardly have dreamed of making a bigger impact. Paul Heald rolled the ball out of the area and kicked it long. I read the flip from Neil Heaney, and the ball just popped up behind me and I went into overhead mode and connected perfectly. It was the sweetest of contacts – the ball just went flying over my head and into the net.

You try that sort of thing at that age. It was the kind of goal you dream of scoring – 30 yards out, and bang. I can't recall ever seeing another goal like it, but that's thennaïvety of youth, I don't think I would try it now.

Marcus Gayle was closest to me, and I just jumped on him, and it was just mayhem – everyone mobbed me. For that second, I couldn't have been happier. But it wasn't all great – we ended up losing 2-1.

I only found out the day before that I was playing. I was training in the reserves on the Friday. Meanwhile, in the first team's session Efan Ekoku got injured, so Joe called me over and said I would be starting, I couldn't believe it. I had been in the squad before, once at home and once away. I think that was more of a learning curve to see what it was like.

I remember going into the dressing room before the game and thinking how amazing it was just to be involved in the warm-up, but it didn't really click that I was playing until the kit man handed over the shirt and I was going out there.

My family and friends went to a lot of games back then anyway, but as soon as I found out I was playing I tried to get as many tickets as possible so everyone could watch. I had been at Wimbledon for seven years and this was my pinnacle.

I was lucky that I came through the ranks. Every time there was a new signing, their clothes would get torn up, their cars would get trashed. You learned to expect the unexpected and all the jokes and prankster stuff made the club unique. And after my goal against Southampton I was firmly part of it.

◆

EKOKU SEALS YORKSHIRE COMEBACK

Wimbledon's season had been littered with more lows than highs, yet Joe Kinnear's side occasionally showed glimpses of what was to follow in the 1996/97 season. One such time came at the McAlpine Stadium when the Dons found themselves 2-0 down to Huddersfield Town in the FA Cup. An early exit was beckoning, step forward Efan Ekoku...

17 FEBRUARY 1996
FA Cup fifth round
Huddersfield Town 2 Wimbledon 2
By Efan Ekoku (player)

We were bashing them all game, but somehow they were leading 2-0. They must have had only two chances – it was one of the most one-sided games I had ever played in, but for 70 minutes we just couldn't score. Then finally I made it 2-1, and that set up the grand finale. We lay siege to their goal, and with time almost out we won a corner. As Alan Kimble went over to take it, I remember clear as day going over to the referee and asking him how long was left. He said: "We're in the last minute."

And that's when I knew it was now or never. We had this belief at Wimbledon, and the last thing we wanted to do was to go out to a lower-division side having dominated the game – that would have really hurt us.

Everyone was back in their area for the corner. Alan swung it in. The goalkeeper charged out to try and claim it, but it went over him and fell perfectly for me. It was quite an easy header really, one of those you just try to get on target and hope it gets through the crowd. It did, and they barely had time to kick-off before the final whistle went.

On paper, a 2-2 draw with Huddersfield doesn't look that hot, but it was one of the best performances we ever produced. If I was to pick one game that proved Wimbledon had a never-say-die attitude, this would be it.

When you are playing a team a division below you, you have to expect a fight, you have to expect them to come out and attack. But at Wimbledon we were used to battles and we were well up for this one. We knew what to do.

I remember coming in at half-time 1-0 down. Joe Kinnear would normally go off at us in those circumstances. But he was quiet, and just said: "Keep going. You're playing well enough – it will happen."

It had been a disastrous start. After just five or six minutes Neil Sullivan let the softest of shots creep through his legs. I then had a goal disallowed for offside, which was never offside. Mick Harford hit the bar. Then straight after the break, Oyvind Leonhardsen wasted two glorious chances.

Then it just went from bad to worse. Five minutes after the break their left-back, Tom Carr – all 5ft 5in of him – scored with a header from a corner. He looped the ball over everyone. How he out jumped our defence I will never know. We looked around, wondering how the hell we were 2-0 down.

We had no choice then but to go for it. The number of chances we kept missing was just amazing. Joe Kinnear was on the touchline. Normally he would be animated, jumping up and down, but he just stood there with his hands in his pockets. He couldn't do anything except watch.

Midway through the half Andy Clarke came on for Dean Holdsworth. He was a natural left-footer and he gave us this little extra bit of pace. He played in a good cross, and I got in a downward header. It was a good goal. It's pretty rare that I remember my goals, but that one is clear in my mind. I could name 10 misses just like that, but 10 goals is a different matter.

Then came my late equaliser. We knew we would finish them off at our place. They actually scored first, but in the end it was very comfortable and we won 3-1.

That season was the beginning of something special at Wimbledon. We were starting to gel and there were a few times when we clicked and we felt we couldn't lose to anyone. Against Huddersfield was one such time. And I suppose it was a marker to what was to follow the following season.

✦

The Spirit of Wimbledon

CHAPTER ELEVEN: THE FAILED PROMISE

BECKHAM RUINS THATCHER'S DAY

The 1996/97 season was to be arguably Wimbledon's finest ever. It began at home against Manchester United. The game will always be remembered for David Beckham's goal from the halfway line. But it was also Ben Thatcher's debut. And despite the defeat, the Dons' new left-back was settling in well at the mad world of Wimbledon.

17 AUGUST 1996

Premier League

Wimbledon 0 Manchester United 3

By Ben Thatcher (player)

It's not really what I would call an ideal debut. At home to the champions, Manchester United. In terms of big games it was amazing, certainly a step up from what I had been used to at Millwall.

But they absolutely destroyed us – and then there was David Beckham's goal. It was a great goal, but it's also a bit embarrassing to concede one like that too. It was the final minute. They were already 2-0 up so we were all pushing up to try and get a consolation and, well, we were just caught. The ball fell to Becks on the halfway line and the rest, as they say, is history.

I honestly thought then what the hell had I got myself in to. A few weeks earlier, when I signed, there hadn't been any doubt. I turned up at Sam Hammam's house in London. Me and Joe went for a walk around the streets of London and we talked about football, while my representative and Sam sorted out all the finances of the deal.

I had been living in digs in Sidcup while I was at Millwall, and then the club got relegated and all of a sudden they needed to raise £2m quickly. I went up to Leicester to talk to them, but I really wanted to stay in London. I didn't want to go to a new city and live on my own without knowing anyone.

It was then that I was told that Wimbledon had come in for me. It was perfect. It was all sorted out in 20 minutes. Sam said it was the quickest deal he had ever done.

I had heard what Wimbledon was like. I knew Jon Goodman and Kenny Cunningham from my days at Millwall, but I didn't really know what to expect.

Icon: David Beckham celebrates after scoring for Manchester United from the half-way line in their opening match of the 1996/97 season against Wimbledon. (Getty Images)

I was just 21. I remember going away on a pre-season tour with the likes of Alan Reeves, Stewart Castledine, Andy Thorn and Vinnie Jones. Those guys were absolute monsters, nutcases really. They would get up to anything and everything. It was a total eye-opener.

Everyone looked like animals. They were all 6ft 2in and there was absolutely no professionalism at all in pre-season. I had heard about the spirit, but this was just crazy. It was madness.

The first day of training after the tour, the lads got me good and proper. I had a shower, and when I came back in all my clothes were gone. I went outside with just my towel. My shorts were tied to the back of one car. My shoes were on the bumper of another, and my boxer shorts were hanging off an aerial, and my team-mates just drove round and round the gravel car park. Everything was ruined. I had to drive home with just my towel. It was all part of the way Wimbledon was. And it didn't stop when the season started.

Central to it all was Joe Kinnear. I have nothing but respect for Joe. I could fall out with him on a Monday morning and still be fuming at him in the afternoon. But there was something about him that meant you just couldn't hold a grudge against him. Joe valued the spirit of the club above everything else.

Banter goes on at every club, but Wimbledon took it to another level. There were no rules, no limits.

You had to take it or suffer. I remember Michael Hughes went mad once when someone cut his trousers up. And because he moaned for the next few weeks it happened to him every day.

But everything didn't always go smoothly. When John Hartson signed for us, I got a lighter and some fuel and set light to his suit. But the whole changing rooms caught fire too and I nearly killed six of the first-team squad.

But I loved the banter at Wimbledon. It was non-stop, and anyone could be behind it. Even the quietest of players used to get involved.

They used to take my passport away from me every time we went abroad and I used to get in a right panic. Then there was the time when they tied all my clothes together and had them dragged around the hall. They'd cut the handles off your bag. Something used to happen every day. You could be sitting down and take a bite out of your roll and someone would have put a tea bag in it. It could have been anyone out of 20 players, but most of the time it was Sam Hammam.

That spirit lifted us. So even though the United defeat was followed by defeats at Newcastle and Leeds, and even though we were propping up the whole table, we knew we would come back. And we did.

✦

ARDLEY'S EVERTON MASTERCLASS

After three defeats in a row, few people would have predicted what was to follow. A 1-0 win over Spurs gave a hint, but the 4-0 demolition of Everton put Wimbledon back on the map.

7 SEPTEMBER 1996
Premier League
Wimbledon 4 Everton 0
By Neal Ardley (player)

I f I was to pick one game out in my career at Wimbledon this would be it. I scored the first and set up the other three, two corners and a neat through ball to Efan Ekoku. Everton had finished sixth the year before and a lot of people believed that that season would be their renaissance. But we swamped them. Every pass went to feet, every tackle was clean and, most importantly, I seemed to be able to find the heads of our players from every cross.

My goal was not exactly a classic, but they do say when you take a free-kick whip it into the far post because if no one gets a touch then it's got a fair chance of going in. So there I was, more or less on the touchline about 40 yards out, and I hit it and no one got a touch.

We were a very set-piece oriented team then. That season, when I played, we would normally have Oyvind Leonhardsen on the left. He was not a natural crosser of the ball – he liked to cut inside and do short passes – so most of the set pieces and crosses were my responsibility.

We had two players who were great in the air: Robbie Earle, who scored 15 goals from midfield that year, and Marcus Gayle. Both of them scored from my corners that day.

It hadn't been the greatest start to a season. We had been beaten in our first three games and everyone was predicting we would go down. After the win at Spurs and the 4-0, we won the next five. It was the start of an 18-match unbeaten run that was to take us to two semi-finals.

I remember as the run stretched on and on, we began to feel invincible. We were taking huge pride in not getting beaten. By the middle of December we were right at the top. There were some people even suggesting we could win the title. It was all too much to believe. But I think deep down we knew there would be a point where we would slip up.

THE GRIT OF THE DONS

The 18-match run had come to an end with a 5-0 defeat at Villa Park, and in the League Cup the Dons drew Bolton away. The hosts were flying in the First Division, and an upset seemed to be on the cards. But Wimbledon had other ideas.

8 JANUARY 1997
Coca-Cola Cup fifth round
Bolton Wanderers 0 Wimbledon 2
By Robbie Earle (player)

It was easily the best season I enjoyed at Wimbledon. At Christmas we were just a few points behind the leaders with three games in hand. If we had won all of those we would have been something like five points clear at the top. And then there were the cup competitions too. We'd go on to reach the semi-finals of the both the League and the FA Cup.

That year we had great wins over Arsenal, Liverpool and Chelsea, but the victory at Bolton in the fifth round of the League Cup was just as special. They had a decent side then and went on to win the First Division championship. Earlier they'd beaten Southampton and Liverpool and they really fancied it.

They were a bit arrogant in the papers and were convinced they were going to beat us. And that just played into our hands. On the way up on the coach, the boys were just getting more and more pumped up – we wanted to show them. We wanted to prove what we were capable of.

And within 10 minutes they knew they were not going to win the game. Efan gave us the lead really early on and then Leo doubled it.

Every now and then you can sense when you are going to win a game even before it starts, and this was one of them. If I knew why that happens I'd have bottled it, and made my millions and I'd be sitting on a beach now. It's just one of those things.

That night we were awesome, everywhere you looked on the pitch Bolton were not going to get through.

In the end I suppose it was the success in the cups that ruined us. We were close to getting into Europe. It was Sam Hammam's last ambition for the club and it was mine too, but we just ended up playing too many games.

Perhaps, in hindsight, if we hadn't played so well at Bolton then maybe we would have been able to focus on the League and maybe Wimbledon would not have got into such a mess.

✦

EARLE'S OLD TRAFFORD REDEMPTION

Cup fever was now gripping the Dons. In the FA Cup they were given the hardest draw imaginable: away at Manchester United.

It is the final minute. It is the FA Cup. It is Old Trafford. Paul Scholes scores to make it 1-0. Surely there is no way back? Tell that to Robbie Earle.

25 JANUARY 1997
FA Cup fourth round
Manchester United 1 Wimbledon 1
By Robbie Earle (player)

For me there is only one game in my domestic career that truly sticks out. And this was it. We had been working on a game plan all week. We had it all sorted, we knew what we were going to do. We were going to shut them off at the back and hit the ball long down the channels. The intention was to stop them playing and to concentrate. And then, with about a minute left, Paul Scholes scored.

They had a free-kick – I can't remember who took it, but more than likely it was David Beckham. The defence pushed out as one, as they'd practised, but for some reason I stepped back. I knew I played him on, I was absolutely gutted.

We had worked so hard. We deserved something out of the game and I go and do something stupid like that. I was mad with myself. After all that, I thought we were going to lose. But then there was Alan Kimble's free kick. It was deep into injury time, deep.

I always had the same policy on free-kicks. There was always someone assigned to pick me up, so I'd try and stand next to someone else and hope the person who was supposed to be on me would see I was marked and leave me alone. So I went and stood next to Dennis Irwin, and it worked. Just before the ball came in, I drifted away from my marker. When the ball came to me I was actually free.

But then Alan also knew where to deliver the ball. I'd always try and get in line with the kick and the goalkeeper, and Alan knew to put it there.

As soon as the ball came in, I knew I was free. I took one glance to see where Peter Schmeichel was and that was it. I just concentrated on heading the ball into the corner and I knew he wouldn't get it. It was a really satisfying moment. It was great. I've seen videos of it since and it still makes me smile.

Redemption: Robbie Earle is swamped by team-mates after scoring a late equaliser against Manchester United in the fourth round of the FA Cup on 25 January 1997. (Getty Images)

I have always supported the underdogs. I like proving people wrong. And this was one of those moments.

I ran to the 1,000 Dons fans sitting up in the corner. There were 60,000 in red, but all I could see was the blue of Wimbledon. I loved it and they loved it. That moment said: "Little old Wimbledon is here and we're still fighting."

People didn't really take us seriously and that suited us. They used to have the impression that we were a glorified pub team, but that was a long way from the truth.

We'd work hard on tactics and systems, we were very thorough. And the Crazy Gang tag helped us immensely – people just underestimated us. Terry Burton is as good as there is tactically, but that would vastly underestimate the importance of Joe Kinnear. Joe would set the game plan and Terry would implement it. It was a real shame when that partnership came to an end. In my view they still had a lot to offer.

They would also let the players have their input, and we would debate it. Everyone was encouraged to air their opinion, from the youngsters like Jason Euell to the senior pros. So when it came to the game on Saturday, we were all thinking along the same line.

There was no room for blame culture. If the team didn't do well it was everyone's fault as we'd all agreed to the tactics, and that was the case with the draw at Old Trafford.

To concede a goal in the final minute was like a defeat for them. Psychologically, we'd won the tie.

By Martin Drake (supporter)

In the last minute Scholes prodded home a shot. I was distraught after the way we had played, but not as distraught as Robbie Earle, who had played Scholes onside.

A few minutes later, deep into injury time with the home fans whistling, Ole Gunnar Solksjaer mistimed a tackle on Kenny Cunningham on the near touchline and we won a free-kick. Eric Cantona rushed over to berate the referee for daring to award anything to us. His petulant and unnecessary intervention would prove costly to his team.

In what seemed like slow motion, Alan Kimble swung the ball in and Robbie Earle connected with a trademark header of such power that it seemed to go through Schmeichel and into the back of the net. Robbie ran to the ecstatic Wimbledon fans squeezed into the corner of the ground and the rest of the team mobbed him. I will never forget the look on Eric Cantona's face as he realised he should have been marking Robbie.

✦

GAYLE BLOWS OVER UNITED

After Robbie Earle's heroics at Old Trafford, it fell to Marcus Gayle to complete the job – and United, the League champions, were out.

4 FEBRUARY 1997
FA Cup fourth round replay
Wimbledon 1 Manchester United 0
By Marcus Gayle (player)

The ball just went straight to the centre of my head, Peter Schmeichel had no chance. It was just a case of being in the right spot at the right time. We had deserved to win at Old Trafford and in the end we had to work hard to get the replay. Robbie Earle's late header had saved us, but we had deserved so much more. We knew that, and this was the chance to put things right. It could have fallen to anyone, but I was the one who got the decisive goal in the replay.

I went to my mum's house the day after. She had bought every paper known to mankind, from The Sun to The Guardian and everything in between. I couldn't even see the carpets. She had the biggest smile on her face.

After the final whistle, I had been mobbed by the press and it was all "Marcus won the game", "Marcus did this" and "Marcus did that". But we were a team and it annoyed me that the rest of the side weren't getting the credit they deserved. One man cannot beat Manchester United on his own. It needed all of us – and we did it.

Joe Kinnear loved the big games. He loved rubbing their noses in it. He would gee us up and that night he instilled the spirit of Wimbledon in all of us. He didn't want us to try anything clever. We just stuck to our game and when the chance came we took it. The spirit was unbelievable in the side. We had a settled starting XI and we got on with it. And that helped in the big games.

We had been under the cosh the whole game, defending resolutely, and then midway through the second half Vinnie Jones took a short throw deep in their

Yes: An overjoyed Marcus Gayle punches the air in delight after scoring the winner in the fourth-round replay against Manchester United in the fourth round of the FA Cup on 4 February 1997. (Getty Images)

half to Kenny Cunningham, which I think surprised them as they were all expecting his usual long one. And then Kenny put in this wonderful curling cross. I could tell straight away that I was going to be on the end of it, and that was 1-0.

But you can never take anything for granted against Manchester United. Peter Schmeichel scored an overhead kick from a corner in the final minute. I remember his celebrations, but we were smart. We'd seen him come up and we played the offside trap. It worked and we held on.

I always go round to my family the day after a game. They are my biggest fans. They are also my biggest critics and they help keep my feet on the ground. But the day after the Manchester United game my mum was in the clouds. The morning after the game, she went into work, as a secretary in Kent, and they gave her a round of applause. It was like she had scored the goal herself. I think they gave her an extra hour off. I'd made her feel proud and that made me feel good.

It capped my season. It was my first as a centre-forward and for the first time I ended the season as the top scorer for Wimbledon. It was my most productive ever in the Premier League and I have very fond memories of that season and that goal.

My life changed after that. With all that media coverage, the anonymity I had enjoyed had gone. People started to notice me when I went to the shops. I suppose it's a fair price to pay for scoring the winner against Manchester United. And even now I get stopped in Kingston and reminded about that goal.

✦

DEANO KEEPS THE DOUBLE DREAM ALIVE

It was a huge week for Wimbledon. On the Sunday there was the FA Cup quarter-final against Sheffield Wednesday, and then two days later was the second leg of the Coca-Cola semi-final against Leicester City. First the quarter final…

9 MARCH 1997
FA Cup quarter-final
Sheffield Wednesday 0 Wimbledon 2
By Dean Holdsworth (player)

I was coming towards the end of my career at Wimbledon. I had had a brilliant time, but injuries kept plaguing me and I wasn't really fully fit for the trip up to Hillsborough. Sheffield Wednesday were a far better side then than they are now, and the stadium was full. It was an unbelievable test.

I was on the substitutes' bench. I wasn't the happiest substitute. Sometimes you don't agree with the manager and that was one of those times. But I was part of the team, part of the club. No one wants to be on the bench, but it's part of being in a squad – you have to accept it.

Robbie Earle had just given us the lead when Joe Kinnear came over and asked me to go on. I remember saying to the physio, Stevie Allen: "I bet I score." He wouldn't take it though.

They were desperate to equalise and that left loads of space up front, and I could tell that I'd get a chance.

Goalscorer: Dean Holdsworth, who scored the crucial second goal against Sheffield Wednesday in the 1997 FA Cup quarter-final. (Getty Images)

And sure enough, with time almost out, I scored. To score in such an important game, a quarter-final, is very special. Especially as it meant we were into the semis.

The game was on television, and I remember Leo had the broadest grin on his face as he jumped on me. I can still picture the delight on all the players' faces. We all started to think of Wembley. But amidst all the joy, bad news was beginning to dawn on me.

Moments before I scored, I got a bad knock on the chest. At the time I just ignored it. You just play on, especially in cup ties. The adrenalin gets you through it. But I had a couple of tests later and it was bad. I was out of Tuesday's match against Leicester and I was out of the FA Cup semi-final against Chelsea. I was inconsolable. Everyone wants to play in the big games and I'm no different.

The Premier League was our bread and butter, but the cup was special. We had built a reputation for rising to the big occasions. The two semi-finals should have suited us perfectly, but something somewhere went wrong.

✦

Frustration: Oyvind Leonhardsen (left) in action against Leicester City in the first leg of the Coca-Cola semi final on 18 February 1997. (Getty Images)

THE HEARTACHE OF LEICESTER

Could this finally be the season Wimbledon broke through? Two semi-finals awaited. The Dons had already held Leicester to a 0-0 draw at Filbert Street, surely they could complete the task at home? When Marcus Gayle gave Wimbledon the lead, the dream seemed to be turning into reality. Then came Simon Grayson's equaliser. Wimbledon poured forward looking for the vital second goal, but it would never arrive.

11 MARCH 1997

Coca-Cola semi-final second leg

Wimbledon 1 Leicester City 1

(after extra time; score at 90min; Leicester won on away goals)

By Chris Perry (player)

There wasn't that much hype before the game. It was the Coca-Cola Cup. It was over two legs and it was only Leicester and Wimbledon. The build-up was very lacklustre in the press. But for us the match meant the world. It was the dream of everyone at the club to get into Europe. We were doing well in the League and the FA Cup, but we all knew our best chance was the Coca-Cola Cup.

After we got the great draw at Leicester, we all felt that this was our year. We thought we had done the hard work. In the other semi-final, Middlesbrough had beaten Stockport County 2-0 away in the first leg so they were more or less already through. And we would have beaten them in the final.

After our victory over Sheffield Wednesday in the quarter-finals of the FA Cup, we knew we had Chelsea next, but that was going to be a much tougher route to Wembley. So the focus for us was really on the second leg against Leicester. And it is a game we should have won.

There was no lack of desire from the Wimbledon team. I grew up as a fan of the club – I used to stand on the terraces – but I didn't stand out in the dressing room. Every player at Wimbledon that night went out with the same passion for the club as I had. We were up for it.

Marcus Gayle gave us the lead midway through the first half and we looked like we were cruising. They weren't even in it. And then they scored straight after the break through Simon Grayson.

It was the luckiest header I have ever seen. It went in off the underside of the bar. Half a millimetre higher and it would have stayed out. Any lower and Sully would have saved it. We were camped in their half for the remaining 40 minutes of normal time and all of extra-time.

Efan Ekoku and Marcus Gayle were fantastic up front for us that year. They were the best forward partnership Wimbledon had ever had. With Alan Kimble and Neal Ardley's crosses and Vinnie Jones' long throws, the whole team was scoring for fun. You always felt we would get something from a set piece. Even I got a goal that season. We were an exciting team to watch. But sometimes it just doesn't happen for you, and the second leg against Leicester was one of those times.

We had chance after chance. We hammered them all night, but we just couldn't get the ball into the net. Kasey Keller was inspired in goal for them. I think he thwarted Marcus Gayle and Robbie Earle in normal time when I'd have put my house on them to score.

The agony only seemed to get worse as the game wore on. In the final two minutes Marcus had a header cleared off the line from Garry Parker, and then moments later he did it again this time denying Efan Ekoku. Nothing was dropping for us. Our luck had run out.

At the end I was gutted. We were all gutted and I left thinking: "What's this away goals thing all about?" The hardest thing about it was that we hadn't actually lost a game. It didn't seem fair that we were out. But I suppose it just wasn't meant to be.

The atmosphere was terrible in the dressing room afterwards. You could have heard a pin drop. In all my years at Wimbledon – and I had been at the club as a schoolboy – I had never known a dressing room so quiet. We were devastated. It was hard to take.

By Mark Lewis (supporter)

History books do not record the blood, sweat and tears of football matches very well. The 1966 World Cup Final result reads simply England 4 West Germany 2, with no mention of the dodgy third goal or the Russian linesman. The result of the Wimbledon-Leicester tie reads 1-1, but that does no justice at all to the valiant efforts made by all Wimbledon players and fans that night.

In all the years that Wimbledon played at Selhurst, there were very few games with any decent atmosphere – this night was one of those rare occasions.

Marcus Gayle put us ahead in the first half. Gayle's goalscoring ratio had tailed off badly after Christmas that season, but at the time this seemed like his most important goal ever for the Dons. With away goals counting double, a 1-0 lead seemed precarious. Simon Grayson confirmed our fears. The last 10 minutes, so nervy at Wembley in 1988, were soul-destroying that night.

At the final whistle it was Leicester who progressed to the final and ultimately they won the trophy and made it into Europe.

Wimbledon were arguably never the same again. Jones moved on the next year, Ekoku and Gayle's partnership was never as fruitful, and slowly but surely Kinnear's reign – and Wimbledon in general – came to a sorry end.

THE COLLAPSE AGAINST CHELSEA

After the disappointment of the Coca-Cola Cup, Wimbledon's season nose-dived. Of the five games that followed the Dons failed to win one. The focus was now on the FA Cup. But Chelsea changed their game plan, and what could have been the saving grace of Wimbledon's season turned into a rout. The heart and passion that had been so evident earlier in the season had simply worn itself out.

13 APRIL 1997

FA Cup semi-final (Highbury)

Chelsea 3 Wimbledon 0

By Chris Perry (player)

We had had such a fantastic season. We had had so many great results and we had played with such self-belief. It seemed almost inconceivable that we would end the year with no reward for our endeavours.

We had some great players – I was linked to England at the time – but the key to that season was that we all played well above ourselves. The spirit was great. The relationship between the manager and the players was fantastic. We were all friends. Everyone went out together. We would lie down and die for each other. We were all pushing for the same thing. We wanted to take the club into Europe.

After the hurt of Leicester, we were really up for the Chelsea game. We had beaten them 4-2 earlier in the season at their place and we went into the match full of confidence. In hindsight, perhaps we were too confident and maybe we allowed a bit of complacency to slip in.

The other big difference was the way they played. They changed their system completely. They went into the game to stifle us. No one had really done that to us before and we just didn't know what to do.

Game over: Wimbledon's Chris Perry (right) tussles with Mark Hughes during the FA Cup semi-final with Chelsea at Highbury on 13 April 1997. (Getty Images)

There's no hiding the fact that we were totally outplayed. No one really performed that day. If only we had got to half-time at 0-0 we would have been able to adjust a few things and have a real go at it. But Mark Hughes scored just before the break, and at 1-0 down in a semi-final we really didn't have any choice other than to start chasing the game. And we got caught.

I don't want to say too much about the second goal, to save Dean Blackwell's embarrassment. But there was little we could do about the third from Gianfranco Zola – it was a touch of class, a few nice moves and then an unstoppable shot.

We took the defeat far better than the loss to Leicester. We knew we didn't deserve anything. Of course we were despondent, but it was nothing like the gloom after the Leicester defeat. We had been beaten by the better team.

By Dean Holdsworth (player)

I was bitterly disappointed not to play against Chelsea. I wanted to take on the likes of Ruud Gullit, Gianfranco Zola and Mark Hughes. I had an injection in my shoulder the day before the match and I had no chance of playing.

It was so painful to watch. After all the hard work getting there we just didn't perform. Chelsea were simply better than us and they won 3-0. It was hard to take.

The season had promised so much and we finished with nothing. We drifted down to eighth in the table and didn't even get a Uefa Cup spot.

✦

CHAPTER TWELVE: THE FINAL FALL

ENTER THE NORWEGIANS

Sam Hammam had big ambitions for Wimbledon. The previous season had seen the club go tantalisingly close to his dream of European football. It was on the back of that success that he persuaded two Norwegian businessmen, Kjell Inge Roekke and Bjorn Rune Gjelsten, to pay a reported £30m for an 80 per cent stake in the club.

SUMMER 1997

By Sam Hammam

When I came to Wimbledon it was no bigger than AFC Wimbledon is now, except we were a few divisions above where they are now. For me my greatest achievement was to take the club into the Premier League and to keep it going there. A miracle happened. A dream happened. It was the most miraculous achievement in sport, not just in football. A fairy-tale happened, but it had a tragic ending like Swan Lake or Romeo and Juliet.

In my opinion, what screwed Wimbledon was the Norwegians. I wanted to secure the future for the club and they had the money to do it. I wanted to take the club to a new dimension. But I fell out with Kjell almost immediately. He wanted to sell a lot of players and I said that was suicide. If the club got relegated we would lose £10-15m a season, but he wouldn't listen.

I was still there, but I was gone. I had no involvement. I stayed to try and keep my family happy but I was doing nothing.

I remember meeting Louise Carton-Kelly a year or two later. I told her Wimbledon had gone. It was dead. We couldn't return and we couldn't stay at Selhurst. Either way Wimbledon dies. We spoke for three hours and we talked about the possibility of setting up a new Wimbledon.

Viking support: Wimbledon fans welcome the arrival of the Norwegians in 1997. (Getty Images)

THE DUBLIN FIASCO

In the stands, the arrival of the Norwegians – and all the money they had – brought a new sense of optimism. It was to evaporate almost immediately when the club proposed a move to Dublin. It seemed ridiculous, but the idea had the backing of Sam Hammam, the new owners and leading Irish politicians. The Saturday after the news broke – at home to Southampton – the Wimbledon stands were awash with anti-Dublin banners, and chants of "We'll never go to Dublin" echoed out.

7 DECEMBER 1997
Premier League
Wimbledon 1 Southampton 0
By Robert Dunford (supporter)

December 1997, a period for traditional festivities, like putting up Christmas decorations, carol singing, excessive shopping and – for us – protests against Wimbledon. It started at the Southampton game, but it went on for weeks after too. Banners at games, badgering Merton Council, media coverage – you name it, it was good practice. However, while all this was going on in London, questions on the other side (so to speak) were being asked. Had the FAI clubs been bought off by promises of good times by the Dublin Dons? Anyway, two concerned Wombles, plus myself, were contacted by the state Irish broadcaster RTE to give our side of the story for the Gaelic language programme SportIris. We agreed, and after some cross-sea communications, we all congregated on a chilly December afternoon at Waterloo station.

The presenter for RTE, a nice woman called Deirdrie niFloinn, had an impressive ability to find us in Waterloo station. Well, not quite – we were in the bar. After the Irish government lubricated three Wombles with alcoholic beverages (a good start), we were all taken to a lovely spot on the Thames by the Houses of Parliament.

Were we about to be used as pro-Dublin propaganda? Bertie Ahern was in favour of the move, Hammam was claiming wide support and we were just fodder, weren't we?

We all spoke eloquently about our plight (well, two of us did anyway), about why it was wrong and why Irish football would suffer. The same old reasons. It all went on tape, and to our surprise they showed the utmost sympathy for our plight.

It turned out that earlier that day, Ms niFloinn had made the pilgrimage to Plough Lane to do some filming. I have no idea what effect this had in the editing of the piece, but our propaganda fears proved to be unfounded.

The high point of that afternoon was when the film crew's driver, a London man no less, said to us: "Good luck, hope you beat them and stay in London."

Although none of us wanted to believe it, it felt as if we had won over RTE. The proof was in the pudding. A polite request saw a copy of the programme (broadcast 18 December 1997) sent over. In between reports for rugby in Limerick and a snooker competition, there we were. The report (subtitled in English) featured ourselves, an interview with a rather moribund Joe Kinnear and some FAI top brass. It seemed to dwell on our side of the story, and best of all it wasn't a cheerleading pro-Dublin Dons piece.

We had penetrated an important audience, namely the ordinary sports fans of Ireland, and they got to hear what we thought of Hammam's plan.

To this day, we have no idea what effect that programme had or how many people watched it, but at least we had done our bit against Dublin. When hearing the news that Dublin was finally dead in the water – due to a stadium casino plan being rejected, officially – amongst the jubilation and relief was a wry smile or two. Much worse wars were to be fought, but at least the money RTE paid us came in handy...

Anger: Wimbledon fans protest against the proposed move to Dublin. (Getty Images)

LEABURN BECOMES A TRUE DON

The arrival of the Norwegians had promised so much, but with power struggles off the pitch and the shadow of the previous season's success hanging over the club, it was inevitable that Wimbledon would struggle on it. The club finished the season in 15th place – their lowest position in 12 years. Joe Kinnear tried everything to rally his team. His usual foil, Terry Burton, had been given a year's sabbatical to study coaching methods overseas, and left to his own devices Kinnear failed to find the necessary inspiration. The season would have few highlights, the most memorable of which was provided by the club's latest signing, Carl Leaburn.

9 FEBRUARY 1998
Premier League
Crystal Palace 0 Wimbledon 3
By Carl Leaburn (player)

I had been at the club just a matter of weeks without doing too much, so by the time of the Palace game I was keen to prove myself. I had been at Charlton for such a long time; it was a very difficult decision to leave. But I remember speaking to Sam and he said: "Carl, just give Wimbledon a chance and it will get into your blood." My first game was at Anfield (I came on as a substitute and we lost 2-0) and then I had my first start at home to Derby. We drew that 0-0.

Then came Palace. It was a great game and to score twice took the pressure off me. Michael Hughes was the provider for both of them. They were both headers, and if I'm going to be honest the goalkeeper probably should have stopped them, but each time they slipped from his grasp and went in. And that just cranked up the derby atmosphere a little bit more.

For the third I got the knock-back for Jason Euell to tap in. And that just sealed a great all-round performance for me. Winning derby matches is always special, but winning 3-0 is even better, and to play such a key role in it as well...

I fell in love with Wimbledon very quickly. The club had such a unique spirit. It wasn't just the players. It was all the staff, the fans and everyone all the way up to the chairman. And that's what helped the club achieve so many great results.

When I arrived the players cut up all my clothes, but apparently that was quite mild compared with what happened to some of the other players.

In those days the club was more or less run by the senior players. The father of the club was Robbie Earle, and Vinnie was there as the elder statesman. They made sure everything ticked over.

But in terms of antics you didn't really have to look much further than Ben Thatcher. Ben, Andy Roberts, Brian McAllister and Peter Fear – they were the pranksters.

Celebration time: A jubilant Carl Leaburn celebrates scoring against Crystal Palace on 9 February 1998. (Getty Images)

If something happened usually Ben was behind it. In the outside world most people didn't really know much about what Ben was getting up to and he wasn't really regarded as one of the characters. But those in the know knew.

The club was just all so different from Charlton. Superficially, the two clubs were quite similar then: small, family-oriented clubs in South London. But whereas Charlton were the well-adjusted hard-working club, Wimbledon was the naughty schoolboy. The pranks and jokes that went on at Wimbledon, I honestly think the players at Charlton wouldn't have been able to cope. It was literally the Crazy Gang.

What Sam had said to me was true. Wimbledon did get into my blood. And the best compliment I can pay to Wimbledon is that I didn't miss Charlton at all. I stayed in touch with the players there and I still love the club, but Wimbledon was just so different.

I was quite lucky that I was able to integrate quickly into the Wimbledon way. Within a few weeks, I felt like I had been at the club for ages. Perhaps those two goals against Palace helped more than I ever knew.

✦

EARLE'S SLICE OF WORLD CUP HISTORY

After a disappointing League campaign, the domestic season was put to one side as the World Cup in France took centre stage. The former Dons captain, Robbie Earle, is arguably the greatest player never to be capped by England, but that summer he was to get his moment of international fame. It came for his adopted country Jamaica in the small stadium of Stade Félix-Bollaert in Lens with 44 minutes gone.

14 JUNE 1998
World Cup finals
Croatia 3 Jamaica 1 (Stade Félix-Bollaert)
By Robbie Earle (player)

When you've played with certain players long enough, you build an understanding. You can tell what they are going to do in certain situations. And when I saw Ricardo Gardner on the flank, I knew what was coming. I knew he was going to hit the ball in early. I could tell by the shape of his body. And from that I knew instinctively what I was going to do.

Igor Stimac was marking me, but he had no idea what was coming. I knew we were going to score from that move even before Ricardo had crossed it. I could sense it.

I jumped early and I remember seeing the flight of the ball and as soon as the ball hit my head I knew straight away.

I turned away as soon as I headed it. I knew it was in; I didn't have to see it hit the net. When it works right, you don't have to look. You just know. On that occasion I knew.

It was a classic header. Any Dons fan must have seen me score hundreds of goals like that, but then I don't expect the Croatian management had been to many games at Selhurst Park.

It was a big vindication for me. I'd been so close to the England squad on so many occasions. I'd won a smattering of England B caps and had been on standby for the senior squad a couple of times. I knew I had something to offer at that level.

When I got back into the changing room, I had a message from John Rudge, who had been my manager at Port Vale. He was ecstatic. He'd had faith in me from when I was a youngster. I remember him saying: "I told you you had it in you, Robbie. I told you."

There was also a message from Sam Hammam. He loved moments like this. "You done it Robbie, you done it," he said. "You've put Wimbledon on the world stage."

Looking back on it all now, it was an unbelievable feeling. I wish I had taken it in more. I got phone calls and text messages galore from the players at Wimbledon. They were calling from bars in Spain and Corfu where they'd been watching the game with a Bud. Even the Prime Minister of Jamaica sent his regards.

The magnitude of it all didn't really hit home until much later. I've met hundreds of people since, who can recall exactly where they were when I scored. And that's made me realise how important it really was.

For Jamaica, it was huge. There was a sense of real pride. It was the breakthrough the country had always wanted. Cameroon and Nigeria had shown they could compete on the world stage and now we had done it too.

We lost the game 3-1 in the end, but we had not been disgraced. For us all, it was overwhelming. This was the World Cup. It was an amazing atmosphere; none of us had ever played on a stage like that. And I think in the end our inexperience told. We didn't know how to control the excitement.

History maker: Robbie Earle (right) makes history for Jamaica by scoring their first World Cup goal at the Stade Félix-Bollaert on 14 June at France '98. (Getty Images)

We were holding our own when Mario Stanic gave them the lead just before the half hour. And when I scored to equalise just before the break, the boys started to believe in themselves. We became too adventurous. Not over confident, but perhaps over ambitious. We were all convinced we could go out and win the game. If my goal had come in the 80th minute perhaps then we would have decided to hold on. But we wanted to win and our lack of patience and discipline costs us.

Robert Prosinecki scored shortly after the interval, and when Davor Suker made it 3-1 that was basically it. I was substituted shortly after.

A week later we were given a lesson by Argentina. Gabriel Batistuta got a hat-trick as we lost 5-0. But the tournament ended on a high when we beat Japan 2-1 with Theodore Whitmore scoring both.

But the highlight for me has to be that goal against Croatia; it will live with me forever. And in the record books it will always say that Robbie Earle scored the first World Cup goal for Jamaica.

✦

EKOKU SEALS THE AMAZING COMEBACK

By the start of the 1998/99 season, Wimbledon had reverted to type. They were once more the bookmakers' favourites for the drop. The rest of the Premier League had seen an influx of new talent. The Argentinians, the French and the Italians were arriving. Wimbledon did nothing. It was to irk with some of the players, but the old never-say-die attitude was still there, even though Vinnie Jones had gone. It was put to the sternest of tests at Upton Park, when the Dons found themselves 3-0 down.

9 SEPTEMBER 1998

Premier League

West Ham United 3 Wimbledon 4

By Efan Ekoku (player)

It's always difficult watching as a substitute. You always want to be out there playing. They had out-passed us in the first half. They'd had three chances and taken them all, Ian Wright scoring twice and John Hartson getting the other. They must have thought the game was over.

Marcus Gayle gave us a bit of hope with a header before the break, but at 3-1 down we were shell-shocked.

Joe Kinnear didn't say much at half-time. I admired Joe and what followed in the second half was an example of the spirit he brought to the side. He said: "Just get a goal and we're back in it." I was sitting there thinking: "He's bound to bring me on, he's bound to bring me on." I just had a feeling that I would do something.

West Ham hardly had a kick in the second half. Marcus and Jason made it 3-3 and once I came on I knew I would score.

There was only five minutes left. West Ham had a corner and almost everyone was in our box. Neil Ruddock was the only one back for West Ham defending.

The ball was cleared to me out on the edge of the box. I toyed with the idea of running 60 yards with it, but I had only just come on as a substitute and I wasn't really into the flow of the game yet.

Jason Euell was furthest forward for us, so I hit a long diagonal ball towards him, more to relieve the pressure on our defence than anything else. I just followed it up.

Jason managed to control it and I was the quickest up there in support. He hit the ball straight to me. I could see the shape of the

Late strike: Efan Ekoku (centre) celebrates his late winner against West Ham United on 9 September 1998. (Getty Images)

cross, so I decided it was going to be a diving header. I probably had time to control it and have a shot, but I had made my mind up.

I remember David James coming out so I headed it back across him.

It was incredible and it sealed an amazing comeback. We were 3-0 down after half an hour, and few teams will ever come back from that to win away from home.

Personally, the goal had huge significance as well. It was a difficult time for me at Wimbledon. I had said I wanted to leave. The fans didn't take it that well and Joe had dropped me to the bench. So it was extra-sweet for me. A lot went in to that goal. It was probably the most satisfying goal I have ever scored.

Off the pitch, all these promises were being made about how the club would be improved. The Norwegians were saying this and that, but I was getting sick and tired of all the empty promises.

I wanted to stay as long as they rewarded the players who had shown such good service over the years. Things were stuck in that respect, and I was well within my rights to leave.

The club talked a lot about losing £2m a year, but that was never really the case. They were in a position to offer more money. They had the cash, but they never looked to invest – they weren't interested in the playing side.

I felt after the two or three years we had had that with just one or two more additions we could have broken into the top six and made it into Europe.

We couldn't rely on the same players year in year out. If Arsenal, Liverpool and Manchester United felt they needed to strengthen each year, then clubs like Wimbledon certainly needed to as well.

But the Norwegians didn't share that vision, and that's why I decided to leave.

My transfer request angered Joe. I suspect that's why I was on the bench, and that made my winner all the more special. It justified my place in the side and it also said to the Norwegians that I had a point.

Overall though, I loved my time at Wimbledon. It just soured in those last few months. By the end of that season the writing was already on the wall and I was off.

I remember talking to some of the players in December 1999 and they were already talking about relegation. In three seasons the club had gone from challenging for three trophies into freefall.

✦

ANOTHER SEMI, ANOTHER HEARTACHE

Despite mediocre form in the League, Joe Kinnear had once more rallied his team in the cup. This time it was Spurs, and again Wimbledon drew 0-0 in the first leg. Surely this time they would make it. The answer was no, and for Kinnear it was to be his last big game in charge of the club.

16 FEBRUARY 1999
Coca-Cola Cup semi-final second leg
Wimbledon 0 Tottenham 1
By Ben Thatcher (player)

At the time every game seemed to be against Spurs. We had drawn them in the FA Cup and that went to a replay, then there were the two semi-final legs of the Worthington Cup, and I think we played them in the League as well – all that in the space of a month. It was mad, but there was no doubt what was the most important of the lot: the semi-final.

The cups were always going to be our best chance of success, but the problem with Wimbledon is that the '88 Cup final always hung over us. There was always this anticipation around cup ties.

And what's worse is that it wasn't the greatest Spurs side ever, and we really fancied our chances. A lot of the players weren't even concentrating on the League; it was all about the semi-final.

Joe Kinnear had everyone pumped up. Robbie Earle and Kenny Cunningham were the calming influences, but we were all so determined.

The week before the first leg at White Hart Lane I was unwell during training. Joe asked me if I'd be all right. I said: "Yeah." So, he decided to risk it. I'd have been happy to come off if it didn't work, but I was fine and we got what we were after. We dug deep and held them 0-0. It wasn't a classic, but it was all set up for us for the return.

I remember the crowd was buzzing for the second leg. Wembley was beckoning. We already knew that we would face Leicester in the final. It was as good chance as we would ever get to reach the final. It was those sort of games you live for, the chance to get a medal, and we were close, very close.

We were all working 110 per cent. We were throwing our bodies in front of the ball, getting the blocks in, getting the tackles in. It was relentless. We so wanted it. And then it went wrong.

The ball fell to Steffen Iversen; he looked offside to me. Dean Blackwell got the challenge in as he shot and the ball just deflected off him and over Neil Sullivan. It was heart-breaking. You can accept defeat if a player beats two and scores or if someone scores with a 30-yard shot, but a goal like that – it was so disappointing.

We spent the last 10 minutes laying siege to their goal, but nothing dropped for us. Kenny Cunningham and I were acting as wingers, the whole idea of trying to defend had gone. We desperately wanted to score. I remember Robbie Earle went close deep into injury time, and then it was over.

Tottenham fans will probably talk about the fact that they lived with us, they survived the Wimbledon assault and earned their place in the final. But in reality it was just a lucky break.

We never really recovered from that. We had put so much effort into the semi-final and the first half of the season, and now we were exhausted mentally.

Then came the blow that tore the club apart: Joe Kinnear's heart attack. Joe had been vital to the team spirit and, although we had been going through a bad spell, you always felt with him in charge we could turn the corner. But with Joe off the scene, you could sense the spirit seeping out of the club.

✦

HARTSON – AND KINNEAR'S HEART ATTACK

The season had promised so much. A few months before the club reached the semi-final against Tottenham, Joe Kinnear had smashed the club transfer record to sign John Hartson for a staggering £7.5m from West Ham United. It was part of his masterplan to take the Dons into Europe. And even after defeat in the semi-final, the Dons were still sixth; a place in the Uefa Cup was still achievable. And then it all came to an end. Joe Kinnear had a heart attack.

3 MARCH 1999
Sheffield Wednesday 1 Wimbledon 2
Premier League
By John Hartson (player)

Heart attack:
Joe Kinnear.
(Paul Willatts)

Joe's heart attack was a huge blow. A lot of the players knew Joe a lot better than I did, but you didn't have to spend long at the club to realise how much of an influence he was. I had had a fair few meetings with Joe before I signed, and that's when I really got to know the man. It was a big, big decision to join Wimbledon FC. Joe spent a lot of money on me.

I signed at Sam Hammam's house in St John's Wood. Joe Kinnear was there as well, and the pair of them said they wanted to spend a lot more money. They had big ambitions. We were going to push for Europe. The club was sixth in the League and still in both cups. The future looked rosy and their dreams seemed achievable. The club had some great players and I could see the potential.

They were an excellent pair. And then there was Mick Harford. I'd worshipped him at

Luton – I used to clean his boots. He was a legend. The move seemed perfect.

The club had all these great players and all these great characters. There was Ben Thatcher. He is a great mate of mine still. We'd played against each other numerous times as youngsters; Ben at Millwall and me at Luton. Our girlfriends became friends as well. I also got on great with Marcus Gayle. Robbie Earle was fantastic too; he was a great captain. He's gone on to great things now on TV. He would make a great manager. There was Alan Kimble. We both bought greyhounds at the same time. And then there was Dean Blackwell. Deano had been there and seen that. He was the link to the old Plough Lane days. He knew Wimbledon, he knew what the club really meant. You had to respect him.

The list went on and on. They were all great players and great characters. And the fans at the club were among the most loyal I have ever known – they were superb to me from day one. That's what I loved about the club. It had such a unique spirit, from the fans to the players. It's a spirit I have never experienced before or since. I would love to have played in the great Wimbledon sides with the likes of Lawrie Sanchez, John Fashanu, Vinnie Jones and Dennis Wise when the spirit was at its peak. That would have been some experience. And behind it all was Joe Kinnear. He was a great man-motivator. He inspired the team.

I felt that under Joe we could really do something. I wasn't fully fit at the time, but I knew that once I was, and, with the rest of the players who were there, we could make Europe.

And then Joe had his heart attack.

It happened just before the Sheffield Wednesday game. I was suspended or injured for the game, I can't remember which, but I wasn't there and I remember clearly seeing it break on the news. It hit me hard straight away. Joe had spent all that money on me. Joe had shown faith in me and now he was in trouble. Joe epitomised everything that Wimbledon stood for. He was easily the best manager Wimbledon ever had. Bobby Gould may have won the FA Cup for the club, but it was Joe who was able to get the best out of his players. Under Joe, the club used to finish in the top 10 as a matter of routine.

If Joe Kinnear had stayed healthy and fit I would have stayed; it could have been so different.

We were sixth at the time and were still in the chase for a Uefa Cup place, but we went on the slide after that. We failed to win any of our remaining 11 matches that season and only just avoided relegation.

◆

THE EGIL LANDS AS PERRY DEPARTS

Joe Kinnear's heart attack left the club in turmoil. The Norwegians avoided the temptation to promote from within. They wanted to bring in a high-profile manager. They turned to their homeland and persuaded the former Norwegian national coach Egil Olsen to take over. He failed to click with the players. The club's central defender Chris Perry didn't like what he saw, and after just one day under Olsen he left. He was right to be concerned – the club would slide to relegation.

JULY 1999

Wimbledon's training ground

By Chris Perry (player)

When the Norwegians took over it all started to go wrong. Little things were happening all over the place. All the routines we had become used to were slowly being altered. I just didn't think it was going to get any better. I could see the end was coming nearer. I remember the day Egil Olsen turned up. There he was with his green wellies. He wanted to make his mark on the club straight away and he called all the players together and made a speech. He explained what ambitions he had for the club and the direction he saw the club heading in. He obviously didn't mention relegation.

It wasn't the kind of speech we were used to hearing. There was none of the banter and the passion. I just looked around and I knew it was time to leave. I joined Tottenham for £4m the next day. I could see the problems ahead and I didn't want to be part of it all.

No one likes to be relegated, and I'm lucky it's never happened to me in my career. But as a Dons fan I was so sad the day we went down. The injuries didn't help, but that happens to every club. You have to cope with it – and Wimbledon didn't.

Spurs played Wimbledon a few weeks before the end of the season, and I would love to have done them a favour. It really hurt me to see the state they were in, but you have to be professional about it. Spurs won 2-0.

By John Hartson (player)

The problems were mounting all over the place, once the club changed management. I had my knee operation. Kenny Cunningham, Robbie Earle and Ben Thatcher all picked up long-term injuries and suddenly the heart of the team had been ripped out. All the responsibility fell to the younger players. And we just kept sliding. It was all very sad for the club.

Sam was on his way out too, and the club spent most of that season trying to off-load me. I didn't understand it. I wanted to do all I could to lift the club, yet it seemed that every week I was attending another medical to join another club. I kept failing them and that just made it even more difficult. It must have looked like I didn't want to stay, but I did.

Given all that, my record at the club wasn't too bad. I scored something like 23 goals in 50 odd games. It wasn't prolific, but given what was happening off the pitch it was still respectable. My regret is that it wasn't enough.

✦

THE ELBOW

Egil Olsen's appearance failed to impress the press, who were used to the charisma of Kinnear. They were after Egil from the off, and at the turn of the year they got a gift courtesy of the elbow of Ben Thatcher. It was an image emblazoned across all the back pages.

3 JANUARY 2000

Premier League

Wimbledon 1 Sunderland 0

By Ben Thatcher (player)

It was just one of those things that happen. I regret it massively. It was a big game for us. They were rising up theere at the top of the Lleague and looking to move into the top three. WAnd with about half an hour gone I went charging down the left., I tangled with Nicky Summerbee and I caught him with my elbow. The major problem was that we scored from it. I fed Martin Andresen and he chipped the ball in for Carl Cort to score the only goal of the game. If that hadn't happened then maybe ithe incident wouldn't have got all the coverage it did.

But I knew I had done wrong. I came off and straight away I apologised to Sam Hammam. And all he said to me: "What are you sorry for, Ben? We have got the three points."

I'm not sure if he had seen the incident, he must have, but I'm not sure. And then I got my bad news. I had taken a knock and it turned out to be a broken ankle. I didn't play again until the final two games of the season.

It's among the most painful experiences a footballer can ever go through, sitting on the sidelines as your team loses game after game and slips closer and closer to relegation.

While I was out, Sam finally sold up and left. He hadn't really been running things for a while, but with him gone the final ties to the old Crazy Gang were being severed.

But things had been going wrong off the pitch for months before that.

The spirit that had kept us going for all those years was on the wane. It had been on the wane even before Egil Olsen arrived, but once he was in it almost disappeared completely.

Everything was new. Being a foreigner, he had a very different mentality to what some of us were used to. Not to say he was wrong, or Joe Kinnear before him was wrong, it was just different. He also brought a load of Scandinavians with him and that watered down the Crazy Gang way of life as well. They had their own humour and their own jokes and it didn't blend well with ours.

Some of the players had issues with him, but I never had a problem with the man. I got on fantastically with him. I fundamentally believe you have to adapt your game to the way the manager wants to play and I was able to do that. For others, it wasn't so easy.

Things were changing, you could sense it. Most of the players had lost interest, and when I came back, Egil had gone and Terry Burton was in charge. I wasn't 100 per cent fit, but I wanted desperately to rescue the situation and Terry knew that.

✦

Anger: Ben Thatcher catches Sunderland's Nicky Summerbee with his elbow during the Dons' 1-0 win in the Premier League on 3 January 2000. (Getty Images)

BURTON TAKES CHARGE

The Dons travelled to Valley Parade two points above Bradford City, who occupied the last relegation place with three games left. After a 3-0 defeat there, relegation beckoned, and with the last throw of the dice Wimbledon turned to Terry Burton.

30 APRIL 2000
Premier League
Bradford City 3 Wimbledon 0
By Terry Burton (manager)

It was only when the shit started hitting the fan that I finally got involved with the first team. I had spent the year as director of the academy – a million miles away from the first team. Then Egil Olsen called me in and asked me if I wanted to come and work for the first team. The team only had three games left and relegation was looming. The very next match was the key: away to Bradford, who were battling with us to avoid the drop.

I remember travelling up for the game – there was Egil, a couple of other coaches and myself. We had more staff than players.

The game itself was a debacle. There was a bad penalty, John Hartson got sent off and somehow we ended up losing 3-0. Yet, we had played well and deserved to get something out of the game. That was the defining moment of the season: it sealed our fate.

Straight after the game my mobile rang. It was David Barnard, the club's chief executive. He explained that the club's owners wanted me to attend a meeting in central London as soon as I got back to the capital.

So I went, and they got straight to the point. They said they were sacking Egil and would I look after the last couple of games?

My relationship with Egil Olsen was a bit distant, but that was to be expected. We were doing very different jobs. There were the common courtesies, the hellos here and there, but that was it.

You could tell things were going wrong. The spirit on the pitch had gone. There was nothing stopping the players having the same camaraderie off the pitch, but the football habits we had developed over decades on the pitch were on the wane.

The players were getting away with murder. Nobody was taking responsibility. Their application and attitude was not the same and a few of the players had given up the fight. They had almost accepted relegation. The fear had gone out of them.

They had become lazy, the caring side had gone. A lot of them thought they were better than Wimbledon.

Egil didn't help, he wasn't clamping down on them. If a manager does nothing, no one is going to get a grip, and all of a sudden we were on our way down.

When I came in I tried desperately to re-instill the fear. I painted the picture for them. I explained that we had two games left to try and save our Premiership status. I made it very black and white.

But team spirit is built over years and it can be lost in a very short space of time. You can't just switch it back on.

A few of the players rallied and we tried to prove that we were strong enough to stay up. Against Aston Villa we did that, but at Southampton their legs went to jelly. They bottled it.

Changing times: Terry Burton (left) shouts words of encouragement to the Wimbledon players against Bradford City on 30 April 2000 as Egil Olsen sits down in what turned out to be his last game in charge of the club. (Getty Images)

HARTSON'S HEADER

Cometh the hour, cometh the man. With seconds left, John Hartson's header seemed to have salvaged Wimbledon's season. The Dons were back above Bradford and the escape seemed on.

6 MAY 2000

Premier League

Wimbledon 2 Aston Villa 2

By John Hartson (player)

It was a huge occasion. There was a big crowd and a massive anticipation. I had only been on for 20 minutes. We were trailing 2-1. There were just seconds left. We knew Bradford were losing and we knew a point would take us out of the relegation zone and give us some hope of survival. And then I scored.

It should be a great memory, but hindsight tarnishes it. It was great at the time, but it was all to no avail – we still went down. And now it is hard to separate the joy of the day from the pain that followed.

Of course, we never should have been in that situation. Egil Olsen was a nice man, but he had lost the dressing room and when that happened he had to go. I mouthed off about it after the Bradford game and I regretted it straight away. Despite his faults, Egil didn't deserve that.

The Bradford game had been shocking – their penalty, my sending off – nothing went right for us. We were 1-0 down at half-time and straight after the break Carl Cort fired a shot over. We felt we were really in it. And then I got sent off. We lost 3-0.

I carried a lot of the blame for that defeat on my shoulders. It really hurt me. I felt responsible. I wanted to make amends. I knew I would miss the last game of the season through suspension. So the Villa game was really my last chance to do something. And here I was sitting on the bench watching helplessly as we were trailing 2-1 to a very good side. It was agony for me. I so wanted to be out there.

By the time I came on we were camped in their half, but nothing was really falling for us. And then it came. It was deep into injury time. The ball came across from a corner. I headed it and in it went. I honestly thought that was it. I had made up from my indiscretion at Valley Parade.

The celebrations were fantastic. It gave us a glimmer of hope. It was a lovely memory, but it was also not a lovely memory. All the celebrations and all the joy that followed, would ultimately mean nothing.

I remember the changing rooms after the game. I had Ben Thatcher jumping all over me – he was delighted. All we had to do was match whatever Bradford did the next week…

By Sam Elliott (supporter)

Ask any Dons supporter and they would be able to count on one hand the number of enjoyable experiences at Selhurst Park. The penultimate match of the 1999/2000 season was one of them.

As I arrived at a sun-baked Selhurst, there seemed something different about the surroundings not felt for a few seasons. With the Dons now perilously close to the Premiership trapdoor after being beaten by Bradford City, the need for a win against Aston Villa was clear. Everyone was tense, but the appointment of Terry Burton had brought a new level of optimism.

Our hearts may have been fixed on the action in front of us, but our ears were listening to news from Bradford's trip to Leicester.

After a few close scares, the Dons grabbed the critical advantage. A swinging cross by Neal Ardley aimed at Marcus Gayle was turned into his own net by Ugo Ehiogu. But relief was to turn to despair as a second-half collapse handed the lead to Aston Villa.

Time was running out for Burton and the Dons. First Division football was beckoning. But Bradford were losing, so a point would take us out of the relegation zone, just one point. There was only one option. Burton called for Hartson.

Chances came and went for both sides, but the running of Francis and Ardley gave the smallest flicker of hope. As 90 minutes came, all eyes were on the fourth official with the board. The illuminated three minutes were greeted with a roar of hope. It was now or never. The seconds trickled away and the third minute of time added on was about to start when Hartson's half-hearted attempt deflected off Southgate for a corner.

This was the last chance and the players knew it. It was time for a defining moment in our history. It was a time for heroes. It was time for Hartson. As Ardley was roared on by the hordes of supporters behind the goal to deliver the perfect corner, nearly every player was camped out in the box hoping, praying for a miracle. As the corner was delivered time stood still.

The ball flew beyond a stranded David James. Hartson fought off the challenge from Southgate and his header sent the home support into raptures. We had equalised. All the emotions of a tedious season were released. The celebrations all around the stadium were like none witnessed before at Selhurst Park.

Hartson ran to the crowd clutching his shirt. Hysteria set in as people jumped rows of seats to hug and kiss perfect strangers. This was football at its finest, and for a moment the 16,000 Dons fans in the crowd of 20,000 forgot their homeless existence and basked in the glory of their late, late saviour Hartson. Months previously some of the fans had ridiculed him for his excessive weight problem. He was now hailed as our knight in shining armour.

Looking back at the video of the goal, I'm sure I am not alone in having a slight tingle run down my spine as I again see the ball ripple the net. The equaliser was just reward for the passionate, under valued and dependable supporters. The spirit and determination shown by both players and spectators that afternoon typifies what it means to be associated with football at Wimbledon.

The celebrations that night were immense. We partied in the street, we drank and drank. But the high of that night was to be surpassed by a huge low just eight days later.

✦

THE TEARS AT SOUTHAMPTON

After 14 years in the top flight, the dream was over. A 2-0 defeat at Southampton, coupled with Bradford's unexpected win over Champions' League chasing Liverpool, meant the Dons were down. For some it was simply too much to take…

14 MAY 2000

Premier League

Southampton 2 Wimbledon 0

By Neal Ardley (player)

I t was tough, and yes, I'll admit there were tears. I had been at the club for the best part of 20 years and I had seen nothing but success. But that whole year was so painful. It was my worst season. I was made to feel like an outcast. I had been sidelined by the new regime and yet I knew I still had so much to offer.

I was slowly watching the club breaking up under Egil Olsen. The big mistake was bringing in someone who didn't know the English game. It was a gamble and it backfired. He had a great record at international level, but he wasn't used to dealing with players on a day-to-day basis and he wasn't used to Wimbledon.

The thought that we could actually go down still took a while to hit home. In the last couple of months I just watched as the team suffered defeat after defeat, unable to do anything.

I finally got my chance when they got rid of Egil Olsen, but by then our fate was almost sealed. There were only two games to go. Terry Burton was put in temporary charge. He had been my manager at youth team level and he had faith in me. I came in and gave everything. I wanted desperately to save the club and keep Wimbledon in the top flight.

I honestly thought that John Hartson's last-minute goal at Aston Villa in the penultimate game of the season would be enough. It took us back above Bradford City on goal difference, and the relief that day was immense. I can vividly remember seeing the joy on the fans' faces as we left the ground. They too thought we had done it.

And then there was Southampton. And it didn't happen. I sat down at the final whistle. We had lost 2-0 and I just couldn't believe the news that Bradford had won. They had beaten Liverpool, who were chasing a place in the Champions' League. It was gutting.

I had hardly played that season, but I'm sure I felt it more than most. I had been at the club since the age of 11.

I felt so sorry for the fans. They had been short-changed under Egil Olsen. The discipline had gone out of the team, the spirit had gone. The players weren't playing for the manager. All the things that had made Wimbledon special had disappeared. For ages I had watched it all happening from afar for ages and being on the sidelines made it all the more painful as there was nothing I could do.

At Southampton after the final whistle, the mood in the changing room was terrible. There were some who were able to dust themselves down in the days that followed and lift themselves up, but for others, like myself, it was not that easy.

I remember looking around the room and in my head I knew that five or six of the players would not be there next season. That friends like Neil Sullivan and Ben Thatcher would be gone.

After such a painful year, I was unsure whether I would stay. It all depended on who they decided to appoint. And when they named Terry Burton I knew I wanted to play on.

By John Hartson (player)

I was down there watching and it was painful, very painful. I was suspended after my sending-off against Bradford and I just felt I could have done something. It was a case of if only…

I'm not sure if we would have recovered the following season if we had not gone down. The mentality behind the scenes had changed. Things happened which the fans and even the players never knew about. I don't really want to say too much about the Norwegians; they paid my wages. But I had a gut feeling that with Terry Burton in charge we would have come back so much stronger.

It had been such a great time, but it had turned sour. It wasn't all that long ago that Wimbledon were flying. The side that went down wasn't all that different from the one that had reached the semi-final against Tottenham the season before. And I believe that if we had been able to hold on to the likes of Marcus Gayle, Hermann Hreidarsson, Neil Sullivan, Ben Thatcher and myself we would have gone straight back up – of that I'm convinced.

But the owners wanted to cut the wage bill, and I left a few months into the next season to go to Coventry.

By Terry Burton (manager)

Relegation was the most difficult day of my life. I had been in charge for only 10 days and we had to go and talk about the reasons why it had happened. There was so much going on in the background. Several of the players didn't care enough. It was inevitable that things had to change.

By Sam Hammam (ex-owner of Wimbledon FC)

I had left the club a few months earlier, but my heart was still there and when Wimbledon were relegated I went to Plough Lane at 3.30am all alone. I often go back to the old site, even though it's all rubble now, for that's where the heart of Wimbledon is.

It was a damn lovely, lovely story. Like Romeo and Juliet, the story was lovely, but the end was tragic. But the memories and the glory are still there. In my office in my home in London, I have three items in front of me. There is a small piece of blue timber taken from the old hut that housed the offices at Plough Lane – a hut I bought for £800. And from that £800 hut we reached the Premier League. I have the pennant from when we won the FA Cup hanging above my head. And I have an aerial picture of Plough Lane framed on the wall, the way it used to be.

I felt after I left Wimbledon that I would not be involved with football ever again. But the amount of letters I got from Cardiff changed my mind.

✦

REALITY BITES

The 2000/01 season was the first in over 20 years that beguan without Sam Hammam at the helm. In his place the Norwegians appointed a little-known South African, Charles Koppel, as chairman. He was introduced to the fans in pre-season and promised a swift return to the top flight. But after relegation the First Division was an eye-opener. Gone was all the glamour, and gone too were most of the first team. John Hartson, Neil Sullivan and Ben Thatcher were among the more high-profile departures. The club captain Robbie Earle had retired through injury. Terry Burton was left with a complete re-building job. It took him a while to get the club going again, but by the end of the season the club was to go agonisingly close to a place in the play-offs.

28 APRIL 2001

First Division

Fulham 1 Wimbledon 1

By Jason Euell (player)

Relegation hurt all of us and I was no exception. The Wimbledon I had grown up with had disappeared in that final season in the Premier League under Egil Olsen. He had wanted a new era. Under him the Crazy Gang had gone. When he left, it was impossible for Terry Burton to recreate the old spirit. Too much had changed. Terry tried to blend the young players he knew from the academy with the older ones who stayed.

In the end, given everything that had happened, we nearly did it. We nearly got back up, and Terry deserves an enormous amount of credit for that. It would have been easy for the club to tumble down the divisions.

Personally, I had become frustrated. I'd spent most of my last 18 months at the club on the transfer list. But I never stopped loving Wimbledon and the fans. I was annoyed by the lack of ambition shown by the club's new owners.

I put in my transfer request in January 2000. It was just after they tried to sell John Hartson to Tottenham. I couldn't understand why the club was trying to do that. It was not the way to move forward.

We had a good team. We were only a few players short of being capable of challenging for Europe, but there was no ambition. Selling John Hartson was like taking a huge step backwards, and I am an ambitious person, so I put the transfer request in.

I grew up with Wimbledon. But a lot of things happen in football. I had spent ages deciding on whether to put in the transfer request. It was the most difficult decision I have had to make in my career. But the fans understood where I was coming from. They knew that every time I put on the shirt I would give it my all. I still wanted to guide Wimbledon back up and we came so close.

The crucial game was at Fulham. We were just outside the play-offs and a win was a must. About half-way through the second half, there was a great through ball to Kevin Cooper. He picked it up on the edge of the box, tricked his way in brilliantly and then got brought down to win the penalty.

The last penalty in regulation play we'd got had come against Wycombe in the Cup and Neal Ardley had missed it. And after him I was next in line to take one. You have to be confident when you step up for a penalty. I hit it down to the keeper's right. He got a hand to it, but it still went in.

The match was our last chance. Fulham were already up as champions and the ground was partying. We had to go and try and do the right job and concentrate. And for 89 minutes we had done just that.

Then came Boa Morte. We all knew he was great at placing penalties and also great at winning them, so we made sure he didn't get the chance. The referee had other ideas.

Darren Holloway was running with Boa Morte. Boa Morte just tumbled. He started falling before he even got into the box.

The tears: Distraught Wimbledon fans react to the reality of relegation after a 2-0 defeat at Southampton on 14 May 2000 (Getty Images)

It was never a penalty, but the referee disagreed. It was just one of those days; we just didn't get the luck.

It was a sickener, and with that one goal our play-off hopes evaporated.

We'd been confident of getting back up via the play-offs if we could get the chance. To miss out like that was hard to take.

The dressing room was really low. We had given the season our best shot, but it was not good enough.

Over the summer, things were to change even more. Wimbledon seemed always to be connected with this place and that place. When I first got into the first team it was Dublin and that passed. Whispers about Milton Keynes surfaced mid-way through the season, but there wasn't anything concrete and I am not sure if anyone took it that seriously. By the time it was finally announced, I had already signed for Charlton.

◆

CHAPTER THIRTEEN: MILTON KEYNES

THE ANNOUNCEMENT

Most people had dismissed the rumours linking the club to a move to Milton Keynes. The proposed move to Dublin had been defeated and this just seemed the latest silly scheme to come out of the Wimbledon boardroom. Then on 2 August 2001 it became reality. Every Wimbledon season ticket holder and club member received a letter that day saying simply the club was going to relocate to Milton Keynes. The club's unofficial websites went into overdrive and in the months that followed, the supporters fought hard to oppose the move.

1 AUGUST 2001
Jay Jays, Wimbledon Broadway
By Kris Stewart (chair of WISA)

The Wimbledon Independent Supporters Association had been told a few times in the weeks before what was coming. We had got leaks from journalists in Milton Keynes and we had been given information from a pretty good source that confirmed it. We knew to expect an announcement. But we couldn't get anything on record. We wanted someone to quote, someone who could say it was happening. We didn't want to jump up and down without any evidence.

We were ready for it. But that didn't take away any of the shock when it was there in black and white – a letter from the club chairman Charles Koppel saying the club had to move to Milton Keynes to survive.

I remember feeling really sick. I have been politically active in my past and I didn't have a very high opinion of people like Charles Koppel. Even with all that, I still find myself getting caught out by how appalling people can actually be. There are still some things that I think: "Bloody hell I was not expecting that". And moving to Milton Keynes was one of those.

WISA were meeting regularly then, our meetings had become almost daily. The whole board was unanimous in our opposition. I remember the meeting the day before they announced it. I was there with Nicole Hammond, Lee Willett, Laurence Lowne and Kevin Rye in a bar called Jay Jays next to Wimbledon Theatre.

There was no doubt whatsoever what was coming, we just sat there and tried to work out how to counter it.

On a purely tactical point of view, the timing of the decision had given us a great opportunity. The Nationwide League started a whole week before the Premiership, so for a week the First Division would be the focus in all the papers. If the decision had been delayed a week or two we would never have got the coverage that we got.

In Jay Jays, we were all suggesting ideas. Not so much the technicalities exactly, but general themes. We agreed that protesting at games was a must and that we needed to get as much publicity as we could. But there was also the importance of talking to the football authorities.

The first time the idea of moving to Milton Keynes surfaced as a rumour we spoke to the Football League and that was back in the January. The Football League pointed us to their rules and the implication was that it couldn't happen.

We had also held meetings with the club's Chief Executive, David Barnard and the new owner, Bjorn Gjelsten. They said they hadn't done anything about a football ground, but added that lots of people had come to them. And that's when Bjorn said: "If it is Milton Keynes, it might as well be Oslo."

All the way through we had a number of formal meetings, and all the way they had been refusing to rule out Milton Keynes. It was impossible to work out whether they were denying it because it was ludicrous or because they were working on it.

In the past we had had rumours linking us to Hull or Basingstoke and this just seemed the latest mad idea, so we didn't really take it all that seriously at first. But slowly it began to dawn us that this time it was for real.

I remember being late for work on the day of the announcement. A friend of mine had got the letter through from Koppel announcing the decision, and he read it to me over the phone at home while I typed it up and posted it on all the websites.

That day at work was spent mainly on the phone talking to the press and other members of the WISA Committee, seeing what we could organise in time for the pre-season friendly against Brentford the following night. It wasn't much really, but we did manage to persuade a lot of people to go.

Black day: Black balloons fly over Selhurst Park as Wimbledon run out against Birmingham City for the first game of 2001/2002 season. (Neil Presland)

And then we started really working hard. We started preparing stuff and talking to the Football League. Then there was the first League game and the black balloon protest. The idea of the black balloons had surfaced on Weird and Wonderful World. Balloons always seemed to be a good thing to do, but there was also a feeling it might be a bit tasteless. In the end it worked really well. The wind blew in the right direction, and the air was awash with black balloons.

Then there was also the publicity side, Laurence and Kev were talking endlessly to the press. We had begun our battle to get our point of view across and to get the media to realise that fans mattered.

✦

THE FINAL SPLIT WITH SAM

The day after the proposal was announced Wimbledon travelled to Brentford for a friendly. To the surprise of numerous Wimbledon fans, Sam Hammam was among the attendees. The fans believed Hammam was responsible for the decision. After all it was he who had sold the club to the Norwegians. Hammam's view was very different. So when he spoke to Wimbledon fans at a pub before the game, the confrontation became ugly. It was to sour his view of the fans forever.

3 AUGUST 2001

Brentford 0 Wimbledon 4

Friendly

By Sam Hammam (ex-owner of Wimbledon FC)

My treatment that night was very very cruel, what was said about me then still hurts. At this moment it's all behind me and I have accepted it. The influence was from negative people and not the silent majority. The negative people are the people who love Wimbledon, who love the club, but who see everything in black or dark grey. They dissipated their views and I was the easy target. They blamed me for the club's fall. That evening was the start of the split and I found it very difficult.

I had been thrown out of the old Wimbledon and that night I was thrown out by the new Wimbledon, the Wimbledon that was to become AFC Wimbledon.

I remain the father of Wimbledon and I wanted to be their hero. But sometimes your children hurt you and that is the situation between me and the new Wimbledon. I feel bitter about it and I feel it was unfair. Would those supporters have dreamed as a non-league fan to have got all those memories of the Premiership?

I want AFC Wimbledon to be successful and to find a home in Merton. I have a lot of love and happiness for AFC Wimbledon. I am very positive about what they are doing and they are always welcome to talk to me.

People who love Wimbledon, love Wimbledon as long as it is in Wimbledon. I feel strongly about it too, very strongly.

I could see the split happening and there is a part of me which is AFC Wimbledon. We are together in mind. AFC Wimbledon is part of my life, my history. Everything that is a fragmentation of the old Wimbledon is a part of me. I still feel it is mine even though it will never be again.

✦

THE BIRTH OF YELLOW AND BLUE

The websites had gone mad. Everyone seemed determined to do something to help. And out of those days of despair, the first alternative matchday programme in Britain was born. It was to be full-colour and contain everything that you would expect from a programme, except this one would have the voice of the fans at its heart.

9 AUGUST 2001
Jay Jays, Wimbledon Broadway
By Niall Couper (Editor of
Yellow and Blue)

I was just an ordinary Wimbledon fan. I had got used to my seat at Selhurst Park. I was on vague nodding terms with the six or so supporters who sat around me. I was not part of any big group. I knew a few other faces from the old days at Plough Lane, but that was it. I was there because I had always been there.

And then came the news that Charles Koppel wanted to move the club to Milton Keynes. It totally destroyed me. I was devastated. I wasn't a member of the Independent Supporters Association. I didn't know what to do. I hadn't even been that involved with the protests against the proposed merger in 1987 or moving away from Plough Lane in 1991. Both times I was too young to really understand the significance of it all. By 2001 I had grown up. I understood and I was furious. But I didn't understand how they

Captive audience: AFC Wimbledon Supporters at Kingsmeadow read Yellow and Blue, the programme that began as a protest against the Wimbledon chairman Charles Koppel. (Getty Images)

could take away my club. I didn't understand the logic of it all. Surely the example of Charlton proved that if there was the will, a return to Wimbledon could be achieved? I had to do something. I hit the websites.

I am not even sure if I knew of the existence of Weird and Wonderful World before that fateful day on 2 August, but by the end of the day that's where I was camped.

Ideas were flying off from all angles over the next few days and there was one that caught my eye: an alternative matchday programme. WISA had the merchandise boycott already in place so this just seemed the next logical step. The idea had come from Ashley Parker-Smith and it was inspired. Alex Kirk and him were already in discussions about it when I leapt on board. And within a day, a group of seven of us were in email contact: Mark Lewis, Ashley, Alex, Charlie Talbot, Marc Jones, Richard Pope and myself. We were to meet seven days later in Jay Jays on Wimbledon Broadway. Well I say all – Ashley, whose idea it was, had to

yellow and BLUE matchday programme

programme sponsor

KISS 100
livesexy

saturday 25th august 2001
WIMBLEDON v NORWICH CITY
nationwide division one
KO 3pm £1.5

stay away as it turned out later he was just 14. We quickly dismissed the idea of getting a programme ready for the first game of the season; that was only two days away. So we targeted the Norwich game on 25 August. Mark Lewis would organise the distribution and sale, while Ashley was to be one of the first programme sellers. I am a qualified journalist and had helped edit a series of football magazines on Arsenal. I had the template ready to roll. We had even knocked together a rough pagination. But the problem was none of the seven of us even had QuarkXPress, the industry standard page-design programme. And then of course there was the issue of cash. A quick call to a series of printers had made it clear that we would need £1,000 up front to get going. That's where Richard Pope stepped in. Pope had no idea who we were. He had no idea what we were capable of producing, but here he was happily writing out a cheque.

The next few days were mayhem. We got a copy of QuarkXPress, and the four designers – myself, Alex, Charlie Talbot and Marc Jones – set to work. Pages were sent over the internet in zipped files to Oxford, where Charlie was studying and editing their student newspaper, to Putney, where Alex an ex-journalist lived, and to Wimbledon, the home of Marc Jones, the webmaster of Weird and Wonderful World. We opted for a 32-page full-colour glossy magazine. We knocked out the content and printed 2,000 copies all of which went on sale on the Walk to Selhurst from Wimbledon – the latest WISA-backed protest. We sold out before we reached the ground. Yellow and Blue was to expand to 48 pages.

We were keen to present the alternative view to Charles Koppel and over the season we included celebrity columns from the likes of Jonathan Pearce, Jim White and Rodney Marsh. We had columns from WISA, the Dons Trust, Merton Council and interviews with a stream of ex-players and all the usual content you would expect from a programme. It would earn praise from the Evening Standard, the Guardian, numerous websites and even got a mention in the House of

The start: The first issue of Yellow and Blue.

Commons. But most amazing of all was that Yellow and Blue would go on to outsell the official matchday programme by three to one.

In a personal capacity I like to think that in our own way we helped change the minds of the sceptics in the Wimbledon crowd. For by the season's end where there had been apathy there was now full support for the protests.

✦

LIBERAL DEMOCRAT CONFERENCE

The anti-Milton Keynes' movement spread quickly into the field of politics. Later Tony Blair would praise Wimbledon fans for their resolve, but it was the Liberal Democrats who were the first to put football franchising on the agenda.

26 SEPTEMBER 2001

Bournemouth International Centre

By Alex Folkes (Liberal Democrat delegate and Dons fan)

I hadn't really been involved in any of the protest activities before. I had shouted and sung along with everyone else on the Holmesdale, but not gone to any WISA meetings or taken part in any of the demos. But I was the Chair of Lewisham Liberal Democrats and the Party's annual conference was coming up. The General Election had taken place earlier in the year so it was one of those conferences when you could get away with a bit more as the party was not overly concerned with scripting every speech.

I have a bit of a history with causing trouble at conferences. In 1995 I was part of the party's youth wing which put forward motions to decriminalize cannabis (now party policy) and abolish the monarchy (still waiting).

So I got a couple of other people in my local party to agree and we put forward an emergency motion on the subject of franchising in football. It didn't just refer to Wimbledon, but to Brentford too, who were being linked to a move to Woking at the time.

Lo and behold, the other emergency motions submitted for debate were so awful that they had to take mine. Not that this guaranteed any attention. Emergency debates are traditionally held at 9am on the last morning, whilst everyone is still nursing hangovers from a party the night before.

But I went around to a few of the press people who I knew and told them what I was doing and why. I needn't have worried as they were soon after me. They asked: "What on earth was I doing and why did I think politicians should give a damn about football?" I explained to them that I thought football clubs were community assets and you can't strip the assets without properly consulting the community.

I also asked around a few of my friends and got a few more people lined up to speak. And they all promised to wear their shirts for the occasion.

But I faced two concerted opponents. The first was the local party from Milton Keynes. Some of them were in favour of Wimbledon's move and wanted to tell me so. They wanted me to withdraw the motion. I said that I supported the idea of football in MK, just that I wanted them to grow their own club, as we had done.

The second opposing force was the party's press office. Did I not know that this was not in their script for conference? They wanted the media to concentrate on other things. Sorry, said I, but the media will focus on whatever they want and this at least was a subject that would reach new audiences who do not usually listen to politics.

As the time for the debate came, the main conference hall was not exactly packed, but there was enough of a crowd to make me feel a bit nervous. I spoke and then watched as the motion was debated passionately. The arguments were either from genuine football fans (on my side) or from those who felt football should be allowed to act as a business and do what they want (opposed to me).

In a typical Liberal Democrat way, somebody then moved a reference back – voting to send the motion to a party policy committee. Although we opposed that formally, we knew that it would allow the party's sport spokesman, Bob Russell MP, to decide on interim policy. So the reference back passed, our opponents enjoyed about 30 seconds of victory and then Bob announced that interim policy would be to oppose franchising in football. Since then, Bob has continued to oppose football franchising.

After that, all that was left was the media scrum. I did 12 interviews in half an hour. Since then I got a bit more involved in the campaigning work associated with both Wimbledon FC and AFC Wimbledon. The only downside is I got saddled with the nickname of Lib Dem Don.

✦

THE PATH TO THE DONS TRUST

From the moment Charles Koppel announced the proposed move to Milton Keynes, he continued to state that the club would go into liquidation if the move was not given the go ahead. With this backdrop, the Wimbledon supporters began to look at ways in which they could take over the running of the club.

25 OCTOBER 2001
The first Dons Trust meeting
Wimbledon Community Centre
By Lou Carton-Kelly (chair of Dons Trust Steering Committee)

The events of August 2001 rocked me to the core. I had followed the Dons for 15 years and now the club wanted to relocate to Milton Keynes. I was the vice-chair of the Wimbledon Independent Supporters Association at the time and I was determined to do all I could to stop the proposal.

I organised the Walk for Wimbledon which took place before the second 'home' match of the season to highlight our homeless plight – 10 years since the Dons left Plough Lane for Selhurst Park. It was a great success, but we had to keep on going and I kept looking for new avenues to explore.

It was around that time that I went to the Supporters Direct conference at Birkbeck College. I was there with Nicole Hammond, Luke Mackenzie and Mags Hutchison and we all took part in workshops, spoke to fans of clubs in administration or receivership and most importantly discovered how to set-up a supporters' trust. After that I was convinced. I went back to the WISA committee and said: "We need to have a supporters' trust."

We were all so terrified of Wimbledon FC going into administration or worse still liquidation. But with a trust set up we knew we could be in a position to take over if Koppel decided to carry out his often voiced threat of putting the club into liquidation if the move to Milton Keynes was blocked by the Football League or the FA.

The WISA committee backed the idea and I was appointed chair of the steering committee which was set up to take the Trust to launch.

The first public meeting was on 25 October 2001 at the Wimbledon Community Centre

The main hall was packed. Myself, Dave Boyle, our caseworker from Supporters Direct, and the inspirational Brian Lomax all sat on the stage and explained the potential role of the Trust and the work that would be required by the fans to bring it to fruition.

I remember there were also great speeches from Richard Lillicrap of Swansea City's Trust and Steve Powell from the Arsenal Independent Supporters Association. You could sense the feeling in the room that the Dons Trust was a goer.

It was to prove to be the first of regular weekly meetings. In the weeks that followed I remember sitting upstairs at The Thomas Farley – the pub Wimbledon used as home before Selhurst Park matches – collecting membership fees for an organisation that hadn't even been launched yet. We ended up having over 400 pre-launch trust members.

✦

KOPPEL'S FANS FORUM BACKFIRES

In the first half of the 2001/02 season, the Wimbledon FC chairman, Charles Koppel, consistently claimed that the silent majority of Dons fans backed the planned relocation to Milton Keynes. To prove his point he set up the Official Wimbledon Fans Forum.

12 DECEMBER 2001
Selhurst Park
By Sean Fox (OWFF elected Fans' representative)

We had had the black balloons and the march from Plough Lane to Selhurst Park. Every Dons fan who had been interviewed by newspapers, radio and television had come out against the move. The Wimbledon Independent Supporters Association, the largest supporters group, had voted not to meet with the club until the Milton Keynes proposal was renounced. Yet, the club's chairman Charles Koppel repeatedly insisted that the protests against Milton Keynes represented only the minority of Wimbledon fans. It was out of this insistence that the Official Wimbledon Fans Forum was born.

In a letter to season ticket holders and club members, Koppel wrote: "The views of some supporters are being aired in public. The views of others are not..." The letter went on to outline his intention to set up OWFF, which he believed would prove his point. All season ticket holders and club members were invited to join.

The Official Wimbledon Fans Forum was born in September 2001. It was to die in August 2002 when the club ceased to recognise it.

A few weeks after the first meeting, invitations were sent to all OWFF members inviting nominations for the seven elected Council seats. When the manifestoes were published Koppel's misunderstanding was exposed. Of the 30 candidates only one was pro Milton Keynes.

When the results were announced on 12 December 2001 the seven elected candidates were all voiciforous opponents of MK and the pro-MK candidate finished last. I was one of the seven.

The meetings that followed frequently descended into farce. At each we were promised two club representatives. We wanted Koppel to attend but more often that not he wasn't there.

The discussions were not about facilitating the move, as Koppel had hoped, but on rejecting MK and building on Plough Lane or another suitable site.

On one rare occasion that Koppel did attend, the fans representatives encountered the bizarre site of two policemen waiting in the room to "protect" Koppel. Despite the promises of access to information and directors little or none was forthcoming. The "extensive" study of sites investigated in London consisted of a map. The promised "more detailed evidence" was never shown to us.

In March Koppel said that he would happily sell the club for a pound but because of the club's financial plight he wouldn't have any takers. Sadly he declined my outstretched hand with a pound in it.

In the aftermath of 28 May Koppel lost interest in the OWFF as a method of consultation. He refused repeated requests for a meeting with fans' representatives. This resulted in a meeting being held on the first day of the 2002/03 season. The club refused to attend and published a letter on their website derecognising the elected members of the OWFF. In his absence the Forum voted to back a motion to support AFC Wimbledon.

✦

FANS UNITED DAY

By December 2001, the protests had begun to escalate. Before the home game against Nottingham Forest, the Dons played host to a Fans United day. It was a mix of colour and cross-football support, and the day turned into a celebration. Fans from over 90 different clubs attended, all to back the Dons fans' cause. The club refused to help and Wimbledon fans were forced to relocate to the Arthur Waite stand if they wanted to sit in solidarity with the supporters of the other clubs.

16 DECEMBER 2001

First Division

Wimbledon 1 Nottingham Forest 0

By Neal Ardley (player)

Playing in the shadow of the protests against Milton Keynes was very difficult. Emotions were running high all season and I remember getting a fair amount of stick from a couple of fans before one game. They were adamant that I had made pro-Milton Keynes comments and they were furious. I had made nothing of the sort, but there was no way of persuading them.

I had every sympathy for the fans. The club was ripping itself apart, the fans wanted one thing, the chairman another and the players were stuck in the middle.

I was getting paid to do a job. I had my own views on it, but I couldn't be seen to give the fans any sympathy. I tried to sit on the fence and not make any comments on the subject.

It was a no-win situation for the players. The fans, naturally, wanted us to make a stand, but it was our livelihood and I think some of the supporters failed to realise that.

It got a little bit grotty and horrible in the end. I just wanted it all to disappear. I made a conscious decision about half-way through the season not to talk about it.

There were moments when everything felt like it had before. The 1-0 win against Nottingham Forest was one such time. We played really well that day. Chris Wilmott got the winner. Most of the fans were in the Arthur Waite Stand for Fans United Day.

I remember at the end of the game going over and applauding them. I didn't realise how significant that was to the fans, but some of them mentioned it to me later. All I wanted to say was that I knew what they were going through.

The protests were impressive: The black balloons, Fans United Day and the Back to the Game protest in the final match of the season. But it only added to the pain for the players.

Terry Burton was great through it all. He made it clear to all of us that we had to respect the fans. He would say: "Let them vent their anger to the chairman, but let's keep playing football on the pitch."

But there was no doubt that our home form suffered that year. If the whole Milton Keynes scenario had never surfaced I firmly believe we would have gone up.

That said I felt Selhurst Park was not the right place for us. It never had the right atmosphere that a ground of our own would have brought. Having spoken to the chairman he made it seem that Milton Keynes was the only option. Whether it was true or not, I don't know.

Altogether now: Supporters united behind the campaign against the proposed move to Milton Keynes at Fans United Day on 16 December 2001. (Getty Images)

The fans didn't think so. They vented their anger. They did what they believed in and you can't criticise anyone who does that. They made their point and when the decision went against them, they didn't give up, they didn't go back. They got off their backsides and did something about it. How many people can say that?

It was a horrible year for me personally, but the fans stood by their convictions and I admire them for it. I wish them all the luck in the world. They deserve it.

By Richard Bugg (supporter)

The march from the Farley to the ground on Fans United day will live long in my memory. The scarf, the togetherness and the spirit of all the fans was tremendous. That was really the only game I enjoyed that season. The singing and jumping about in the Arthur Waite Stand was electric and the team winning was a bonus. I was actually really pleased we won. Other results that season were meaningless. But I will always remember we won that game.

✦

THE LAUNCH OF THE DONS TRUST

After Fans United day, the focus switched to the launch of the Dons Trust. The Trust was to prove instrumental in the months that followed. Its launch was a milestone and within three months it was to become the largest supporters' trust in the country.

10 FEBRUARY 2002

The launch of the Dons Trust

Wimbledon Theatre

By Lou Carton-Kelly (chair of Dons Trust Steering Committee)

Take over 1200 Wimbledon fans, add in a liberal sprinkling of VIPs including MPs and members of the Council, guest speakers, a passionate MC, over 60 stewards, the FA Cup and a host of ex-players, enclose in a theatre for three hours and gently stir and inflame with emotion. What have you got?

The launch of the Dons Trust on 10 February 2002.

It was a very ambitious launch date, but it was also the only date that the theatre could accommodate us. They gave it over to us for free.

As for the night itself, I didn't really know what to expect. We had various working groups working hard to try and make the day a success and prior to the launch we were all really anxious. We wanted to show the community of Merton that we meant business. Once we knew the FA Cup and a number of ex-players would be there we knew we would get a fair crowd, but 1200…

I spent the whole night running on adrenalin. I was excited and nervous all at once.

Chris Philips, from Kiss FM, was the MC and he was superb. Then there were the speakers. We had the mayor of Merton, Stuart Pickover, ex-players Dickie Guy and Jeff Bryant, then ex-manager Allen Batsford.

Then it was over to Brian Lomax the newly installed managing director of Supporters Direct. He said that the Dons Trust working groups were more than capable of running a football club with their professionalism and skills. How prophetic those words would prove to be.

Then it was the turn of Dave Boyle, Andrew Judge, the leader of Merton Council, and then the Wimbledon MP Roger Casale. Casale

Dons supporters gathered in Wimbledon Theatre celebrate the launch of the Dons Trust. (Yellow and Blue)

had drafted an Early Day Motion opposing the move to Milton Keynes. It was to become one of the most successful Early Day Motions in the history of parliament.

Finally, we came to Lord Faulkner of Worcester, better known as Richard Faulkner the former director of Wimbledon FC.

His speech was passionate and direct. There were a number there on the day who have known Richard for more than 25 years and his speech summed up exactly what being a football supporter is all about. It was delivered from the heart.

After the speakers, came a parade of former players, a chance to have a photograph with the FA Cup and then the auction, which Jo and Mark Lewis will remember forever for their £3,000 plus bid for a signed picture of Lawrie Sanchez's FA Cup winning goal.

It was an amazing night and one that will live with me forever, but it also said The Dons Trust meant business and we were ready to take over the club.

By Carl Leaburn (ex-player)

The day Egil Olsen arrived the spirit began to fade away. He had a different, more professional approach and it just wasn't Wimbledon. When Terry Burton took over the Crazy Gang was almost dead and he wasn't all that keen on reviving the kind of antics we used to get up to. He liked the professionalism that Egil had introduced.

It was around that time that issues in the boardroom were also beginning to surface. As players all we ever heard was the chairman's perspective and I really wanted to hear the other side of the coin.

At the time I couldn't really speak out because I was still employed by the club, but once I left I was free to do what I wanted. And I still wanted to know what was going on. I knew quite a few of the club's supporters, so when they invited me down to the launch of the Dons Trust I didn't hesitate.

A couple of the players wanted to come too, but they couldn't because they were still employed by Wimbledon FC.

What I remember most of the meeting was the passion of the supporters and I was surprised to be dragged onto the stage.

It was good to at last get the other side of the argument. Undoubtedly, they were half-truths told on both sides, but at last I could start to see the whole picture.

I still find it difficult to make a fully informed decision. But I have nothing but admiration for the supporters. It is just a shame that the fans were forced to go down that route, but the reality is Wimbledon FC has moved.

The fans are what are left of the spirit of Wimbledon.

✦

THE TEARS OF KEVIN COOPER

In March 2001 Kevin Cooper, the popular Wimbledon winger, was sold to Wolves for £1m. He had been the runaway favourite for player of the year. A WISA poll confirmed it and with the help of the staff at Wolves, WISA presented Cooper with the award at Molineux. Wimbledon FC were never told.

14 APRIL 2002

First Division

Wolverhampton Wanderers 1 Wimbledon 0

By Kevin Cooper (ex-player)

It may have only been 12 months, but I was playing the best football of my career and it was the best year of my life. And receiving the award from the fans at Molineux having just left was… well, I can't quite explain how I felt. It was so emotional, it was a wonderful experience. I remember Kris Stewart giving me the Player of the Year award in front of thousands of cheering Dons fans and I'll be honest the tears were streaming from my eyes.

The emotion then… it's just so hard to describe. It's better than winning games and scoring goals.

To be appreciated by the supporters of the club you have just left in such a way; I just don't think anything in football can better that. It was amazing.

I knew how the fans were feeling, I knew it had been a difficult year for them and I felt for them. I could feel the emotion from the fans as I walked over. And to be honoured like that, I was overwhelmed.

I first got an inkling that I might get the Player of the Year award when I first arrived at Wolves. One of the officials there said he wasn't sure whether I'd still get the award after the move. I knew I had played well, but I just thought that the fans would give the award to a player

Emotion: Kevin Cooper walks towards the Wimbledon supporters to receive his 2001/02 player of the year award at Molineux on 14 April 2002 just a few weeks after joining Wolves and (below) with his award. (Aideen Rochford / Yellow and Blue)

still at the club. And after that there hadn't been a whisper until the day of the game itself.

I found out later how much work had gone into organising it all but they kept it all secret from me.

The whole game had been overwhelming, every time I touched the ball I got a cheer from the Wimbledon fans. It was really nice. I'm glad Wolves won the game though as I'm not sure how well they would have reacted to me receiving an award from the opposing fans at the final whistle! That said I think a lot of Wolves fans developed a soft spot for the supporters because of that game, certainly the ones that I've spoken to.

On the day the players from Wimbledon were fine. Personally, I had only just left so it was a strange feeling to see them all again.

I think the Wolves players were more overwhelmed by the reaction I received than the Wimbledon guys. Most of the Wolves team had never seen anything like that.

But I remember Kenny Cunningham saying something similar a few weeks earlier when I got substituted against Stockport and the whole ground rose to applaud me. I had been at Stockport for four years and they had just got relegated and that was a nice gesture.

Some players claim that they don't hear the fans, but that game against Stockport I was fully aware that the two sets of fans were on the same side and that endeared me even more to the fans of Wimbledon and Stockport.

I hadn't wanted to leave Wimbledon. I was 100 per cent happy there. The supporters at Wimbledon were second to none and my heart is with them. But in the end I was asked to make a choice and as a professional footballer there are times in life when you have to do what is right for you family and yourself in the long term. It was the hardest choice I have ever had to make.

It's a difficult subject for me to go into in depth. I have to be careful in what I say. But in my mind it would be nice to see a club called Wimbledon playing in Wimbledon and in the First Division.

I have nothing but respect for the fans; they are the bread and butter of the game. And I think it's good for football what AFC Wimbledon are doing.

I'm willing to do anything to help the fans there. After all the supporters at AFC stood by me and it's the very least I could do in return. They deserve the best.

✦

THE DISMISSAL OF TERRY BURTON

The final game of the 2001/02 season was a mix of emotions. Five minutes before half-time the fans turned their backs on the play. It was a symbolic gesture. The fans still backed the players and the manager, but the owners had failed to listen to every other protest. At the end of the game, the owners of Wimbledon FC turned their backs on Terry Burton.

21 APRIL 2002

First Division

Wimbledon 0 Barnsley 1

By Terry Burton (manager)

After the game I was sacked. Their public stance was simple: it was all about results. They said to the press we hadn't won promotion and that wasn't good enough. But if that was the case 90 per cent of managers would be sacked each year. There were a lot of other things that happened that I can't go into. I'm still sorting out my pay-off from the club. I know the real reasons behind it. I knew what was going on.

But that whole season had been overshadowed by Milton Keynes.

The disappointing thing was that over two years I had given 13 players their debuts and in Neil Shipperley and David Connolly we had a forward line with prospects. If there had been some investment then we would not have been that far away. We had even identified a couple of players that would have been perfect.

Final outrage: Wimbledon fans turn their backs on play 21 April 2002 against Barnsley, the final game of the season. (Neil Presland)

But the owners weren't thinking about football, Milton Keynes was the big thing for the club. And for the supporters there were simply not going to go there. It was the big issue. We couldn't come out and say what we did or didn't want to do. The club paid our wages. It was difficult.

Those last two seasons were very hard. Playing in the First Division was a massive change for all of us. Half the squad had gone, we were trying to play a new style, we were playing different opponents and financially we were hamstrung. We weren't going to be able to adjust overnight.

I didn't want the club to fall through the divisions, like Barnsley or Sheffield Wednesday. That was my fear, that not only would we lose our top players, but that we would collapse. We tried to keep some stability; it was a difficult juggling act. There was a three-year plan. The club wanted to reduce the wage bill and re-build in the third year.

The expectation from the fans was that we would go straight back up. But if you let half your team go, it was always going to be difficult.

Then Milton Keynes arrived. It was a crazy crazy season. All the chants about Koppel and about not going to Milton Keynes. It was difficult.

It did take our eyes off the ball, it was impossible for it not to, but it was something we grew to understand and deal with.

It was not the best background, hearing all that barracking every game. We were thankful it wasn't against the team and the players. We knew where the criticism was directed, but it didn't help the atmosphere at the ground.

The Backs to the Game demonstration in that final match was just the latest in a long line of protests. All I could do was to try to focus on the way we were playing. If only the situation hadn't arisen, we would have benefited from the fans' full support.

Even after that final game there was still no decision on whether the club would move to Milton Keynes or not, but at least it was now a problem I didn't have to deal with on a day-to-day basis.

✦

The Spirit of Wimbledon

CHAPTER FOURTEEN: 28 MAY 2002

MILTON KEYNES MOVE WINS APPROVAL

Since the announcement on 2 August 2001, Wimbledon fans had battled hard against the proposed uprooting of the club. The Football League had even voted 9-0 against the move, but an appeal by Charles Koppel persuaded the Football Association to set up a three-man commission to re-consider the case. The three were the Ryman League chairman Alan Turvey, the Aston Villa secretary Steve Stride and the media lawyer Raj Parker. They began their deliberations on 14 May 2002. On the same day, Wimbledon fans began a vigil outside the headquarters of the Football Association in Soho Square.

Two weeks later the news leaked out: the move had been approved by two votes to one. By 9am it was on the Evening Standard website. It took another four hours for the news to become official. For Wimbledon supporters across the world, it was beginning to sink in.

Peter Davis: Football had ended. The World Cup didn't matter, and all I wanted to do was grab people and shout at them. The Football Association and Charles Koppel had ruined everything. A lawyer and a secretary had decided that Wimbledon Football club should be allowed to move to Milton Keynes. Where were the football people in this decision-making process?

Fazal Ahmed: During the course of that last season, the football had become boring, trudging to Selhurst was tiresome, and any hope that we'd ever get any sense out of the club owners had vanished. We had our own voice in Yellow and Blue, the best programme the club has ever had. In the last issue, I'd even had a letter published in which I suggested that if we the fans were allowed to run our club, we could be bigger than Real – and how soon we'd start living that dream.

It was a bright sunny day. I was working in a dull office next to the Madejski Stadium in Reading. The World Cup was looming. Having recently been on the demo at Soho Square, I was confident. I'd discovered the chat rooms and was eagerly waiting for news.

When I finally got a phone call from my wife about the decision, it felt like part of me had died. Amazingly I'd turned the whole office to our cause. Many of them (mainly Brentford fans) signed the postcards to the FA that WISA had made, so when news spread across the building, a crowd gathered offering condolences to me. The only way I can describe it is like a bereavement. All the old names and matches flashed through my mind. I never thought I'd watch football again.

Neil Presland: The news broke on the Evening Standard website. I immediately took a half-day holiday and made my way up to Soho Square to join the swell of other supporters who were there praying that the Standard had got it wrong. We waited and waited, but no official statement. Eventually we were forced to "invade" the FA headquarters. That got their attention, and finally we were handed a printed statement confirming that our club was dead. Unbelievable! Here we were outside the offices of the authority that was supposed to protect football, and they had sold us out to appease a bunch of businessmen. What did I feel? Anger and despair. The despair has now gone, but the anger will stay forever.

Ray Armfield: Working in and around Central London, I was able to attend the vigil at Soho Square for at least an hour most days. It was strange initially, just standing around with fellow Dons fans, most of whom I barely knew, corralled into a corner outside the FA headquarters, draped with "Show Me The Way To Plough Lane" and other protest banners.

Soho is a cosmopolitan area, and playing "spot the celebrity" raised the spirits. An eclectic mix of Noddy Holder, Ken Bates and Howard Wilkinson passed by, together with bemused tourists, cheeky van drivers, supporters of other clubs and the odd wino.

Adam Crozier stopped for a chat, organising drinks and cakes for us. Although he wouldn't be drawn on possible outcomes, he appeared sympathetic. A visitors' book was started, which deserves a place in any future AFC Wimbledon museum.

Little did we know then that the dirty deed was taking place in a solicitor's office in Fleet Street and not Soho Square. I did, however, see Alan Turvey, the Ryman League chairman and reportedly the panel member who voted against MK, leaving the FA in a taxi one day.

I gave him an "I know who you are" nod and a smile, as he passed. He looked embarrassed. Days went by, and the place felt like a mini Greenham Common. A van driver dropped off some bottled water for us and just said: "From Brentford – good luck." Terry Eames turned up for a couple of hours in his red Elonex WFC top.

Eventually, whispers were heard that a verdict would be announced on 28 May. Then rumours of the worst kind began. An article appeared in the Evening Standard followed by feverish activity on the internet, announcing that MK had been approved.

Unsurprisingly, a larger than average crowd began gathering on the final day. Koppel had expensive lawyers and a glossy brochure on his side; we had hard facts and morality on ours. Wasn't that enough?

I don't know what I expected in terms of an announcement: papal white smoke from the roof of the FA, a general election style returning officer? In fact, we got a terse statement from a lowly minion thrust at us. Before this, media crews began arriving, all with the same opening line: "You've heard they've voted for MK, haven't you?" The mood became depressed. A few eggs were thrown, and some fans briefly gained entrance to the building, but they were token gestures.

And so to home. My wife, who'd been updating me from Sky News during the day, was a bit cautious around me. My daughter didn't really understand the implications of it all, but just said: "That's not fair, Dad". My 13-year-old son's reaction was the most interesting. But for school, he was up for joining me at the vigil, having taken part in all of the post-match MK demonstrations. I opened his bedroom door, and saw that he'd taken down every single WFC picture and poster that had covered the walls. At that point I wished I had Pete Winkelman next to me so he could explain how "deserving" Milton Keynes was to take our football team away, but I couldn't have vouched for his safety if he'd tried.

I still feel very, very bitter and angry about the whole issue, not least the way the authorities tried to hide the news "Jo Moore" style beneath World Cup stories about David Beckham's foot and Roy Keane's tantrum.

Dean Parsons: When I heard it on the radio after camping out at the FA headquarters the day before, I couldn't believe it. I remember the exact moment it was announced – I was at work in the warehouse and I had to sit down. I really was in shock that the FA were allowing this tragedy to happen to our club, a club I had loved since my first game against Mansfield in 1981. It was as if my whole family had been shot down in front of me and I began to cry uncontrollably. It was like when we were relegated, but 10 times worse.

Alasdair MacTavish: I left work early to walk from Covent Garden to Soho Square, shitting myself. I turned into Soho Square and immediately I knew it was bad by the look on people's faces. It was the culmination of the worst year of supporting the Dons. I knew that afternoon that I'd never see WFC play again. They just weren't my team any more.

Matt Couper: I was at work – not that I was really working. I was on-line and I was just so anxious, very anxious. Up until the last minute I completely believed that the decision would go our way. The Football League had voted 9-0 in our favour back in August, and every other time the authorities had backed the fans. I couldn't understand why anyone would back the move to Milton Keynes. It just didn't make any sense.

On line, everyone was saying that the decision was due in half an hour. That deadline would come and go and then it would be another half an hour. It kept dragging on and on.

And then, on the Weird and Wonderful World website, there was a simple message saying something like: "It is official. The decision has gone against us."

I refused to believe it, so I phoned the FA and was put through to a press officer who said that the decision hadn't been made yet. But I was fuming and said: "Look, there's this rumour going round – if it isn't true why don't you deny it?" But he couldn't.

I was shaking, I was angry and I was really, really nervous. I tried to calm down, and just kept logging on again and again. I was meant to be working, but I couldn't do a thing.

When it became real I was numb. I just couldn't believe it. The only thing I knew was that I had to get up town, so I left over an hour early. I don't remember anything about the journey. When I got to Soho Square, there were loads of people in tears. My overriding feeling was one of betrayal. I felt betrayed by the FA, by the Football League, and most of all by the owners of Franchise FC – the new name for Wimbledon FC. I was there long before they were, and I would have been there long after they left. They had no right to do this to any of us.

Mark Chapman: It is a day I will never forget. I went to work as usual in the morning, but even now I remember that things didn't feel quite right. I didn't think an announcement was imminent, although talk on Weird and Wonderful World the night before had indicated that bad news would be released shortly.

A phone call from a friend related the breaking story. In a cliché moment, I dropped the vase I was working on, smashing it to pieces. It didn't bother me – all that mattered was how soon I could get to Soho Square. I knew there would be other people there feeling exactly the same, and it seemed so poignant that we should all be together.

Arriving at the FA, I found exactly what I'd expected. One thing that I remember vividly is cars and vans still beeping their horns as they passed, unaware that the fight was lost. A Crystal Palace fan was there, sympathising, yet he may as well have been talking Swedish for all the attention I paid him.

The tears were for later...

Claire Richardson: I only missed one day of the vigil. The amazing response of the passers-by made me feel that we were not only right but we also had the support of the British public. When I heard the decision on 28 May, I cried. I felt I had been part of the biggest injustice – it was wrong, and everyone knew it. I cried, not for me but for the people who had been watching Wimbledon for decades, people who had just had a huge part of their lives ripped away from them, and for the people who had been campaigning for years to bring Wimbledon back home, where the club belongs. The day only got worse as I travelled for one last time to Soho Square. I was not the only one who had felt the need to be there. The emotion was thick in the air, my friends were hurt, and I was tired and angry. It was over.

Paul Raymond: I was sitting at work keeping an eye on the websites, and at about 11.50am the message came up that permission for the MK move had been granted. I was stunned. I don't know how I got through the next 10 minutes. At noon I got up and said: "I'm off to lunch." I went out and walked around, thinking of the good times that I'd had, and wondered what I would do in the future.

Mark Hodsoll: I always look forward to 28 May. I should do, because 28 May is my birthday, along with Kylie and the late Thora Hird. No prizes for guessing which I'd rather spend a joint party with. And this year was no different with my 38th year dawning.

I'd spent the preceding weeks with more important things on my mind, sneaking off to Soho Square a few times with my son in full kit to man the barricades. We paraded with the faithful to a chorus of toots from passing drivers, and even had our pictures taken for Jockey Slut magazine, blissfully unaware that for much of the time the dirty deed had already been done. To think I even told my son off for kicking the football against the FA window – if only I'd known.

So there was I, looking forward to an Italian meal for two and everything else you'd expect on your birthday, especially with the kids at the in-laws, when BANG – the news I didn't want to hear. The feeling I had in the pit of my stomach is as indescribable today as it was then.

I spent the evening staring out of the restaurant window, drifting in memories from Windsor and Eton to Andy Sayer to Robbie's header at Old Trafford and Hartson's equaliser... and on and on. My poor wife couldn't raise my spirits at all. Cheers, I thought, happy birthday!

Adam Russell: Strangely, I didn't feel anything when I saw the news on Teletext – I just felt blank. It still puzzles me even now. I was extremely angered when I first heard of the plans, spending a few days in an internet café in Cesky Krumlow (in the Czech Republic) instead of enjoying my holiday. When the MK move was sanctioned, I felt disappointment at such a poor decision being reached, rather than anger.

Trevor Pearce: Fittingly, news of the murder – or at least the attempted murder – of my club reached me in a scrappy manner, by rumour and from no official sources.

As I had done every day since the start of the three-man commission's deliberations, I logged on to the net from work, and went to look at the WISA site, expecting to hear nothing, but finding a succession of posts from sources of varying repute saying that the battle had been lost. No official announcement, nothing from the daily papers (they had a broken bone in David Beckham's foot to keep them occupied), no clap of thunder or dimming of the lights.

While I can't actually remember the moment when I actually accepted that we'd lost, I do remember being unable to think about anything else all day, unable to hold a coherent conversation much less concentrate on work. I remember going to the gym at lunchtime and mindlessly pushing weights up and down, not knowing whether I'd lifted 10 kilos or 100, twice or 100 times.

Later that day, I played football in the park and went to the pub with fans of other clubs, friends who would send me abusive texts after a 5-0 home defeat by Palace. One of them, a Spurs fan, had vowed revenge when he received a cheery message from me 10 seconds after the final whistle of that year's Worthington Cup final defeat by Blackburn, and I was steeling myself for the banter. But even he could only say: "It's not what you sign up for, is it?" saying in nine words what I've since said in many, many more.

A few pints later, I walked down to the FA to tape my shirt to the window, with a message reading "Wimbledon FC – RIP. FA Sellout" underneath. And that was 28 May 2002.

I'd like to say that I've put all that behind me, that I never give the Franchise a second glance now, that my focus is on AFC Wimbledon, but it's not true. I still have sleepless nights. I know it's just a game. I know that in a world that rushes into war, where people starve because of their political allegiance, where people in my city can't find work or enough money to support their families, that it just isn't important. But I cannot get over the fact that the very people whose privileged existence revolves around my game just capitulated and allowed this to happen.

That one man, whose sole claim is that he has more money than I do, can take 113 years of history, can take the team that I have spent my adult life obsessing about, can tell me and thousands (yes thousands) of others that we don't deserve a professional football team when he'd never been to a football match before 1997. And that the people who we relied on to sit him down and quietly tell him exactly what this game is about waved him through and then sat back and washed their hands of the whole thing – it's all beyond belief. Truth be told, I still can't believe that it is being allowed, that there are still a handful of Franchise supporters who will tell you that they can't be disloyal or that football is a business and I should just live with it.

It just isn't what you sign up for, is it?

Richard Bugg: The day started in good spirits, but the rumour went round that we had "lost". The Sky crew asked us for comments, but I refused and said they should wait for Kris Stewart. When he appeared, ashen-faced, and spoke to them, we knew it was all over.

We never really believed the verdict would go against us. It was like having your guts ripped out. I swear that if Charles Koppel had walked by at that moment he would have been torn to bits by the people there.

But it's what being a Dons fan has always been about. We react best with our backs against the wall. Put us down, and we come back better than before. We never know when we are beaten.

Mark Lewis: Strange as it may sound now, I had been looking forward to 28 May 2002 for quite some time. I had spent the past six months working hard on an exhibition my company was running in Germany, and as a German-speaker it was partially my responsibility to ensure that all ran smoothly when the show opened on 28 May 2002.

So, when a friend sent me an innocent text saying "we have lost…" I was thrown into panic. I was shocked, devastated and surprised. Unlike all my football mates, though, who could get out of work and march to the FA, jam the phone lines of all radio stations and make a vocal protest, I was stuck with 300 international exhibitors and nine non-football-supporting colleagues in picturesque Lübeck in northern Germany.

Now, Lübeck in late May is pleasant enough, with warm sunshine and a breeze from the nearby Baltic Sea to welcome its tourists. But I would NOT recommend spending one of the most emotionally traumatic days of your life there. I called home several times to check that the text I had received was right. It was – and I went into autopilot for the rest of the day. What I said to clients and colleagues I have no idea, as my mind and soul were far away, floating somewhere over Plough Lane.

Callum Watson: We had protested outside the headquarters of the Football Association in May 2002 for two weeks. I had been there for at least three full days. I had waved to numerous taxi drivers, white van drivers and members of the public who had tooted their horns in support of our cause: to stop Wimbledon moving to Milton Keynes.

I had eaten cakes sent down from Adam Crozier, had laughed with two down-and-outs who had volunteered to storm the roof of the FA in return for two cans of beer, and met many fellow Wimbledon fans who I hadn't met before, but who I now count as good friends. Nothing, however, could have prepared me for the shock of the decision of the FA three-man commission who sanctioned the franchising and destruction of a 113-year-old club I had supported with a passion since 1983.

My support for the Dons came quite late in life when, after completing my degree in Edinburgh, I moved to Kingston upon Thames and started work in London. Being a keen football fan, I went to quite a few games – Charlie Nicholas at Arsenal, the Shelf at White Hart Lane, the West Ham "football academy" – but none of these so-called big clubs felt right. The club I was looking for was in fact only a few stops away by train from Kingston to Wimbledon, followed by a short walk past a graveyard. After watching Wimbledon FC only twice, once at Plough Lane and once away (at Orient), I found my passion and the football club I would come to love.

Everything was special: the fans (meeting the Batsford Boys and the Epsom Dons on my first away trips helped), the players (Alan Cork walking in to the Sportsman pub with his copy of Sporting Life pre-match still makes me smile), the club staff (Eric Willcocks, the link between the fans and the club, made me so welcome) and an atmosphere between manager, fans, players and club that was special and unique. Wimbledon FC was everything you could ever want in a friendly family club.

So on Tuesday 28 May, why did I feel so bad when the decision to move the club to Milton Keynes was announced? I had never lived in Wimbledon, had no family ties with the area, had started supporting the club aged 21, and now lived 50 miles from Wimbledon in Hampshire. Quite simply, my football club had been destroyed – rubbed out and cancelled at a whim. It didn't feel nice then and it feels just as bad now.

Some of our fans were in tears, some were pretty damn angry, some rather shamefully threw eggs and objects at the FA building, and a few even jumped into a taxi and sped off to confront our unpopular chairman, Charles Koppel, at a TV studio south of the river. I was just numb and in shock. During the many months of protesting I had never even considered the decision going against us. We were right, and the club and the authorities were wrong to destroy our history and heritage. I slipped away as quickly as possible.

Peter MacQueen: A few weeks earlier I'd lost my job as a designer and I was having a pretty torrid time of it. I'd been doing temp work, and now I was the lowest of the low, working for a debt collection company.

I was sat at work when my girlfriend Audrey phoned me to tell me what had happened. She said: "Wimbledon have got permission." I said: "You must be kidding, don't you mean they turned it down?" And she said: "No, no, it's been granted. They are going to Milton Keynes."

I went on the internet straight away and found out it was true. I was literally shaking after that. I had to go and hide in the toilet. I held my head in my hands for five minutes. Afterwards, everyone at work just laughed – they just didn't understand.

Adam Procter: I have only a hazy memory of the actual day. I thought then that I would try and remember it all. It was a strange week, and it had been an even stranger season that seemed to be leading to that day.

That whole season was all about 28 May. If you were to ask me where we finished in the League, I can't remember off the top of my head. If you were to ask me to describe Soho Square that week, then I could.

When the news finally came through I remember feeling numb and in shock. I could not understand how such a decision could be made on the basis of all the lies I had heard all season. I wondered what lengths Koppel had gone to to make sure his spin machine worked on the three men appointed to decide the future of my club. I think I managed one drink that evening, and wondered what I would do with all that spare time on a Saturday.

I had a strange conversation with my dad as I realised that he would not be making the trip to every home game to sit with me and cheer on the Dons. I wished I had seen more games over the years, or at least some of the games my dad had been to. I remember thinking I would probably only watch the FA Cup final and the World Cup now. Shock is the only word I can think of to describe it. I think my dad likened it to losing a family member.

Martin Drake: Not a normal Tuesday. Joe Blair texted me late that morning. His text simply read: "Oh shit." I didn't need to ask what that meant.

I was stunned, surprised and very annoyed all at once. How could the FA sanction such a move when it patently went against everything they are supposed to stand for? Hiding behind an independent commission was no excuse.

I couldn't work, so I headed straight for the Central Line and Tottenham Court Road. A brisk walk took me to the FA's soulless corporate-style headquarters in Soho Square. There were already around 50 Dons fans there, and the atmosphere was one of righteous indignation. The decision had been announced to the media, but no one from our wonderful FA had bothered to tell the assorted Dons fans outside.

As our numbers grew, we put posters up shouted songs, but still no official notification. Only when we took over the lobby did the FA provide us with a worthless photocopy of their press release. It was over.

The crowds eventually dispersed, to convene at the Fox and Grapes up on Wimbledon Common, the pub where the original Wimbledon Old Centrals used to change and drink back in 1889. The general feeling of outrage and disappointment after putting up such an imaginative and intelligent campaign for an entire season soon turned to determination and optimism. Marc Jones was there, full of hope, and people suggested starting a new "Wimbledon" football club that would replace the one whose League place had been franchised to Milton Keynes. This time we would truly own OUR club, and we would never allow anyone to take it from us.

Karen Hardy: I was at work. Someone sent me an e-mail about going to MK. I was so shocked I emailed Niall Couper, who confirmed the awful truth. I couldn't work. I had to tell a few friends. I was sick, cold and in disbelief. Then I asked myself: "Well, what are we going to do?" I'm not a member of WISA but I decided then to go to the momentous AGM on the Thursday.

Matt Akid: My memories of 28 May are snapshots, moments of clarity snatched from amid the mundanity of everyone else's lives carrying on as usual.

I remember making my way to the FA HQ at Soho Square in my lunch hour, talking to a few fellow supporters huddled in the rain, and knowing instantly from the subdued mood that, even though no announcement had yet been made, the unthinkable was happening.

I walked back to the tube station, through the lunchtime crowds of office workers and tourists, not really knowing what to do with myself. After work I had a drink with a friend and saw the news coverage of the decision on a TV screen in the corner of the pub, but still I could not quite believe what had happened.

My overriding emotion was resignation, defeat, a feeling that part of my life – a hugely important part – was over and that my life would now continue minus *my* team.

I am so grateful that other people kept the faith and refused to buckle, so that two days later I was able to join more than a thousand fellow Dons in Wimbledon Community Centre to witness the rebirth of our club.

Andrew Harris: I first heard the news from a patient when I was doing my afternoon surgery. He knew that I was a Wimbledon supporter, so asked if I had heard. My reaction was shock, disbelief, anger and horror. Needless to say, it was extremely hard to focus on what I should have been doing after that. I drove home that evening wondering where and who I would be watching next season. Fortunately, two days later AFC Wimbledon was formed – and the rest, as they say, is history.

Robert Smith (chair of Wimbledon Down Under Supporters Association): On the day of the FA Commission decision, I wondered what would become of the Wimbledon Down Under Supporters Association (WDSA). After all, WDSA had been going continuously since October 1985, drawing together Wimbledon FC supporters in this part of the world.

Long-standing friendships had been made, and we all had a common purpose. Now that was in peril. There was a fear that this disparate group of ex-pats, Aussies and Kiwis would become a victim of the shameful FA sell-out to franchise football.

But that changed for many of us with the birth of AFC Wimbledon. Disenfranchised Dons fans in Australia and New Zealand now had an alternative to dropping out of the game entirely, or even, perish the thought, following some other team who were once our rivals.

There were a few who no longer wanted to be part of WDSA, and went their separate ways, but the great majority pulled in behind AFC. Why? Because we now had something with which we could identify, even if it was six leagues below where the old Wimbledon played.

Oliver Cooper: As I lay in Cyprus soaking up the sun, I caught a glance of the back page of a newspaper on holiday in 2001. The key words I noticed were "Dons" and "Milton Keynes". I went in to a shop to buy a paper, and indeed there it was: Wimbledon FC had planned to relocate to Milton Keynes. I was very blasé about Koppel's plans. My friends (Fulham, Brentford, Arsenal and Spurs fans) asked me what I thought. I confidently predicted: "It's a disgrace, there's no way the FA will allow it."

On 28 May 2002 I received a text from a Fulham supporting friend. "Will ya go to, will ya go to, will ya go to Milton Keynes? Heard on radio, ur def moving." I switched on the radio at lunchtime, and there it was on the 12:30 news. It was official. If only I had stayed longer at the protests, if only I had volunteered to help WISA, if only I had attended the vigil outside the FA, then I might still have my club.

Two days later at the WISA AGM, its members voted to start a new club. Just five weeks after that, AFC Wimbledon played their first game. Over 4,500 turned up. It was emotional, but I predicted that the support would not last.

Now, I've started to enjoy going to football again. I do still have my club, and I've realised that the FA are useless and I'm crap at predicting things.

✦

The Spirit of Wimbledon

CHAPTER FIFTEEN: THE BIRTH OF AFC WIMBLEDON

THE FIRST STEPS TOWARDS THE NEW DONS

It is well known that AFC Wimbledon was born out of the fateful decision on 28 May 2002. The speed of it all surprised many, but the reality was that the plans for setting up a new club had begun six months earlier.

NOVEMBER 2001
By Ivor Heller (supporter)

The idea of starting a new club came to me in November 2001, in the middle of that last ghastly season at Selhurst, and I started to do some research. I wanted to find out whether we would be able to get into a league and what we would need to do. I talked to Trevor Williams about it and we sounded out a few others and got some positive feedback. So I always knew we had a chance of creating our own club. But it all depended on what the Football Association's three-man commission said.

I knew about the decision on Monday the 27th, the day before it was officially announced. I never said a word to anyone. I'd heard several rumours before saying we'd lost, but there were loads of rumours flying around then.

That night I put a call into Trev and we arranged to meet at 8.15 in the morning at my factory on Haydons Road. By the time we met, I was resigned to the fact that I had lost my club. I didn't want to do any more protests. I didn't want to go up to town and join the vigil at Soho Square. I wanted to do something positive. I'd made up my mind that I wanted to start a new club, and I needed help.

After Trev, I called up Marc Jones and he joined us later that day. The three of us were totally focused. We made a list of things we thought we needed to do to make the club a reality and within 30 minutes we were making calls.

It soon became a clear that we needed to apply for senior status, and we were told that the London FA would be the best bet. So we spoke to David Folkes at the London FA. He explained that to get senior status we needed a league to play in, a London FA form, and a groundshare agreement.

They were the initial stages we aimed for and by the end of 28 May we had them all under control. We had made contact with the Ryman League and spoken to their chairman, Nick Robinson. I had asked Niall Couper, who I knew lived near the London FA headquarters in Lewisham, to pick up the form. He got it to us a day later. I then made an appointment with the Khoslas, the owners of Kingstonian, for Friday the 31st. All that was why Marc went to the Fox and Grapes that Tuesday night so enthused. He knew it was all falling into place.

It's my one regret that I never made it up there that night. I'd arranged to meet Kris Stewart, the chairman of WISA. He loved the idea of a new club. At my factory there was an office put aside for the use of the Dons Trust and WISA, but it was never manned, so I said to Kris: "I'm either shutting it down or you are using this to set up the new club."

To his credit, Kris rolled up his sleeves and got stuck in. By the time of the crucial WISA meeting on the Thursday we had the AFC Wimbledon office up and running, with computers and phone lines fully operational.

The name itself was the hardest part – we had to get it sorted out by the time of the WISA meeting. David Folkes was passing on the Wednesday and he helped us with the form. We wanted to be Real Wimbledon, but David said: "No, the London FA wouldn't sanction that."

There were a lot of other names being thrown around. Some were really silly, like "Anti-franchising FC", but we felt that Wimbledon had to be the focal part of the name. We plumped for AFC Wimbledon.

The next question on the form was: "What is your start-up date?" Kris didn't hesitate, he said: "1889." David said: "Yes, that's it", and put it on the form. That was a real catalyst for me. We weren't a new club – we were still Wimbledon. Kris had made it sound like a joke, but as soon as David had said we could do it, I just thought: "God, we will have some of that!"

We had to move at a pace. It helped hugely that Kris and I gelled perfectly in those early days –

if we hadn't, AFC Wimbledon may never have happened. In those first few weeks Trevor Williams was hugely important. Trev was doing all our administration, and there were tonnes of it. We needed to raise £30,000 to pay for the groundshare agreement, and the only way to do that was to sell season tickets. Within a day we had season ticket applications flooding in and they all needed to be processed. It was all coming together, but not everything went smoothly. It took some persuading to get the Dons Trust board fully onside. We couldn't wait for them, so to get things moving we had to set the club up in our own names and sell it to them later for £1. And then we had the knock-back at the Ryman League meeting. Thankfully the Combined Counties League came to our rescue, and we owe them a great debt of thanks.

Once we got the groundshare agreement sorted, it was left largely to Trevor to arrange pre-season friendlies – though I made the fateful call to Bruce Elliott, the chairman of Sutton. We had called him several times before to ask for advice. I explained that I thought we should be playing them in our first match. I could tell he was sceptical, and he asked how many I expected to turn up. I had no idea, so I guessed at 1,000 or 1,500. He said: "No, seriously." I could tell he wasn't convinced. So I upped the ante and said: "Well, OK, probably more like 2,000." That's when we got the yes.

There were quite a few people in the office when I made that call, and they all looked at me as though I was barmy. In the end, I was wrong – more than twice that many turned up. So far I have not overestimated anything: this club has always surpassed my wildest expectations. It has gone so far beyond what I dreamt of all those months ago during the dark days at Selhurst.

✦

"I JUST WANT TO WATCH FOOTBALL"

It was arguably the most famous speech in the history of AFC Wimbledon. On Thursday 30 May, two days after the decision had been announced, the Wimbledon Independent Supporters Association held a meeting at the Wimbledon Community Centre. A thousand people attended, and the first few speakers were sceptical about the creation of a new club. Then Kris Stewart, the then chair of WISA, took the floor…

30 MAY 2001

WISA AGM (Wimbledon Community Centre)

By Kris Stewart (WISA chair)

I decided to make the speech only a few seconds before I stood up. It had been going round in my mind since the FA's decision on the Tuesday. I wanted to be able to say what I thought. As a chair, you're not really allowed to speak out, so when I stood up I asked Nicole Hammond to take the chair.

It was really difficult to judge the mood of a meeting. The first few people who spoke were against the idea of the club. They were saying it was giving in and it was the wrong time to start afresh. They wanted to continue protesting at Selhurst, to spend another year jumping up and down on the seats. That's what finally swayed me to speak. To me, that was very, very dangerous: Charles Koppel had made it clear in the last year that he had no intention of listening to us. Starting a new club a year later would have been so much harder.

I had nothing written down. The thing I remember most about my speech is that I kept saying:

"I just want to watch football." And I really meant it. We would go to games, maybe have a few laughs with friends before or after the match. It was an exciting young side and it should have been a great time to watch the team, but everything else had stopped it being enjoyable.

Sometimes protesting can be fun. At the start of the season it had almost made up for what was going on, but by the end even the protests weren't enjoyable. We could launch black balloons, give out leaflets, organise a Fans United day, even turn our backs on the play. But in the end, what was the point of protesting when Koppel was never going to listen?

Even the normally cynical press were on our side. It was David Mellor and Charles Koppel against the rest of the world.

All this was in my mind when I came to speak. The Community Centre was packed, and it was actually quite difficult to get to the microphone. I remember having a sense of people listening to me – which is quite nice, particularly when you are talking about something that means so much to you. But it was still hard to know what people were thinking. If my speech encouraged people to join in, then that's great.

I wasn't thinking clearly after I finished, it had been emotionally draining. I couldn't tell you what happened after that, except that there was a moment when lots of people put their hands in the air.

I never thought the vote would be unanimous in favour of creating AFC Wimbledon, especially after those first few speakers. But somehow, over the course of the meeting, the idea had captured people's imagination. It was going to be hard work, but it was also going to be hugely enjoyable, and I think people clicked onto that.

After the meeting, I just wanted to talk to everyone. It was really important that everybody had voted so strongly in favour. I had already made my mind up that I was going to back AFC Wimbledon whatever happened, even if only a couple of hundred of people came with us, but to have thousands was amazing. I can still picture all those hands in the air.

Then the hard work began. Ivor Heller, Marc Jones and Trevor Williams had actually started on 28 May. I had joined in the day after, but we really went for it after the meeting.

AFC Wimbledon was up and running, and for the first time in ages I was looking forward to watching football again.

By Dave Boyle (Supporter)

I turned up not knowing what would happen. After the trauma of 48 hours earlier, who knew what to expect?

There was standing room only. Then that filled up. They were packed in at the back of the hall, in the foyer. There was a palpable anger in the room, but a defiance too. Motions to boycott Selhurst Park were passed unanimously. Then came the meat of the night's proceedings – should a new club be formed?

WISA Chair Kris Stewart stood down from the platform to speak as an ordinary member. The room fell silent as he began. When he said: "I'm tired of fighting. I just want to watch football", he seemed to echo many people's thoughts. Kris spoke about getting a new team going, and that too seemed to echo many people's thoughts.

The vote was overwhelmingly in favour, but did anyone fully realise what had just happened? I think they did. Previously tired legs, aching from standing for two hours, now had a spring in their step.

It was a reminder that football wasn't about franchising or freeloaders. It was about fans. End of. In the pub afterwards, those fans were smiling, something you'd hardly have thought possible just two days before.

✦

THE DONS TRUST TAKES OVER AFC

The passion displayed by Ivor Heller and Kris Stewart could only take AFC Wimbledon so far. They needed financial clout behind them. It came in the form of the Dons Trust.

13 JUNE 2002

Dons Trust meeting

Wimbledon Community Centre

By Lou Carton-Kelly (chair of Dons Trust)

There was never any doubt that the Dons Trust would back the decision to own AFC Wimbledon. Really it was the only option. No Wimbledon fan wanted to have their club stolen away from them again, and with a democratically elected body owning the club we could ensure that it could never happen. But even with all that certainty I was still elated that the decision went through. It was the end of a horrible 12 months. I was devastated by the decision on 28 May. On behalf of the Dons Trust, I had put forward the case against the MK move to the three-man commission. Having spent so many months fighting for our club, I simply could not believe that they ruled in favour of the move. And the decision to back AFC Wimbledon put a line under everything that had gone before.

We had always had in the back of our mind that one day we might have to rescue a football club, namely WFC Ltd – but this was far better. This was building a club that would belong to the fans. We already had bank accounts in operation and could start taking donations and season ticket money from people. And once we had the backing from our members, we started moving.

AFC Wimbledon also made a few other key announcements that night that just added to the euphoria: a kit and a manager.

My one regret was that I wasn't around in the days that followed. I was in Japan for the World Cup, and I had to search for internet cafés so I could respond to the emails that were flooding in.

By Matthew Breach (supporter)

The FA announcement really didn't hit home at first. I was numb and just couldn't believe it. The following day I was on a 747 to Japan for the World Cup, and spent the flight wondering if I might never go to a game again on my return. The first couple of days in Tokyo were a blur of new sights, sounds and smells, before the uninspiring England display against Sweden dampened the mood.

I took the bullet train to Sapporo. From my hotel there, I phoned my fiancée back at home, and she read me the letter from the Dons Trust outlining the plan for a new club. After making arrangements to send off the £200 pledge ASAP I went out into the city with a new sense of hope for the future.

My first port of call was the Sapporo Brewery beer garden for an "eat and drink as much as you like in 180 minutes" barbecue-fest. I spotted a lady across the hall wearing a Dons Trust top. I rushed over to impart the glad tidings, and to my surprise I received all the latest insider news – she was none other than Lou Carton-Kelly, the chair of the Dons Trust.

Now on the crest of an emotional wave, I made my way to the Sapporo Dome and screamed England on to an historic win over Argentina. Suddenly, life could hardly be bettered…

◆

THE NAMING OF A MANAGER

So by mid-June AFC Wimbledon was up and running, but who would take charge of team affairs? There were dozens of applicants, but at first the favourite was reluctant even to put his name in the hat.

13 JUNE 2002
Dons Trust meeting (Wimbledon Community Centre)
By Terry Eames (manager)

I had been involved from the very start of the club and I wanted the job, but I still never saw it coming. I got a call from Ivor on 13 June to say there was a meeting of the Dons Trust in Wimbledon that night. He said: "Terry, we really want you to be there tonight. We have got an important announcement to make and we need you there."

I didn't think I could make it. I had meetings until 6pm in Crawley. I couldn't see how I could get to the Community Centre for the start at 7.30pm. So I asked him what the announcement was going to be.

"You're going to be the manager," came the reply. I said: "You've got to be joking!" Naturally I was there for 7.30pm.

I had played for the club in the late 70s, but I hadn't been involved that much until the Fans United day in December 2001. My wife had been a season ticket holder for five years, and she just asked me to come down and show some support. It was that day that I first met Kris Stewart and Ivor Heller. I just didn't like what was happening to the club I had played for 20-odd years earlier. This wasn't the Wimbledon I knew.

The day the decision to move to Milton Keynes was finally announced Ivor came to me and asked me what I thought we should do. It was obvious: we would have to start again. A day after the announcement, I met Kris and Ivor at the Tattenham Corner pub in Epsom. We all agreed that

we couldn't let Wimbledon die. We had made our decision. I had been manager of several non-league clubs and still knew quite a few people in the game. I spoke to the chairmen at Leatherhead and Dulwich, and they were really helpful. I also knew Nick Robinson, the secretary of the Ryman League, quite well so I gave him a call and put the AFC Wimbledon proposal to him. He was really keen and explained what we needed to do. The first priority was to find somewhere to play.

The new team: Kris Stewart (left) and the new AFC Wimbledon manager Terry Eames. (Getty Images)

Ivor contacted Kingstonian about a groundshare. We already knew that Leatherhead and Dulwich would be happy for us to share, but Ks was the ideal location. It was near Wimbledon and it had all the facilities we could want.

But it wasn't all sweetness and light. There was the Ryman League meeting where our application to join was discussed. We had left it late, and we needed the approval of 95 per cent of the clubs to get in. We got 87 per cent. Coming out of that meeting was the lowest low. But then we got the lifeline of the Combined Counties League, who welcomed us with open arms. God knows how we would have coped with a season of nothing but friendlies.

The next big decision was to find a manager. I wanted the job badly, but I decided to sit on the fence and just help out where I could. I didn't want to steal Ivor and Kris' thunder, so I kept quiet and just waited. There were many applicants for the job, and a few of them were really talented people. But Ivor and Kris wanted someone whose heart was in Wimbledon. When they asked me I didn't need to think twice. I just wanted to get the club going. I was part of the history; I had the link with the old times.

At the Dons Trust meeting they called me up to say a few words. I hadn't prepared anything, but I ended up coming out with a great speech, straight from my heart. The reaction was great, and I remember thinking this is me – this is me made for life. I saw the pleasure on all those faces.

In the days that followed I got a lot of backing from the likes of Dickie Guy and Jeff Bryant. I have never enjoyed myself more than in the days, weeks and months that followed. The first two weeks were mayhem. I'd just had a knee operation so I wasn't very mobile.

I had to try to get the best individuals. Lee Harwood, who was at Wimbledon as a player in the 70s with me, was a huge help back then. I hadn't seen him for something like 15 years, but he was the right person at the right time. I needed someone to back me up, someone to support me, and he was perfect.

223

There were one or two players I could trust, people like Trigger (Glenn Mulcaire). I then recruited Paul Bentley and John Egan, who now run the under-11 and under-10 sides respectively. Between them those two have played over 1,500 games in the Ryman League, and they went round trying to get players interested.

Paul and John helped loads in those early days and even more since. I would say that around three-quarters of AFC Wimbledon's players have come through their recommendations. But in the early days the key was the trials. It was like going to a fete. I was expecting 60 players and we ended up with nearly 300. Everything was go. AFC Wimbledon was happening – and I was the manager.

❖

THE TRIALS

The club now had a manager, but no players. It would have been almost impossible to build a squad just through contacts, so the decision was made to hold an open trial on Wimbledon Common. Volunteers were on hand to run the proceedings even the former Wimbledon manager Terry Burton turned up to lend a hand, but the numbers quickly became overwhelming…

29 JUNE 2002
Wimbledon Common Extensions
By Sim Johnston (successful trialist)

I found out about the trials two days before they happened, thanks to my mate Eddie Piggott. We work in the same office and he was listening to Kiss FM, when Chris Phillips came on and started plugging them. Eddie came over and asked if I had heard. He knew I was looking for a team. I'd just moved up from Kent, where I had been playing for Otford United, and I thought: "Yeah, I'll give this a try."

I went down there on my own, on my motorbike. I was like Billy No-mates and I was just freaked out seeing all those people. I thought: "How the hell am I going to show what I can do with all these people around?" The organisers had expected 60 people, and they ended up with over four times that. There weren't enough bibs to go round, which made things even more difficult.

Opposite top
Old and new: Terry Eames (right) in discussion with Terry Burton before the trials on Wimbledon Common on 29 June 2002. (Yellow and Blue)

Right
The dreamers: Terry Eames addresses the AFC Wimbledon hopefuls at the trials on Wimbledon Common on 29 June 2002. Sim Johnston (right of the goalkeeper in the front row) was one of the few successful trialists. (Neil Presland)

I remember walking around, looking to see if any of the players were any good or not. Some people knew each other. There were players of all different standards, none that I recognised though. I heard later that Joe Sheerin, who had played for Chelsea, was there. His presence caused quite a stir apparently, but I was oblivious to it.

The idea of the trial scared me to death. I had always had a nightmare at trials. I'd failed again and again, but this was the first one

where I did myself justice. I got picked out by a guy called Brendon, I can't remember his surname. It was a bit of a weird situation to be honest. He was also trying out and yet he was my group leader.

The day began with everyone being split into two groups. Half did ball skills, while the other half played mini-games. I started in the half doing ball skills – it was basically just hanging about in the sun. But when it came to the mini-games I tried really hard, but as a centre back it's hard to shine. During the day I'd seen that some players had been approached, but no one had come up to me.

Then Terry called everyone over, and there's me thinking: "Shit – that's it" and how bad it had been that I had never really been able to show what I can do. It was then that I got a tap on the shoulder from Brendon, asking me what my name was. I went home on a huge high, I was buzzing. It had been madness, but it was also a top day.

The second trial was a few days later in the same place. We did the same kind of things, but this time it was easier to be seen as there were only 60 of us. There were some new faces that Terry had invited down. I thought: "After all this, here's another big hurdle to cross." But then AFC Wimbledon was the team to join. At the end of each session they would read out a list of names – the ones who would stay on. By the time of the first pre-season game against Sutton they had narrowed it down to 30.

We were all wondering who would play. The changing room was absolutely rammed. Terry Eames still hadn't picked the starting team.

And then came the news that I was in the first ever AFC Wimbledon starting XI. After the nightmare of the trials and being knackered for days after putting all my effort into training, I had made it to the first ever line-up. It was very special – it was like my FA Cup final.

My family were watching, and they just hadn't expected the whole AFC Wimbledon experience to be as big and as huge as it was. They were proud of me and they were amazed. That completed a very special few weeks for me.

✦

The Spirit of Wimbledon

CHAPTER SIXTEEN: AFC WIMBLEDON'S DEBUT

CHAMPAGNE AND FOOTBALL CHAIRMEN

In the morning of AFC Wimbledon's first ever match against Sutton United, the Wimbledon Independent Supporters Association took a hired double-decker bus to ambush a protest by Football League chairmen against the collapse of ITV Digital. The bus trip was to prove a complete success.

10 JULY 2002

Carlton TV Studios

By Callum Watson (supporter)

Six weeks after the fateful decision, I was back at the FA headquarters. A new club had quickly been formed. It was started, run and owned by the fans. AFC Wimbledon had their first game, a friendly against Sutton at Gander Green Lane that night, but first there was a bit of unfinished business.

WISA had hired an open-top bus and were planning to gatecrash the Nationwide League chairmen's protest about the collapse of the ITV Digital deal. The prospect of paying the FA a visit en route was really too good to turn down.

Our double-decker bus circled Soho Square while we handed out our flyers advertising the game and waved at office staff we recognised from the two weeks of the vigil. We put up our banner outside the FA building and sang our songs. We were back. We had not been defeated. We had saved the traditions of the club I loved and we had got rid of the money-men who had never listened to us.

Later, we opened bottles of champagne and joined the crowds heading for Sutton. But first it was to the Carlton Studios on the South Bank, and the Nationwide League chairmen.

Mischief makers: Wimbledon fans ambush the Football League chairmen's protest outside Carlton TV Studios on 10 July 2002. (Neil Presland)

We drink champagne: Wimbledon fans on the bus down to Sutton swig away on champagne. (Alex Folkes)

By Alex Folkes (supporter)

The chairmen were protesting at the decision by Carlton and Granada to shut down ITV Digital and leave all the clubs out of pocket. We were protesting at the decision by the Football League to allow Franchise FC to move to Milton Keynes.

I got there and saw a few photographers around, but nobody else. I didn't have to wait long, as an open-top bus soon appeared, bedecked in banners. However, it was not the chairmen, but Dons fans. We had to wait a bit longer for the chairmen, who arrived in a couple of executive coaches and were all given identical placards. More incongruous protesters have never been seen before. These were barons of local industry, owners of Lancashire mills and Yorkshire steelworks. Holding placards. Trying to chant in unison. Looking embarrassed.

We gave them our protest postcards and asked them to support us. A few of them said that they were on our side and disagreed with the decision which had been taken, but others clearly resented our presence. One told us to "Bugger off", because we'd had our day. Needless to say, we made sure that we stayed and mingled with them so that the press pack could not film them without filming us.

By Dave Boyle (supporter)

I hardly slept the night before. It was a surreal day, and it started with the Football League chairmen.

I couldn't help thinking as I looked at the frankly rather grey and uninspiring collection of suits that we had something so much better. The contrast between them, as they shuffled onto their coaches and us, in our bright yellow T-shirts, was noticeable. On the one side of the road, the past; on the other side, the future – about to get onto their own bus full of hope and vitality.

Our bus was the same open-top affair that had seen regular action throughout the campaign against Milton Keynes. With anti-MK banners strapped to it, we made our way towards Sutton.

By Alex Folkes (supporter)

The bus wasn't full, but everyone was determined to enjoy the party. We spent most of the journey from Central London trying to figure out new versions of our old songs – you'd be amazed how much difference the extra "A" makes. We stopped at an off-licence in Clapham and bought what seemed like their entire stock of champagne. But not the cheap stuff. Between the 30 or so of us, we must have got through almost three cases of bubbly, including six bottles of Bollinger bought at a wallet-wincing price.

228

It must have taken about two hours to get to Sutton, but we weren't in a hurry. We sang, we ducked low branches, we waved at bemused motorists and people waiting at bus stops. The low point of the journey was passing Plough Lane. From the top of the bus it was painful to see the rubble where just eight months earlier our stadium had stood.

We arrived at Gander Green Lane just as the crowds that would eventually fill the ground started to gather. This was a new experience for me. Throughout my days of following the Dons we have rarely had large crowds, and even when we have, they've mostly been away supporters. But here we were, ready to fill the place. And smiling. There was nobody involved in this club who we hated. We almost forgot about Franchise and Koppel for a day.

By Dave Boyle (supporter)

I went to where the pre-match press conference to announce the sponsors was being held. Everyone was nervous, excited, stunned and a thousand other emotions. The big guns were in their Sunday best. Kris Stewart was having trouble with his tie, and I offered to help. It wasn't my best effort, but when I saw the AFC Wimbledon half-season DVD with footage of the press conference, I smiled at my extremely small contribution to the day's events.

◆

THE MATCH

And so to the inaugural game: Sutton United v AFC Wimbledon. The atmosphere around the ground was electric and expectations were high. A crowd of 2,000 had been predicted. The official attendance was put at 4,657 – though it was rumoured to be a lot higher than that.

10 JULY 2002
Friendly
Sutton United 4 AFC Wimbledon 0
By David Fry (AFC Wimbledon player)

From fan to player: AFC Wimbledon's David Fry. (Yellow and Blue)

When I think back to that first game, it sends a shiver down my spine. It was very special for me. I arrived at about 5.30pm and there were already a few fans walking about. It was all part of a crazy day.

I used to watch Wimbledon at Plough Lane when they played teams like Doncaster Rovers and got only 1,000 people. I went to Plough Lane for years. As a teenager in the mid-80s I used to go to every game home and away. I remember going to midweek games against Millwall, Gillingham, Orient and Nottingham Forest, and of course the FA Cup final in 1988. I only stopped going when I started playing regularly on Saturdays.

It was always great watching Wimbledon and being part of that crowd, so to actually play in front of those same fans… it was like a dream come true. Say you support Portsmouth, and you come to the age of 30 and then you *play* for Portsmouth. It was incredible. It's like I'd turned into a pro-footballer over night. As a Dons fan, this was too much. Seventeen years after starting my career, I was a Wimbledon player.

And then there was the crowd. I was told to expect about 2,000 fans, and then 3,500. It turned out to be more like 5,000. The kick-off just kept on getting put back. We went out for the warm-up and were promptly told to go back in. Then there was another warm-up, and again we went back to the dressing room. The buzz was getting bigger and bigger. My heart was in my mouth.

I can remember clearly standing in the tunnel. It was just amazing, waiting there while both sides lined up next to each other. I could sense the anticipation of the crowd. Then there was the roar, a massive cheer as we walked out. There were yellow and blue balloons everywhere. It was simply breathtaking.

Even the dressing room was packed. Terry Eames wanted to play two separate teams, one for each half, so there were 24 of us in there. I played in the first half and another team played the second. We didn't even have enough shirts, and had to swap them between us, but I don't think anyone cared.

We had never played together as a team. We didn't know each other. So to be holding a full-strength Sutton side to 0-0 at half time was an amazing achievement. We ended up losing 4-0, but that didn't really matter. The whole day was for the fans. For me, it was the highlight of my career.

It helped that I "got it". AFC Wimbledon is about Wimbledon reclaiming its identity. You can't have a team called Wimbledon playing in Milton Keynes. But for me it goes back further than that.

I went to Selhurst four times, when I was either injured or suspended and Ivor Heller had got me a ticket, but it was never like watching at Plough Lane. It didn't feel like Wimbledon FC. You'd drink in the Steve Coppell Bar; you'd be served by people in red and blue stripes. The photos on the wall were all of Palace in various cup finals. It just wasn't Wimbledon FC – where were the photos of 1963, of 1988?

The owners of the club had just forgotten about the fans. But fans make a club. They are the most important part. At AFC Wimbledon the fans would rather have their own identity and watch Viking Greenford than change identity and watch Crystal Palace or Wolves. If AFC Wimbledon hadn't started, I wouldn't have gone to another Wimbledon game. All the Dons fans I knew felt the same, and that's why AFC Wimbledon was so important.

After the final whistle we walked round the pitch and applauded all the fans. The fans ran on from everywhere, and I remember looking at all their faces – everyone was smiling. Everywhere was yellow and blue. These were the proper Wimbledon fans. The fans I had known from my days at Plough Lane, the fans who had been there against Doncaster Rovers. The club had been reborn.

I did many interviews after the match; I could have stayed there all night. It was breathtaking, the most amazing night of my life. I have played in cup finals, I have won league titles – but none of that can ever compare.

The adrenalin didn't stop flowing. I just couldn't sleep. I kept telling my wife about it all: about all the crazy scenes, about AFC Wimbledon and about the sheer happiness on everyone's faces. Wimbledon were back and I was a part of it.

By Kevin Cooper (Sutton United player)

There's always some excitement around the first pre-season game, but this was off the scale. At Sutton we were hearing stories all the time about the new AFC, things like they'd sold 800 season tickets and that they were attracting this and that, but it was all hearsay. We didn't really know what to believe. Personally, I was a bit dismissive. I didn't believe all the rumours.

I had been at a few clubs: Aldershot Town, Charlton and Wycombe. In reserve and testimonial games, I'd played against the likes of Dennis Wise, Matt Elliott, Julian Dicks, Tony Cottee and Alan Shearer. I'd seen a lot in football and I viewed the AFC Wimbledon game as just another pre-season friendly. It was great to be playing football again, but it would be nothing special. I was wrong – very wrong.

I could tell something special was happening from the moment I arrived at Gander Green Lane. There were already loads of people there, and the game wasn't due to start for another two hours. And then the rumours of the crowd numbers started to filter through. We were originally told to expect around 2,000. When we first walked out for the warm-up there were about that many in the ground already, and I was thinking: "That's nice, a decent crowd to play in front of."

It was then that the tannoy announced there were hundreds more outside, then that edged up to thousands. It was like being part of a carnival. For most of the team the wait was frustrating. It wasn't so bad for me – I'd only come back from my holiday a few days before, and I knew I was only going to play the second half. It meant I could take in the occasion far more than the other lads.

By the time we kicked off the ground was full, and there were even fans hanging from the trees. I'd never seen anything like it. It just made me want to play as well as I could – and I suspect I probably annoyed a few people that day as I scored twice! The first came courtesy of Matt Hanlon. He headed the ball into my path and I nodded it down before firing it low into the net. The second I really enjoyed. I beat two men and then wrong-footed the keeper. It was a good feeling, scoring two goals in front of such a large crowd, but each time only 100 people cheered.

We missed all the scenes that followed on the pitch, as we had gone straight in. I saw it all later on television and it just looked amazing. We could hear it clearly from the dressing room, and the buzz was still there when I left the ground.

At the time my mind wasn't on joining AFC – it was on the next game for Sutton, against Leicester. But I thought to myself: "I wouldn't mind playing in front of that sort of crowd every week." So when Terry Eames spoke to me and asked me to join AFC Wimbledon, I was sold straight away. Who wouldn't be?

Introducing the new Dons: Joe Sheerin (right) leads out the teams in AFC Wimbledon's inaugural match against Sutton United on 10 July 2002. (Getty Images)

By Kevin Bagnall (supporter)

"So let me get this right. You're going to drive all the way to London on a Wednesday afternoon, picking up two people you've never met in two places you've never been to, to watch a friendly match between two non-league teams in the middle of summer? And then you're going to drive all the way back here to Stockport after the game so you can go to work the next day? I think you're silly!"

At the risk of sounding sexist, sometimes wives don't quite grasp just how important some things in life are. And there are those events that are *important* as opposed to important. The call of AFC Wimbledon had to be heeded. How could I face my children in future years and admit that I wasn't there? Simple. I couldn't.

A sunny day. Not a lot of traffic from Manchester to Birmingham (despite the usual M6 antics), and then a quick kip while waiting for Mr Peach. Decision time. "A" road to Leamington, or motorway? Motorway shorter. Wrong choice. End of slip road – gridlock. Two hours to Leamington, including finding the "mansion" inhabited by a certain Leamington Pete. After a tour of the back roads of Leamington we've just over an hour to get to Sutton. Honestly officer, we kept to the speed limit all the way.

The main road to Sutton. Radio Five Live has a live report from Gander Green Lane as the teams run

out. There's a Mr Kris Stewart being interviewed. Blimey! It's hard to describe that feeling of pride and pleasure that one moment brought three men in a car who'd never met before that day. If the car itself could have swelled with pride, it would have.

Three miles to go. Kick-off delayed, not once but twice, due to crowd congestion – at a non-league friendly game. Three miles is a long way when you're late for history. And just for fun, let's try parking the car near the ground.

Queues to get in. It's gone 8 o'clock. Kick-off was supposed to be 7.30. Get those programmes. How do I keep them pristine? I'll manage.

In at last. Our line-up? Who cares? It's our team – AFC Wimbledon. It's not just a match out there on the pitch. It's a new life for us. We score. It was the big bloke up front. Someone says his name's Dean Martin – are they taking the mick? Our first ever goal… is disallowed. We sing, we chant, we laugh, we banter. We are one. In passion. In Yellow. And Blue. And a borrowed kit.

I've lost Pete and Peachey. I've found others – until now, just names on a guestbook. But we are not just names – we are the club.

Half-time wander. There is such a feeling in the ground. A family feeling. The warmth of the summer night mixes with the warmth of the people.

Second half. They score. Irony of ironies – it's a bloke called Kevin Cooper. They score again, and then a couple more. But it doesn't matter – never before has the result of a match mattered so little in comparison with the fact that it was played.

And it never will again. Because that night something was born that can never die. *We* were born, and I never thought that would ever happen. It was a long journey home, but nothing compared to the journey ahead.

"Was it worth it?" as I climbed into bed at four in the morning. I think my smile said it all.

By Dave Boyle (supporter)

I remember seeing fans wearing other clubs' shirts, I remember being on the pitch at the end. Everyone was smiling, in some Stepford Wives fashion. After all the pain and all the despair, it was a joy to behold the joy of others.

Debut: The first AFC Wimbledon line up. Back Row: Mehmet Mehmet, Dean Martin, Glenn Mulcaire, Daniel Jones, Chris Theodore, Dave Fry, Sim Johnston, Andy Hunt, Kevin Tilley. Front row: Neil Northcott, Drew Watkins, Daniel Scottow, Akin Gallimore, Craig Carly, Joe Sheerin, Carlo Castronovo, Julian King, Dave Towse, Daniel Couch. (Getty Images)

By Ian Hidden (supporter)

The excitement of what was going to happen that evening had got to me so much that I skived off work a little after lunchtime and made my way to Ivor's office to see if there was anything I could help with. There was. Would I be prepared to drive Kris and Ivor to the ground, collecting Marc Jones and the players' kits en route?

We got to Jonesy's place. There was just enough room in my boot for everything, and we set off for Gander Green Lane. Twenty minutes later and we pulled into the car park. Kris and Ivor said their thanks and dashed off to meet the assembled press. Jonesy and I unloaded the boot and had the kit stowed in a room under the main stand for collection by the players.

I dashed home – I live near the ground – for something to eat and a change of clothes. I was halfway through eating when there was a din from a little way down the road. Gander Green Lane gets very busy around 6pm, and my wife called me to the front door. I was as amazed as her when an open-top bus appeared, and I was recognised by some of the fans on the top deck, and they chanted my name. My wife thought we were all mad, but she got caught up in the euphoria.

When I left for the ground, I was amazed at the number of people making their way up the road. Nobody cared about the start being delayed. Nobody even cared about the result, but everybody cared about AFC Wimbledon.

The official attendance was 4,500 or thereabouts, but a senior official at Sutton United told me that they stopped counting after the tickets ran out, and their estimate was a crowd of over 6,000. A hazy day that led to a hazy season.

By Robert Dale (supporter)

"Oi," someone shouted.

I carried on walking down the platform at London Bridge station. It was Tuesday evening, 9 July 2002, and I was on my way home from work, wondering what rubbish was on the box that night.

"Oi," someone shouted again, "Bert!" and tapped me on the shoulder. It was an erstwhile work colleague, an occasional drinking buddy and Palace fan who I'd bump into three or four times a year at best. It was fate.

We shook hands, exchanged our hellos, and then he asked me the question that was destined to plunge me into a different world. "Are you off to see the new Wimbledon tomorrow night then?"

My match-watching days had ended over a decade previously, but my interest was sufficiently piqued. My friend was in a bit of a rush, but managed to mention "AFC Wimbledon" before shooting off. I spent the 30-minute journey wondering what the hell he was on about. I almost jogged down the road from the station to home and fired up the browser before I'd managed to take my coat off. Search: "AFC Wimbledon".

An hour or so and several websites and chat-rooms later, and I was up to speed. Another hour or so and the arrangements had been made.

And so it came to pass that three Wimbledon fans, three Palace fans, a Chelsea fan and a Man United fan found themselves in a crowded in a pub in Sutton High Street early the following evening. There was an atmosphere of anticipation I hadn't felt for years. There was also plenty of beer. This was to become a recurring theme as the season progressed! Nobody really knew what to expect. I'd been to a couple of Sutton's pre-season games at Gander Green Lane, and the Chelsea fan lived nearby, so we thought we had an inkling of what to expect. Given the obvious buzz generated by the game I confidently predicted a crowd of over a thousand, and was laughed down by most of my companions.

As the car nudged yard by yard towards the Borough Sports Ground, they stopped laughing. Everywhere was yellow and blue. And red, green, orange and claret. After half an hour of edging round backstreets we finally found a parking space slightly closer to the ground than the pub was, and set off for a liquid top-up in the Plough. Turning the corner onto the main drag revealed a queue of people halfway down the road, but luckily that was for the ground, so we managed to squeeze up to the bar for a couple more jars. Everywhere I looked there were old Plough Laners proudly sporting their tops, hats and scarves. All the time I was nodding at dimly recognised faces.

I'd been at all our promotion games over the years and, of course, Wembley, and it's no exaggeration to say that the atmosphere inside the ground was at least on a par with anything I'd experienced before. People were shaking hands everywhere, slapping each other on the back, and broad grins were radiating from every face I saw. The match was delayed by half an hour to allow everyone to cram in, speeches were made and balloons let loose, and we played "spot the kit" but gave up when we reached 50.

The game itself was a bit of a blur, a noisy blur, although not in any anti-climactic way – reminiscent, in fact, of the best Plough Lane days. By the end I'd managed to work out who Joe Sheerin, Dean Martin and Trigger were, and that we'd lost, rather unluckily, to a Ryman Premier team. And it didn't matter in the slightest. If anything, the grins were broader and the back-slapping a little harder. For the first time in history a 4-0 defeat was greeted by a spontaneous pitch invasion.

So that was the rebirth of a football club. Then, next Saturday, it was Dulwich Hamlet...

By Pete Baker (supporter)

It was a long time since I'd been to a match, the last having been at Plough Lane in 1991. My kids ribbed me about going back on the terraces, but in the end they came with me. The blue and white strip – the same colours we had worn as a Southern League side – brought a lump to my throat, and for the first time in years I went home hoarse.

By David Honour (supporter)

As I joined the train at Merton South that lovely summer evening, memories of the previous few seasons supporting my local football team came rolling past. Most of the memories were none too pleasant. Joe Kinnear's heart attack, his replacement by a Norwegian figure of fun in green wellies,

the constant aggro at home games, very little to enjoy on the pitch, and finally the decision that it was OK to take our club away from us.

The Dons are re-born: Supporters gather for AFC Wimbledon's first game on 10 July 2002 against Sutton United. (Getty Images)

A notable highlight for me was a confrontation at one game between several supporters and Charles Koppel. Leading the verbal attack was a tiny chap who I'd seen several times before, but I didn't know his name. Little did I realise that he was Ivor Heller and that he would be the salvation of our club and, with others, would restore my faith in the joys of being a football supporter.

All these thoughts went through my mind as the train rumbled on to West Sutton station. I was met by the staggering sight of huge crowds surrounding Sutton's ground and the pub on the other side of the road. Huge AFC Wimbledon banners adorned the walls and railings, and it was evident that a massive party was about to begin. Queuing for 15 minutes to see a friendly between clubs that were more or less "amateur" (whatever that means today) seemed a bit ridiculous, but once inside the ground it was well worth while. Balloons, speeches and the teams out on the park signalled the start of the party. OK, so we lost 4-0, but the pitch invasion at the end showed what we had and what Franchise FC had lost. And we've been partying ever since.

By John Woodruff (supporter)

It was my first football match for over five years. I was there out of curiosity and to lend support to a new venture. I still counted myself as a Dons supporter – I'd been a regular from the last Southern League season until promotion to the old Second Division, when starting a family and self-employment put paid to free evenings and weekends.

I went to a handful of Second and First Division games at Plough Lane, and just two or three games at Selhurst. I continued to look out for Wimbledon's results, and was sad (not gutted) to see the club relegated from the Premiership. I was concerned (not angered) at the management blunders, but not at the talk of a move to Milton Keynes: after all, that had first been suggested years ago, and nothing happened then, so why should it now?

I'd always enjoyed lower-level football more, and I didn't like Selhurst Park. I'd moved to Carshalton, and was thinking about going to the occasional game at Carshalton or Sutton. Then came the astonishing FA decision of 28 May – and that *did* get me angry. But I was seeing events from the outside looking in. I knew little of the communication breakdown between the club and its fans.

But what was this – a kick-about on Wimbledon Common to select players for a new team called AFC Wimbledon? My initial reaction was: "It'll never work."

Anyway, come 10 July, there I was in Gander Green Lane, with Kevin O'Keeffe – another drifted-away Don, one of my daughters, and Kevin's daughter and her boyfriend. The pub opposite the ground was full to bursting, so we relieved the local offy of its remaining cold lagers. The queue for tickets was huge, but we found a turnstile at the back of the ground with no queue, and the remaining lagers got into the ground undetected.

Inside, there was a real buzz about the place. Lots of vintage Dons apparel, as well as colours from many other clubs. The game itself was what I'd expected – a win for Sutton, but AFC did remarkably well for a scratch team, and the performance by the first team in the first half was good. The reserves didn't do so well in the second half, but no matter. I'd never seen such post-match celebrations for a 4–0 defeat: pitch invasion, lap of honour, the lot. I was back in the fold.

By Steve Meyer (supporter)

I remember my brother-in-law, five minutes after the final whistle of the FA Cup final. He sat on the terracing crying his eyes out. "Martin," I said: "Enjoy this moment – this is as good as it gets." So it proved, until Gander Green Lane on the night of 10 July 2002, when it was my turn to shed tears.

✦

The Spirit of Wimbledon

CHAPTER SEVENTEEN: PRE-SEASON MADNESS

THE FIRST GOAL

The 4-0 defeat at Sutton was followed by a 1-0 loss at Dulwich. When would the first AFC Wimbledon goal arrive and who would score it? A trip to Bromley in AFC's third game would provide the answer.

17 JULY 2002

Friendly

Bromley 2 AFC Wimbledon 1

By Glenn 'Trigger' Mulcaire (player)

I can't quite explain it, but I had a feeling from the moment I woke up that something special was going to happen that day. It's a feeling I have not had since and had never had before. I remember Dave Towse went down injured and we got a free-kick just inside our own half. Andy Sullivan chipped it in. It was headed out and it came back to me.

I knew instinctively what I was going to do. Usually three out of five times when I hit a long-distant shot it either goes in or hits the post.

But I knew this one was going in. I could tell by the leverage and the way my knee was over the ball that Glyn Shimell in the Bromley goal wasn't going to get to it.

It was such a great way to open the AFC Wimbledon account. Top quality finishing is captivated in the volley. So many different aspects have to be in place for it to be properly executed: the knee, the leg, the right spot on the foot, the shape of the body.

It is almost impossible to describe how I felt when it went in. I tried to sprint away, but Joe Sheerin just held me back. I remember clearly him saying: "You don't know what you have just done. That's the first goal. That's what legends are made of. I would rather have that then any of the next 50."

It was a surreal few seconds. You see it in films, but the world did seem to stop. Everything just panned in, with Joe's words ringing in my ears. It was weird. The only word to describe it is unbelievable.

Shims said to me later that he had made history too: The first goalkeeper to let in an AFC Wimbledon goal!

I dedicated the goal to my late brother Stephen Mulcaire. He died in a car crash in 1981, driving back from watching Chelsea play Shrewsbury in the FA Cup. My dad and Simmo have always backed me, but it would have been nice if Stephen could have been there too.

My path to AFC Wimbledon was quite an unusual one. I was drinking in the Red Lion pub in Cheam and I got talking with the barman, Mark Lockett. He explained that Terry Eames was the manager of AFC Wimbledon and that he was going to meet up with him a day later. I knew Terry from my Dorking days, so I said: "Just say hello from Trigger."

Mark gave him my number and in that next week I had a series of calls from Terry. It was enough to persuade me to go down to the trials. It was great to be there from the start.

Terry knew what I was about. He knew I could perform in front of crowds. I loved the Sutton game – Trigger loves a stage. Those first few weeks were just an amazing sequence of events. I had fallen in love with the club.

By Paul Jeater (supporter)

A drive through the leafy suburbs of Bromley did little to prepare me for my first visit to Hayes Lane. Long before kick-off Dons fans were arriving clad in the yellow T-shirts that during pre-season became our matchday uniforms.

Once the game began Bromley took an early lead through a penalty. A diabolical decision, I thought, from a distance of 80 yards. In truth we rarely threatened in the first half, but not long after the restart the ball came over from the right, and there was Trigger on the edge of the box to volley it into the top corner. The Dons had scored.

Behind that goal we celebrated like never before, jumping up and down. The bloke behind me leapt onto a plank of wood masquerading as a bench, and the guy at the other end was launched like a missile into the air.

OK, Bromley got a winner and their keeper had to endure discussions about how his ears resembled a trophy we won in 1988, but he obviously enjoyed the experience because Shims joined us a couple of weeks later. At the end of the game, we had lost but who cared – we had got a goal, and of course "I was there when Trigger scored."

Above
Elation: AFC Wimbledon supporters celebrate AFC Wimbledon's first goal. The Dons still lost the game, against Bromley, 2-1. (Niall Couper)

Opposite
Goalscorer: Glenn Mulcaire, scorer of AFC Wimbledon's first goal on 17 July 2002. (Alex Folkes)

✦

THE RETURN OF THE WIMBLEDON SPIRIT

The first few pre-season games had been one-sided affairs. The players were still strangers to the supporters, who had yet to see any sign of the fighting spirit that had made the Dons so famous. In the second half against Kingstonian it was back.

30 JULY 2002
Friendly
Kingstonian 2 AFC Wimbledon 1
By Matt Akid (supporter)

A beautiful summer evening, a lush green pitch and more than 2,000 people paying to watch a pre-season friendly – all the elements were in place to make AFC Wimbledon's first ever game at Kingsmeadow a special occasion.

This was an "away" game for us and I remember taking up a position at the Athletics End of the ground. It was also my first AFC game since the first ever fixture, at Sutton United. I had read about a succession of defeats in friendly fixtures against superior sides and a fairly bewildering succession of players who were tried out and then either discarded or retained by Terry Eames. So it was almost like seeing a different team when the Dons came out onto the Kingsmeadow pitch – I recognised some familiar faces like Joe Sheerin, Dave Fry and Trigger, but there were also some new names to learn like Simon Bassey and Kevin Cooper. The atmosphere in the crowd was lively, full of anticipation, but the big difference from the Sutton game was the pace and nature of the play – this may have been a friendly between the new tenants and landlords, but somebody must have forgotten to tell the players.

The first half settled down into a predictable pattern as Ryman Premier League Kingstonian – two divisions further up the non-league ladder than the new boys AFC Wimbledon – took control. In midfield in particular Ks were first to the ball and more capable of doing something with it when they won those challenges.

Passion play: Kevin Cooper (centre) holds off the challenge of a Kingstonian player at Kingsmeadow on 30 July 2002. (Yellow and Blue)

Kingstonian scored first to take a 1-0 half-time lead and they doubled their advantage at the start of the second half as the Dons struggled to keep up with the pace. But the game suddenly changed when young Daniel Jones set up Dave Fry for a spectacular strike to halve the deficit.

For me this was the moment when I got *that* feeling – a renewed bond between me and *my* team – which proved that AFC Wimbledon is merely the continuation of Wimbledon FC before Charles Koppel and his Norwegian friends sunk their claws into our beloved Dons.

There's no logic to explain why you stick with your team, through all the ups and downs, but *that* feeling is at the heart of it.

The Sutton game had been a statement of intent, a media event, with the actual football relegated to a supporting role, but the Kingstonian game was very much a real match.

Dave Fry's moment of magic galvanised the team and they started playing with passion, determination and a spark of menace. The Dons were now winning the midfield tussles and a succession of dangerous corners rained down on the Kingstonian goal.

An equaliser, which the new Dons would have deserved on the basis of their second-half performance, just would not come but that didn't matter too much. What mattered was that this game proved we could compete with a team two divisions above us and that a strong bond was developing between players and fans.

✦

THE FIRST WIN

Nine pre-season games, nine defeats for AFC Wimbledon. When would the first win arrive? The answer came courtesy of the inaugural Supporters Direct Cup final.

12 AUGUST 2002

Supporters Direct Cup

Enfield Town 2 AFC Wimbledon 3

By Andy Sullivan (player)

Losing your first nine games is hardly the greatest of starts for a new club, but it never really worried the players. For the fans, I suspect, it was different. AFC Wimbledon was so new. The side we had was very raw and we knew that in every game Terry Eames was going to bring in new players. I have nothing but respect for Terry. He had an almost impossible task in pre-season. Sure, all non-league or professional managers get trialists to look at but they all have a core squad already in place., Terry just had a blank sheet of paper.

By the Enfield match we were still trying to get a nucleus to the side. Given all that, to actually go and beat an established side was an amazing achievement. But for three of us it so nearly didn't happen. I remember myself, Danny Roberts and Tony Readings were all late. We got caught up in traffic on the M25 and only just made it in time for kick-off.

When we got there I remember looking around the ground, and the majority of the spectators were wearing the yellow Dons Trust T-shirts with the "I was there" logo on them.

I can't quite describe what that means to a player. I just loved the fact that people who had supported Franchise were now watching The Real Dons in large numbers and I was a part of it. Mental.

My first taste of AFC Wimbledon came after the club's first game against Sutton United. My two best mates, Danny Roberts and Andy Hunt, were at the trials and played in the first game against Sutton. I spoke with Neil Robson the night after and he explained how amazing the whole experience was and said that I should come down.

I was going through a period where I was fed up with my football. I had had a disappointing season at Staines and I was going through the motions with other non-league clubs. So I called Terry and we had a chat about the club and my CV. I'd played in the Conference for Kingstonian and Farnborough and I'd also won five caps for England schoolboys back in 1994. After that he asked to take a look at me against Dulwich in the second pre-season game.

Come the Dulwich game, I knew I was starting – Terry had told me as much in that first phone conversation. The amazing thing for me was the roar from the Dons fans when both sides came out. It was incredible and I thought to myself: "God, they haven't seen me play yet, they might boo soon." Thankfully I had a good game and Terry kept me on.

The Enfield game itself was a good test for us as they played in a similar league to the Combined Counties. Every other side we had played previously was either a Ryman Premier side or a Ryman First Division side.

As a side we wanted to win big time. It was also the first time the team met Danny Oakins and Lee Sidwell.

We started strongly and we were constantly at Enfield's defence. Ten minutes hadn't even gone when I received the ball from Lee Passmore out on the left. I only had the right-back to beat. I did a little step-over, dropped my shoulder and beat him, and drilled the ball low into the path of Joe Sheerin for him to stroke it into the net. I was chuffed, 1-0 and I had supplied it. Kevin Cooper then scored a good goal to make it 2-0. I can't exactly remember how the scoring went after that but I know Lee Sidwell got the winner.

At the final whistle, it was madness. We lifted the Supporters Direct Trophy. The fans went crazy. They were coming up to all the players and thanking us for our efforts so far and wishing us all the best for the season. It just made me want to do more and more for the club.

We were elated. I was delighted for Terry too – he had put his heart and soul into the club and at last we had given him some reward. Personally, I was on cloud nine and I remember the shivers going down my spine, I just couldn't wait for our first League game against Sandhurst.

We knew the first win was going to be an important milestone. It was great to get it, but you could also feel the sense of relief too.

By Iain McNay (supporter)

Our first Combined Counties League match against Sandhurst Town was looming large. I'd been to most of the friendlies and I had been far from impressed with what I had seen. Apart from the second half against Kingstonian, I hadn't felt much of the famous Wimbledon spirit. We had frequently been shambolic and just looked out of our depth.

I felt the Enfield game was the big one. They too had been formed by disenchanted fans (of Enfield, who play in the Ryman Premier), and the Essex Senior League was on a par in the football pyramid system with the CCL. The other nine friendlies had been against teams from higher leagues.

It was a beautiful Monday summer's evening when I set off for Cheshunt, where the match was being played. I was driving leisurely along the M25 when I hit a traffic jam. Apparently a lorry had overturned several miles further on and blocked the road. I patiently waited for nearly 30 minutes until the next turning. The clock was ticking by and time was running out. I sped through small country lanes, got lost, found Cheshunt and after stopping twice to ask directions finally found the ground. The car park was full and I ended up parking nearly a mile away and running back to the ground. Breathless I arrived 15 minutes late and was told we were 1-0 up. I should have been pleased but all I could think of was that this was the first AFC Wimbledon goal I had missed. But we scored again. We were looking good. We had spirit, confidence and even some reasonable ability. Enfield pulled one back, but we scored again and eventually won 3-2.

It took a little time for it to sink in. We had *won* a game! In fact we had even won a trophy. Everyone was ecstatic. After nine straight defeats we had won, and won in reasonable style as well.

The nicest touch of all was walking back through the dark car park towards the exit where several Enfield Town supporters had gathered to wish us the best for the forthcoming season. "See you in the Ryman Premier in two or three years," they shouted. And they meant it.

It was a night to touch the heart of true football supporters.

By Adam Russell (supporter)

Of all the pre-season games, Enfield was up there with Sutton. I remember Coops walking round the outside and speaking to him, and I was just overawed, I could hardly speak! Then the final whistle had gone and I ran on the pitch and hugged one of the players. It was probably my all-time favourite night as a Wimbledon fan. I left singing "AFC Wimbledon" out of the window of a Mini.

✦

The Spirit of Wimbledon

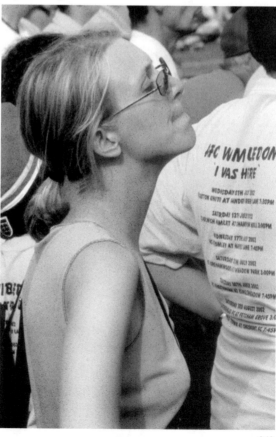

CHAPTER EIGHTEEN: ONE AMAZING YEAR

THE PERFECT START

After the pain of 28 May 2002, all the hard work over the summer and all the pre-season friendlies, this was it: AFC Wimbledon's competitive debut. A glorious hot sunny day. Sandhurst away in the League. A huge crowd and a win.

17 AUGUST 2002

Seagrave Haulage Premier Division

Sandhurst Town 1 AFC Wimbledon 2

By Keith Ward (player)

Everything that had happened in the two months before, all the emotions, all the training – now everything was focused on this one game. I remember getting on the coach at Kingsmeadow to head off for the game. You could feel the sense of anticipation. We were all hyped up. The friendlies had been great, but they were more often than not just another chance for Terry to try something out. This one, however, would count.

There was a lot of nervous banter on the way to the game. When we got there everywhere was yellow and blue. We all expected some sort of crowd, but this was overwhelming.

There were 2,500 people there, basically standing in a field. I have no idea how the fans must have felt.

Stretching: Jo McEwan tries to peek through the crowds at Sandhurst. (Marcus Massey)

A year earlier they had been watching Nationwide football in state-of-the art stadiums and here they were crowded six or seven deep around a metal railing in a ground with no seats to speak of.

It was a boiling hot day and we started off really well. Kevin Cooper scored almost immediately. I ran the ball down the line and fed the ball into him, and he just slid it under the goalkeeper. Then there was my second. The contact was superb; it just flew into the net. It came five minutes after the first one. We had a corner, the ball went from left to right, it went over all of us and back to Coops. He crossed it back in and I got between two defenders and just powered it in.

When it hit the net I just didn't know what to do. I remember there was a split second where I was just stunned. This was our first League game and here we were 2-0 up inside the first 25 minutes. Then the roar of the crowd got into my ears and I just ran into them. It seemed the only place to go.

The biggest thing for me was the supporters. I have played against a few teams with big support. I've played for Tooting against Wycombe in front of 3,500 and I played in an FA Vase semi-final at Whitley Bay for Banstead, but before AFC Wimbledon I had never had a big crowd cheering me on. It makes the world of difference.

As the game wore on I was just thinking we just have to get the win, we just have to get the win and get the three points under the belt.

When they got the goal back we really got the jitters. The pressure on us was immense, but we held out. At the final whistle, the crowd celebrated as though we had won the Premier League. The songs, the chants, the passion at that Sandhurst match will live with me forever.

The celebrations that night were also legendary. We ended up in Wimbledon Village until the small hours, celebrating with the supporters. I don't remember a great deal about the night, but it must have been a good one as I remember waking up with curry down me. That night helped us bond as a team and a club.

With all the press coverage the next day I got quite a lot of stick from my mates. They were all asking how to spell my surname so that they could put it on the back of their shirts. My work mates took the piss too. I walked in on the Monday and they were all chanting my name.

Of course it had been a gamble to join a totally new team, but I saw it as a new challenge. I liked what I saw at the club and after the Sandhurst game I knew I hadn't made a mistake.

In a way it seemed inevitable that I'd end up at Wimbledon. The Wimbledon connection has kept re-appearing throughout my life. I was born in Tooting and the estate I lived on was just full of Chelsea fans so I became one myself, but I used to go and watch Wimbledon with my dad when they were in the Southern League.

I made my debut at the age of 18 for Tooting and Mitcham against Hitchin Town and I scored the winner and we won 1-0. The manager that day was Dave Donaldson and his assistant was Jeff Bryant, both Wimbledon legends. And now I too was part of the legacy.

By Matt Rickard (supporter)

On 17 August 2002 Wimbledon FC, the team I had worshipped for over 20 years, visited Vicarage Road. The year before 2,000 of us had used this match to protest against the folly of moving our local club 70 miles north to Milton Keynes. We had even hired a plane to fly over for the duration of the game proudly displaying our "MK NO WAY" slogan.

Except it wasn't a folly. Not to the secretary of Aston Villa and some faceless lawyer. These two men had been allowed to sit in judgement and, incredibly, felt that Charles Koppel's terrible investment decision was a more pressing concern than 113 years of history and the aspirations of football fans everywhere.

So Vicarage Road on 17 August was an eerie place, 35 Wimbledon fans remained. Fifty miles away in the Surrey village of Sandhurst, the mood was somewhat different. A huge beer tent was straining under the demands of a thousand summer thirsts, the clubhouse of the local village football club had been renamed the Batsford arms in honour of Allen Batsford – the man who had indelibly stamped his mark on Wimbledon history by winning promotion to the Football League in 1977 – and some 2,500 fans were rejoicing in the re-birth of Wimbledon – AFC Wimbledon.

I felt at home at Sandhurst. The same people I had stood cheek to cheek with at Plough Lane, at Wembley and latterly at Selhurst Park were here. The community camaraderie that had first drawn me to my local team was in evidence and the traditional badge was back, emblazoned on our shiny new yellow and blue kit.

The only thing missing was the players – the spineless, believe in nothing players who took their money and lapped up the adoration but when we needed their support, the silence was deafening.

Power header: Keith Ward, No 6, heads in AFC Wimbledon's second goal and winner in the Dons' first competitive match, against Sandhurst on 17 August 2002. (Yellow and Blue)

By 3 o'clock the crowd was some 10 deep around the metal bar that surrounded the perimeter of the pitch. Myself and eight others had

Making hay: An AFC Wimbledon fan gets a prime spot to watch the Sandhurst match on 17 August 2002. (Yellow and Blue)

perched on a park bench. We christened it the executive lounge and as the action unfolded all the old emotions returned. Incredible surges of passion and despair, anger and ecstasy. The same jokes and songs echoed around the field and the referee was every bit as inadequate as his professional predecessors.

And then we scored. Not a work of art by any means, but as the ball nestled in the back of the net involuntary actions took over: a leap into the air, arms flailing and a lap of the far end of the pitch – embracing strangers as I went, screaming and roaring. The goal was celebrated harder and more intensely than a Lawrie Sanchez header 14 years earlier.

When it happened again moments later, the realisation that we were going to romp this non-league business fleetingly entered my reasoning. Even a soft goal conceded failed to bring me back to earth – that happened the following Tuesday when Chipstead failed to understand the romance of the situation – and I spent the rest of the day basking in the August sun and the righteous glow that I wouldn't want to be anywhere else in the world – and especially not in Watford.

Terry Eames is swamped by AFC Wimbledon supporters as he leads his side off the pitch after the 2-1 victory over Sandhurst. (Getty Images)

By Dean Parsons (supporter)

It was a lovely sunny afternoon. I managed to find a space by the corner flag, and while the lads warmed up we sang "AFC Wimbledon" as if our lives depended on it. But it wasn't until the lads ran out before kick-off that we got to see them in our new yellow and blue kit in all its glory. I was so glad that we had gone back to that lighter blue, as it was how I remembered our kit from when I first fell in love with the club. I've never had such an emotional day since, well, the FA Cup or when we beat Huddersfield to get promoted. And when Uncle Keith powered in the winner, the atmosphere, the emotion was just like '88. Except it was better, because this was *our* club winning.

✦

A SELL-OUT AND A DOSE OF REALITY

AFC Wimbledon's first home game will always be remembered as a momentous occasion. There were the thousands of fans locked out and the amazing buzz inside the ground – but there was also the first League defeat.

21 AUGUST 2002
Seagrave Haulage Premier Division
AFC Wimbledon 1 Chipstead 2
By Joe Sheerin (captain)

I was expecting a big crowd, but I wasn't expecting this many. The official attendance was put at 4,262, but I heard later that there may have been many more than that inside. I remember about two miles away from the ground I started to see the odd couple of fans heading towards the game. A mile later and there were dozens. By the time I had turned into Kingston Road everywhere was yellow and blue.

Sell-out: The queue to get in weaves its way out of the main gates at Kingsmeadow as AFC Wimbledon prepare to play their first home game in the Seagrave Haulage Combined Counties League against Chipstead on 21 August 2002. (Getty Images)

I had played in a pre-season friendly for Chelsea against Kingstonian in 1997 and that had had a big gate, but this was huge.

It was amazing. People were waving to me as I drove in. It got the old nerves going. I remember walking in and everyone was wishing me good luck. It was such a huge occasion.

The Sutton game had been big too, but I had arrived two hours before kick-off then and I had missed all of the build-up to the game outside the stadium. I didn't get the same buzz then as I did for the first home game at Kingsmeadow.

I suppose in a lot of ways I was lucky. I knew Kingsmeadow well, as I had driven down there so many times to play for Chelsea's reserves. I was there almost every Monday night. But in those games we were lucky to get 100 people watching – against Chipstead the ground was packed.

Even by the time of the warm-up the ground looked full and yet there were thousands still outside. And then we were told the kick-off was being delayed. It was then that we started to realise that this was going to be a unique occasion.

I remember being in the changing room waiting to go out. I didn't want to let on I was nervous. I was the captain, I was supposed to be composed, but I was shitting myself. I had missed the Sandhurst game so I knew less than the others about what to expect. But looking around the dressing room, it was clear that I was among the more relaxed players. You could tell by the looks on some of their faces that they were petrified.

I had never led a side out to that kind of roar before. It was deafening. Kingsmeadow is a small compact ground and it was packed, and all these cameras were flashing. It was also an evening game and that always adds to the atmosphere. The hairs on the back of my neck were standing up.

The whole captain's experience was so new to me as well. I remember just putting on the captain's armband felt weird. I wasn't used to having anything on my arm and it just felt uncomfortable. And then there was the mascot. He was a 10-month old baby called Elliott Brown. His dad came into the dressing room before the match and I remember him telling us all that he had been the last ever Southern League mascot for Wimbledon, and that touched quite a lot of the players. It made us realise that little bit more what AFC Wimbledon were about. I was really quite nervous about carrying little Elliott. I was so worried about dropping him, but in the end, thanks to the noise of the crowd, I think Elliott was more scared than I was.

The worst part of the night was the result. Considering we were quite nervous, we had played fairly well, but we didn't take our chances and made silly mistakes. They won the game with a last-minute winner. I was gutted. But in a way the defeat was almost inevitable. There was such a big expectation, but we had only been together as a side for a month. There were a lot of people thinking we were going to win every game and it brought a lot of people down to earth. It was helpful for our development. It was a release and lifted a burden from all the players. But my one lasting memory of that night was the reception we got from the fans at the end. It was superb. We had lost, but the love was still there and that spoke volumes for what we meant to the fans. After that I vowed that I would not let them down again.

By Kris Stewart (AFC Wimbledon chairman)

Given how many people had come to the Sutton game, I had always thought we might have a sell-out. But it was only in the last week that we began to realise how big the game was going to be. We were keeping in touch with the police and we were really worried.

Four or five days before the game we took the decision to try and dampen things down because we knew it was going to sell out. We were saying: "If you haven't got a season ticket then we can't guarantee you can get in." And we were telling people to get there as early as they could. In hindsight we would have made the match all-ticket, but by the time we realised that it was too late.

On the night itself, it just got bigger and bigger. We had expected a crowd, but not this many. I remember around the time we delayed the kick-off for the first time the senior police offer turned to me and said: "That's it, you have to shut the gates and tell everyone to go home." There were still thousands outside.

I went out with him to the gates and we were counting back from the turnstiles. We got to a certain number and he said: "You can have up to there but no more." It was left to me to tell everyone after that they couldn't come in.

I borrowed a megaphone and said: "I'm really sorry. The ground is full and you guys are not going to get in." No one wanted to miss the game and it was really tough to send people home. In the end I had to go into the queue and tell people face to face what was happening. It was horrible. Everyone had a reason to be there and it was really painful turning them away.

There was one guy who had brought his son and had driven all the way down from the Midlands. It was a birthday treat for his son. It was really difficult to turn them away, but I couldn't show any favouritism and I couldn't break the rules as the police and the local council were watching us really closely, especially as this was the first match we had ever put on. I found it heartbreaking, but the ground was full, really full. You couldn't walk around it. It was a massive event. I remember very little about the match itself, apart from losing. But it was a great night. It showed AFC Wimbledon could be a success and, of course, personally I was glad we beat them in the return.

✦

FRIENDLY FRIMLEY

Frimley Green had more reason than most to oppose AFC Wimbledon's election to the Seagrave Haulage League. They had spent eight years battling to return to the League after the financial burdens of senior status had forced them to opt for relegation.

28 SEPTEMBER 2002
Seagrave Haulage Premier Division
Frimley Green 0 AFC Wimbledon 5
By Mark O'Grady (Frimley Green secretary)

We had joined the Combined Counties League in 1980, but the financial implications of senior football proved too much for us to handle and we relegated ourselves down to the Surrey Intermediate Western League in 1994. We finally returned in 2002 after five years in the Surrey Intermediate and three in the Surrey Senior League. It was the completion of a long battle back up football's pyramid and a remarkable achievement for everyone at Frimley Green. It was the same year the CCL elected North Greenford United and AFC Wimbledon.

There were never any doubts about us going up. We were in the pyramid, we had made the necessary ground improvements and they couldn't really refuse us. So when the time came we replaced Cranleigh.

We may have worked hard to get back into the League, but there was never any bitterness towards AFC Wimbledon. In fact we viewed it totally positively. The publicity that AFC Wimbledon gave the League gave us more clout with the local council and it helped us get more local coverage. Then of course there was the money side of it all.

We were strapped for cash, having spent it all on the ground improvements, and the 28 September fixture with AFC Wimbledon stuck out a mile.

Frimley goalscorer: AFC Wimbledon's captain Joe Sheerin. (Yellow and Blue)

We would have loved to play the game at our own ground, but it didn't take us long to realise that that was just not possible.

There are only a small number of us that actually run the club and it's very hard work to keep the club going at a senior level. Week in week out, the majority of the work is done by just three people: myself, the vice-chairman Steve Giddings and Craig Fennell, the chairman.

The idea of doing all the work that was needed to host AFC Wimbledon was far too much for us to take on. We could have got 2,000 people into our ground, but there are no car parking facilities. There's also a huge hill overlooking the ground so we would have had to have block off the whole park. The police wanted us to have stewards everywhere. There is only one public toilet. And then there was the catering. The logistics of it all were a nightmare. It was far easier to switch it to Farnborough.

It wasn't a big disadvantage – many of our players have played cup finals at Farnborough so they knew the set-up there. The big difference was the crowd. It affected the youngsters and some of them froze. We also had a new manager, and he changed a few things round and that didn't help either. I suppose we were almost lucky to escape losing only 5-0. But then I didn't see any of the game. I spent most of that afternoon in the boardroom sorting out the money. Then I had to deal with the stewards and the programme sellers. The game was almost an irrelevance.

I remember the beers afterwards in the boardroom, and thinking it was a really friendly atmosphere. Frimley Green is a family club and although AFC Wimbledon had brought over 1,000 people to the game, they too had a family feel. It was all very welcoming and I remember thinking how much admiration I had for what AFC Wimbledon had achieved and also, to be honest, how much financially they had helped us.

✦

DONS SHOW FIGHTING SPIRIT

Fightbacks have always been a part of Wimbledon's history, and the victory over North Greenford United was AFC Wimbledon's turn to acknowledge the legacy.

21 SEPTEMBER 2002

Seagrave Haulage Premier Division

AFC Wimbledon 4 North Greenford United 3

By Andy Sullivan (player)

There are comebacks and there are comebacks, but to be trailing 3-1 with just over 30 minutes to go and then to win 4-3 takes something special. Personally the game was among my best for the club. As a winger you look to set up chances and I was the provider for all four of the goals. I've always prided myself on my delivery; it was something I learnt as a kid at Southampton. The ex-Villa winger Ray Graydon was a coach at the club at the time and he taught me to aim for the area between the six-yard line and the penalty spot. And against North Greenford our first three goals all came from that area. But the match couldn't have started much worse: we were 1-0 down within two minutes.

From there you can only react in one of two ways: you can either dwell on it, or accept it and take the game to them. At AFC Wimbledon we only know the one way: we took the game to them.

About 10 minutes later we won a corner on the right, I swung it in and Sim Johnston powered it home. But back came North Greenford and just before the break we were 2-1 down. I can't remember exactly what Terry said at half-time, but it clearly didn't work straight away as within 10 minutes of the re-start it was 3-1 and we were staring defeat in the face. But that's when the spirit kicked in.

They then got a player sent off and that helped too and, although our defending wasn't great, we kept attacking at an unstoppable rate.

Then there was Keith Ward's goal. I whipped the ball in from a corner, it was nodded down by Oakins and Wardy produced a spectacular overhead kick. The boys still don't believe he meant it. It came at the perfect time, just a couple of minutes after the sending-off. After that they couldn't cope with us.

The West Bank was going crazy. It always helped when we attacked that end. The West Bank is like a 12th member of the side and that day they were in full voice. The ball was being literally sucked into their net. I fired in another cross, Ally Russell headed it against the post and Danny Oakins rifled it in to make it 3-3.

Ally Russell got the winner with about seven minutes left. I had just fed him the ball in the centre of the pitch and watched as he beat one man and closed in on the goalkeeper. Players are like fans in situations like that, you're just praying he scores.

It wasn't the greatest of shots, and I'm sure that if Ally was honest he'd admit he mis-hit it, but it didn't matter. It ended up in the back of the net and we had completed an amazing comeback.

We all just piled into the West Bank after that, fans and players together celebrating. It was an incredible buzz.

We played some great football in the second half, good passing and moving. You could sense the confidence flowing through the side and through the crowd as the half went on. By the final whistle the noise was deafening.

The club has come back from deficits countless times since and that's all just part of AFC Wimbledon. The club was born with a special spirit. The club has a team of players who want to win, who will wear their heart on their sleeve and will play with passion from the moment they pull on the yellow and blue.

There have been a lot of changes in personnel since the first game back in July 2002, but everyone who has worn the shirt knows what the crowd, the club and the other team members expect. AFC Wimbledon will always be about being in it together.

I love the club, what it represents, what it stands for, and I am proud and glad to be a part of its history.

Provider: AFC Wimbledon's Andy Sullivan, who set up all four goals in the Dons 4-3 victory over Viking Greenford. (Alex Folkes)

✦

THE GREAT GOAL FRENZY

In the space of a few weeks at the start of their inaugural season, AFC Wimbledon scored three amazing goals. Each one would have easily graced a national goal of the season competition. The three players involved describe their efforts...

GOAL ONE: Sim's Thunderbolt

31 AUGUST 2002
Seagrave Haulage Premier Division
AFC Wimbledon 3 Hartley Wintney 1
By Sim Johnston (player)

As a kid, I loved to have a pot from long range. I remember the week before the Hartley game my dad was nagging me, moaning about the fact that I didn't shoot as much as I used to. He was right, and I suppose that might have had something to do with it. I remember picking the ball up inside our half, having intercepted it from one of their players, then a guy came in from the left. I cut in on my right. My first touch took it into my stride and I found myself slap bang in the middle of the goal 35 yards out.

I remember thinking: "Why not?" So I hit it. I couldn't have dreamed of hitting it more sweetly.

I'd love to say I was aiming for the top corner, but I just gave it a belt and it flew in.

Everyone bombarded me after it. I think they were more surprised than I was. Nine times out of 10 the shot would have ended up on the athletics track. I have never scored a goal as good as that one and I doubt whether I ever will. But it wasn't all congratulations. Terry Eames shouted at me after the game. He wanted to know what the hell I was doing that far forward.

The Channel 4 breakfast show, RI:SE, were showing highlights of our games every Monday morning and I had set my tape to record it, but it didn't record. I was gutted, so I phoned up Channel 4 and they sent me the video. And whenever I feel a bit low I put it on.

The whole TV thing was another example of how big the club had become. The whole media thing was weird. I never expected to be signing autographs, being on TV and in DVDs. It was like being a little superstar. I'd explain it to my friends and they couldn't believe it was happening. It's just crazy, but I loved every minute. All my life I had wanted to play professional football. I always wanted to play in front of a crowd and this was a dream come true. The goal was just another highlight.

A few weeks later, Ally Russell and Danny Oakins scored a couple of long-range efforts, but neither of them were as good as mine and they know it!

The blaster: AFC Wimbledon's Sim Johnston. (Marcus Massey)

GOAL TWO: Russell's volley

26 OCTOBER 2002

Seagrave Haulage Premier Division

AFC Wimbledon 4 Cobham 0

By Ally Russell (player)

It was definitely the best goal of the season. It was a long ball over the top from our defence. Kevin Cooper was chasing it down, their goalkeeper rushed out to head it away and it came straight to me. I controlled it on my chest and volleyed it in. It was a nice sweet volley. It was one of those that as soon as I kicked it I knew it was in.

It was part of a perfect day for me; I ended up getting a hat-trick, the first hat-trick for AFC Wimbledon. The other two goals were headers. For me normally a header is a header, it's pretty routine, but the second header in that game was special – it completed the hat-trick.

The lads all knew how important the first hat-trick for the club was and they were doing everything they could to set me up. I think the Cobham players realised that too and they started to try and stop me, but in the end they couldn't do anything about it. It was a bit of quality work from Danny Oakins – he hit the cross straight at my head. I couldn't miss. The roar from the crowd was immense; they were just so supportive that day. You could tell they too wanted to see the first AFC Wimbledon hat-trick. I've got the ball up in my room. I will be keeping it for some time – I reckon in a few years it might be worth something!

It was easily my best game for the club, and I remember Terry was really pleased for me. He was my old manager at Forest FC in Horsham and he was well chuffed. It was Terry who got me down to AFC Wimbledon. I think the club had a few suspensions and injuries up front and he asked me if I wouldn't mind coming down for a few weeks to cover. I ended up staying for the rest of the season.

Hat-trick hero: Ally Russell is congratulated by Kevin Cooper, No 10, after completing the first AFC Wimbledon hat-trick in the 4-0 win over Cobham on 26 October 2002. (Yellow and Blue)

As for whether my volley was the best goal of the season... Well, I didn't actually see Sim's goal as I wasn't at the club at the time, but from what I've seen of it on the DVD mine was far better. Danny's doesn't even come close. It was just fluky, it was just jammy. He mis-controlled it and had no other option other than to hoof it towards goal and somehow it went in.

GOAL THREE: Oakins from the half-way line

30 OCTOBER 2002
London Senior Cup
AFC Wimbledon 4 Woodford 0
By Danny Oakins (player)

I was near the dug-out on the half-way line when the goalie cleared the ball. It bounced once and I just drilled the ball goalwards. There was no-one around me. I remember the ball bounced before it went in and I was a bit worried that it was going to bounce over the bar. Luckily it hit the underside of the bar and went in. I don't know where the goalie was, but frankly who cares?

Some people say it was a bit jammy, but it was all about vision. That said, I have never scored a goal like that before. I have had a few go out for throws from that distance, but never in. It was certainly not the kind of goal I normally get. I normally get the scraps from corners and set plays. Terry likes to have me on the goalkeeper for that exact reason.

But we were 3-0 up at the time and they had just had a player sent off, so it didn't really matter what I did with the ball – so I just hit it.

The long-range effort: AFC Wimbledon's Danny Oakins. (Yellow and Blue)

I was giving it large for days after that. Ally had the hump as he had scored from the edge of the centre circle a couple of days earlier and he kept calling my goal a fluke.

I wouldn't like to judge which was the better goal, mine, Ally's or even Sim's. Mine was certainly from the furthest out.

✦

A THOUSAND CHEESE ROLLS

In a season of welcomes, the arrangements made by Merstham FC surpassed all others. The Merstham chairman was so overwhelmed by the occasion that he took it upon himself to shake the hand of every AFC Wimbledon supporter.

9 NOVEMBER 2002

Seagrave Haulage Premier Division

Merstham 0 AFC Wimbledon 2

By Ted Hickman (Merstham FC chairman)

It was a wonderful, wonderful day. I was so proud. I had a feeling it would be a great day, but not everyone was as convinced as I was. The surrounding neighbourhood were really worried about it. They were concerned that football thugs would invade their town. They had read the newspapers and watched the TV and seen pictures of Millwall and Birmingham fans causing loads of trouble. They thought all football fans were a load of thugs. I remember in the weeks and months before the game everyone was coming up to me and saying: "Are things going to be alright, Ted? We're not going to have the thugs here are we?"

There were also worries about car parking and congestion. There were fears being voiced that were just unfounded. In the end the biggest problem on the day was the trains. They were running late so we took the decision to delay the kick-off by 15 minutes.

It was a damn lot of hard work to organise everything, but it was a fantastic day. Our home pitch is part of an open park, so we had to close in the ground. We hired fencing that slotted into large concrete blocks, without that we would never have been able to collect the gate money. It was going to be a bonanza.

Goalscorer: Kevin Cooper, who scored one of the two AFC Wimbledon goals against Merstham. (Marcus Massey)

The money itself was a big concern. We had to organise a way of looking after it. Fears were creeping in that someone might steal it.

Then there was the catering. We had a small social club, but that was too small so we hired out the hospitality suite connected to the local Age Concern Centre, and it was there that we made the famous cheese rolls. We had an army of ladies making them from 6.30 in the morning: cheese and onion, cheese and pickle, ham and pickle, ham and tomato – the list was endless. Our club secretary was up even earlier than that to pick up all the rolls. The ladies were doing a conveyor belt system: one would cut the rolls, the next would butter them, the next would fill them and the next would wrap them. They were at it for hours and hours.

We also had a huge marquee erected in the ground to sell teas, coffees, chocolates, soft drinks and the famous cheese rolls. We hired a hamburger stall and extra toilets. It was an organisational nightmare, but in the end everything went smoothly.

We had to deal with the local police. We knew our beat policeman Steve quite well, and he was involved with everything all the way through. We also had a few specials in. At the start they hung around the hospitality suite, but they had bugger all to do so they all trotted off to watch the match.

I was so proud of everything everyone had done and I was so proud that all these people had come down to visit us. The Dons fans were superb. I walked around the edge of the pitch and I remember all the big smiles on everybody's faces. I introduced myself to everyone: "I am Ted Hickman; I am the chairman of Merstham FC, welcome." I shook hands with all the fan. It was just something I wanted to do. It was a pleasure to have people participate in the event. I wanted to thank everyone. It was the biggest thing that had ever happened in the history of Merstham FC and it proved that we can put on a show.

I had such a wonderful time with the Wimbledon fans, players and officials. I will always remember Kris Stewart and my little friend Ivor. They were really, really superb.

If football was to ever become like that… Forget the £200 to take your family to a big game. This was what football should really be like. We may have lost the game 2-0, but we won so many friends the score was irrelevant.

At the final whistle, the fans were coming up to me and to anyone connected with Merstham to say thanks. The mere thought of it brings a lump to my throat. I cannot remember meeting so many nice people in such a short space of time. There was even hardly any rubbish to clean up. It all just went perfectly. I used to be a press photographer, but I had so much to do and had so much fun that I didn't even have the chance to take my camera out.

A few weeks later I stopped at the traffic lights round the corner from the ground. I saw a motorcyclist with a Wimbledon sticker on his number plate. I stopped him and asked him if he was an AFC Wimbledon fan. He was, and he said: "Bloody hell, you are the chairman of Merstham FC." We had a good natter; the lights must have changed two or three times.

I have had similar experiences a number of times since and I had a wonderful time when we came to Kingsmeadow. I spoke to our players and they all said that those two games against AFC Wimbledon will live with them forever. It was simply wonderful.

✦

THE GLOOM AT WALLINGFORD

The match had promised so much: a top-of-the-table meeting between AFC Wimbledon and the unbeaten League leaders AFC Wallingford. However, it was to be marred by a sending-off and an ugly fight at half-time. The match was to end with police helicopters buzzing overhead. It was hardly the ideal background for Sean Daly to make his debut.

23 NOVEMBER 2002
Seagrave Haulage Premier Division
AFC Wallingford 3 AFC Wimbledon 0
By Sean Daly (player)

I only really got involved because of Simon Bassey's suspension. Terry was looking for a left back and ironically it was (the then left back) Bass, along with Neil Robson, who recommended me to him. Terry rang me up on the Wednesday and asked if I could play on Saturday. I signed on the Thursday and that was that. But it was a bit of gamble. An ankle injury meant I hadn't played for a year and a half. I had only just started kicking a ball again. And I hadn't even met the players before I got on the coach.

Bassey told me what to expect. So I was a bit prepared, but still to see a crowd of 2,000 plus in an Oxfordshire village takes some getting used to. The whole place was buzzing.

Then there was this family who recognised me from my time at Wimbledon and that was really strange. That was over 10 years ago, yet they still recognised me. I had been on schoolboy terms with the club from age nine to 14. Wimbledon then sent me up to Lilleshall, and when I came back, they wanted me to sign associate schoolboy terms, but I wanted to get a proper contract. I had Arsenal, Chelsea, Tottenham and West Ham interested in me. But I finally opted for Crystal Palace. I should have gone to Arsenal. It didn't work out at Palace or at Fulham after that. So I ended up drifting round the non-league circuit. I have had more clubs than Nick Faldo.

I went on to Carshalton where I picked up my ankle injury. I tried to rest it, but that didn't help. And after a failed pre-season with Tooting I finally had an operation on it.

I was just getting my fitness back up to scratch when Terry called.

As for the match itself, we were disappointed that we didn't win. The turning point really came with Joe Sheerin's dismissal. We were on top before that and we even created more chances than they did afterwards, but it just wasn't our day. They had three breakaways and scored each time.

The magnitude of the club only really began to hit home that next week. I am an electrician by trade and we do a lot of loft conversions. Two days after the Wallingford game, I went round to this house full of mad Wimbledon fans. The wife was there and she kept asking me about everything to do with the club, the players, the League, everything. And that's when it clicked that this was really big.

By Andy Nobes
(Wallingford supporter)
It's difficult trying to explain the strange mix of feelings that I felt after the election of AFC Wimbledon to the Combined Counties League. Although being essentially a passionate supporter and committee member of my local side, AFC Wallingford, I had followed Wimbledon since 1995 in the days of Earle, Holdsworth, Jones and Perry. I regrettably never made it to a live game, but I wore my three replica kits with pride (even when the white third kit was mistaken for a Spurs top) and had a real Elonex red match shirt as worn by Gary Elkins.

Gary was at the time the only link between Wimbledon FC and AFC Wallingford, having been born in Wallingford and living locally when he was playing for Wimbledon in the Premiership. He later came to play for his home town when he retired from professional football.

Debut Don: AFC Wimbledon's Sean Daly. (Yellow and Blue)

Although my interest in Wimbledon slipped somewhat in the disastrous Olsen/relegation season and the frustrating season in the First Division that followed it, I thought the fans' decision to form AFC Wimbledon was one of the most daring and exciting moves in football. It was an adventurous new chapter in the already fascinating history of Wimbledon Football Club. But I never expected for a second that I would end up watching AFC Wallingford v AFC Wimbledon, and that very season.

When the fixture list was announced, I could barely wait. After three months of hype, 23 November finally arrived.

This was like a dream – the legacy of the famous Wimbledon, with the bulk of its hardcore fan base, visiting the Hithercroft, the ground that I had spent most of my youth in, watching hundreds of AFC Wallingford games, sweeping the stands before the game, playing in the goals (and getting bollocked by the groundsman), smoking fags in the stand late at night, and so on. And this visit was not in the context of a big club sending their reserve team down for a friendly, but in a crucial, much-hyped competitive top-of-the-table clash, with my team the unbeaten League leaders. The atmosphere was fantastic. The ground was absolutely packed with 2,350 people, easily the biggest in our history. The visiting fans were making plenty of noise, but we managed to rustle up about 300 home fans, and even managed to sing a couple of songs.

Sadness: The AFC Wimbledon chairman Kris Stewart. (Marcus Massey)

We won the game 3-0 – a score which probably flattered us after AFC Wimbledon had missed several chances. The game had swung heavily in our favour with the controversial sending off of Joe Sheerin. Andy Shildrick scored with a cracking scissor-kick to make it 2-0 just before half-time. To be honest, I wanted AFC Wimbledon to score in that first half because it would have made for a much closer exciting game that would have better fitted the occasion.

The violence in the bar outside the ground (which involved fans not related to either club) spoilt the occasion for some people, but for me it was a memorable day. One of the most vivid memories of the day was near the end of the match. With the somewhat anti-climatic second half petering out, an eerie atmosphere filled the ground with the rain pouring down on the dispirited, wet and muddy footed Wimbledon fans. A sound began to rise from the far side of the ground, starting as a half-hearted murmur, but growing into a passionate and defiant: "AFC Wimbledon, AFC Wimbledon, AFC Wimbledon…" I have to admit that moment gave me goose pimples. I felt a kind of allegiance with the visiting fans and wished they could have enjoyed the day as much as I did.

In the end though, I was delighted with the victory, and happy with the way Wallingford put away their chances. At the end of the day the creation and arrival of AFC Wimbledon reminded me even more about the importance of following my local team, and following them through thick and thin.

By Kris Stewart (chairman of AFC Wimbledon)

I hardly saw the game. The violence in the bar at half-time spoiled everything. We had gone there full of high hopes and bubbling with enthusiasm.

We were told later that the violence was caused by a group of people not connected with either club. The police explained that they were local idiots who just saw the opportunity for a ruck. But after seeing scenes like that, it was little consolation that both clubs were innocent. The concept of searching out violence is pretty sick and it ruined everything.

It was a surreal day. The ground was full, very full and it was very wet. You could feel the tension around the ground. In the first half, there had been a problem with one of our fans getting attacked and his friends were getting upset. There was a lot of needle in the atmosphere which I hadn't felt before or since.

I was walking through the bar at half-time when it kicked off. I was right in the middle of it. The surprising thing was how long it went on for. It may have only been a couple of minutes, but it felt like ages. I remember some chairs and table got broken and then there was blood and broken glass. My mum was in the bar when it kicked off and she was petrified. There were people put off going to away games after that.

It took a long time to calm people down, and there were a lot of people who were quite upset. As chairman of AFC Wimbledon it was horrible for me. There were lots of people who come to our games who have never seen a nasty fight in a pub and I was one of those – just ordinary people who love football.

I just wanted to go home, but there was still the second half and I had to wait for the coach. The game then was pointless – we were losing and a man down. The hype and enthusiasm before the game had gone so flat.

It was a really low experience. I spoke to their chairman afterwards. It was a communal head-shaking. We stood and commiserated each other.

It was easily the hardest day I've had to deal with as chairman of AFC Wimbledon. Thankfully a lot of people knew nothing about it.

The match was to end in a surreal atmosphere. Dark clouds above, a police helicopter hovering overhead, a car park packed with police and thousands of dejected fans who cared little about the result. This was not what AFC Wimbledon was about.

❖

THE ST PAULI TIE-UP

The match itself was a key defeat for AFC Wimbledon, but it also marked the arrival of a group of fans from the German team St Pauli. It was the culmination of a bizarre link-up between the two sides.

22 FEBRUARY 2003

Seagrave Haulage Premier Division

AFC Wimbledon 0 Withdean 2000 2

By David Boyle (supporter)

How did a small club in the Combined Counties League get involved in a love-in with a bunch of anarcho-syndicalists playing in Germany and better known for their link-up with Celtic? It all started several years ago when, I was doing a master's degree in cultural studies. I decided somewhat spuriously to do my dissertation on the cultural aspects of watching Euro '96 in pubs, which was a joy to research. In the course of the studies though, I'd read about fan culture in other countries and came across this team from Hamburg who played in brown – a brave choice, aesthetically and historically – and had the best slogan I'd ever seen: "Never again racism. Never again fascism. Never again the Second Division." I immediately adopted them as my German team, and like most second teams, were followed via the occasional glance at the European league tables in the Monday papers, like Lens and Viktoria Zizkhov.

Link up: Dave Boyle of Supporters Direct speaks at a Dons Trust press conference. Boyle organised the link between AFC Wimbledon and German side St Pauli. (Yellow and Blue)

My Scottish team happened to be Celtic, who had got into a thing with St Pauli, and when I worked at a place with internet access, started to see links on Celtic fansites to St Pauli sites. Sadly, I couldn't delve any deeper as I don't speak a word of German. Luckily though, their main messageboard had a section called "for our visitors from abroad", which was in English.

St Pauli are the outsiders of German football, loathed for their propensity to defy the odds, and resented for refusing to get with the slickness of the Bundesliga. Their fans are renowned for being, well, unhinged. They care about more than just their team and to them football isn't just about watching 11 men kicking a ball around. They have a real sense of community, and have lots of fun into the bargain. I started to post on the messageboard, and mentioned about what had happened at Wimbledon and what we'd done with AFC Wimbledon. I suspected that it might just be up their alley – fans taking on the established

order, doing it their way and damn the consequences. It's also a bit of a mad story too, and I was sure that aspect would appeal.

And so it did. Soon afterwards, a fellow poster contacted me to say that there was a posse of St Pauli fans coming over the see the game against Withdean at Kingsmeadow. Sofas and floorspace in Clapham, Walthamstow and Blackheath were secured and then here they were. They loved it. They loved the bars. They loved the atmosphere, despite the defeat. They managed to get served in an off-licence on Wimbledon Broadway at 1am. And they promised they'd be back.

In the meantime, I'd identified a weekend when we had no game, and started to arrange a trip out there. A post on WISA Chat indicated that there'd be about 10 people up for a visit to the Millerntor Stadium. I then found a Ryanair flight for 99p each way. A deadline was posted and anyone wanting to go had to let me know by 5pm on a Thursday. I was away from my email all day and by 5pm, I switched on to find about 83 people wanting to come along! Flights were booked and match tickets were reserved. Obviously, being a team of left-wing subversives, the game was then moved due to TV. Unfortunately, AFC Wimbledon by then had arranged a game and most of the now 94 people wanted to see that too. What to do?

Happily, the St Pauli people had a plan. We'd go on a barge trip around Hamburg harbour and drink lots of beer. Sounded like a great plan to me. And so 10 set off as an advance party to do some reconnaissance. They discovered that St Pauli fans drink like fish, love football and go mental when their team scores a vital last-minute goal. I mean really, really, mental. Hamburg is after all the city in 1978 where punk turned up in, liked the licensing laws and stayed to have a family.

Two days later, the Womble horde arrived, red-eyed and hungover. We piled onto the boat and the madness began. Official signed shirts were swapped, beer was drunk, and two hours later, a group of supporters from SW London were singing about a German team most had never seen, and 40 Germans were extolling the virtues of AFC Wimbledon. Loudly. This carried on into the night at the 'Jolly Roger', one of the main St Pauli bars. Did I mention that the club emblem was a skull and crossbones?

St Pauli sent over a deputation to watch the final two games of the AFC Wimbledon's inaugural season and some Wombles went to see the final home game of the season at the Millerntor. St Pauli were relegated unfortunately. They were in the top flight in 2001, but in 2003 they were playing in a regional league, where their crowds were about 10 times bigger than the other teams in the league. Sound familiar?

✦

THE SMILE OF FRANKUM

Halfway through AFC Wimbledon's first season, Terry Eames signed Noel Frankum. It was to be a stroke of inspiration. Frankum was to add an extra bit of spirit to the club and, against Cobham, a delightful goal.

8 MARCH 2003

Seagrave Haulage Premier Division

Cobham 0 AFC Wimbledon 5

By Noel Frankum (player)

I don't score that many goals and all that was going through my head was: "Shit – I am going to miss in front of all these people!" Actually it was a huge shock that I even got the ball. I remember laying the ball into Coops, and thinking: "He is not going to give this back to me, because he never does." But he did, which was a massive surprise, and the rest as they say is history!

I couldn't have got a better contact on the ball. The goalkeeper came racing out, and I got a perfect dink on the ball and it looped beautifully over him and into the net.

It was easily the best goal I'd ever scored. My last goal before that had come over a year before when I was at Tooting, but I had been drinking the night before so didn't really remember it! But that one I'll remember forever. It was a great way to finish off a great win.

What's weird is that I can remember thinking that their pitch wouldn't suit our passing game, but we ended up totally playing them off the park. We had been threatening to give someone a good hiding for weeks, but the chances never really seemed to drop for us. Against Cobham it all fell into place.

Matt Everard gave us the lead after seven minutes – a soft header, but you take it. Then Joe Sheerin scored, and it was 2-0 before the game had even started.

Gavin Bolger got the third, after great work from Coops. Then Sully made it 4-0. Now at that stage everyone wanted it, and that's what made Coops' pass even more amazing.

And after it went in, I remember reeling away with the biggest smile on my face – I just wanted to get my photo in the programme!

Seriously, I hadn't been playing all that well up until then, but that day I was bang on form and it was just nice to show the fans that I can play a bit.

Deft touch: Noel Frankum (centre) lobs the ball over the advancing Cobham goalkeeper for the Dons fifth goal. (Yellow and Blue)

It was the attitude of the fans that really persuaded me to join AFC Wimbledon. You only have to come down to one game to fall in love with the club. The spirit of all the supporters is amazing and it's hard not to want to be a part of it. It's just a massive buzz to play in front of such a big and passionate support. I have been at Burnley, Kingstonian, Carshalton and Tooting, but AFC Wimbledon is truly unique.

The spirit is great. Everyone there in my first season was a character: Simon Bassey, Sean Daly, Danny Oakins, Gareth Graham, Glyn Shimmel and Mark Nicholas. But it's the fans that make the club. Wimbledon FC failed to realise what a great asset they had. I think it's absolutely scandalous how they can take something people loved and believed in and one day say: "Unlucky, we're moving." But the fans are with AFC now and as far as I am concerned, AFC is Wimbledon.

✦

EVERARD BURNS ASH

Ash United had been among the early pace-setters in the Combined Counties League in the 2002/03 season. Earlier they had beaten AFC Wimbledon 3-2, and that day a certain Matt Everard impressed. He was to join the Dons later and was to prove instrumental as AFC Wimbledon gained revenge.

12 MARCH 2003

Seagrave Haulage Premier Division

AFC Wimbledon 5 Ash United 3

By Matt Everard (player)

I had been at Ash for five seasons, and now here I was lining up against them. It was bizarre. Everyone at Ash was a mate and playing against them was a weird experience. I was expecting it to be like that, but it didn't make it any easier.

In the days before the game I got a few text messages, all taking the piss really, and one that said I was going home in an Ash ambulance. I also got a few e-mails, saying how nice it would be to benefit from a Matt Everard own goal for once.

I remember Terry speaking to be before the game. He knew what it would mean to me and he just told me to concentrate on my normal game and try and treat the match as any other game. I think in the end I managed to do just that, but it was difficult.

Then there were also the comments from Mickey Wollen, who had been the manager of Ash at the start of the season. He'd ruled out AFC Wimbledon from the title race. In hindsight it was probably not the wisest of things he's ever said and it came back to haunt him a little bit. Those words helped stoke the Wimbledon lads up even more, and we got off to a flyer. Kevin Cooper, in particular, was on fire that night. He ended up with a sweet hat-trick. He scored the first with the outside of his right boot from about 30 yards. You see him trying it in games and they go all over the show, but this one came off and it gave us a nice platform to build from as he scored so early in the game.

And then I made it 2-0 almost immediately. It wasn't the prettiest of goals and I didn't really know what to do to celebrate. In the end I kept it pretty minimal. I was trying not to laugh at the fact that I'd just scored against them.

It was a real toe ender of an effort. Sully whipped the ball over from a corner, and Wardy tried to volley it but it just caught the outside of his boot. I got on the wrong side of Ian Jopling, the guy who was marking me, and just hung my right leg out. I'm not sure what hit the ball, my studs or the end of my boot. The contact wasn't the greatest, but somehow it was enough to take it in.

At that point we were coasting and maybe we took our foot off the pedal a bit as they pulled one back just before the break, but that was merely a blip.

The third came just after half-time. A nice break down the right, between Noel Frankum and Joe Sheerin. Noel whipped the ball in for Coops who just had to tap it in. The crucial goal was the fourth: it just killed the game. We had a throw-in on the left touch line. It went deep to Coops, who took the ball in one move and spun the defender and shot. Andy Hunt saved it, but it popped up for Lee Sidwell to head in.

And the fifth, well that was Cooper's party piece. Sully won a free-kick, about 25 yards out, and with Coops on a hat-trick no one else was going to get a look in. He bent it round the wall and in to the bottom right-hand corner, classic Coops. By then we were in total control. But by that time my shins were heavily bruised where I had caught the bottom of one of the Ash boys' studs in the first half. We were 5-1 up at the time and it made sense just to come off and rest. It would have been nice to see out the game though, especially as I had to watch Ash score twice more while I was on the bench.

Arched leap: Matt Everard (No 5) leaps to win a header as darkness draws in at Kingsmeadow. (Alex Folkes)

But even with those two late goals we were never really in trouble. I got a lot of stick from the Ash boys in the bar afterwards, especially when I was seen signing a couple of the young kids' programmes with a cigarette hanging out of my mouth.

Joining AFC Wimbledon was too good an opportunity to miss, to play in front of a superb crowd, week in week out, and the chance to be a part of something that will go down in history. That said, I had been at Ash for years and it is never easy to leave.

A seven-day approach had been put in for me on Wednesday 5 February; I was informed by Ash's club secretary of the approach. I then had to wait the seven days before I could speak to Terry. I spent the whole of that first day dwelling on whether to stay or go. I wanted to meet Terry with my mind made up one way or the other. And in my heart I knew I had to go.

The hardest part was not letting the news leak out. I'm well connected at work and I'd been a regular poster on the AFC Wimbledon website Weird & Wonderful World. There were a few rumours being bandied about anyway. And even before the approach it was being openly discussed on W&WW. Then on the official site they put a note up saying that a seven-day approach had been put in for me. That got it stoked up a bit more. I was quite happy keeping silent about it all, because I think it would have been disrespectful to Ash and my old team-mates if I started discussing a proposed move on the internet, especially as I had already made up my mind to go. And once I spoke to Terry, I knew it was the right decision. I received a transfer request form, completed it and was signed on in time for the Saturday game against Chessington & Hook.

◆

THE DONS FIND A HOME

In 1991 Wimbledon FC left Plough Lane. In 2002 an FA commission granted Wimbledon a move to Milton Keynes on the grounds that the club's continuing homelessness made it a "special case". The club chairman Charles Koppel had insisted that no site was available inside the M25. But within nine months of their formation AFC Wimbledon had put in place a deal that would secure them a stadium that was just two miles away from Wimbledon Common, where the club had first played in 1889.

24 MARCH 2003

Dons Trust SGM

Wimbledon Theatre

By Lou Carton-Kelly (chair of Dons Trust)

It was a momentous night. I was nervous, of course, but I was also confident. The Dons Trust's Stadium Working Group had put a lot of time and effort into the motion and I was convinced that what we put forward was the best option: to buy the lease at Kingsmeadow.

The SWG had looked at all the other options, but one by one they were ruled out. The dream of course was to return to Plough Lane, but realistically it was too expensive. The land itself was too pricey and then there would have been the stadium-building costs on top of that.

We considered six other options, but for one reason or another they were ruled out. The only other serious option, other than buying the lease at Kingsmeadow, was a groundshare with Tooting & Mitcham.

It had a lot going for it. The romance of a return to the London Borough of Merton, our spiritual home, was of course the biggest appeal and we considered the groundshare very seriously. The Dons Trust board even approved a payment for traffic studies to support Tooting & Mitcham's application which, if successful, would have allowed Merton Council to lift the restriction of only one club playing at their ground, Imperial Fields.

We had wanted to give people both options to consider, but Merton Council's planning committee vetoed the idea of the groundshare 11 days before the SGM and so we were left with Kingsmeadow. For most of us on the Board it was our preferred option, but we wanted to have both available, if only to help our bargaining position.

It was hard work getting a deal with the Khoslas, the owners of the Kingsmeadow lease. Ivor Heller, Kris Stewart, Erik and I worked endlessly to get the best deal for the club. Throughout we continued to refer to our Financial Working Group to see what was feasible and what was not.

And so to the night itself. I suppose I feared that we might get a more negative response and I thought that there were going to be a few more dissenting voices, but it never transpired and when the vote came it was almost unanimous: the members of the Dons Trust wanted us to buy the lease at Kingsmeadow.

It would take three months of hard work and, after a successful share issue that raised £1m in three weeks, we took control of Kingsmeadow in mid-July 2003 and in the process secured the

The appeal: AFC Wimbledon fans queue up to get into Wimbledon Theatre on 24 March 2003 for the vote on whether the Dons Trust should buy the lease at Kingsmeadow. (Alex Folkes)

...and the decision: AFC Wimbledon fans vote in favour of buying the lease at Kingsmeadow. (Alex Folkes)

future of Kingstonian FC. After 12 years of pain, we finally had a place we could call home. Who would have thought it possible 12 months earlier when we were starting out?

Merton of course remains the dream, but at Kingsmeadow we are only one mile away from the border of the Borough. And in fact Kingsmeadow is covered by the Merton Fire Brigade. Besides, what is a borough boundary? They change all the time. Who knows, in a few years Kingsmeadow may even be in the London Borough of Merton.

✦

DONS ANSWER DOUBTERS

AFC Wimbledon had won dozens of matches, but when the big challenges arrived the side failed to live up to expectations and had lost. Questions were being asked about the club's big-match temperament. The victory over Wallingford answered them all. And after the vote to buy the lease at Kingsmeadow it completed a perfect week.

29 MARCH 2003
Seagrave Haulage Premier Division
AFC Wimbledon 3 AFC Wallingford 2
By Matt Everard (player)

The Wallingford game was far and away the most enjoyable game that I've ever played in. I remember my goal, the winner, clearly. We won a free-kick out on the left. I think Andy Sullivan put a deep ball across, Coops peeled off on the back post, took it down well and then chipped a sweet ball to the opposite post, where I just backed off my marker and got matched up with one of their smaller defenders. I got the jump on him and knocked it in.

The crowd went mad, but I didn't celebrate much. I've never really been one to celebrate my goals. I give it more of a Stuart Pearce celebration.

It was a massive victory for the club. It proved to a few of the doubters that we were a side to be reckoned with, that we could compete in the big games, fight for each other, play well and get the right result.

I hadn't played in the first game at Wallingford, so it wasn't really dominating my thinking as much as the other guys. But I distinctly recall the players talking about what went wrong at their place and how much they were looking forward to the game.

They felt the pressure more than I did. We had just lost to Withdean and the question marks were there: "Could we really beat the big clubs?"

Goal one: The ball creeps into the AFC Wallingford net direct from an Andy Sullivan corner to level the scores at 1-1. (Alex Folkes)

I remember the atmosphere clearly, not just from the West Bank, but from the whole of the ground. The noise was relentless for the whole game and the place was just rocking. We desperately wanted to win for the fans as well as Eamo and ourselves, just to get the buzz going, especially after we let ourselves and everyone else down during the Withdean game.

Goal two: Joe Sheerin (centre) rises above the AFC Wallingford defence to head the Dons into a 2-1 lead. (Alex Folkes)

Personally, and this may seem a bit weird, but I was more interested in beating the sides we had to play before to the Wallingford game. About three weeks earlier, we had let ourselves down badly against Farnham and I was determined to get that result out of the system. But I could sense how big the Wallingford game was. We didn't need to get pumped up for it and in the end we just totally dominated.

At the time, I had no idea my goal was going to be the winner. That said I didn't think Wallingford would score again as we'd done a good job of containing them.

Apart from the two free-kicks and the one scuffed shot in the first half, they didn't have a shot on target the whole game. I just thought, with the way we were playing, there were definitely more goals in it for us and we had three or four good chances to make sure of it in the last 15 to 20 minutes. But in the end I think we were just happy to take the win.

Goal three: Matt Everard powers home AFC Wimbledon's winning goal against AFC Wallingford. (Alex Folkes)

It was really satisfying to score. I had a lot to make up for. I was totally to blame for their first goal. I was all over him and the referee had no choice but to give the free-kick. It was still quite a difficult angle, but the guy goes and puts it in the top corner.

Thankfully Sully equalised almost immediately, direct from a corner. I'm not quite sure how it went in. I suppose a lot of it was down to Danny O, who just stood in front of the keeper and backed him further away from the ball, allowing it to creep in at the near post.

And then Joe scored to put us ahead. It was a great header. We had a corner which Sean Daly sent over to the back stick. I contested it with Andy Shildrick, who got the jump on me and knocked it back out to Sean. He got it back in and Joe got up well and got a real deft flick on it that sent it in to the top corner. And the whole West Bank went mental. That makes up for my foul, I thought, but I was wrong.

I got a clean header on the ball with about four minutes left of the first half, and two of their players collided with each other and the referee gave a free-kick. I couldn't believe it. It was 30 yards out, but after the first one, I just knew what was coming. And there it was, 2-2. Gutted.

And it nearly got even worse for me. In the dying seconds of the half, me and our goalkeeper Ray Merry went up for the same ball. I got a late shout from Ray to get it away, but by that time I was already in the process of trying to knock it back to him. I got the flick on it, looked up and Ray was about a yard away. It went over him. It looked like an own goal all the way, but Wardy came out of nowhere, got back, hooked the ball over his shoulder and I managed to hoof it away.

To be honest from where I was standing, the ball looked at least half a yard over the line. Wardy hooked it backwards and it still hit the underside of the bar. I suppose after what happened before we were due our slice of luck. To go in 3-2 down would have been devastating.

That scare woke us up and we totally dominated the second half. After I scored, we had loads of chances. Ally missed a sitter. He tried to lob the keeper but ended up lobbing the stadium. Coops went through on goal – the angle was getting a bit tighter for him – and he blazed it across the goal. And then Gavin Bolger had a good chance but he hit it straight at the keeper. They had a man sent off at the end, but by then the game was already over.

The celebrations that night were superb. We left the clubhouse when we got kicked out at about 8pm, and I was absolutely hammered.

By Matt Rickard (supporter)

Wallingford had it all. Before this season, I had never even heard of Wallingford but here I was, acutely anticipating a game against them, as if Chelsea and their lavish assemblage of exotic, ball-juggling, slightly-past-their-prime mavericks had just rolled into town.

Job done: Matt Everard leaves the field in jubilation after the Dons 3-2 win over Seagrave Haulage Premier Division leaders AFC Wallingford on 29 March 2003. (Alex Folkes)

In fact, Wallingford came second only to Sandhurst for the event of the season. It had atmosphere – with some 3,500 people packed into Kingsmeadow, most of them seemingly wedged onto the West Bank. A terrace not designed for watching football admittedly, but acoustically up there with Roker Park.

It had a victory… for Wimbledon. Ok, we had 36 of them that season but this was against a good side, in a game we had to win. I have witnessed every abject surrender from various Wimbledon teams in the last 10 years and fully expected us to continue this fine tradition. In fact, after falling a goal behind after just 10 minutes, I was waiting for four of the players to hail cabs, and a couple to nip back to the changing room to start running the bath, leaving the other five to remain and wander about aimlessly, huffing and puffing.

It had a sending-off. Admit it, no game could ever be complete without one. Ignore the po-faced commentator who decries that it has ruined the game. All sending-offs are entertainment of the highest kind. If your team suffers the loss of a man, it unites the crowd, galvanises the team and more often than not leads to a glorious victory against all the odds – Watford in the quarter-final anyone? Whereas, if the opposing team loses a man the hilarity that ensues, is up there with sharing a beer with Tommy Cooper.

It had great goals. Joe Sheerin's leap to flick home a Lee Sidwell cross was spectacular – Fashanu-esque even – though he probably has a phobia about that sort of thing now. Meanwhile, Shane Small-King enjoyed his swerving 25-yard free-kick into the top left corner so much that, he did it again half an hour later. Ray Merry did not even move during the repeat so as not to miss anything.

It also had life-enhancing amounts of alcohol. That wasn't just me, was it?

It really did have it all.

✦

THE MERTON DERBY

The significance of this match was not lost on Wimbledon fans. Two clubs playing each other, both whose spiritual home was in the London borough of Merton. The match was due to take place in the borough, but a late request from the police saw the match switched to Carshalton.

21 APRIL 2003
Seagrave Haulage Premier Division
Raynes Park Vale 0 AFC Wimbledon 5
By Lee Dobinson
(manager of Raynes Park Vale)

I t was weird to lose so heavily and to enjoy the day so much. It was easily the biggest attendance in the club's history. I was looking forward to the game hugely, not so much for myself but for my players. This was the biggest game of their lives.

Raynes Park Vale are one big family – and in my case then, literally. My son Darren, who like me joined AFC Wimbledon in the summer, was in the team. No one gets paid for anything at Raynes Park. Everyone mucks in, including the players. They even rotate the bar manager's job. They do it for the love of the club. But it still took ages to organise the game. We had our first meeting about it six months before the game finally took place. I went to other AFC away games to see what they were doing to cope with the crowd.

Andy Sullivan prepares to whip in a corner against Raynes Park Vale at Carshalton FC on 21 April 2003. AFC Wimbledon won the match 5-0. (Marcus Massey)

At their Grand Drive ground Raynes Park Vale normally get around 20 spectators, 50 if they are lucky. And to be honest sometimes on bleak days it has been one man and his dog. Raynes Park Vale could open the gate 10 minutes before kick-off and have no problem getting everyone in.

I was convinced we could hold the game at Grand Drive, and I had several meetings with our committee and they'd agreed. We were all gearing up for it and then we had trouble with fly-tipping at the ground. I still wanted to go ahead, but the police refused. There were bricks amongst the earth dumped at the ground and the police came out with all the worst-case scenarios. We had no choice but to move the game and Carshalton was the best option for us.

It was still hard work. We had to ask AFC Wimbledon and Carshalton to provide the stewards as we don't have enough fans to organise everything. My wife Julie and our centre-back Lee Cox's mum Chris made all the food. They were cooking non-stop on the day before the game.

It felt like far more than the 1,871 attendance that was declared. My one regret is that we froze. Our goalkeeper was violently sick with nerves before kick-off. You just can't pick the ones that are going to be terrified. None of the players had ever experienced anything like that before. A few of them really loved it, but for most of them it was just too much.

For me, it was an amazing experience and I wanted to taste it all over again in the return three weeks later.

◆

THE SIDWELL HAT-TRICK

The story of Lee Sidwell is perhaps among the best examples of how much AFC Wimbledon changed the lives of so many people. The 3-0 win over Walton Casuals was to be his best performance of the 2002/03 season.

26 APRIL 2003
Seagrave Haulage Premier Division
AFC Wimbledon 3 Walton Casuals 0
By Lee Sidwell (player)

Sometimes you had to pinch yourself. I used to play in front of five or six people. To play in front of 3,000 – I can't describe how that feels. You know, all the AFC Wimbledon players are just ordinary people. Every player has a day job, six days a week they're just like everybody else and then on Saturday they're treated like pro footballers.

The whole experience totally changed my life. I used to go out and have a few drinks on Friday and eat whatever I wanted during the week. And now I stay in on Fridays and spend the week watching my diet.

As for the Walton game, well, I have scored a few hat-tricks before, but never in front of 3,000 people. I got all the boys to sign the ball after the game and it's safely tucked away now.

By 2003, I had been playing for 10 years and there was no club like AFC Wimbledon. It was not just the fans and the set-up: it was the players and the personalities in the team. I don't know whether it was accidental or not, but the spirit in the first season was sensational. Everyone backed everyone.

There was also the level of talent in the side, it was just amazing. Most of the players at AFC Wimbledon had had a taste of the professional circuit. I wanted that too, but I never had the chance.

When I went to Netherne I gave up on doing anything different. I had a few offers from the Ryman League. Tooting & Mitcham asked me to go there but I never really fancied it.

And that's why I can't thank Nicky English enough. He spoke to Terry about turning Netherne into the club's reserve side. So Terry came down to have a look just to see the set-up and he came away with me and Danny Oakins signed up for AFC!

Netherne was just about enjoying it and having a drink with your friends. My attitude changed totally when I joined AFC. I think I missed just one training session.

As for the Walton game, well, for the first goal I remember cutting in and going past two players. There was no option, other than to shoot. So I went for it, and it got a bit of a deflection and went in.

And you could feel the relief all around the stadium. It had looked like being another 0-0 Farnham Town type match before that.

The second came when I nicked the ball off the left midfielder's foot. I cut in slightly and shot, and it went in the bottom left-hand corner.

The third was a penalty. I did a few twists and turns and got brought down in the box. It was a definite penalty and there was no way anyone else was going to take it.

I always know which way I am going to put a penalty, and that was it – 3-0 and I was delirious.

I don't know what the future holds, but I would like to be involved in the club for ever more. I think most of the lads would. We were there at the start and we we want to be there to help guide the side up through the leagues.

Lee Sidwell (left) reels away in delight after scoring against Walton Casuals on 26 April 2003. Sidwell finished the match with a hat-trick. (Alex Folkes)

✦

THE READING ANTICS

Off the pitch, the spirit at AFC Wimbledon was building up. A victory for Wallingford over Feltham the same day ended the Dons' hopes of promotion. It should have been a gloomy day, but it wasn't.

3 MAY 2003

Seagrave Haulage Premier Division

Reading Town 0 AFC Wimbledon 2

By Jill Stratton (supporter)

The one thing that had always worried Wimbledon fans about starting a new club was whether the old spirit and passion that was the Wimbledon we knew in the 80s and 90s would resurface. As a fan from the Plough Lane days I had seen the antics and the pranks of the old Wimbledon. The jokes and the laughter at Wimbledon had been such a key part of the spirit of the club.

I'd heard rumours of similar things going on at AFC Wimbledon but I wasn't convinced. The journey back from Reading Town dispelled all those concerns. This club wasn't as crazy as the old Wimbledon – it was even crazier.

The journey really has to be put into context. We may have won the match 2-0, but Wallingford's win at Feltham meant our hopes of automatic promotion had gone. The fans and the players should have been despondent. At any other club I'm sure that would have been the case, but this was AFC Wimbledon.

Aideen Rochford and I had been due to travel back on the supporters' coach, but it left without us. We had no choice but to ask Trevor Williams, the club secretary, if we could travel back with the players. He agreed, so we clambered on to an empty coach and waited for the players to appear.

Relaxed: Terry Eames (centre) with pint in hand after the victory over Reading on 3 May 2003. (Alex Folkes)

First to appear was Lee Sidwell sprinting around the corner with about 10 Wimbledon fans in hot pursuit. Apparently he had sided with a rival set of Wimbledon supporters when the two sets had launched into a singing competition in the bar. Sids of course was far too fast for that lot and managed to jump onto the safety of the coach.

The rest of the team followed soon after with a large number of fans walking up with them. Lads being lads they all piled on to the back of the coach, but straight away you could see that Danny Oakins and Gareth Graham were scheming.

It was like watching a duel: 20 AFC Wimbledon fans lined up along the road, backs turned to the coach, and on board the majority of the first team with their backs up against the window. And as the coach pulled away there was a mass trouser drop. It was like being at Alan Cork's testimonial all over again!

The journey back was full of jokes and banter and the beer continued to flow. You would never have guessed that this side had just missed out on automatic promotion.

The players ran their own awards ceremony. I remember bald-headed Keith Ward won the award for "the player who spends the longest time doing his hair and then leaving it at home".

Even the toilet break turned into a farce. The whole team on the hard shoulder all decked out in yellow and blue AFC tracksuits watering the grass for all and sundry to see. Danny Oakins found the urge to push the players down into the ditch too hard to resist. While most of the players got away in time, Gareth Graham wasn't so fortunate and ended up being pushed straight in. The sight of Graham, ever so slightly the worse for wear, scrambling around grasping onto tufts of grass to pull himself back up will live with me for ever.

The journey back to Kingsmeadow was to end with a range of songs from Simon Bassey, each one about one of the players. None of them are printable.

After we got off the coach at Kingsmeadow the lads were scheming again. They wanted to go to the Robert Peel and watch the strippers. Their girlfriends were none too pleased and the lads backed down. We left in a big cab convoy: the boys in the cabs behind the girls.

Leaving Ks it looked good, they were indicating that they were turning right to head into Wimbledon with us but as soon as we turned they changed the indicator, turned left and headed straight into the Peel with mobiles turned off so they couldn't be contacted.

An hour or so later they trundled in to Jaspers in Wimbledon as if nothing had happened – trying to convince everyone they had in fact been in Kingston for some dinner. It would have worked except for one tell-tale sign – the smiles on their faces!

That journey was a real eye-opener. After watching the Dons since 1986, seeing the antics they got up to, it was like being back in the era of Wise, Fash, Vinny and the others. I realised that this side has the passion for this club on and off the pitch. The spirit and togetherness is so apparent. The Crazy Gang is alive again at AFC and it feels fantastic to be able to be a part of it.

✦

COOPER'S DOUBLE HONOUR

The day after the Reading game, the Observer newspaper named AFC Wimbledon's front man Kevin Cooper as their player of the year. On the same day, Chelsea's Gianfranco Zola beat Cooper to the BBC Radio London award by just 2.8 per cent.

4 MAY 2003
By Kevin Cooper (player)

It was a mad few weeks. I first heard about the award a couple of weeks earlier. But when I found out that I had been nominated, I was so surprised I thought it was a wind-up. But then Radio London called me up and I realised it was real. I remember sitting by the radio listening to it. The results were announced around 3.15pm. When I heard the guy from QPR had finished third, I was gutted not to win it, but to come second was amazing. I got 35.2 per cent. Chelsea's Gianfranco Zola won it with 38 per cent. It would have been great to win it, but Zola is Zola. To be even considered in the same breath was amazing.

It was just an amazing day. For the rest of my life, I can say that in 2002 I came second only to Gianfranco Zola in the whole of London. That's just madness. Earlier in the day, I was named the Observer Player of the Year and that was just crazy. I didn't know anything about that.

Looking back on it, I really have to pinch myself. Ten months earlier I was just an ordinary Sutton United player, and I couldn't have imagined any of this in my wildest of dreams. It says so much for what AFC Wimbledon achieved in such a short time.

Naturally, the Wimbledon fans helped massively. Details of the poll were on every Wimbledon website. And then there were the fans walking round with "Vote Coops" on their backs. It was just so surreal. Of course I also told everyone I knew to vote for me, once I was nominated.

Humour: Kevin Cooper, right, is hugged by AFC Wimbledon supporter Paul Farrance sporting a "Vote Coops" logo in an attempt to rally votes. (Alex Folkes)

And then there was all the television and radio coverage. Tom Watt from Radio London did a long interview with me. He was just overwhelmed by the whole atmosphere at the club. Then there were Sky Sports and the BBC. It was just unrelenting.

It had been an amazing year, yet those last few days of the season surpassed it all.

Media man: AFC Wimbledon's Kevin Cooper talks to the media after the final home game of the 2002/03 season against Raynes Park Vale on 5 May 2003. (Alex Folkes)

I was so glad to sign off with a couple of goals too. I ended the season with 41 in all competitions – far more than I could have possibly hoped for. My one regret is that I failed to beat Eddie Reynolds' league goalscoring record of 40 goals in a season. I managed 37, and I'll be honest that the pressure of chasing that target got to me in the last few weeks of the season. I so badly wanted that record that it began to play on my mind. I've been looking back at the season ever since and thinking that if only I had got that chance or this chance I could have made it.

But 37, is still a great total, and on the way I passed Alan Cork's one season record for League goals and that meant a lot to me too.

I equalled Cork's record of 29 with a hat-trick against Ash United in March. Then I passed it with a goal against Bedfont. I remember it came across the six-yard box and I put it in the far corner. What made it even more special was the presentation on the pitch at the next home game. It was an AFC Wimbledon shirt signed by Alan Cork congratulating me on beating his old record. That was the best achievement I have ever had in football.

✦

The Spirit of Wimbledon

CHAPTER NINETEEN: 5 MAY 2003

THE PERFECT SEND-OFF

5 MAY 2003
Seagrave Haulage Premier Division
AFC Wimbledon 5 Raynes Park Vale 1

AFC Wimbledon's season ended in a festival of football and fun. The match sold out 20 minutes before kick-off. The team won 5-1. Dozens of old Wimbledon players turned up. Kevin Cooper scored with a header. Lee Sidwell won the player of the year award. The antics off the pitch reached new levels. Even the Womble was back, and the smiles were everywhere.

THE BUILD-UP
By Terry Eames (manager)

It was an amazing day from the moment I turned up at Kingsmeadow to the journey home from the Hand In Hand pub on Wimbledon Common over 12 hours later.

It all began at 10.30am with the revival of an old Plough Lane tradition. In the old days on the final day of the season, all the staff, volunteers and players would gather together for a big photo session, and it was great to recreate that moment at Kingsmeadow. The club would have been nothing without its legions of volunteers and this was just a small way of saying thank you. It meant as much to me as it meant to anyone else.

That first season was the greatest period of my footballing life, and in my life overall it ranks in the top five. AFC Wimbledon began on day one with nothing, yet by the end of the season we had achieved so much.

Key to all our success was keeping our tradition and rediscovering the spirit that had served Wimbledon so well for decades.

By 11am there were loads of people milling about and the ground was already buzzing in a way that I had not known all season. Then there was the presentation of the future youth teams on the pitch. Watching them as they paraded around the

Womble return: AFC Wimbledon's commercial director Ivor Heller, right, hugs a Womble before the Raynes Park Vale game on 5 May 2003. (Alex Folkes)

Joyous Dons: Danny Oakins, left, is congratulated by Gavin Bolger after scoring for the Dons against Raynes Park Vale on 5 May 2003. (Alex Folkes)

ground made me feel so proud. These kids wanted to be a part of AFC Wimbledon. They were smiling and they were chasing autographs. They were cuddling the Womble that had just swapped allegiances from Wimbledon FC to AFC Wimbledon. You could tell they "got" AFC Wimbledon and that they are our future. There were moments like that throughout the day.

When the news filtered through that the game had sold out 20 minutes before kick-off, I took the time to look around the ground. The crowd had fluctuated all year between 2,500 and 4,000, but they all wanted to be there for the final game. I remember walking round and seeing faces I hadn't seen for years, some of them not since my days at Plough Lane. I can only thank all those people who turned up and made the day so special.

◆

HAPPINESS IN DEFEAT
By Lee Dobinson (Raynes Park Vale manager)

I think we had learnt a lot from the previous game and to have an even bigger attendance helped us. Many of the players said they couldn't hear the crowd. It was just one solid noise; you just couldn't hear the specifics. In a normal game, you can hear individuals really clearly, especially the one guy from Ash United.

After the first game we expected quite a lot of barracking, but it was a good feeling all day and it was a great vibe. I knew there were going to be a lot of people there, but it far exceeded my expectations. It took me several minutes just to get into the ground. I had posted a few times on

Weird and Wonderful World and people were stopping me and introducing themselves. There was a real buzz about the place and I thoroughly enjoyed it.

It was a big game for them, but we wanted to win too. We played well and the result didn't do us justice – 5-1 flattered AFC Wimbledon. Perhaps 2-1 would have been fairer.

Having AFC Wimbledon in the Combined Counties League had been a great experience. It was a long season and it was made a lot more enjoyable by having AFC Wimbledon in it.

◆

SIDWELL NAMED PLAYER OF THE YEAR
By Terry Eames (manager)

The game itself wasn't the greatest. We won 5-1, but it was about the day more than the match. The scenes after the final whistle were fantastic and two or three of the boys were in tears. Tom Watt was dumbfounded on Radio London.

After the game, Lee Sidwell deservedly got player of the year. He was a player who no one had given a second look to before, but he's a fighter. And what he lacked in ability, he gave in passion and spirit. It didn't surprise me that the Wimbledon crowd warmed to him. They saw in Lee Sidwell what they had seen in Wimbledon players throughout the ages, and that was why it was so important to me that Dickie Guy presented the award – from one passionate Wimbledon hero to another.

The club didn't want Dickie to present the award, but I insisted. Dickie is a great man and a great inspiration for anyone connected with AFC Wimbledon. He had been there for me since the start. If I've needed someone to call, I've been able to call him. Dickie didn't have to be there, but he was. I can't think of a better candidate to be made the club's first life president.

By Lee Sidwell (player)

I didn't expect to be named player of the year. I thought Coops or Danny Oakins would win it. The whole day was overwhelming. The atmosphere was the best I have ever known.

Getting the award at the end was a proud moment. The squad had all these players with a lot more experience than me, so to come in from a league lower than the CCL and to win the award was unbelievable.

The AFC Wimbledon players gather in the centre circle awaiting the awards ceremony. (Alex Folkes)

A lot of good players will come through this club. AFC Wimbledon will one day have players playing for England. So to be the first AFC Wimbledon player of the year means the world to me.

The spirit this club creates is very important. I think most of the players feel that if you can't enjoy it, you shouldn't be playing. That's what Wimbledon is about.

◆

THE OLD PLAYERS RETURN
By Kevin Cooper (Wimbledon FC 2001 player of the year)

All the old boys who were at Kingsmeadow they were the real heroes. The ones who won the FA Amateur Cup, the ones who took the club in to the Football League and the ones who won the FA Cup. And then there were the fans – they too were heroes. I was just honoured to be considered in the same company.

I had wanted to come down for months and months, and as soon as I heard this match was on a Monday and the kids were off school I knew I was going to be there. After that day at Molineux the year before when the fans honoured me, I wanted so badly to show my appreciation to them.

I kept an eye on what was going on on-line. The Wolverhampton Wanderers fans also kept me informed, and the support they have offered to AFC Wimbledon is unrelenting.

I was really looking forward to coming back, and it proved to be everything I hoped for and more. It was such a wonderful day. The club is simply fantastic. AFC Wimbledon has the whole spirit of the club I played for. It is Wimbledon.

You look at the fans, the set-up and the passion and you know this club has the capability to go very far.

It was also the first time I ever heard the song: "There's only two Kevin Coopers."

The two Kevin Coopers: Kevin Cooper of Wolves, right, with Kevin Cooper, of AFC Wimbledon, and his golden boot award. (Alex Folkes)

By Roy Law (captain of FA Amateur Cup winning side in 1963)

The atmosphere was brilliant and I was so proud to be part of the day. My respect and thanks go to all the people who work so hard to keep the club going. They are the true heroes.

It was a spectacular day and it was all run so professionally. I have so many good memories of the day, it's impossible to list them. It was so nice to meet up with so many of my old colleagues: Bobby Ardrey, Dickie Guy, George Coote and so many of the 1963 team were there.

It was a full programme of events. It epitomised perfectly what AFC Wimbledon have achieved. They are a credit to football.

By Dave Beasant (captain of FA Cup winning side in 1988)

It was a good day. The football wasn't the greatest, but that wasn't the point. It was a celebration of the amazing achievements of AFC Wimbledon. These were the fans of Wimbledon who had supported the club through thick and thin. They were saying: "This is our stance, we're here at AFC and we're proud."

There were 4,500 inside the stadium and loads more locked outside. I just found it all amazing and I have nothing but respect for the fans.

They were typical Wimbledon fans, the ones I knew from my days at the club. They were humorous with their chants and their songs. It took me back to my days at Plough Lane. It was emotional.

By Glenn Mulcaire (scorer of AFC Wimbledon's first goal)

The final day epitomised everything the club stands for. The whole is bigger than the sum of its parts. The Wimbledon fans are intelligent and caring people, and for me that's what shone through.

While the awards were going on Robbie Earle came over to me and he said: "I may have got the first World Cup goal for Jamaica, but I didn't score the first AFC Wimbledon goal with a 30-yard volley."

That was just unbelievable. Robbie is a Wimbledon legend, yet I felt on a par with him because of the respect from the fans.

Hero visits: Dave Beasant at Kingsmeadow for the final game of the 2002/03 season. (Alex Folkes)

COOPER'S HEADER

By Kevin Cooper (AFC Wimbledon player)

I may have scored a lot of goals that season, but before that day not one of them had been with my head and, well, some of the fans had organised a bet. If I could score a goal with my head they would give some money to the Stadium Fund. By that Monday the total had reached £1,200.

I can't think why, but Niall Couper, who was behind the idea, didn't have much faith in me. So he set up a little bit of fun in case I didn't score with my head in the match.

I didn't – and that's why after the final whistle me and Andy Sullivan trotted back out. It was going a bit too far when I found out he had persuaded Ivor Heller to go in goal!

To be honest I could have scored with the first cross, but that would have taken away the fun of it. I was quite happy to get a bit of stick. So I did a couple of diving headers and the like. After I missed the first couple I had to admit I started to try. I'm just glad it didn't go beyond the five attempts it took me!

It was great fun and capped a great day. It was a privilege to meet all those ex-players and especially nice to meet the "other" Kevin Cooper. I told him he had a great name. He was a real nice guy.

The celebrations went on and on, and I was nursing a hangover for weeks after.

✦

THE EVENING

By Terry Eames (manager)

Later that night, the news filtered through to the Hand In Hand pub, where we'd all gathered, that Charlton's pre-season fixture with Franchise had been called off after pressure from Charlton fans. There was a huge cheer, and what was notable was that it came as much from the players as it did from the fans.

The players at AFC Wimbledon care. They "get" what AFC Wimbledon is about. They oppose franchising and that's why the news about Charlton, Tottenham and then Luton pulling out of the pre-season games cheered them all.

They are not here for the money. If it's money they are after, there are plenty of better options open to them. They are here because they can have a good time, because they can enjoy their football and because they love the Dons.

Of course, they still like to mess about and they were up to their tricks again on that day too.

At the final whistle, two supporters tried to pick up me and carry me on their shoulders. My trousers ripped. The trouble was that Lee Sidwell and Danny Oakins saw the rip. And later on that night in the pub I was standing up making a speech and the two of them crept up and used the rip to tear my trousers off. I ended up having to walk home from the Hand In Hand across Wimbledon Common with no trousers. At least my wife Anne was there.

When they are messing about it is best to keep out of the way and let them get on with it. But when they need to buckle down and work hard they all do it willingly. They are just like the old Wimbledon.

The boys are a group and they are always doing things together. When we first started Andy Sullivan and a few others would come in and have one drink and then go. Lee Passmore and Tony Readings sometimes didn't even stay for a drink. That's all gone. The unity is there now.

✦

THE ANTICS

By Noel Frankum (player)

I was a schoolboy at Wimbledon FC. I was in the same year as Neal Ardley, Stewart Castledine, Justin Skinner and Chris Perry. I've always known what Wimbledon is supposed to be about. It's about being a community, enjoying yourself and having fun.

In my years at Wimbledon we were just kids, but there was still all this banter going on. We liked having a laugh. It was just the culture of the club. We'd be doing our own session and we'd see all the professionals mucking about. They used to set fire to training bags, cut up people's clothes. Anything and everything was happening. The whole club was mad. I learnt from that and I have mucked about ever since.

AFC Wimbledon in that first season was as mad as anything I have ever known, and none more so than on that final day of the season. Loads of stuff was going on. We just wanted to enjoy ourselves.

Danny Oakins kicked it all off by showing his arse to the crowd mid-way through the game. We knew from then on that everything was fair game. Once we got back into the changing room I tried to

Fundraisers: Kevin Cooper and Ivor Heller embrace after Cooper scores a header to help raise money for the ground fund after the final game of the 2002/03 season. (Alex Folkes)

Jokers: AFC Wimbledon's Simon Bassey, Danny Oakins, Noel Frankum and Gareth Graham outside the Kingsmeadow bar on 5 May 2003. (Marcus Massey)

shave off Kevin Cooper's hair, but that just backfired on me. Keith Ward and Danny Oakins pinned me down I ended up with a St George's cross shaved on my chest. But that was just the start of it. Within a matter of minutes hair was all over the floor. We shaved off Ally Russell's chest hair. Then it was onto goalkeeper Ray Merry. You just had to take it.

Then there was Simon Bassey. He was getting loads. We'd labelled him a non-drinker, but he was having none of it and was pouring pint after pint down his throat. There was lots of other stuff going on, but most of that will have to remain secret.

There's a bit of the Crazy Gang about us. In fact we're probably crazier than the Crazy Gang. I was serious once. I think it was back in October 87 – it lasted about 20 minutes.

By Joe Sheerin (captain)

It was a perfect end to a perfect year. We had been used to big crowds and even huge roars. The Wallingford game sticks out in my mind, but this was even better. There was an excellent buzz around the game – it was a carnival atmosphere. It was a game we wanted to win and we really enjoyed it.

Even though we had finished the season in third, we had improved throughout the year. We had broken club records – highest points tally, most goals scored – and most importantly of all we had proved that we weren't a flash in the pan. Attendances didn't drop off as some had predicted. The whole day turned into a huge celebration of everything that everyone had achieved over the previous 11 months.

The team had developed, and the dressing room was the best one I have ever known. There were no prima donnas. Everyone was out for a laugh. Noel Frankum, Simon Bassey and Gareth Graham are hysterical. Danny Oakins is a total loon.

A couple of weeks earlier, we all agreed to do a naked calendar. We rolled up on the Sunday morning still drunk from the night before. They provided us with loads of beer and it just turned in to one big laugh. They got us to do all these dodgy poses, but by the end of it we couldn't take anything seriously and it ended up with us all running around the pitch at Kingsmeadow naked and lagered up. The residents must have been getting a right eyeful! It was one of the funniest days. But that final game surpassed even that.

We had the best bunch of lads. Maybe we weren't quite up to the Crazy Gang level yet, but we were getting there.

The AFC Wimbledon manager Terry Eames. (Marcus Massey)

THE OVERVIEW

By Terry Eames (manager)

The first season at AFC Wimbledon epitomised perfectly the spirit of Wimbledon. There was the ability to defy the odds, the determination to succeed and, most importantly, there was the passion of a community.

AFC Wimbledon was born out of the will of the supporters. It thrived because of the togetherness of the club: the supporters and the players. It was very much like the old Wimbledon.

Together we defied the sceptics. Back in August 2002, there were so many people saying that by November our attendances would have died off. But that never happened. The fans that came down grew to love the club more and more.

But it was not an easy year. Sometimes, I found it really hard to be manager of AFC Wimbledon and hold down a full-time job as well.

The icing on the cake came in mid-July 2003 when we finally took over the lease at Kingsmeadow; that was one of the proudest days of my life. How many other clubs could have raised £1m in three weeks? And after 12 years of pain, Wimbledon had a home base once more.

✦

The Spirit of Wimbledon

EPILOGUE

So there you have it: the story of Wimbledon told through the eyes of the players, managers and supporters who were there to witness it. The story of Wimbledon FC is an amazing tale, from park football to the Premiership, from the Clapham League to the FA Cup final, from treks to Willington to trips to Old Trafford. It's a tale that will probably never be repeated – a tale of the spirit of Wimbledon.

So why is it that after all that, after 113 years of history, I freely gave up my season ticket to support a club that hadn't even played one game? That is a question I have been asked again and again. But then few fans will ever experience the emotions Wimbledon supporters suffered from 1999 to 2002. That period changed my view on football.

In 1999, I watched powerlessly as the club fell into a slumber that would lead to relegation. After the decision to relocate to Milton Keynes a year later, it could not have been any clearer what scant regard the club had for its own supporters. And it hurt. At the end of that period, I was asking myself: why be a fan at all?

I loved my club, but did they really love me? Did these players care how I felt? Did the owners care for the ordinary fan? Every time, I felt the answer was no.

By the end of the 2001/02 season the only reason I was still in my seat was out of habit. It was irrational. It was all one way. The Wimbledon fan, it seemed, had no place in the vision put forward by the club's chairman Charles Koppel. So why was I there at all? I was asking fundamental questions. I wanted to remember why I was a fan.

I had grown up watching football at Plough Lane. Back then Wimbledon was a little family club with the community at its heart. I was born in Wimbledon and I loved watching my local team battling the odds and defying the critics. Wimbledon was in my blood. I had grown up on a never-say-die attitude and a style of football based purely on passion. In the last few years at Selhurst Park, I had forgotten all that. And that's when I realised why it hurt so much; the club was betraying its legacy.

My mindset had been transformed. I was no longer the apathetic fan that I was in 1999. The Wimbledon I identified with had died. But I also realised that to give up was not the Wimbledon way. I wanted to fight. I refused to lose. And thankfully the likes of Ivor Heller, Kris Stewart, Terry Eames and Trevor Williams were two or three steps ahead of me. They too had been infected by the never-say-die attitude and the community spirit of the Wimbledon of old. It is thanks to their vision that I now have a club that is living the legacy of Wimbledon. And AFC Wimbledon is Wimbledon. We never left.

In the months and years ahead I know AFC Wimbledon will not be a unique case. In these days of multi-millionaire chairmen, who use clubs as executive playthings, our tale will be repeated.

There may never be a club that will repeat the meteoric rise of Wimbledon FC, but given the financial whims of today's football chairmen there may well be the need for many more clubs like AFC Wimbledon. And in my experience that's no bad thing.

If AFC Wimbledon has proved one thing, it is that the fans can run a football club far better than any multi-millionaire chairman. The supporters of AFC Wimbledon have kept the spirit of Wimbledon alive and the same passion exists inside every football supporter – it can never die.

Niall Couper

♦

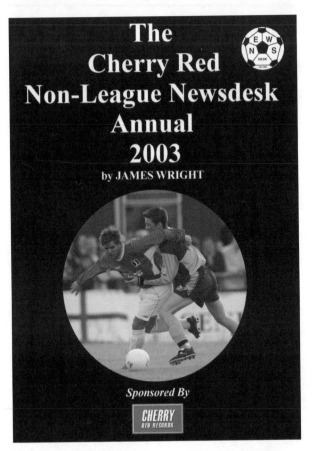

The
Cherry Red
Non-League Newsdesk
Annual
2003
by JAMES WRIGHT

Sponsored By

CHERRY
RED RECORDS

The Cherry Red Non-League Newsdesk Annual 2003 by James Wright

This is the fourth edition of the Cherry Red Non-League Newsdesk Annual comprehensively covering the world of semi-professional and amateur football. Compiled by experienced Non-League journalist James Wright, the Annual is a concise but thorough statistical review of the 2002-03 season, and an essential companion for the 2003-04 campaign.

Crammed into 256 pages are:
- ■ Tables and all league and cup results from senior English and Welsh pyramid leagues
- ■ Round-by-round results for the FA Cup, FA Trophy and FA Vase
- ■ 2003-04 mini-directories for senior leagues
- ■ Full, hot of the press, details of all summer inter-league club movement
- ■ Numerous tables from minor leagues - in all over 5,500 teams are featured
- ■ Results from a myriad of county and local cup competitions

Order the book by post from Cherry Red Books, Unit 17, 1st Floor, Elysium Gate West 126/128 New Kings Road, London SW6 4LZ
Credit card hotline: 0207 371 5844 Fax orders: 0207 384 1854 E-mail orders: infonet@cherryred.co.uk
Online orders with Visa, Mastercard, Switch at www.cherryred.co.uk
Cheques should be made payable to Cherry Red Records Ltd
UK £8.95 Europe £9.95 Rest Of World £10.95 (prices include postage & packing)

Non-League Newsdesk Annual 2003 is also distributed to book shops by Turnaround.

www.cherryred.co.uk

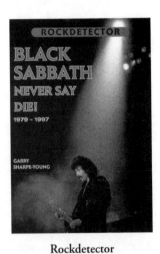

CHERRY RED BOOKS

We are always looking for interesting books to publish.
They can be either new manuscripts or re-issues of deleted books.
If you have any good ideas then please
get in touch with us.

CHERRY RED BOOKS
a division of Cherry Red Records Ltd.
Unit 17, Elysium Gate West,
126-128 New King's Road
London SW6 4LZ

E-mail: iain@cherryred.co.uk

Web: www.cherryred.co.uk

www.cherryred.co.uk